For Sharron Bishop

A Bibliography of
Shelley Studies: 1823-1950

A Bibliography of
Shelley Studies: 1823-1950

Clement Dunbar

with a foreword by
Donald H. Reiman

DAWSON
1976

TABLE OF CONTENTS

FOREWORD

Many scholars carry out research and produce books on subjects that everyone knows in advance will be useful and for which the basic materials have already been identified. Some study Shakespeare's use of the Tudor historians and of Plutarch, while others examinethe influence of Godwin and of other radical theorists on Shelley. Clement Dunbar, a more imaginative young scholar, saw a need where his elders (most of us, at least) thought none really existed. He has performed his work so well that I must retract my previously published opinion that in 1970 there were adequate enumerative bibliographies of publications discussing Shelley.

The present volume contains more than seven times the number of entries in any previous bibliography of Shelley; among these are some five hundred items not listed elsewhere, as well as all those genuine items from previous bibliographies that fall within its basic guidelines—the significant mentions or discussions of Shelley published in English from 1823 through 1950. These chronological limits bridge the gap between the comments during Shelley's lifetime (most of which appear in Newman Ivey White's *Unextinguished Hearth*) and the inclusive bibliography of "Keats, Shelley, Byron, Hunt, and Their Circles" published annually in the *Keats-Shelley Journal*.

With the great number of new items that Dr. Dunbar has discovered and the wealth of additional information that he has compiled as to exact dates, volume numbers, and specific pages

[ix]

on which references to Shelley are to be found, he has clearly made life much easier for the student of Shelley. He has provided the raw materials for a new estimate of Shelley's reputation in England and America from the date of the poet's death to 1950. His chronological arrangement and excellent cross references to reprintings and to the earlier items that are the subject of reviews enable a scholar to identify immediately any book, article, or review on Shelley from the most oblique allusions. The index to names makes it easy to locate all items by a particular author or in a specific periodical. But the basically chronological arrangement also enables the reader to identify the particular earlier writing that may have provoked a hostile reaction on the part of a later writer. In short, both the scope and arrangement of Dunbar's *Bibliography* enable us to reconstruct critical history in the most efficient possible way.

Years ago I thought of compiling a new enumerative bibliography of Shelley. Not only did I not have the time to attempt it, but in checking Dr. Dunbar's manuscript, I realized that I would never have done it so well. I am grateful to him for having provided all the students of Shelley with so imaginatively conceived and carefully executed a work as this volume.

Donald H. Reiman
New York, New York
July 8, 1975

ACKNOWLEDGMENTS

I am grateful to a number of institutions and people without whom this work could not have been completed. I am indebted first to staffs of the many libraries where I have worked: the Bodleian Library, Oxford; the British Museum; the Columbia University Libraries; Cornell University Library; Duke University Library; the Huntington Library; the Keats-Shelley Memorial House, Rome; the Newberry Library; the New York Public Library; Pennsylvania State University Library; The Carl H. Pforzheimer Library; Trinity College Library, Hartford; Wisconsin University Library; and Yale University Library.

I am indebted to Carl R. Woodring of Columbia University for his assistance, his guidance, and most of all his patience, while this bibliography was still in its dissertation stages. And I am equally indebted to Eugene P. Sheehy of the Columbia Library Reference Department, who also guided the dissertation; but far beyond that I am indebted to him for his sympathy, his help in threading the maze, and the many hours he has so freely given to me in the preparation of this manuscript for the press, including several weeks of invaluable proofreading. To Donald H. Reiman of The Carl H. Pforzheimer Library I am grateful for finding a publisher, for many hours of advice, and for many pages of detailed, thoughtful criticism which have improved this book.

Last, I am thankful to family and friends who have

given me moral support and practical help as well: to my mother, who paid tuition bills without complaining and watched the years drag by without nagging; to Jim Bilbao, Martin Minsky, Francine Ovius, and Marion Solomon, who distracted me when I need distraction, and who glued, copied, sorted, and alphabetized cards when I needed that; to Sharron Bishop, without whose friendship and assistance neither dissertation nor book would ever have been finished.

INTRODUCTION

Five predispositions or motivations loosely charac-
terize the critical approaches to Shelley in the seventeen-year
period from his death in 1822 to the publication in 1839 of
Mary Shelley's edition of his works: 1) political affiliation,
2) moral and religious concern, 3) social or class bias, 4) literary or critical doctrine, and 5) personal connections with the
poet. These are not discrete phenomena, for the motivations
often overlap, and one position may masquerade under the protec-
tive coloration of another.[1]

Political motivation is apparent in the correlation of
the political affiliations of the major journals with their
reviews of *Posthumous Poems* [item 49] in 1824. The *Quarterly Review*,
spokesman of the Tories, confined its remarks [item 71] to
Shelley's translations from *Faust*, damning Shelley with faint,
generalized praise, and concluding that the world had lost a
potentially great translator—not a hint of the radical, atheist
poet. *Blackwood's Edinburgh Magazine*, offering a more popular brand
of Toryism, prided itself on championing young writers, but con-
tented itself on this occasion with an attack [item 30] on the
Edinburgh Review, twitting its New Whig opponent for its earlier
silence on Shelley, slurring Bryan Procter—a young poet who
helped underwrite the publication of *Posthumous Poems*—for his
support of Shelley, and joking feebly that the weight of Keats'
poems in Shelley's pocket had caused the fatal boat to sink.[2]

[xiii]

The *Edinburgh Review*, major organ of the New Whigs
and rival to the *Quarterly*, was equivocal [item 24]: though
Shelley was "extravagant," "incomprehensible," even "abortive,"
he was, nonetheless, "a man of genius," and "was what he pro-
fessed to be, a sincere lover of truth, of nature, and of human
kind." The *Edinburgh Review* did not wish to condemn Shelley, but
to praise him outright would have provided the Tories of the
Quarterly with free ammunition in their running battle. A leading
Liberal journal, the *New Monthly Magazine*, printed a review which
epitomizes the difficulty of the middle-of-the-road position
[item 25]. Despite the impression that Shelley's "speculative
opinions" might make, the reviewer asserts that "no one will
. . . deny his high and peculiar merits as a poet. . . ." This
critical approach was to prevail later in the nineteenth century,
evolving into the general view of Shelley as a master lyricist,
the content of whose poems was incidental to their worth and need
not be considered seriously. Other liberal periodicals of
narrower circulation and less impact took a similar approach
[items 26, 29].

Of the radical journals, only *The Examiner*, owned by
Leigh Hunt's brother John, reviewed *Posthumous Poems*, for the volume
contained none of the material on which radical interest centered.[3]
The Examiner had personal as well as political motives for its
unqualified praise [item 20], but the reviewer stressed the man
over the poet: Shelley was possessed of a "benevolent and exalted
spirit," and " his mental independence subjected him to the

rancourous virulence and calumny of those who knew him not."

There were other political forces whose precise influence is immeasurable, forces of a liberalizing nature that
were simultaneously the effects of and contributory causes to the
broad trend of emancipatory toleration discernible in the social
and political climate of England. The Tory repression that had
followed Waterloo and characterized that climate during the years
of Shelley's adult writing career culminated in the Peterloo
Massacre and the Cato Street Conspiracy. The political tide
turned with the death of Castlereagh. Peel's reform of the
criminal code, Canning's policy of non-intervention internation-
ally and his movement away from alliance with the reactionary
governments that had convened the Congress of Vienna, Huskisson's
modifications of the Corn Laws and easing of the Navigation Laws,
the Catholic Emancipation Act, the triumph of the Whigs in 1830,
the Great Reform Bill, and the abolition of slavery were all
creating an England better prepared for Shelley's views.

There was a slower shift in religious tolerance:
blasphemy was still illegal, and atheism unthinkably wicked. The
Literary Gazette, which regularly devoted its columns to the excori-
ation of the vicious and the extirpation of the ungodly, produced
the most virulent response [item 27] to *Posthumous Poems*; its indig-
nant and righteous reviewer found page upon page of blasphemy, but
was charitable enough to grant an occasional piece the "negative
merit of having in it nothing to offend." Such censure yielded
slowly, silenced finally by the mid-Victorian conviction that

Shelley would have evolved into a professing Christian, his heterodoxy being commensurate with the naturally rebellious skepticism of youth. Even in 1824 voices were being raised to exonerate Shelley of atheism: the *Literary Magnet* devoted much of its review to an explication of *Queen Mab*, finding the poem mistaken speculation rather than atheistic avowal, and terming it a poetic masterpiece, despite the failure of its argument [item 23].

Social or class prejudice in the reviewing periodicals is more difficult to pinpoint, and unlike political or religious predispositions, such prejudice worked in Shelley's favor. While Keats and Leigh Hunt were derided as the "Cockney School," the birth, breeding, and education of Shelley exempted him from inclusion. The witty, urbane Lockhart, principal reviewer for *Blackwood's Edinburgh Magazine*, was an inveterate social snob. He accorded Shelley perceptive and appreciative critical treatment while the poet lived, and probably contributed strongly to the generally favorable treatment Shelley later received in *Blackwood's*.

Journals attempting a genuinely literary assessment of *Posthumous Poems* were of less prominence, smaller circulation, and a more ephemeral nature. Their technique was almost invariably to quote extensively and praise briefly. The *Somerset House Gazette* was cautiously favorable about its long extracts, seconding its own judgment by quoting Wordsworth as saying, "Shelley was by far the most promising young poet of the day" [item 22]. The *News of Literature and Fashion* printed sizable portions of "Julian and

Maddalo," praising Shelley as a friend of liberty whose works
seemed "unfinished" [item 21]—a convenient way to avoid judgment.

Personal connections with Shelley surely influenced the
review in Hunt's *Examiner*, and may also account for the ambiguity
of Hazlitt's remarks for the *Edinburgh Review*; however, the most
important contribution of his circle was not the reviews, but Mary
Shelley's "Preface" to the *Posthumous Poems*. Here Mary laid the
foundation for all future references to Shelley as an angel: he
was a "bright vision. . . worth all the realities that society can
afford," one whose "unearthly and elevated nature is a pledge of
the continuation of his being, although in altered form." No mere
canonization, but a full-scale apotheosis. Mary's was not a mindless outpouring though, for her insistence on Shelley's innocence
and altruism was to reappear in many reviews as extenuation for
Shelley's less acceptable views. She chose the notes of her
threnody wisely: her vision of the persecuted angel was an inspired answer to those critics by whom Shelley had been depicted
as a fallen one.

As we move beyond *Posthumous Poems*, the most important
writings on Shelley were produced, directly and indirectly, by
four friends—Hunt, Medwin, and Hogg directly; Byron indirectly.
Byron's contribution was the most far-reaching. While he wrote
nothing for publication about Shelley, the linking of their names
created a steady flow of incidental mentions of Shelley—fully one
reference in three in the first two years after he died, and
nearly one in six in the first decade. Shelley profited by the

contrast with Byron's reputation for rake-hell profligacy: more
than one critic was to find Shelley the lesser of two moral evils,
and perhaps Mary had intuited this in stressing Shelley's virtuous
life in her "Preface."

Hunt's contributions were direct: he was responsible
for the *Examiner's* incidental references and Shelley quotations;[4]
he devoted more than seventy pages of *Lord Byron and Some of His Contemporaries* to a treatment of Shelley [item 116]; and, in 1832, he
edited Shelley's *Mask of Anarchy* with a thirty page preface containing significant biographical information [item 191]. This preface
was most important for its depiction of Shelley as a level-headed
and clear-sighted political thinker, rather than a wool-gathering
utopian or a radical bent on revolution. Hunt's critical remarks
handle Shelley's failings as forthrightly as they demonstrate his
strengths, and Hunt's insistence on close and reasoned examination
of the texts is unique in Shelley criticism of this period.

Medwin's service was two-fold. He wrote a ten page
memoir of Shelley as a footnote to *Conversations of Lord Byron* [item
48], and more than thirty-five scattered pages of additional
anecdotes, valuable for presenting Shelley as intellectually the
equal of Byron, and morally the superior, rather than the simple
camp-follower or minor protégé that many had thought him. Medwin
also produced a series of articles for the *Athenaeum*: an expanded
memoir in six installments [items 174-175, 180-183], followed by
eleven installments of unpublished poems and prose remains [items
184-188, 192-193, 199-201, and 221]. Public interest warranted

issuing the series in book form later the same year, 1833 [item 242]. Medwin offered his readers a dreamy-eyed, melancholic Shelley, an other-worldly spirit of spotless virtue whose mental balance was tenuous at best—a variation on the seraph *qua* poet already offered by Mary, and seconded by Leigh Hunt.

Of greater biographical importance, and more readable too, were seven installments on Shelley's Oxford days by T. J. Hogg that appeared in the *New Monthly Magazine* [items 175, 176, 180, 184, 202, 215, and 233]. Hogg's portrait, despite its distortions, inaccuracies, and exaggerations, had a flair and a spiciness that none of the other accounts duplicated. Here was a Shelley slightly mad, more than slightly impractical, an alchemist burning holes in his rug and nearly quaffing poison, a physically uncoordinated genius, amalgam of quick mind and clown.

The friends' influence extended beyond their own works, for Leigh Hunt and Mary each assisted others with memoirs which circulated widely [items 164 and 141]. And the connection with Byron continued to augment the biographical picture: Moore and Galt produced lives of Byron in 1830, each devoting considerable space to Shelley [items 162 and 160].

While the friends were primarily concerned with the life of Shelley, and with promoting publication of his works, genuine literary criticism, relatively free from political or moral motive, began to issue from other quarters with increasing regularity. The first such criticism of importance was John Wilson's "Preface" to the January issue of *Blackwood's* in 1826 [item 64]. Surveying his contemporaries, Wilson gives Shelley prominence and praise—the praise only slightly marred by questioning Shelley's sanity: "He had many of the faculties of a great poet. He was, however, we verily believe it now, scarcely in his right mind. . . ." Further comments are favorable to Shelley, but damning of the "Cockneys."

In France the following year, Amédée Pichot wrote a balanced, thoughtful estimate of Shelley for an anthology of English poetry [item 93]. With rare perspective, Pichot discusses Shelley's atheism as a product of eighteenth century rationalism and skepticism—the Gallic temperament was, perhaps, inherently better disposed to accept Shelley's moral and religious speculation. Ranking Shelley only slightly below Byron in genius, Pichot gives intelligent consideration to Shelley's major works. Attention to the longer works saves Shelley from appearing the mere lyricist that so many English critics seemed set on making him.

An anonymous critic in the *National Magazine* termed Shelley "an elegant and profound metaphysician," and placed him above Byron and Wordsworth [item 151]. Coleridge, Shelley and Wordsworth as "metaphysical" poets are favorably contrasted with Donne, whose metaphysicality is too "erudite and pedantic." While Coleridge emerges as the greatest of these three in poetic terms, more space is devoted to Shelley than the others, and the commentary is both positive and perceptive. Shelley's broad humanitarianism and ameliorism are clearly understood and properly contrasted with the central tendencies of Wordsworth and Coleridge.

Macaulay, reviewing an edition of *Pilgrim's Progress* for

the *Edinburgh Review* a year later, made a startling comparison of Shelley and Bunyan [item 174]:

> Bunyan is almost the only writer who ever gave to the abstract the interest of the concrete. [...] Personifications, when he dealt with them, became men. [...] In this respect, the genius of Bunyan bore a great resemblance to that of a man who had very little else in common with him, Percy Bysshe Shelley. The strong imagination of Shelley made him an idolator in his own despite. Out of the most indefinite terms of a hard, cold, dark, metaphysical system, he made a gorgeous Pantheon, full of beautiful, majestic, and life-like forms. He turned atheism itself into a mythology, rich with visions as glorious as the gods that live in the marble of Phidias. . . . Some of the metaphysical and ethical theories of Shelley were certainly most absurd and pernicious. But we doubt whether any modern poet has possessed in an equal degree some of the highest qualities of the great ancient masters.

It is an apt and astute comparison which reveals one of Shelley's greatest poetic strengths.

In the same issue of the *Edinburgh Review* Carlyle damned Shelley in a line second only to Arnold's famous dictum in the canon of remarks endlessly iterated by his detractors: "Hear a Shelley filling the earth with inarticulate wail; like the infinite inarticulate grief and weeping of forsaken infants" [item 173]. Like Arnold's "ineffectual angel," Carlyle's "inarticulate wail" is not only ungenerous, but generally inapplicable; unfortunately, it is the kind of waspishness that is not any the less painful for being so small a puncture.

In 1833 John Stuart Mill wrote a valuable critique for the *Monthly Repository* [item 236]. Distinguishing two types of poet, one "born" and the other "made," Mill exemplified the one with the evanescence and inspiration of Shelley and the other with the ponderousness and power of Wordsworth. Selecting *The Cenci* as Shelley's masterpiece because of its restrained and severe simplicity, Mill intimates that had Shelley lived to develop his control, he would have outstripped Wordsworth.

In the same year, in a general estimate of England [item 239], Bulwer-Lytton pronounced Wordsworth and Shelley the two most influential poets of the age, their real importance still obscured by the fashionable popularity of Byron and Scott. Like Mill, Bulwer-Lytton singles *The Cenci* out for praise, but unhappy with Shelley's subject matter, he prefers Wordsworth as the more "salutary" poet of the two.

The first substantial American criticism, a review in the *American Quarterly Review* in 1836 [item 274], again pitted Shelley against Wordsworth for pre-eminence:

> The three greatest poets of this century are, we think, Shelley, Wordsworth and Byron. We place them in what seems to us the order of their merit, though this of course will be a matter of dispute—and it will be a very difficult thing to reconcile opinions where the question concerns minds of such various and different powers. Between the first and the last, there can hardly be a doubt as to which deserves pre-eminence—the difficulty lies between the first two.

The critic praises Shelley for the "enquiring and doubting" spirit of his poetry, but cautions that Shelley, like Milton, will only be read by a select few.

Another American critic chose to contrast Shelley with the minor poet Robert Pollok [item 280]. Condemning Shelley for "extravagancies," and mourning that he was an "unbeliever," the critic admires Shelley as a poet and feels he "often exhibits much more true Christian faith, than many, who scoffed at him, as an atheist and outlaw." Singling out Shelley's longer works for particular praise, the critic firmly states that he would rather be damned with Shelley than go to heaven with the likes of Pollok and John Calvin—surely a daring view for 1837.

In England the following year an important article appeared in *Fraser's Magazine* [item 289], almost certainly by Medwin. As in the American article, there is a deep concern with depicting Shelley as a true Christian whose speculations did not lead him from the virtuous path. By a manipulation of Shelley's intentions, the writer offers *Queen Mab*, *The Revolt of Islam*, and even *The Cenci* as works advancing the cause of Christianity. Claiming, for example, that the characters in *The Revolt of Islam* are only apparent atheists, the writer asserts that "the pious reader will find himself able to explain the apparent contradiction [i.e., after reading this critic]; and out of its solution extract wholesome though bitter medicine, which shall elevate his Christianity and purify his religion." The writer is determined to make Shelley acceptable to Christian readers, and if that requires making him a Christian into the bargain, so be it. This is no longer literary criticism in anything like a pure form, but rather a special pleading intended to counteract continuing moral and religious bias. The moral outrage and pious indignation of the 1820's give way, for the most part, in the next decade to the mollifying tones of the apologists. A critic in the *American Biblical Repository* in 1839 [item 304] can condemn *Prometheus Unbound* as pure blasphemy, and praise *The*

Cenci and *The Revolt of Islam* as thoroughly moral works. The writer finds Shelley infinitely the superior of Byron, but not the equal of the "sublimely pious" Wordsworth. While still judging morally, the critic is able to condemn the part without damning the whole.

The most politically motivated material came from the radical press whose hopes and demands were far from satisfied by the broad changes sweeping England. Richard Carlile, in a series for the *Newgate Monthly Magazine*, examined Shelley's works as radical doctrine, contending that Shelley's obscurity at the time was the result of conservative powers suppressing his writings [items 57, 70, 72, 73, 75]. Another series appeared in the Owenite *New Moral World*, depicting Shelley as the "total poet," the writer as social reformer. Extensive quotation, summary, and explication of *Prometheus Unbound* and *The Revolt of Islam* emphasized the social visionary elements of the works [items 296, 297, 298, 306, 311, 324, 325].

As Shelley's moral and political opponents waned in importance, a new force emerged, one destined to be more dangerous than his foes had ever been. This was the band of devout Shelleyans. Offspring of the all too worshipful attitudes of Mary and Leigh Hunt, they were a line of well-meaning sentimentalists and unquestioning enthusiasts whose effusions account for more than half of the material written on Shelley. Like the Liberal journals which had eschewed consideration of Shelley's ideas to protect their flanks from Tory attack, the Shelleyans avoided his content; they wanted beautiful poetry from a bright angel, not revolutionary doctrine from an atheist. Consistently they chose

[xxiv]

the shorter, more musical and emotional lyrics, weaving their praise from three strands, Shelley's lyricism, his purity, and his persecution. Typical examples are found in *The Metropolitan Quarterly Magazine* [item 81], *The Athenaeum* [items 101, 103], *The Censor* [items 109, 111], and *Tait's Edinburgh Magazine* [items 351, 388].

The Shelleyans did not limit themselves to essays; they rhapsodized in verse as well. One sample, a sonnet by Thomas Wade [item 269], should suffice:

Shelley

Holy and mighty Poet of the Spirit
That broods and breathes along the Universe!
In the least portion of whose starry verse
Is the great breath the sphered heavens inherit—
No human song is eloquent as thine;
For, by a reasoning instinct all divine,
Thou feel'st the soul of things; and thereof singing,
With all the madness of a skylark, springing
From earth to heaven, the intenseness of thy strain,
Like the lark's music all around us ringing,
Laps us in God's own heart, and we regain
Our primal life ethereal. Men profane
Blaspheme thee: I have heard thee *Dreamer* styled—
I've mused upon their wakefulness and smiled.

Would "Mad Shelley" have smiled to see himself soaring from the sonnet's alembic as a rarefied "mad skylark"? This allusive tribute is superior to most of the awkward and adoring lines that Shelley inspired.[5]

In this first period, one other group of material merits mention: literary histories and reference works. Whether because Leigh Hunt and Mary were their principal sources, or because editorial policies dictated balance and neutrality, such works gave Shelley generous treatment, favorable to his reputation. He was

called "a poet of considerable eminence" by the *Encyclopaedia Londin-
ensis* [item 115], which noted a "charm" in his writing that would
make him "a favourite and profitable study for the poet, though
he many never become generally admired." Literary histories, too,
were cautiously positive. In his *History of the English Language and
Literature* [item 285], Robert Chambers said, "The poetry of Shelley
has a mystical grandeur, which alike recommends it to the more enthusiastic lovers of verse, and disqualifies it from giving general pleasure." Allan Cunningham wrote a peculiarly apt summary
of contemporary reaction to Shelley in his *Biographical and Critical
History of the British Literature of the Last Fifty Years* [item 255]: "His
admirers, in these mystic strains [*The Revolt of Islam* and *Prometheus
Unbound*], perceived a high and godlike philosophy; others saw a
design to overturn church and state: nor were men wanting who
called the poet mad, and his verses nonsense; but the bulk of mankind agreed that the poems were rapt, fiery, and energetic."

* * * * * *

The editions of Shelley's poetry and prose which Mary
edited in 1839 marked the beginning of a new era in Shelley study,
a second period which closes with the inauguration of the Shelley
Society in 1886. In simple quantity this period produced more
than the others, a reflection as much on Victorian publishing and
literary trends as on the growing reputation of Shelley. To the
modern scholar, the works of enduring importance in these years

are textual and biographical.

Foremost are the texts Mary edited in 1839, beginning with a four volume edition of the poetry [item 345]. Despite her censoring of *Queen Mab* and omission of the political satires, Mary gave the public a sound edition, enabling critics to assess the corpus meaningfully. Repairing her omissions, she re-edited the poetry later that year in one volume [item 346], and published two volumes of the prose [item 344], reminding readers that Shelley was a persuasive essayist, translator and thinker. Mary's short-comings, her caution and reverence, are more than compensated by a knowledge of the text, a unique intimacy, that no other editor could possess. Her extensive annotation is not analytical, but broadly interpretive and biographically illuminating; her notes are regularly cited and reprinted as an indispensable adjunct to the texts.

Textual scholarship proceeds in 1862 with Richard Garnett's *Relics of Shelley* [item 734], a potpourri of textual variants and fragments gleaned from the Shelley papers at Boscombe Manor. The first scholarly text was Rossetti's edition of the poetry in 1870 [item 839]. Rossetti's free-handed corrections and emendations were challenged by scholars, notably Mathilde Blind [item 824]. The critics and Forman's more exacting edition in 1876 forced Rossetti to temper his emendatory eagerness in a revised edition in 1878 [item 1033]. Such tampering as Rossetti's has been unacceptable practice ever since—until, sad to say, the edition presently in preparation by Oxford University Press.

In 1876 the first volumes of H. B. Forman's edition of
the poetry appeared; the following year it was complete [item
1008]. In 1880 the prose followed [item 1079], and then both were
reissued as an edition of the works [item 1081]. Though the prose
canon has since been enlarged and improved, so scrupulous was Forman that no edition of the poetry since his is more reliable—
indeed, none is so reliable.

Our second period began with personal authority for the
text; it closes with scholarly authority. In biographical writing
there is something of the same progression. We begin with Mary's
"Notes" to her editions, which constitute a wondrous and authentic
spiritual biography of Shelley. They are touching and intense,
and her sympathy evokes her finest writing. Everywhere they con-
vince us of the inseparability of Shelley's life and work. They
idealize, but they are profoundly sincere and moving.

Medwin, Hunt, and Hogg, familiar already, are heard from
again, with Trelawny and Peacock joining the chorus of friends.
Medwin writes the first full biography in 1847 [item 477], a pad-
ding of his earlier work for the *Athenaeum*, perpetuating and adding
errors, recreating the dreamy and drooping poet, as virtuous and
ethereal as ever, yet managing some intelligent literary criticism
and a consideration of Shelley's reading and its influence. Hunt,
too, added little in his *Autobiography* [item 522] to what he had
said in 1828, but Hunt, a better writer, offered more sophisti-
cated understanding of Shelley's personality, and a more compre-
hensive estimate of his achievements. Trelawny, whose account

had been retailed by Hunt in 1828, widened his scope in 1858 in
Recollections of the Last Days of Shelley and Byron [item 669]. Here
Shelley is innocent and rather effeminate, but Trelawny shows too
a practical side to Shelley in contrast with Byron. Trelawny's
swaggering virility is contagious, and Shelley emerges from the
rough-and-tumble prose as a man, not a celestial visitant.

Hogg's biography [item 664] appeared the same year and
generated a storm. The family had given Hogg materials for an
'official' life, counting on him for a sprightly narrative that
would encourage the 'right' kind of popularity. They misjudged.
The book was sprightly and popular, but the near-caricature of
Shelley, antic and foolish, led the family to withdraw materials
and sanction. Many find Hogg delightful, many find him malicious.
Altering letters and minimizing Shelley's radicalism, he improves
himself at Shelley's expense. But he has been the most influential biographer, for others have relied too uncritically on his
vivid narrative, and from them his conception has passed into
textbooks, anthologies, and popular works like Maurois' *Ariel*.

Peacock wrote five articles on Shelley between 1858 and
1862. Two corrected distortions and errors of the biographers
[items 653, 684]; two reprinted letters [items 687, 688]; the last
defended Harriet from her detractors [item 721]. Though clearly
a Shelley partisan, Peacock remains objective and uneffusive; he
is more accurate and unbiased than the others, despite preoccupa-
tion with Shelley's hallucinations.

In 1859 Lady Jane Shelley published *Shelley Memorials* [item

683], containing, with connecting narrative, the materials Hogg had abused. The book was a failure: Lady Jane could not produce what she had promised would clear Shelley of deserting Harriet, and readers preferred Hogg's lively version. Hogg's antic image was supported in 1860 by Garnett's reprinting of articles containing early letters which had appeared in 1826 and 1827 [item 689].

From outside the circle of family and friends came items of importance. Coining the "eternal child" epithet, Gilfillan's essay in 1845 was a bland compilation of Hogg, Hunt and Medwin, but it reached a wide audience, for Gilfillan was a standardizer, read and quoted as a reliable authority [item 434]. Robert Browning's essay in 1852 was critical in intent, but stressed the interdependence of Shelley's life and work [item 573]. Browning found Shelley practical in his attempts at reform, and strongly contended that Shelley would have become a Christian, a reminder that Shelley's views were still disturbing in 1852. A full-length biography by C. S. Middleton in 1858 [item 665] conflated the work of the friends with added snippets from other published sources—"a mere compilation," Peacock called it.

Rossetti's memoir, written for his poetical edition of 1870, was the first independent, carefully researched biography. He represents a new generation, for his work depended on research, not on memory. The memoir [item 839] was thorough for its time: until Dowden's biography in 1886, Rossetti's was the soundest account available. His balance and caution in dealing with the life did not extend to his critical remarks; there he was unstinting, almost indiscriminate, with superlatives. He is unusual, however, in praising the use of the grotesque in the political satires.

In a study of the early years in 1872 [item 876], Denis Florence MacCarthy underlined the non-lyric Shelley. His careful research uncovered much of Shelley's Irish political activities and corrected numerous errors in Hogg. His emphasis on Shelley as a practical, cogent politician is important, for in Victorian times this was the neglected side of Shelley.

By their very publication in a single decade, four other works indicate Shelley's growing reputation. Biographies by Smith [item 1011] and Stoddard [item 1012] added nothing: Smith reworked Lady Jane's materials; Stoddard, intending only a scrap-book approach, further disseminated the livelier parts of Mary and the friends. John Addington Symonds' biography [item 1036] appeared in the English Men of Letters Series and was extensively reprinted. Like Gilfillan's essay, it had a standardizing impact: in a popular series of short, inexpensive books, by a recognized literary figure, it reinforced the general conception of Shelley in clear, pleasant prose. John Cordy Jeaffreson's biography, *The Real Shelley* [item 1239], was concentrated sensationalism, a dynamiting of the seraphic image so long fostered by family and friends. Jeaffreson charged all but Hogg with concealing the truth: the 'real' Shelley was weak, effeminate, unreasonably rebellious against a loving father, treacherous to the innocent Harriet, unfaithful to Mary, untrustworthy as a friend, and probably certifiably mad. A carefully negative biography might have balanced the treacle and tears of the intemperate Shelleyans and prevented the critical backlash that soon began, but the cure that Jeaffreson offered was worse than the disease.

An amusing adjunct to these biographies are numerous *memento mori*—notes, tributes, and effusions of admirers cherishing sites associated with Shelley, notably his grave in Rome. Alfred Austin, later laureate, was a typical pilgrim in 1863. Notables had preceded him—Dickens in 1846, the Brownings in 1854—but he versified his visit:

> When men by knowledge shall be drawn,
>   Not driven by the goad,
>   This spot apart,
>   Where sleeps his heart,
>   Deaf to all clamour, wrong, or rage,
>   Shall be their choicest pilgrimage.

Others came as well: Coventry Patmore, Thomas Hardy, Aubrey De Vere; and the less known, like Walter Crane, Augustus Hare, and St. Clair Baddeley. Even Matthew Arnold came avisiting, but found the grave of Goethe's son more to his liking. Many, like Austin, misconstrued the "Cor Cordium" inscription, treasuring the spot where they supposed the poet's heart to lie. The real whereabouts of that disembodied organ provoked a controversy all their own, reaching a kind of climax in 1885, when A. S. Bicknell [item 1220] speculated that what Trelawny had snatched from the funeral pyre was more likely the liver than the heart.

While pilgrims pressed violets from the borders of the grave, critics at home were busy with the proliferating editions and biographies, and busy too writing assessments and comparisons.

The essays abound, but they are of little value to the modern scholar, except as they reflect the changing fashions in critical writing and the Victorian penchant for broad generalization and stately pronouncement. Because they have been scrutinized and summarized at length elsewhere,[6] only the most striking and influential need be noted here.

In the 1840's the important English commentary was by G. H. Lewes, Gilfillan, and De Quincey. Lewes' essay, a review of Mary's editions, was the first balanced appreciation of Shelley as poet and reformer [item 379]; Lewes subordinates biography to a consideration of the poet's content. Gilfillan's essay, mentioned as biography, was critically important too, for Gilfillan contends that the difficult passages in Shelley are products of subtlety of thought and not confusion—a common and persistent charge against Shelley [item 434]. In reviewing Gilfillan, De Quincey repeated the "eternal child"—resulting in its common misattribution to De Quincey—adding the memorable "lunatic angel" of his own [item 4 2 8]. Contesting Gilfillan, De Quincey tried to show how central to Shelley's thinking his antagonism to Christianity had been.

Several American critics stand out in the 1840's. Henry Tuckerman, in the influential *Southern Literary Messenger*, urged that Shelley be judged by his practice, not his principles; dismissing *Queen Mab* as crude and youthful rebellion, Tuckerman praised the lyrics and, surprisingly, the prose [items 361, 374]. In the New England Transcendentalist organ, *The Dial*, John M. Mackie stressed Shelley's courage in publishing his radical opinions, patiently

[xxxiii]

explaining the sources of Shelley's religious errors. Mackie saw
in Shelley's political views an utopian socialism akin to that of
Sir Thomas More [item 380]. Margaret Fuller, commenting on British poets of the time, spoke sentimentally of "the gentle, the
gifted, the ill-fated Shelley," whose lyrics were second only to
Shakespeare's, but she was most impressed by him as the poet of
nature [item 453]. Edwin Percy Whipple, an early champion of
Wordsworth, contrasted Shelley with Longfellow, with admiration
for Shelley's "strength and daring" and his superior imagination
[item 408]. In another review, Whipple found Shelley a man of
such extreme genius, so unhypocritically and naturally moral, that
his detractors looked foolish beside his example [item 424]. On
the whole, American critics, like their English counterparts, were
content to praise the melody and imagination, pity or excuse the
atheism, and ignore the social message whenever possible.

Neither Emerson nor Poe wrote a formal essay on Shelley,
but their comments, scattered over decades, should not go unnoted.
Emerson had no sympathy for Shelley at all:

> Shelley, though a poetic mind, is never a poet. His muse
> is uniformly imitative; all his poems composite. A good
> English scholar he is, with ear, taste, and memory, much
> more, he is a character full of noble and prophetic traits;
> but imagination, the original, authentic fire of the bard,
> he has not. [Item 364]

Later Emerson wrote in his journal, October 30, 1841: "Shelley is
wholly unaffecting to me. I was born too soon: but his power is
so manifest over a large class of the best persons, that he is not
to be overlooked" [item 1975]. By contrast, Poe admired Shelley

and was strongly influenced by him, not only in poetry, but in critical theory. Julia Power explores the influence fully, and she speculates that Poe strove to conceal it [item 2857]. Poe, in a comparison of Shelley and Tennyson [item 501], concluded that the ideal poet was "that mental and moral combination which shall unite in one person (if ever it shall) the Shelleyan *abandon* and the Tennysonian poetic sense, with the most profound Art (based both in Instinct and Analysis) and the sternest Will properly to blend and rigourously to control all." Again, Shelley is not a poet of thought or substance, but of unregulated impulse.

The 1850's were marked by essays of Browning, Kingsley, and Bagehot. Browning's essay [item 573], already mentioned, shows a salient danger in the biographical approach. Categorizing poets as objective or subjective, he found Shelley the epitome of the latter, and contended that man and poet were, in such a case, inseparable, the work being a projective outpouring of an inner vision. Later, confronted with Shelley's culpability in the separation from Harriet, Browning was ashamed of his earlier enthusiasm for the poetry. The circular reasoning which defends the life by the work and the work by the life is a result of the tenuous assumption, dear to the Victorians, that great poetry is written by men of purity—a problem that Shelley himself wrestled with in the *Defence of Poetry*. In Kingsley and Bagehot, Shelley had damaging detractors. Kingsley, defender of Byron, was tired of the contrastings of the two poets' vices, contrasts increasingly favoring Shelley as Byron's fame declined [item 582]. Iterating familiar

[xxxv]

moral charges against Shelley, Kingsley champions 'virility'—a
substitute for purity in the equation—and calls Shelley weak,
wailing, and effeminate. After pages of sarcastic ranting, he
still terms Shelley a great lyric poet: when he "leaves philosophy and politics, which he does not understand, and shriekings and
cursings, which are unfit for any civilized and self-respecting
man—he is perfect." Bagehot's essay was the most influential of
the decade [item 614]. Here Shelley was a creature entirely "impulsive and childlike"; his interest in reform was the same: "The
love of liberty is peculiarly natural to the simple impulsive
mind." Bagehot's view of the life was based primarily on Hogg;
judging the poetry accordingly, he dismissed Shelley's thought
with an impatient wave of the hand, praising only short poems and
lyrical passages of the longer works.

        In the 1860's prominent voices were raised in Shelley's
favor; the numerous biographies and reviews were making possible a
clearer understanding of Shelley. David Masson, writing in *Macmillan's Magazine* in 1860, found Shelley's philosophy consistent, his
atheism a misnomer for Platonism and pantheism, his politics practical, and his long poems his great achievement [item 694]. In
the same year, James ("B. V.") Thomson expressed indignation at
the treatment Shelley had been receiving [item 697]:

>   Emerson is serenely enthroned above hearing him at all;
>   Carlyle only hears him 'shriek hysterically'; Mrs. Brown-
>   ing discovers him 'blind with his white ideal'; Messrs
>   Ruskin and Kingsley treat him much as senior schoolboys
>   treat the youngster who easily 'walks over their heads'
>   in class—with reluctant tribute of admiration copiously
>   qualified with sneers, pinches, and kicks.

Thomson pleads for a serious consideration of Shelley's subject matter, but in vain. Three years later, R. H. Hutton, reviewing some of the biographies [item 738], finds Shelley's mysticism "either the cravings of an expectant rapture, or the agony of a severed nerve," and like Bagehot, he thinks Shelley ruled only by the "authority of impulse." *Adonais* is "only a rainbow of beautiful regrets"; *Prometheus Unbound* is meaningless because, to Hutton, Demogorgon is "pure nothingness," and where is the drama in the triumph of nothing? But Hutton concludes by placing Shelley in the "front rank" because, of course, he wrote great lyrics.

By the late 1860's Rossetti was at work on his edition, and he wrote to *Notes and Queries* with a series of suggested emendations [items 789, 790, 791, 792], which prompted a major reply by Swinburne in the *Fortnightly Review* [item 802] urging editorial caution. Critically, however, Swinburne was no more restrained than Rossetti; rejoicing that Shelley was now a "classic" warranting such textual scrutiny, Swinburne called him "the master-singer of our modern race and age." Excess follows excess: Shelley is "the poet beloved above all other poets, being beyond all other poets—in one word, and the only proper word—divine." Fifteen years later Swinburne was defending Shelley against Matthew Arnold's famous gibe, perhaps never appreciating how comments like his own had provoked Arnold and others to depreciate Shelley, and made such depreciations welcome in many quarters when they came.

In the last sixteen years of this period, Shelley was again read for political reasons when new utopians, new spokesmen for reform, and a newly emerging socialist left proclaimed him a prophet and seer; typical are Mathilde Blind, Charles Sotheran, and Henry S. Salt [items 836, 968, 1129]. The radical poems are still occasionally thought morally unsafe, with warnings that they be kept out of young hands [items 813, 871]. And respected men like John C. Shairp and Leslie Stephen echoed Bagehot's estimate of Shelley as impulsive, mindless lyrist [1046, 1043]. But new notes are also struck. In 1880, John Todhunter's *Study of Shelley*, the first book-length critical study, grouped Shelley with Victor Hugo and Walt Whitman as the greatest poets of the democratic ideal; while asserting the importance of the poet's thought, Todhunter relents in the end and rests his case on the lyric genius of the mistaken visionary [item 1084].

Foreign criticism has its first impact with Taine's *History of English Literature* and Brandes' *Naturalism in England* [items 863, 1869]. Taine follows the English stereotype, noting that Shelley allowed "his conduct to be guided by an enthusiastic imagination which he should have kept for his verses," and suggesting that Shelley had a weak hold on the actual. Brandes, in a chapter entitled "Radical Naturalism," claimes startlingly that Shelley's life was "of greater and more enduring significance in the emancipation of the human mind than all that happened in France in August of 1792." But Brandes seconds Taine in concluding that "where [Shelley] fell short was in his grip on reality."

This is a period of numerous Shelley anthologies, among which the most influential was one edited by Stopford Brooke. His

introduction, appearing first in *Macmillan's Magazine* [item 1061],
is as balanced a set of remarks as the biographical approach ever
achieved, and it was fortunate for Shelley's reputation that this
should be the most reprinted of the anthologies. Brooke saw Shelley as a poet of nature, a moral poet interested in reform, and a
poet of the abstract. To Brooke, Shelley is not sufficiently personal in his major works; he speaks to mankind and for mankind,
but he converts the individual to the universal by a submergence
of self, and in this respect is inferior to Wordsworth, for whom
that conversion did not result in abstraction and depersonaliza-
tion, but rather in a magnified intensification of the reality of
experience.

There are a few attempts to develop critical alterna-
tives to the biographical approach. Thomson, for example, closely
considers the structure of *Prometheus Unbound*, foreshadowing the for-
malist approach in his concern for the poem's organic unity [items
1094, 1095, 1098, 1101, 1102]. John Mackinnon Robertson tries a
comparative evaluation: in two-thirds of his space he demolishes
the *Revolt of Islam*, then perversely adopts it as a yardstick to
measure other works, finding Shelley inconsistent, confusing and
confused [items 1196, 1197, 1198]. In the midst of this shambles,
Robertson compares Shelley to Keats, to the detriment of Shelley
and the glory of Keats. From this time on, Shelley's name will
be linked more and more with that of Keats and contrasted more and
more with that of Byron—a recognition of stylistic and conceptual
affinities replaces the earlier concern for shared political view.

[xxxix]

In our own century, when Keats' reputation eclipses Shelley's, the pairing culminates in the *Keats-Shelley Memorial Bulletin* and the *Keats-Shelley Journal*. A shared graveyard in Rome sentimentalizes the link —on the evidence of *Adonais* and the Protestant Cemetery, more than one critic assumed they had been fast friends. The Shelley of the *Defence of Poetry* is better yoked with the Keats of *Hyperion* and the letters than with the Byron whose literary ideal was Pope.

To the contrasting of Shelley and Byron we owe Arnold's famed remark, the most quoted of all about Shelley. More than a clever turn of phrase, it is a touchstone of the predominating view articulated by Victorian critics. In his "Preface" to a Byron anthology [item 1103], Arnold wrote:

> . . . As a man, Shelley is at a number of points immeasurably Byron's superior; he is a beautiful and enchanting spirit, whose vision, when we call it up, has far more loveliness, more charm for our soul, than the vision of Byron. But all the personal charm of Shelley cannot hinder us from at last discovering in his poetry the incurable want, in general, of a sound subject-matter, and the incurable fault, in consequence, of unsubstantiality. [p. viii]
>
> . . . I for my part can never think of equalling with them [Byron and Wordsworth] any of their contemporaries; —Coleridge, poet and philosopher wrecked in a mist of opium; or Shelley, beautiful and ineffectual angel, beating in the void his luminous wings in vain. [p. xxxi]

This is the traditional biographical approach, nothing novel, nothing strange: Mary had made Shelley an angel, Leigh Hunt seconded, and Medwin confirmed; Hogg had shown Shelley ineffectual; any number had insisted he was airy and ethereal. The remark distills sixty years of opinion epigrammatically; it is rhetorical flourish, not prejudiced attack. The words have a different cast if we note how they echo a comment by Joubert that Arnold himself had earlier translated as: "Plato loses himself in the void . . . but one sees the play of his wings, one hears their rustle" [see item 2839]. Who would mind beating his luminous wings in the same void with Plato? Surely not Shelley.

There is a poetic justice to the popularity of Arnold's epithet. It was a sad reverse for those who had worked so hard to secure Shelley's place among the seraphim: with the deft turning of a phrase, angelhood had now become a poetic liability. Fond of Milton's Satan, Shelley could have counseled them, "Better to reign in Hell than serve in Heaven."

* * * * * *

By 1886 Shelley's fame and popularity reach their high-water mark. Now a Shelley Society is founded, Dowden writes the 'official' life, and soon the poet's centennial is celebrated. A little further on, and the 'world's slow stain' begins, the corrosion of the halo as literary tastes change, the attack and counter as adjustment is made to the false Victorian conception.

The Shelley Society first met on March 10, 1886. In its initial years activity was intense: numerous facsimile reprints of the less-known works, the first stage performance of *The Cenci*, and assistance in compiling the concordance [item 1603]. Its history is chronicled in its *Notebook* [item 1373], and recounted with delightful irreverence by Sylva Norman in *Flight of the Skylark*.[7]

[xli]

Dowden's biography appeared later that year [item 1283].
In many ways a success, it stood without challenge as the defini-
tive scholarly life until Newman Ivey White's *Shelley* in 1940.
White's own estimate of it is a fair one:

> Professor Dowden, Shelley's authorized biographer,
> successfully maintained his independence of Lady Shelley's
> control, but he could not be independent of the dominant
> tendency of the age. His treatment of Shelley is apolo-
> getically and sentimentally protective. To him Shelley
> was great and good not because of, but in spite of, his
> major beliefs. He did not sufficiently perceive either
> the guiding purpose of Shelley's life or the strength of
> that purpose. This may explain why one so admirable in
> the collection and presentation of factual detail could
> be at the same time so glossily mediocre in his critical
> treatment of Shelley's ideas. [Item 2863, II, 417]

Reviewers were strong in their praise [e.g., 1266, 1271, 1323],
though Mark Twain was disgusted by Dowden's handling of Harriet,
contending that it was not necessary to destroy Harriet to love
Shelley [items 1656, 1658, 1659]. The *Quarterly* too was in the
minority when it faulted Dowden for neglecting the negative in
Shelley's life and repeated the earlier image of Shelley as an impulsive, near-mad child who had propounded wickedness while writing gorgeous lyrics [item 1332]. And Matthew Arnold regretted
knowing the facts of Shelley's life; he credited Dowden with try-
ing to destroy the lovable and angelic Shelley of the earlier accounts [item1386]. He was irritated by what he called "Dowden's
pleadings for Shelley." Reading the life had not changed his former judgment, and he quoted himself emphatically at the end of his
review:

> The man Shelley, in very truth, is not entirely sane,
> and Shelley's poetry is not entirely sane either. The

> Shelley of actual life is a vision of beauty and radiance, indeed, but availing nothing. And in poetry, no less than in life, he is "a beautiful *and ineffectual* angel, beating in the void his luminous wings in vain."

The majority, however, concurred that Dowden's biography was the authority for the facts of Shelley's life.

In the remaining years of the century there are two other biographies: one, by William Sharp, was a popular, short volume in the Great Writers Series [item 1377]; the other, by the Frenchman Felix Rabbe, was the first translated work on Shelley [item 1425]. Both were favorable and familiar material. Even the entry in the *Dictionary of National Biography* supports the general critical view: "Opinion seems to be agreeing to recognize Shelley as the supreme lyrist, all of whose poems, whatever their outward form should be viewed from the lyric standpoint" [item 1709].

In the twentieth century, important information has come from previously unpublished sources. We now have the diaries of Edward Williams [item 1808], John Polidori [item 2035], and Mary herself [item 3140], and the voluminous correspondence of the whole circle of family and friends . The accounts of Hogg, Medwin and Peacock have been edited with annotation [items 1849, 1890, 1973, 2620, 2071]. And information recovered from the legal files of the family solicitor by Roger Ingpen has clarified Shelley's years in England [item 2124].

Among the numerous biographical attempts, some stand out for their influence. To correct for Dowden's protectiveness, Arthur Clutton-Brock stressed Shelley's faults, which produced the

impractical dreamer again [item 1974]. Widely cited in later
works, A. H. Koszul's thoughtful examination of the early years,
La Jeunesse de Shelley (Paris, 1910), has unfortunately never been
translated. Ingpen's work was a straight-forward, non-literary
account, essentially free from inference and implied judgment
[item 2124]. Helen Rossetti Angeli's retelling of the Italian
years, with new information, was a temperate narrative in which
Shelley appeared a practical thinker in touch with the ideas of
his time [item 2026]. H. N. Brailsford's *Shelley, Godwin, and Their
Circle*, not strictly biography, usefully depicts the intellectual
climate and helps give context to Shelley's thinking in a larger
radical spectrum, despite over-emphasis on Godwin's influence
[item 2069]. Mrs. Campbell's spirited defense of Shelley as ef-
fectual, manly, and possessed of a keen, clear mind, still makes
lively reading; the works strips away Victorian prejudices and
fallacies, but is marred by its enthusiasm and the purchase of
Shelley's greatness at the expense of other Romantic writers
[item 2353].

    The most damaging work has been André Maurois' smooth
fictionalization, *Ariel*, more widely read than any other life of
the poet, and directly responsible for the persistence of the
angelic Shelley [item 2361]. Here at last is the biography Lady
Jane would have rejoiced to read; here is the life story of Bagehot's impulsive child, Kingsley's effeminate lyrist, and Arnold's
ineffectual angel. That such a book should be popular, that it
should shape, if not create, the general image of Shelley is an

understandable misfortune. That it received support by academics is shocking, yet Bernbaum in *Guide Through the Romantic Movement* [item 3267] said: "An historical fiction, based on good sources; delightfully vivid. The interpretation is worldly wise."

The first scholarly biography of the century was also a misfortune. Walter Edwin Peck, a tireless caviler, produced a compendious life full of minor discoveries and errors [item 2452]. He was not able to forge a consistent whole out of his idiosyncratic readings and biographical minutiae.

At last, in 1940, Newman Ivey White published *Shelley*, a dependable factual and critical life [item 2863]. Many have taken issue with White on one point or another, but not without admiration for his thoroughness, care and acumen. An even greater asset of White's is his willingness to entertain doubt, to leave doors open for disagreement; he offers the probable, not the absolute. For every disputed point, he gave all the evidence then available; he was not afraid to conjecture, but he did not confuse his own theories and the facts. His shortcomings, minor ones, stem from a common cause. Earlier work on Shelley's contemporary reputation and Shelley's influence on nineteenth century radicals had given him a special interest in the political, with a consequent shortchanging of literary and philosophical aspects, and more notably the difficult area of Shelley and religion.

The solidity of White's work was made clear when it came under attack in 1945. In a debunking effort reminiscent of *The Real Shelley*, Robert Metcalf Smith and his associates accused White

and Shelley scholars generally of shielding Shelley by the sup-
pression of evidence [item 3046]. Smith's distortions, circular
reasoning, unfounded accusations and misuse of evidence in *The
Shelley Legend* were exposed in three devastating reviews [items
3075, 3080, 3081], which were later collected into a book.[8]

The biographical survey ends with a popular book,
Shelley, by Edmund Blunden, which provides little that is new.
Dependent on Dowden, Blunden writes an entertaining chronicle
with intelligent literary valuations, a decent choice for general
reader and undergraduate alike [item 3095].

Significant textual gains have been scored in this last
period. The centennial brought Forman's "Aldine Edition," the
last refinement of his labors [item 1605], and Woodberry's careful collation, sound and conservative, though excessive it its
repointing of the texts [item 1620]. Key manuscript materials
were edited and transcribed: C. D. Locock, A. H. Koszul, and R.
H. Hill worked on the Bodleian holdings, and Forman deciphered the
notebooks which had migrated to America, lodging later in the
Huntington Library [items 1818, 2008, 2418, 2030]. Most important
of all, Shelley's *Philosophical View of Reform* saw light in 1920. His
greatest statement of political principle, it was unknown aside
from Dowden's summary paraphrase in 1886 [item 2187].

In the 1920's a collective edition was undertaken by
Ingpen and Peck, the Julian Edition [item 2419]. By default, it
is definitive, though marred by the omission of restricted materials now available, and inferior to work already done. It is now

inadequate to the burdens a definitive edition must bear; in light of the numerous subsequent discoveries, and the availability of material formerly withheld, a fresh attempt is needed and overdue.

Further textual advances have resulted from Woodberry's photographic facsimile of the Harvard notebook [item 2511], and additional work on the Bodleian manuscripts by Sir John C. E. Shelley-Rolls and Ingpen [item 2643]. In the steady stream of minor additions, a most welcome one has been accurate texts of Shelley's translations of Plato [item 3217].

In this last period, critical material shifts from the general appreciation, mainstay of the nineteenth century, to close textual readings, source studies, and detailed examinations of large areas of Shelley's thought. The general appreciation did not die out quite soon enough to forestall the greatest gush of grandiloquence produced in the name of Shelley, an essay in the *Dublin Review* [item 1929] by Francis Thompson, whose twenty-five pages of 'prose-poetry' are intense purple:

> . . . The universe is his box of toys. He dabbles his
> fingers in the day-fall. He is gold-dusty with tumbling
> amidst the stars. He makes bright mischief with the moon.
> The meteors nuzzle their noses in his hand. He teases in-
> to growling the kennelled thunder, and laughs at the shak-
> ing of its fiery chain. He dances in and out of the gates
> of heaven: its floor is littered with his broken fancies.
> He runs wild over the fields of ether. He chases the
> rolling world. He gets between the feet of the horses of
> the sun. He stands in the lap of patient Nature, and
> twines her loosened tresses. . . .

Admirers of Shelley continued to quote approvingly from Thompson well into the 1950's.

A major movement in the changing sensibility at the time

of the First World War was the New Humanism, whose leading voices, Paul Elmer More and Irving Babbitt, condemned Shelley for his emotionalism, and for taking his own flights of fancy too seriously [items 2010, 2149]. In contrast with Milton, More found Shelley lacking in maturity and control; Babbitt suggested that any man who had not outgrown Shelley at forty had not grown up. To the defense came Joseph Warren Beach [item 2234], but the attack was renewed by the New Criticism, offspring of New Humanism, which concentrated on the rhetorical and formal concerns of a renascent classicism. T. S. Eliot, key figure in the doctrinal transition, extended the attack of his Harvard mentor, Babbitt. Though many years later Eliot was to credit Shelley's genius, ranking him among the great heretics, in 1933 Eliot found him the poet of adolescence, whose ideas were puerile and offensive [item 2615]. To the defense came Herbert Read with a bit of psychoanalyzing that made Shelley a psychotic with persecution delusions, incestuous desires, and homosexual tendencies [item 2714]. To Read, Shelley's narcissism and undeveloped personality were the sources of his poetic greatness. A more cogent and pertinent defense was offered by C. S. Lewis [item 2836], who stressed Shelley's relationship to the classical tradition from which Eliot would have divorced him. With Lewis the disagreement with Shelley's principles did not preclude admiration for Shelley's poetic greatness, which was not his religious, but his mythic vision.

The strongest attacks came from the major figures of the New Criticism itself. It was to the remarks of F. R. Leavis and Cleanth Brooks [items 2713, 2832] that the later defenders, Richard H. Fogle [item 3025] and Frederick A. Pottle[9] addressed critical responses. Professor Cameron pinpoints the central weakness of the New Critical attacks[10]:

> . . . It is sometimes asked why Shelley scholars have not made a full scale reply to these attacks. The answer is that they are peripheral. The New Critics take no account of Shelley's major works, either in verse or prose, but base their attack upon the stylistic analysis of selected lyrics.
> The fact that the New Critics have frequently misunderstood these lyrics and that their stylistic analysis itself is sometimes open to question. . . is of less consequence than the fact that their judgment has no total relevance.

The attack was in reality an assault on Victorian critical standards and judgments, and the attackers had naturally chosen the minor lyrics so inordinately admired by the earlier generation.

When we seek names the 'size' of Eliot's with which to redress the critical balance, we have the positive remarks of Yeats, Shaw, and A. C. Bradley [items 1825, 2583, 2503]. If we seek close studies of his thought and his poetics, we are also richly provided. Shelley's poetic theory and versification have been analyzed [items 2455, 2589]; his theology has been treated [items 2557, 2585, 2752, 2835]; his political writings, activities and influence have been examined in the works of White and Cameron; and, we have had broader studies linking the life with the poems or tracing the developing expression of his central concepts [items 2222, 2562, 2618, 2715, 2758, 3136].

Two studies stand out above the rest; through thorough and detailed scholarship both succeed in the larger and more difficult task of creating a sense of the whole Shelley from the diverse parts. Carl Grabo's *The Magic Plant* traces the difficult development of Shelley's thought, integrating the poetry, prose, and letters with the essential biography [item 2712]. Carlos Baker's *Shelley's Major Poetry* restricts itself to the core of the canon as it develops the thesis that Shelley is a "profoundly serious philosophical and psychological poet" [item 3170]. Both writers establish Shelley as more than a lyrist in their emphasis on the scope and depth of his thinking.

Shelley is now the classic that Swinburne rejoiced to see him becoming; his life and works are still read for pleasure, but they have become the property of the academic community. The material dealing with him is to an ever greater extent analytical and scholarly, the accumulation and examination of facts by the specialists. The material on Shelley is now a subject of study in itself, and the 'weight of scholarship' is no longer metaphor: the assembled entries of this bibliography would tip the scales at nearly two tons. To borrow from Shelley's *Defence of Poetry*, ". . . Our calculations have outrun our conceptions; we have eaten more than we can digest." There is need now for the kinds of study which will 'digest,' which will integrate the wealth of research. We will always profit from the continuing textual labors and close readings, but "a voice is wanting" to give us clearer assessment of the whole of Shelley's accomplishment, and to broaden and enrich our perspective on each of the mature works.

* * * * *

[1]

NOTES TO THE INTRODUCTION

[1] Much of this early material has been treated in the pioneering scholarship of George L. Marsh in "The Early Reviews of Shelley," [item 2496], and Newman Ivey White in *The Unextinguished Hearth* [item 2797]. White also wrote the best summary and discussion of the growth of Shelley's reputation in the penultimate chapter, titled "Shelley's Posthumous Reputation," of his *Shelley* [item 2863]. The other principal studies of Shelley's reputation and of Shelley criticism are: 1) Francis Claiborne Mason, *A Study in Shelley Criticism* [item 2764]; 2) Willis Winslow Pratt, *Shelley Criticism in England 1810-1890* [item 2679]; 3) Julia Power, *Shelley in America in the Nineteenth Century: His Relation to American Critical Thought and His Influence* [item 2857]; 4) Francis B. Carothers, Jr., *The Development of Shelley Criticism, 1810-1916: A Study of Conditions That Have Influenced His Critical Reputation* (Los Angeles: an unpublished doctoral dissertation, University of Southern California, 1954); 5) Sophia Phillips Nelson, *Shelleyana, 1935-1949* (University Park, Penn.: unpublished doctoral dissertation, Pennsylvania State University); 6) Sylva Norman, *Flight of the Skylark: The Development of Shelley's Reputation* (Norman, Okla.: University of Oklahoma Press, 1954).

[2] The full history of *Blackwood's* vacillations on Shelley has been described by Alan Lang Strout in "*Maga,* Champion of Shelley," [item 2563].

[3] For a fuller consideration of radical press treatment of Shelley, see Newman Ivey White's "Shelley and the Active Radicals of the Early Nineteenth Century," [item 2527].

[4] For a fuller consideration of the *Examiner's* treatment of Shelley see Edmund Blunden's *Leigh Hunt's "Examiner" Examined* [item 2479] , R. Brimley Johnson's *Shelley-Leigh Hunt: How Friendship Made History* [items 2483, 2507], and an article by Walter Graham, "Shelley's Debt to Leigh Hunt and the *Examiner,*" [item 2373].

[5] A more extensive sampling of the verse tributes is available in Newman Ivey White's *Unextinguished Hearth* [item 2797] and his *Shelley* [item 2863], and also, with delightful, skewering commentary, in Sylva Norman's *Flight of the Skylark* (see note 1 above).

[6] The best summaries are in the works of Mason [item 2764] and Carothers (see note 1 above); both provide intelligent quotation and comment. Summaries in Pratt [item 2679] are more superficial; his commentary is generally less apt, and occasionally misleading or misinformed.

[7] See Chapter XIV, "Expansion as Epilogue."

[8] *An Examination of the Shelley Legend* (Philadelphia, 1951).

[9] Frederick A. Pottle, "The Case for Shelley,"*PMLA*, LXVII, No. 3 (September, 1952), 589-608.

[10] Kenneth Neill Cameron, "Shelley Scholarship: 1940-1953. A Critical Survey," *Keats-Shelley Journal,* III, (Winter, 1954), [89]-109.

BIBLIOGRAPHICAL PRINCIPLES

The present bibliography was undertaken to close the gap between the work of Newman Ivey White in his *Unextinguished Hearth* and the work of the *Keats-Shelley Journal* in its annual bibliography of Shelley material. White catalogued material on Shelley published during the poet's lifetime and the first six months after his death; the *Keats-Shelley Journal* has provided an annual cataloguing of material since July of 1950.

To create a catalogue of materials between January of 1823 and June of 1950, I began by collating and verifying all of the entries in the existing partial bibliographies. Every such entry was included here, regardless of its merit, so long as it was written in English. The only exceptions to this rule were patent errors, ghost entries, insignificant editions, and anthologies. This omnivorous approach, the swallowing whole of earlier bibliographies, has clear justification: as a result, this bibliography renders unnecessary the consultation of any of its predecessors. The partial bibliographies subsumed are:

1. *The Cambridge Bibliography of English Literature*. Volumes III and V.
2. *The New Cambridge Bibliography of English Literature*. Volume III.
3. *Poole's Index to Periodical Literature*. The original and revised editions, and supplements.
4. *Nineteenth Century Readers' Guide to Periodical Literature*.
5. *The Magazine Subject-Index: A Subject-Index to Seventy-Nine American and English Periodicals*.
6. *Readers' Guide to Periodical Literature*.
7. "The Romantic Movement: A Selective and Critical Bibliography," in *ELH* originally, and subsequently appearing in *Philological Quarterly*.
8. *Modern Humanities Research Association. Annual Bibliography of English Language and Literature*.
9. "Annual Bibliography," in *PMLA*.
10. *The Year's Work in English Studies. The English Association*.

In addition, the items named or listed in the following works
were included:

1. Alan Lang Strout, "*Maga*, Champion of Shelley," *Studies in Philology*,
   XXIX, No. 1 (January, 1932), 95-119.
2. Willis Winslow Pratt, *Shelley Criticism in England, 1810-1890*. An
   unpublished doctoral dissertation, Cornell University. Itaca,
   New York, 1935.
3. Francis Claiborne Mason, *A Study in Shelley Criticism: An Examination of the Principal Interpretations of Shelley's Art and Philosophy in England from 1818 to 1860*. Mercersburg, Pennsylvania:
   privately printed, 1937.
4. Elizabeth Nitchie, "Shelley in 'Fraser's' and the Annuals," *The Times
   Literary Supplement (London)*, No. 1960 (August 26, 1939), 503.
5. Newman Ivey White, *Shelley*. 2 vols. New York: Alfred A. Knopf, 1940.
6. Julia Power, *Shelley in America in the Nineteenth Century: His Relation to American Critical Thought and His Influence. University
   of Nebraska Studies*, XL, No. 2 (April, 1940). Lincoln, Nebraska:
   University of Nebraska Press.
7. Francis B. Carothers, Jr., *The Development of Shelley Criticism,
   1810-1916: A Study of Conditions That Have Influenced His Critical Reputation*. An unpublished doctoral dissertation, University
   of Southern California. Los Angeles, 1954.
8. Sophia Phillips Nelson, *Shelleyana, 1935-1939*. An unpublished doctoral
   dissertation, Pennsylvania State University. University Park,
   Pennsylvania, 1951.
9. Sylva Norman, *Flight of the Skylark: The Development of Shelley's
   Reputation*. Norman, Oklahoma: The University of Oklahoma Press,
   1954.

When all of the items from these sources were transcribed and
collated, I had a little over two thousand items each of which
I then attempted to verify by first-hand personal inspection.
In the scholarly libraries to which I went in the course of the
verification I inspected the card catalogues for additional po-
tential entries. And, as each individual item was verified, I
also examined it carefully, inspecting footnotes, indices and
bibliographies for further materials. Particular attention was
also devoted to the indices and tables of contents of periodicals.
This added searching produced another two thousand items, only
half of which have been worthy of inclusion.

Essentially, three kinds of items have been excluded. Of the hundreds of reprintings of Shelley's poems, both in books and in the periodical press, only major editions and editions of peculiar historical or textual importance have been included here. I have also excluded the numerous musical settings of Shelley's poetry; they have been given ample treatment in Burton R. Pollin's *Music for Shelley's Poetry (1810-1971)* (New York: Da Capo Press, 1974). As a second group, clearly related to the first, I have excluded textbooks, except those listed in the earlier partial bibliographies. Third, and most difficult, is the loose category of "passing references." I have excluded almost seven hundred minor mentions, even though some of them were no more minor than items which have been included because they previously apppeared in the partial bibliographies. I judged each mention by asking, was the statement important because of the time or place in which it appeared? was the author of the statement himself important enough to warrant inclusion of his repetition of the name of Shelley? was the statement of peculiar intrinsic interest?

I have marked with an asterisk every item which I have not been able to verify by first hand inspection. Constituting about ten percent of the entries, this group of items is not unified by any internal characteristic; they are simply unexamined items. For the most part they are items available in very few libraries, but in many cases they are works which had not come to my attention until after I had moved on from the libraries in which I might have seen them. Naturally, I reached a point at which I had to call a halt to my researches, leaving the library stacks for the typewriter; any item which turned up after that time—for example, two items sent to me by the kindness of Professor Charles E. Robinson of the University of Delaware— and any item which had not been verified already automatically received an asterisk. At least a dozen other asterisks were awarded entries that proved defective, items that I had inspected, but for which my notations proved inaccurate, or occasionally even absurd; they are reminders of human weakness, products of momentary inattention, writer's cramp, tired eyes, or bad light.

I have read, reread, proofread, checked and cross-checked the entries here, yet I know that errors must remain. For these I ask the reader's indulgence. Because I have a continuing interest in the matter of Shelley bibliography, I hope that any reader discovering omitted material worthy of inclusion will publish his findings or forward the listings to me through the publisher.

SIGNS AND SYMBOLS

[ ]   Editorial insertion; used to enclose item numbers, annotations, and cross-referencing

*[ ]   Used to identify items not personally verified by first-hand inspection of them in their original form

[?]   Used in place of missing datum, or to indicate conjectural datum

[B]   Biographical item; an item dealing with the life, the ancestors, the descendants, the grave, the body, or the memorials of Shelley

[C]   Critical item; an item essentially evaluative or interpretive of Shelley's works

[M]   Mention of Shelley; material usually of minor significance

[R]   Review item; an item reviewing a work by Shelley, or a work about Shelley, and cross-referenced to indicate the work reviewed

[T]   Textual item; an edition of the text, or an item dealing with emendation, correction, location, or transmission of the text

[*sic*] An error or anomaly in the spelling which is reproduced as found in the original

(brackets in the original) A compromise attempt to avoid following brackets with brackets where brackets have occurred in the original

( )   Used to enclose bracketed information within bracketed information; with the exception of the phrase identified immediately above, all information in parentheses appeared within parentheses in the original unless the parentheses occur within brackets

A Bibliography of
Shelley Studies: 1823-1950

Periodicals:

[1]   [Anonymous]. "The Candid," *Blackwood's Edinburgh Magazine*,
      XIII, No. lxxii (January, 1823), 123-124. [M]

[2]   [Anonymous]. "Art. XXXIV. *Elegy on the Death of Percy Bysshe
      Shelley.* By Arthur Brooke. 12mo. 20pp. 1s6d. C. &
      J. Oliver [*sic*]. 1822.," *The Monthly Censor*, II, No. 8
      (January, 1823), 101. [R]

[3]   [Signed "Jonathan Oldmixon"]. "Oldmixon on 'The Liberal
      No. II.,'" *The Scots Magazine, and Edinburgh Literary Miscel-
      lany* [later titled *The Edinburgh Magazine*], New Series
      XII [whole number XCI], [No. 1] (January, 1823), 9-16.
      [R; M: 9]

[4]   [Anonymous]. "Letters from Italy. No. VI.," *Blackwood's
      Edinburgh Magazine*, XIII, No. lxxiv (March, 1823), 281.
      [M]

[5]   [Anonymous]. "Valperga," *Blackwood's Edinburgh Magazine*, XIII,
      No. lxxiv (March, 1823), 283-293. [R; M]

[6]   [Anonymous]. "Art. XXVI. The Liberal or 'Verse and Prose
      from the South,' No. I. and II.," *The Monthly Censor*, II,
      No. 11 (April, 1823), 452-456. [R; M: 454-455]

[7]   Soligny, Vicompte de [pseud. of Peter G. Patmore]. "Count
      Tims laudeth the late Mr. Shelley.," *Blackwood's Edinburgh
      Magazine*, XIII, No. lxxvi (May, 1823), 564. [C]

[8]   [Signed "J. Oldmixon"]. "Note on 'The Liberal. —No.
      III.,'" *The Edinburgh Magazine* [*And Literary Miscellany, Being a
      New Series of The Scots Magazine*], [New Series] XII [whole
      number XCI], [No. 5] (May, 1823), 614-616. [R; M:615]

[9]   [?Maginn, William]. "Letters of Timothy Tickler, Esq. to
      Eminent Literary Characters, No. VIII. To the Editor
      of Blackwood's Magazine. On the last Number of the
      Edinburgh Review, and Things in General.," *Blackwood's
      Edinburgh Magazine*, XIV, No. lxxix (August, 1823), 212-
      235. [C: 227-228]

[10] [Hunt, Leigh]. "On the Suburbs of Genoa and the Country
      about London.," *The Literary Examiner*, No. VIII [sub-
      titled *The Indicator*, No. LXXXI] (August 23, 1823),
      [113]-120. [B: 118-119]

[11] Odoherty, M. [pseud. of William Maginn]. "Odoherty on
      Don Juan, Cantos IX. X. XI.," *Blackwood's Edinburgh
      Magazine*, XIV, No. lxxx (September, 1823), 282-293.
      [M: 282]

[12] [Anonymous]. "Sonnet to Percy Shelley.," *The Literary
      Examiner*, No. XII [subtitled *The Indicator*, No. LXXXV]
      (September 20, 1823), 192.   [C]

[13] [Anonymous]. "Art. III. *Flora Domestica*, or the Portable
      Flower Garden; with Directions for the Treatment of
      Plants in Pots; and Illustrations from the Works of
      the Poets. 8vo. pp. xii. 396. Price 12s. London
      [/] 2. *Hortus Anglicus*; or, the Modern English Garden:
      containing a familiar Description of all the Plants
      which are cultivated in the Climate of Great Britain,
      either for Use or Ornament, and of a Selection from
      established Favourites of the Stove and Greenhouse:
      arranged according to the system of Linnæus; with
      Remarks on the Properties of the more valuable
      Species. By the Author of "The British Botanist."
      2 vols. 12mo. pp. 1126. Price 16s. London,
      1822.," *The Eclectic Review*, XX (October, 1823), 319-
      333.   [C: 328-329]

[14] Montgomery, Gerard. "Introductory Stanzas to the Second
      Canto of La Belle Tryamour," *Knight's Quarterly Magazine*,
      I, No. ii (October, 1823), 378-382.   [M]

[15] Montgomery, Gerard. "La Belle Tryamour [/] Canto II,"
      Knight's Quarterly Magazine, I, No. ii (October, 1823),
      383-418.   [C, satire]

[16] Titus [pseud. of Henry Thomson]. "Modern Dramas, and
      Dramatic Writers," *Blackwood's Edinburgh Magazine*, XIV,
      No. lxxxii (November, 1823), 555-560.   [C; M: 555]

[17] [Anonymous]. "Animal and Vegetable Diet.," *The Medical
      Adviser*, [I], No. 1 (December 6, 1823), 13-16.   [M]

Books:

[18] [Kent, Elizabeth]. *Flora Domestica, or The Portable Flower-
      Garden; with Directions for the Treatment of Plants in Pots;
      and Illustrations from the Works of the Poets.* xxxiv +
      396pp. London: Taylor and Hessey, 1823. [M: xx;
      T: 16]

[19] Soligny, Victoire, Count de [pseud. of Peter G. Patmore].
      Letters on England. 2 vols. London: Henry Colburn and
      Co., 1823. [C: II, 112-117]

Periodicals:

[20]   [?Fonblanque, Albany; signed "Q."].   "*Posthumous Poems.
       By Percy Bysshe Shelley,*" *The Examiner*, No. 854
       (June 13, 1824), 370.   [R: item 49]

[21]   [Anonymous].   "IV. Posthumous Poems of Percy Bysshe
       Shelley. 1 vol. 8vo. Hunt. London. 1824.,"
       The News of Literature and Fashion, [I], No. 2 (June 19,
       1824), 29.   [R: item 49]

[22]   [Anonymous].   "Posthumous Poems of Percy Bysshe Shelley.
       London: J. and H. L. Hunt, 8vo. 1824," *Somerset
       House Gazette, and Literary Museum*, II, No. xxxviii
       (June 26, 1824), 177-180.   [R: item 49]

[23]   [Signed "T. G."].   "Posthumous Poems of Percy Bysshe
       Shelley. 1 vol. 8vo. Hunt, London. 1824.,"
       *The Literary Magnet of the Belles Lettres, Science, and the
       Fine Arts*, II, Part XIII, No. 50 (1824), 342-344.
       [R: item 49]

[24]   [Hazlitt, William].   "Art. X. Posthumous Poems of Percy
       Bysshe Shelley. 8vo. pp. 400. London, 1824. J. &
       H. L. Hunt.," *Edinburgh Review*, XL, No. lxxx (July,
       1824), 494-514.   [R: item 49; rptd.: item 1817]

[25]   [?Redding, Cyrus].   "New Publications, English and
       Foreign, with Critical Remarks," *The New Monthly Maga-
       zine*, XII, No. xliii (July, 1824), 313-318.   [R:
       item 49]

[26]   [Anonymous].   "Shelley's Posthumous Poems," *The Scots
       Magazine, and Edinburgh Literary Miscellany* [frequently
       cited as *The Edinburgh Magazine*], New Series XV [whole
       number XCIV], [No. 7] (July, 1824), 11-17.   [R:
       item 49; rptd.: items 39, 59]

[27]   [Anonymous].   "Posthumous Poems of Percy Bysshe Shelley.
       8vo. pp. 415. London. 1824. J. & H. L. Hunt.,"
       *The Literary Gazette, and Journal of Belles Lettres, Arts,
       Sciences, &c.*, No. 391 (July 17, 1824), 451-452.   [R:
       item 49]

[28]   [Harness, William].   "Celebrated Female Writers. No. I.
       Joanna Baillie.," *Blackwood's Edinburgh Magazine*, XVI,
       No. xci (August, 1824), 162-178.   [M: 163]

[29]   Haselfoot, Edward [pseud. of ?W. S. Walker]. "The
        Anniversary," *Knight's Quarterly Magazine*, III,
        No. i (August, 1824), 178-238 [misprinted 328].
        [R: item 49, 182-192; C: 192-199]

[30]   [?Maginn, William]. "Letters of Mr. Mullion to the
        Leading Poets of the Age. No. I. To Bryan Procter,
        Esq., alias Barry Cornwall.," *Blackwood's Edinburgh
        Magazine*, XVI, No. xcii (September, 1824), 285-289.
        [R: item 49]

[31]   [Lockhart, John Gibson]. "Letters of Timothy Tickler,
        Esq. to Eminent Literary Characters. No. XVIII.
        To Christopher North, Esq. On the last Edinburgh
        and Quarterly Reviews, and on Washington Irving's
        Tales of a Traveller.," *Blackwood's Edinburgh Magazine*,
        XVI, No. xcii (September, 1824), 291-304. [M: 292]

[32]   Shelley, W. S. [*sic*]. "Stanzas Written in Dejection,
        Near Naples. By W. S. Shelley," *The Atheneum or Spirit
        of the English Magazines* [Boston], New Series I, No. 12
        (September 15, 1824), 480. [T]

[33]   [Signed "S."]. "To the Editor of the Christian Obser-
        ver.," *The Christian Observer*, XXIV, No. 10 [whole
        number 274] (October, 1824), 619-620. [B]

[34]   [Anonymous]. "Byron-Shelley," *The Examiner*, No. 870
        (October 3, 1824), 635. [Fifty-four line poem]

[35]   [Anonymous]. "The Selecter, or, Choice Extracts from
        New Works. Lord Byron.," *The Mirror*, IV, No. 110
        (October 30, 1824), 312-314. [B; extract rptd. from
        item 46]

[36]   Harroviensis [pseud. of William Harness]. "To the
        Editor of Blackwood's Magazine," *Blackwood's Edinburgh
        Magazine*, XVI, No. xciv (November, 1824), 536-540
        [R: item 48; M: 539]

[37]   [Lockhart, John Gibson, William Maginn, and John Wilson].
        "Noctes Ambrosianæ," *Blackwood's Edinburgh Magazine*, XVI,
        No. xciv (November, 1824), 591. [M; rptd.: item 599]

[38]   [Hunt, Leigh]. "The Late Mr. Shelley.," *The Examiner*,
        No. 876 (November 14, 1824), 724. [R: item 46]

[39]   [Anonymous]. "From the Edinburgh Magazine. Shelley's
        Posthumous Poems," *[Littell's] Museum of Foreign
        Literature*, V, No. 29 ([November], 1824), 458-463.
        [R: item 49; rptd. from item 26]

*[40] [Anonymous]. "[On Lord Byron]," *The Universal Review, or Chronicle of the Literature of All Nations*, [?] (November, 1824), 241-259. [?R: item 48]

*[41] [Anonymous]. "[On Shelley and Mary Shelley]," *The Universal Review, or Chronicle of the Literature of All Nations*, [?] (November, 1824), 676. [?M]

*[42] [Anonymous]. "[On Shelley]," *The Universal Review, or Chronicle of the Literature of All Nations*, [?] (November, 1824), 680. [?M]

[43] [Signed "V. V."]. "Critical Notices. '*Blackwood's Edinburgh Magazine*. Number XCII. September.,'" *The Atlantic Magazine*, II, No. viii (December, 1824), 156-159. [R: item 30; M: 158]

[44] Southey, Robert. "Southey and Byron," *Blackwood's Edinburgh Magazine*, XVI, No. xcv (December, 1824), 711-715. [B]

*[45] Tyler, William. "Conversations of Lord Byron," *The Bucks Gazette, Windsor and Eton Express and Reading Journal*, No. 643 ([?], 1824), [?]. [R: item 48]

Books:

[46] [Anonymous]. *Narrative of Lord Byron's Voyage to Corsica and Sardinia, during the Summer and Autumn of the Year 1821. Compiled from Minutes Made during the Voyage by the Passengers, and Extracts from the Journal of His Lordship's Yacht, the Mazeppa, kept by Captain Benson, R.N., Commander.* viii + 79pp. London: J. Limbird, 1824. [B; spurious]

[47] Hazlitt, William. *Select British Poets, or New Elegant Extracts from Chaucer to the Present Time, with Critical Remarks.* [First edition, suppressed] xxii + 822pp. London: Wm. C. Hall, 1824. [C: xiv; T: 745-753; reissued without contemporary poets]

[48] Medwin, Thomas. *Journal of the Conversations of Lord Byron: Noted During a Residence with His Lordship at Pisa, in the Years 1821 and 1822.* viii + 345pp. London: Henry Colburn, 1824. [B: 248-258; extensive M]

[49] [Shelley, Mary Wollstonecraft, ed.]. *Posthumous Poems of Percy Bysshe Shelley.* viii + 400pp. London: John and Henry L. Hunt, 1824. [C, B, T]

[50] Tyler, William. *Woodland Echoes; with Poetical Sketches of the Scenery and Objects in that highly picturesque Vale through*

which the Thames flows from Medmenham Abbey to Cliefden,
Historical and Topographical Notes; and Other Poems. x +
214pp. London: Harding, Triphook, and Lepard,
[1824]. [M: vi]

1825

Periodicals:

[51] [Anonymous]. "The Philosophy of Contemporary Criticism.
No. XL. *The Quarterly, Edinburgh,* and *Universal Reviews.,*"
The Monthly Magazine, LVIII, No. 404 (January, 1825),
518-523. [C: 520-521]

[52] [Anonymous]. "Reviews [/] Journal of the Conversations
of Lord Byron: Noted during a Residence with his
Lordship at Pisa, in the years 1821 and 1822. By
Thomas Medwin, Esq., of the 24th Light Dragoons,
Author of 'Ahasuerus the Wanderer,' With Additions.
New York. 1824. 12mo. pp. 304.," *The United States
Literary Gazette* [Boston], I, No. 19 (January 15, 1825),
[289]-292. [R: item 48; M: 289]

[53] [Anonymous]. "Intelligence. Lord Byron.," *The United
States Literary Gazette* [Boston], I, No. 23 (March 15,
1825), 365-366. [M: 366]

[54] [Anonymous]. "Adonais, an Elegy on the Death of John
Keats, Author of Endymion, Hyperion, &c. By Percy
B. Shelley. Pisa, 1821. [/] Hellas, a Lyrical
Drama. By Percy Bysshe Shelley. London, 1822.,"
The European Magazine, and London Review, LXXXVII (April,
1825), 345-347. [R]

[55] [Anonymous]. "The Literature of the Nineteenth Century.
With Specimens.," *The Literary Magnet of the Belles
Lettres, Science, and the Fine Arts,* III, Part XXI (1824),
161-173. [C: 163-165]

[56] [Wilson, John]. "Analytical Essays on the Modern English Drama. No. III. On Babington. A Tragedy.,"
Blackwood's Edinburgh Magazine, XVIII, No. cii (July,
1825), 119-130. [M: 119]

[57] C[arlile, Richard]. "The Essayist. No. III. On the
Character and Writings of Shelley.," *The Newgate Monthly
Magazine,* II, No. 1 (September, 1825), 36-39. [C, B,
T]

[58] Shelley, Percy Bysshe. "XIV. Lines Written in Dejection,

Near Naples.," *The Newgate Monthly Magazine*, II, No. 1 (September, 1825), 46. [T]

[59]   [Anonymous]. "Criticism. Percy Bysshe Shelley.," *The New-York Literary Gazette, and Phi Beta Kappa Repository*, I, No. 4 (October, 1825), 53-54. [R: item 49; rptd. from item 26]

[60]   [Norton, Andrews]. "Art. II.—1. *Recollections of the Life of Lord Byron, from the Year 1805 to the End of 1814.* By the late R. C. Dallas, Esq. 8vo. Philadelphia. A. Small, and Carey and Lea, 1825. [/] 2. *Correspondence of Lord Byron with a Friend; including his Letters to his Mother; in 1809, 1810, and 1811.* 12mo. Philadelphia. Carey and Lea. 1825. [/] 3. *Journal of the Conversations of Lord Byron; noted during a Residence with his Lordship at Pisa, in the Years 1821 and 1822.* By Thomas Medwin, Esq. of the 24th Light Dragoons. 12mo. New York. 1824.," *The North American Review*, XXI, No. xlix (October, 1825), 300-359. [R: item 48, 353-354]

Books:

[61]   [Anonymous]. *The Life, Writings, Opinions, and Times of the Right Hon. George Gordon Noel Byron, Lord Byron; Including, in Its Most Extensive Biography, Ancedotes and Memoirs of the Lives of the Most Eminent and Eccentric, Public and Noble Characters and Courtiers of the Present Polished and Enlightened Age and Court of His Majesty King George the Fourth. In the course of the Biography is also separately given, Copious Recollections of the Lately Destroyed MS. Originally Intended for Posthumous Publication, and Entitled Memoirs of My Own Life and Times. By the Right Hon. Lord Byron. By an English Gentleman, in the Greek Military Service, and Comrade of His Lordship. Compiled from authentic Documents and from long personal acquaintance.* 3 vols. London: Matthew Iley, 1825. [Spurious work, pirated from item 48; B: I, 366; II, 116-117, 195-205, 368-369; III, 323-334]

[62]   Brydges, [Samuel] Egerton. *Recollections of Foreign Travel, [/] on Life, Literature, and Self-Knowledge.* 2 vols. London: Longman, Hurst, Rees, Orme, Brown, and Green, 1825. [M: I, 29, 146]

[63]   [Kilgour, Alexander]. *Anecdotes of Lord Byron, from Authentic Sources, with Remarks Illustrative of His Connection with the Principal Literary Characters of the Present Day.* 207pp. London: Knight and Lacey, 1825. [B: 131-133, 139-141, 168]

Periodicals:

[64]   [Wilson, John].   "Preface," *Blackwood's Edinburgh Magazine*,
        XIX, No. cviii (January, 1826), i-xxx. [C: xxvi-
        xxvii]

*[65]   [Anonymous].   "Lord Byron and Percy Bysshe Shelley,"
        The Spirit and Manners of the Age [London], I (March 4,
        1826), 144.   [B]

[66]   [Signed "T. R. P."].   "Poetry and Music.," *The Newgate
        Monthly Magazine*, II, No. 8 (April, 1826), 371-375.
        [M: 375]

[67]   Shelley, Percy Bysshe.   "Political Greatness.,"
        The Newgate Monthly Magazine, II, No. 8 (April, 1826),
        343-344.   [T]

[68]   [Signed "Edgar"].   "My Common-Place Book. No. XII.
        Shelley and Poetry.," *The Mirror*, VII, No. 190
        (April 8, 1826), 215-217.   [C]

*[69]   [Signed "Sigma"].   "Percy Bysshe Shelley," *The Spirit and
        Manners of the Age*, I (April 22, 1826), 241-246.   [B;
        C]

[70]   C[arlile, Richard].   "The Essayist. —No. IV. On the
        Writings of Shelly [*sic*]. —Queen Mab.," *The Newgate
        Monthly Magazine*, II, No. 9 (May, 1826), 415-422.   [C]

[71]   [Lockhart, John Gibson].   "Art. VII. —1. *Faust, a Drama by
        Goethe, with Translations from the German*. By Lord Francis
        Leveson Gower. 2d Edition. London. 1825. 2 vols.
        [/] 2. *Posthumous Poems*. By Percy Bysshe Shelley. 8vo.
        London. 1824. [running title: "Translation of
        Goethe's Faust"]," *The Quarterly Review*, XXXIV, No. lxvii
        (June, 1826), 136-153. [R: item 49; C: 148-153]

[72]   C[arlile, Richard].   "The Essayist. No. V. On the
        Writings of Shelley. —'The Revolt of Islam.,'"
        The Newgate Monthly Magazine, II, No. 10 (June, 1826),
        [469]-476.   [C]

[73]   C[arlile, Richard].   "The Essayist. No. VI. On the
        Writings of Shelley. —The Cenci, a Tragedy.,"
        The Newgate Monthly Magazine, II, No. 11 (July, 1826),
        517-527.   [C]

[74]   [Hazlitt, William]. "Boswell Redivivus.*—No. I.,"
        The New Monthly Magazine, XVIII, No. lxviii (August,
        1826), 113-118. [M: 114; rptd.: item 1817]

[75]   C[arlile, Richard]. "The Essayist. VIII. On the
        Writings of Shelley.," *The Newgate Monthly Magazine*,
        II, No. 12 (August, 1826), 570-571. [C]

[76]   Stockdale, J[ohn] J[ames]. "Percy Bysshe Shelley.,"
        *Stockdale's Budget [/] of "All That Is Good, and Noble, and
        Amiable, in the Country.,"* No. I (December 13, 1826),
        [1]-2. [B, T]

[77]   Davenport, Allen [pseud?]. "Remarks on the Genius and
        Writings of the Late Mr. Percy Bysshe Shelley,"
        The Republican, XIV, No. 23 (December 15, 1826),
        715-718. [C]

[78]   Stockdale, J[ohn] J[ames]. "Percy Bysshe Shelley.
        (Continued.)," *Stockdale's Budget*, No. II (December 20,
        1826), [9]. [B, T]

[79]   Stockdale, J[ohn] J[ames]. "Percy Bysshe Shelley.
        (Continued.)," *Stockdale's Budget*, No. III (December 27,
        1826), 18-19. [B, T]

[80]   [Anonymous]. "Shelley's Epipsychidion," *The Literary
        Magnet of the Belles Lettres, Science, and the Fine Arts*,
        IV, Part XXIII (1826), 79-81. [C]

[81]   C[oleridge], D[erwent]. "An Essay on the Poetic Character
        of Percy Bysshe Shelley, and on the Probable Tendency
        of his Writings," *The Metropolitan Quarterly Magazine*, II,
        No. iii (1826), 191-203. [C]

Books:

[82]   [Hazlitt, William]. *The Plain Speaker: Opinions on Books, Men,
        and Things.* 2 vols. London: Henry Colburn, 1826.
        [M: II, 123-124; rptd.: item 1817]

                                1827

Periodicals:

[83]   Stockdale, J[ohn] J[ames]. "Percy Bysshe Shelley.
        (Continued.)," *Stockdale's Budget*, No. IV (January 3,
        1827), 26. [C]

[84]   Stockdale, J[ohn] J[ames]. "Percy Bysshe Shelley.
        (Continued.)," *Stockdale's Budget*, No. V (January 10,
        1827), 34. [T]

[85]   Stockdale, J[ohn] J[ames]. "Percy Bysshe Shelley.
        (Continued.)," *Stockdale's Budget*, No. VI (January 17,
        1827), 42. [B, T]

[86]   Stockdale, J[ohn] J[ames]. "Percy Bysshe Shelley.
        (Continued.)," *Stockdale's Budget*, No. VII (January 24,
        1827), [49]. [B, T]

[87]   Stockdale, J[ohn] J[ames]. "Percy Bysshe Shelley.
        (Continued.)," *Stockdale's Budget*, No. VIII(January 31,
        1827), 59. [B, T]

[88]   Stockdale, J[ohn] J[ames]. "Percy Bysshe Shelley.,"
        Stockdale's Budget, No. IX (February 7, 1827), 68-69. [B]

[89]   [Anonymous]. "Byron and the North American Review," *The
        Boston Lyceum*, I, No. 4 (April, 1827), 174-183. [M:
        179-180]

[90]   "H.H." [William Hazlitt]. "On Disagreeable People.," *The
        Monthly Magazine*, New Series IV, No. 20 (August, 1827),
        129-137. [C; M: 133; rptd: item 1817]

Books:

[91]   Two Brothers [pseud. of Augustus Hare and Julius Charles
        Hare]. *Guesses at Truth*. 2 vols. London: John Taylor,
        1827. [C: II, 146-147]

[92]   Hogg, Thomas Jefferson. *Two Hundred and Nine Days; or, The
        Journal of a Traveller on the Continent*. 2 vols. London:
        Hunt and Clarke, 1827. [Allusion: I, 285-286]

[93]   "A.P." [Joseph Jean M. C. Amédée Pichot]. *The Living Poets
        of England. Specimens of the Living British Poets, with Bio-
        graphical and Critical Notices and an Essay on English Poetry*.
        2 vols. Paris: L. Baudry, Bobée et Hingray, A. et
        W. Galignani, 1827. [B,C: "Percy Bysshe Shelley (/)
        A Literary Memoir of Shelley," II, (366)-370; T: II,
        (371)-405]

[94]   [Montgomery, Robert]. *The Age Reviewed: A Satire: In Two
        Parts*. xix+339pp. London: William Carpenter, 1827.
        [C: 158-159, 170]

Periodicals:

*[95]   [Anonymous]. "[Leigh Hunt's *Lord Byron and Some of His Contemporaries*]," *The Literary Journal*, [?] (January 5, 1828), 7-8. [R: item 116; M]

*[96]   [Anonymous]. "[Leigh Hunt's *Lord Byron and Some of His Contemporaries*]," *The Literary Journal*, [?] (January 12, 1828), 13-15. [R: item 116; M]

*[97]   [Anonymous]. "[Leigh Hunt's *Lord Byron and Some of His Contemporaries*]," *The Literary Journal*, [?] (January 26, 1828), 25-27. [R: item 116; M]

 [98]   [Anonymous]. "Lord Byron and His Contemporaries," *The Athenaeum*, No. 5 (January 29, 1828), 70-71. [R: item 116; M]

 [99]   [Wilson, John]. "Lord Byron and Some of his Contemporaries. By Leigh Hunt," *Blackwood's Edinburgh Magazine*, XXIII, No. cxxvi (March, 1828), 362-408. [R: item 116; M: 372ff, 375ff, 401ff]

[100]   [Lockhart, John Gibson]. "Art. IV. — *Lord Byron and some of his Contemporaries*. By Leigh Hunt. London, 1828. Quarto. pp. 513.," *The Quarterly Review*, XXXVII, No. lxxiv (March, 1828), 402-426. [R: item 116; M: 413-414; 418-419; 424-425]

[101]   [Anonymous]. "Sketches of Contemporary Authors. [/] No. VIII. —Percy Bysshe Shelley.," *The Athenaeum*, No. 13 (March 7, 1828), 193-194. [C]

[102]   [Anonymous]. "Shelley.," *The Yankee* [Portland, Me.], I, No. 12 (March 19, 1828), 96. [C]

[103]   [Anonymous]. "Sketches of Contemporary Characters. [/] Lord Byron—Shelley—and Keats. [/] To the Editor of the Athenaeum.," *The Athenaeum*, No. 25 (April 18, 1828), 397. [C]

[104]   [Anonymous]. "Poetical Department.," *The Yankee* [Portland, Me.], I, No. 17 (April 23, 1828), 136. [M, T]

[105]   Shelley, Percy Bysshe. "From Shelley.," *The Yankee* [Portland, Me.], I, No. 20 (May 14, 1828), 160. [T, and significant C in two footnotes]

[106]   [?Neal, John]. "Leigh Hunt's Byron.," *The Yankee* [Port-
         land, Me.], I, No. 21 (May 21, 1828), [161]-163.
         [R: item 116; M throughout]

[107]   P., P. [pseud. of Sumner L. Fairfield]. "Percy Bysshe
         Shelley," *The Philadelphia Monthly Magazine: Devoted to
         General Literature and the Fine Arts*, II, No. 4 (July 15,
         1828), 245-247. [C; rptd.: item 110]

[108]   [Jeffrey, Francis]. "Art. III. — *The Fall of Nineveh, a
         Poem*. By Edwin Atherstone. The First Six Books. 8vo.
         Pp. 288. London, 1828.," *Edinburgh Review*, XLVIII,
         No. xcv (September, 1828), 47-60. [M: 68]

[109]   [Anonymous]. "Byron and Shelley," *The Censor*, I, No. 3
         (October 4, 1828), 38-41. [C]

[110]   Fairfield, S[umner] L. "The Young Poets of Britain. [/]
         Shelley.," *The Philadelphia Album, [/] and Ladies' Literary
         Gazette.*, III, No. 19 (October 8, 1828), 150. [C; rptd.
         from item 107]

[111]   [Anonymous]. "Byron and Shelley," *The Censor*, I, No. 4
         (October 18, 1828), 49-51. [C]

[112]   [Anonymous]. "The Keepsake," *The Athenaeum*, No. 55 (Novem-
         ber 12, 1828), 864. [R, C]

[113]   [Signed "Marius"]. "Ode on the Death of Shelley,"
         The Censor, I, No. 6 (November 15, 1828), 86. [Poem]

[114]   [Wilson, John]. "Noctes Ambrosianae. No. XL.," *Blackwood's
         Edinburgh Magazine*, XXIV, No. cxlvi, Part I (December,
         1828), [677]-708. [M: 695; rptd.: items 388, 599, 621]

*[115]   [Anonymous]. "Shelley, (Percy Bysshe)," in Volume XXIII,
         115. *Encyclopaedia Londinensis*. 24 vols. London: [?],
         1810-1829 [Volume XXIII: 1828]. [B, C]

Books:

[116]   Hunt, Leigh. *Lord Byron and Some of His Contemporaries; with
         Recollections of the Author's Life, and of His Visits to Italy.*
         viii + 513pp. London: Henry Colburn, 1828. [B and
         C: "Mr. Shelley. With a Criticism on His Genius, and
         Mr. Trelawney's (*sic*) Narrative of His Loss at Sea.,"
         (173)-245; second edition, 2 vols., London: Colburn,
         1828, I, 294-406]

[117]   Landor, Walter Savage. *Imaginary Conversations of Literary
         Men and Statesmen.* 3 vols. London: Henry Colburn, 1828.

[Vols. I and II, dated 1824; vol. III, dated 1828, xvi + 546pp.; C: "Conversation XIV. Landor, English Visitor, and Florentine Visitor.," III, (375)-448; Shelley: 437-441]

1829

Periodicals:

[118] [Peabody, William Bourne Oliver]. "Art. I. — *Lord Byron and his Contemporaries; with Recollections of the Author's Life, and of his Visit to Italy.* By Leigh Hunt. Philadelphia. Carey, Lea & Carey. 8vo. pp. 440. [running title: "The Decline of Poetry"]," *North American Review*, XXVIII, No. lxii (January, 1829), 1-18. [R, C]

[119] [?Barrow, John]. "Art. VI. —1. *Observations upon the Power exercised by the Court of Chancery of depriving a Father of the Custody of his Children.* London. Miller. 1828. [/] 2. *Observations on the Natural Right of a Father to the Custody of his Children, and to direct their Education.* By James Ram, Esq., Barrister at Law. Maxwell. 1828. [running title: "Parents and Children. Equitable Jurisdiction."]," *The Quarterly Review*, XXXIX, No. lxxvii (January, 1829), 183-214. [M: 193, 200, 210]

*[120] [Anonymous]. "[?]," *The Edinburgh Literary Gazette*, [?] (January 2, 1829), [p?]. [C]

[121] [Anonymous]. " *The Poetical Album; and Register of Modern Fugitive Poetry.* Edited by Alaric A. Watts. 12mo. Boston. Republished, 1828. Wells and Lilly.," *The Critic. A Weekly Review of Literature, Fine Arts, and the Drama,* I, No. 11 (January 10, 1829), 161-164. [M: 161]

[122] [Hazlitt, William]. "Poetry," *The Atlas, A General Newspaper and Journal of Literature* [London], IV, No. 147 (March 8, 1829), 153. [C; rptd.: item 1817]

[123] [Signed "D. M."] "An Ode [/] To the Memory of Percy Bysshe Shelley. [/] By D. M.," *The Lion*, III, No. 11 (March 13, 1829), 346-349. [Poem]

[124] [Anonymous]. "Oddities of Genius," *The Critic. A Weekly Review of Literature, Fine Arts, and the Drama*, I, No. 19 (March 14, 1829), 308. [C]

[125] Carlile, Richard. "Secret History of One of Mr. Shelley's
       Works," *The Lion*, III, No. 14 (April 3, 1829), [417]-
       418. [C]

[126] [Signed "Anon." and "E. R."]. "Stanzas on Shelley," *The
       Lion*, III, No. 16 (April 17, 1829), 512. [Two poems]

[127] [Anonymous]. "The Poet Shelley," *The Edinburgh Literary
       Journal; or, Weekly Register of Criticism and Belles Lettres*,
       No. 32 (June 20, 1829), 41. [C]

[128] [Anonymous]. "The Poet Shelley—His unpublished Work,
       'The Wandering Jew.,'" *The Edinburgh Literary Journal; or,
       Weekly Register of Criticism and Belles Lettres*, No. 33
       (June 27, 1829), [43]-45. [C, T]

[129] [Anonymous]. "The Poet Shelley—His Unpublished Work,
       'The Wandering Jew.,'" *The Edinburgh Literary Journal; or,
       Weekly Register of Criticism and Belles Lettres*, No. 34
       (July 4, 1829), [57]-60. [C, T]

[130] [Willis, Nathaniel Parker]. "The Editor's Table," *The
       American Monthly Magazine*, I, No. vi (September, 1829),
       428-438. [R: item 49; 431-436]

[131] [Anonymous]. "Shelley. [/]Adonais. An Elegy on the
       Death of John Keats, Author of 'Endymion,' 'Hyper-
       ion,' &c. By Percy B. Shelley. 8vo. pp. 36.
       Cambridge, 1829. (Reprinted from the Pisa edition.),"
       The Athenaeum, No. 97 (September 2, 1829), 544-545.
       [R, C]

[132] [Anonymous]. "The Substance of a Diary of Sickness,"
       The American Monthly Magazine, I, No. vii (October, 1829),
       474-482. [M: 482]

[133] [Signed "G. L."]. "Specimen of a Canto," *The American
       Monthly Magazine*, I, No. vii (October, 1829), 483-485.
       [M: 483]

[134] [Willis, Nathaniel Parker]. "The Editor's Table," *The
       American Monthly Magazine*, I, No. vii (October, 1829),
       494-516. [R of unspecified edition of Shelley:
       507-515; C, T]

[135] [Jeffrey, Francis]. "Art. II. —1. *Records of Woman: with
       other Poems*. By Felicia Hemans. 2d Edition. 12mo.
       Pp. 323. Edinburgh, 1828. [/] 2. *The Forest Sanctuary:
       with other Poems*. By Felicia Hemans. 2d Edition, with
       Additions. 12mo. Pp. 325. Edinburgh, 1829.,"
       Edinburgh Review, XL, No. xcix (October, 1829), 32-47.
       [M: 47]

[136]   [Willis, Nathaniel Parker].   "The Editor's Table,"
         The American Monthly Magazine, I, No. ix (December,
         1829), 646-659.   [M: 648]

[137]   [Anonymous].   "Unpublished Poetry.," *The Yankee; and
         Boston Literary Gazette*, III, No. vi (December [mis-
         printed November on first page of issue], 1829),
         295-298.   [M: 295]

[137]   Shelley, Percy Bysshe.   "An Incantation Scene. —A
         Poem, Hitherto Unpublished, By Percy Bysshe
         Shelley," *The Edinburgh Literary Journal; or, Weekly
         Register of Criticism and Belles Lettres*, No. 59 (De-
         cember 26, 1829), 425-426.   [T]

Books:

[139]   [Best, Henry (later Henry Digby Beste)].   *Personal and
         Literary Memorials, by the Author of "Four Years in France,"
         "Italy As It Is," &c.*   xii+496pp.   London: Henry
         Colburn, 1829.   [B: 386, 390-393]

*[140]   Hallam, Arthur Henry.   *Timbuctoo.*   [?]pp.   Cambridge,
         Eng.: [?], 1829.   [C]

[141]   [Redding, Cyrus].   "Memoir of Percy Bysshe Shelley.,"
         [v]-xi in *The Poetical Works of Coleridge, Shelley, and
         Keats. Complete in One Volume.* 3 vols. in one.   Paris:
         A. and W. Galignani, 1829.   [B; rptd.: item 524]

                            1830

Periodicals:

[142]   [Wilson, John].   "The Fall of Nineveh.," *Blackwood's
         Edinburgh Magazine*, XXVII, No. clxii, Part I (February,
         1830), [137]-172.   [R; M: 149]

*[143]   Whittier, John Greenleaf.   "Infidelity," *Essex Gazette*
         [Haverhill, Mass.], [?] (February 6, 1830), [?p].
         [B]

*[144]   [Signed "Justitia"].   "Letter to the Editor," [*Poulson's*]
         American Daily Advertiser, [?] (February 12, 1830),
         3, col. 2.   [B]

*[145]   Whittier, John Greenleaf.   "Percy Bysshe Shelley.," *Essex
         Gazette*, [?] (February 27, 1830), [?p].   [B]

[146]   [Wilson, John]. "Moore's Byron. Part II.," *Blackwood's
         Edinburgh Magazine*, XXVII, No. clxiv (March, 1830),
         [421]-454. [R: item 162; M: 421]

*[147]   [?Morris, Robert]. "Shelley.," *Philadelphia Album [/] and
         Ladies' Literary Gazette*, IV, No. 11 (March 13, 1830),
         86-87. [B, C; reply to item 145]

[148]   A Modern Pythagorean [pseud. of Robert Macnish]. "Poeti-
         cal Portraits," *Blackwood's Edinburgh Magazine*, XXVII, No.
         clxv (April, 1830), 632-633. [M: four line stanza]

*[149]   Hallam, Arthur. "On Some Characteristics of Modern
         Poetry and on the Lyrical Poems of Alfred Tennyson.,"
         The Englishman, [?] (April, 1830), [?p]. [C]

[150]   [Anonymous]. " *The Beauties of Percy Bysshe Shelley; with a Bio-
         graphical Preface*. London, 1830. Hunt.," *The Athenaeum*,
         No. 128 (April 10, 1830), 218. [R: item 164]

[151]   [Anonymous]. "The Works of Percy Bysshe Shelley," *The
         National Magazine [and Dublin Literary Gazette]*, I, No. iii
         (September, 1830), 285-300. [C]

[152]   [Heraud, John Abraham and William Maginn]. "Galt's Life
         of Byron," *Fraser's Magazine*, II, No. ix (October, 1830),
         347-370. [R: item 160; B: 365-366]

[153]   Galt, John. "The Burial of Shelly [*sic*].," *The Polar Star
         [of Entertainment and Popular Science, and Universal Repertor-
         ium of General Literature: Comprehending, Under One Unlimited
         Arrangement, the Most Valuable and Amusing Articles, Selected
         from the English and American Reviews, Magazines, Journals, and
         New Publications of the Day, of Lasting Interest. The Whole Care-
         fully Compiled, Digested, and Methodised.]*, V, (July-October,
         1830), 317. [B; rptd. from item 160]

[154]   Galt, John. "Shelley.," *The Polar Star*, V, (July-October,
         1830), 373-374. [B; rptd. from item 160]

[155]   [?Medwin, Thomas]. "Byron and Shelley on the Character
         of Hamlet," *The New Monthly Magazine*, XXIX, No. cxviii
         (October, 1830), 327-336. [B; rptd.: item 156]

[156]   [?Medwin, Thomas]. "Byron and Shelley on the Character
         of Hamlet. By an Eye Witness.," *The Polar Star*, V,
         (July-October, 1830), 416-421. [B; rptd. from item
         155]

*[157]   [Anonymous]. " [?]," *The Christian Examiner and Church of Ire-
         land Magazine*, [?] (November, 1830), [?p]. [C; reply
         to item 151]

*[158]   [Anonymous].   "Popular Authors of the Nineteenth Century.
          The Reverend George Croly.," *The British Magazine*, [?]
          ([?], 1830), [?p].   [M]

Books:

[159]   Fairfield, Sumner L.   *Abaddon, the Spirit of Destruction; and
          Other Poems*.   157pp.   New York: Sleight and Robinson,
          1830.   [C: "The Young Poets of Britain," 135-150;
          Shelley: 135-142]

[160]   Galt, John.   *The Life of Lord Byron*.   xii+372pp.   London:
          Colburn and Bentley, 1830.   [B: "Chapter XXXIX.   Mr.
          Shelley—Sketch of his life—His death—The burning
          of his body, and the return of the mourners," 255-
          259; M: 247-255]

[161]   [Godwin, William].   *Cloudesley: A Tale*.   3 vols.   London:
          Henry Colburn and Richard Bentley, 1830.   [B: the
          character of St. Elmo, also known as Calmoldel, is
          a fictionalized portrait of Shelley]

[162]   Moore, Thomas.   *Letters and Journals of Lord Byron: with Notices
          of His Life*.   2 vols.   London: John Murray, 1830.   [B]

[163]   [Morgan, John Minter].   *The Reproof of Brutus*.   xxvii+229pp.
          London: Longman and Co., 1830.   [C: 76-78]

[164]   [Roscoe, C.].   "Biographical Memoir of Mr. Shelley.,"
          [v]-xviii in *The Beauties of Percy Bysshe Shelley, Consisting
          of Miscellaneous Selections from His Poetical Works.   The Entire
          Poems of Adonais and Alastor, and A Revised Edition of Queen Mab
          Free from All the Objectionable Passages.   With a Biographical
          Preface*.   xviii+251pp.   London: Stephen Hunt, 1830.   [B]

*[165]   Steropes [pseud. of Theodore Hook].   *Sweepings of Parnassus*.
          [?]pp.   London: [?], 1830.   [?C]

1831

Periodicals:

[166]   [Anonymous].   "Modern Poetry.," *The National Magazine* [*and
          Dublin Literary Gazette*], II, No. ix (March, 1831), 277-
          285.   [C]

[167]   [Signed "N. P. —Genessee"].   "Sonnet to Shelley," *The
          Lady's Book* [known as *Godey's Lady's Book*], II (May,
          1831), 278.   [A sonnet]

[168] [?Heraud, John Abraham]. "New Poem. —By Percy Bysshe
       Shelley. The Wandering Jew. Introduction.," *Fraser's
       Magazine*, III, No. xvii (June, 1831), 529-536. [C]

[169] Hunt, Leigh. "The Character of Shelley.," *The Polar Star*,
       VII, (April-July, 1831), 371-375. [B and C; rptd.
       from item 116]

[170] Shelley, Percy Bysshe. "The Wandering Jew. A Poem. By
       the Late Percy Bysshe Shelley.," *Fraser's Magazine*, III,
       No. xvii (July, 1831), 666-677. [T]

[171] [Jewsbury, Maria Jane]. "Shelley's 'Wandering Jew.,'"
       The Athenaeum, No. 194 (July 16, 1831), 456-457. [C]

[172] [Wilson, John]. "Friendly Advice to the Lords. —Observa-
       tions on a Pamphlet, &c.," *Blackwood's Edinburgh Magazine*,
       XXX, No. clxxxiv, Part II (August, 1831), 330-348.
       [M: 341]

[173] [Carlyle, Thomas]. "Art. IV. —1. *An Essay on the Origins and
       Prospects of Man*. By Thomas Hope. 3 vols. 8vo. Lon-
       don: 1831. [/] 2. *Philosophische Vorlesungen, insbesondere
       über Philosophie der Sprache und des Wortes. Geschrieben und
       vorgetragen zu Dresden im December 1828, und in den ersten Tagen
       des Januars 1829*. (Philosophical Lectures, especially on
       the Philosophy of Language and the Gift of Speech.
       Written and delivered at Dresden in December 1828,
       and the early days of January [running title: "Char-
       acteristics"]," *Edinburgh Review*, LIV, No. cviii (De-
       cember, 1831), 351-383. [C: 375; rptd.: item 340]

[174] [Macaulay, Thomas Babington]. "Art. VIII. —*The Pilgrim's
       Progress, with a Life of John Bunyan*. By Robert Southey,
       Esq. LL.D. Poet-Laureate. Illustrated with Engravings,
       8vo. London: 1830.," *Edinburgh Review*, LIV, No. cviii
       (December, 1831), 450-461. [C: 454]

                              1832

Periodicals:

[175] [Hogg, Thomas Jefferson]. "Percy Bysshe Shelley at Ox-
       ford," *The New Monthly Magazine*, XXXIV, No. cxxxiii (Jan-
       uary, 1832), 90-96. [B; rptd.: items 177, 664, 1849]

[176] [Hogg, Thomas Jefferson]. "Percy Bysshe Shelley at Ox-
       ford," *The New Monthly Magazine*, XXXIV, No. cxxxiv (Feb-
       ruary, 1832), 136-144. [B; rptd.: items 181, 664,
       1849]

[177] [Hogg, Thomas Jefferson]. "Percy Bysshe Shelley at Ox-
       ford.," *The Polar Star*, IX (November, 1831-February,
       1832), 293-299. [B; rptd. from item 175]

[178] Shelley, Mary. "Origin of Mrs. Shelley's 'Frankenstein.,'"
       The Polar Star, IX (November, 1831-February, 1832),
       18-20. [B; rptd. from item 221]

[179] [Anonymous]. "American Lake Poetry," *American Quarterly
       Review*, XI, No. xxi (March, 1832), 154-174. [M]

[180] [Hogg, Thomas Jefferson]. "Percy Bysshe Shelley at Ox-
       ford," *The New Monthly Magazine*, XXXIV, No. cxxxvi (April,
       1832), 343-352. [B; rptd.: items 664, 1849]

[181] [Hogg, Thomas Jefferson]. "Reminiscences of Shelley at
       Oxford.," *The Polar Star*, X (February-April, 1832), 128-
       132. [B; rptd. from item 176]

[182] [Signed "A."]. "Retrospective Criticism," *The New Monthly
       Magazine*, XXXIV, No. cxxxvii (May, 1832), 441-444. [C]

[183] [Anonymous]. "Göthe.," *Tait's Edinburgh Magazine*, I, No. iii
       (June, 1832), 314-320. [M: 317; rptd.: item 187]

[184] [Hogg, Thomas Jefferson]. "Percy Bysshe Shelley at Ox-
       ford," *The New Monthly Magazine*, XXXV, No. cxxxix (July,
       1832), 65-73. [B; rptd.: items 188, 664, 1849]

[185] Medwin, Thomas. "Memoir of Shelley," *The Athenaeum*, No. 247
       (July 21, 1832), 472-474. [B; rptd.: item 242]

[186] Medwin, Thomas. "Memoir of Shelley," *The Athenaeum*, No. 248
       (July 28, 1832), 488-489. [B; rptd.: item 242]

[187] [Anonymous]. "Goethe and His Productions," *The Polar Star*,
       New Series I (Midsummer, 1832), 269-273. [M: 271;
       rptd. from item 183]

[188] [Hogg, Thomas Jefferson]. "Diet of Shelley.," *The Polar
       Star*, New Series I (Midsummer, 1832), 351-352. [B;
       rptd. from item 184]

[189] Blessington, [Marguerite Gardiner,] Countess of. "Journal
       of the Conversations with Lord Byron. By the Countess
       of Blessington. No. II," *The New Monthly Magazine*, XXXV,
       No. cxl (August, 1832), 129-146. [M: 134, 140; rptd.:
       item 253]

[190] Medwin, Thomas. "Memoir of Shelley," *The Athenaeum*, No. 249
       (August 4, 1832), 502-504. [B; rptd.: item 242]

[191]   Hunt, Leigh. "The Poet Shelley," *The Atlas, a Select Literary
         and Historical Journal* [New York], IV, No. 47 (August 4,
         1832), 376. [C; rptd. from item 116]

[192]   Medwin, Thomas. "Memoir of Shelley," *The Athenaeum*, No. 250
         (August 11, 1832), 522-524. [B; rptd.: item 242]

[193]   Medwin, Thomas. "Memoir of Shelley," *The Athenaeum*, No. 251
         (August 18, 1832), 535-537. [B; rptd.: item 242]

[194]   Medwin, Thomas. "Memoir of Shelley," *The Athenaeum*, No. 252
         (August 25, 1832), 554-555. [B; rptd.: item 242]

[195]   Shelley, Percy Bysshe. "The Coliseum. A Fragment. By
         Percy Bysshe Shelley.," *The Athenaeum*, No. 253 (Septem-
         ber 1, 1832), 568-569. [T; rptd.: item 242]

[196]   Shelley, Percy Bysshe. "Original Papers [/] Invocation to
         Misery," *The Athenaeum*, No. 254 (September 8, 1832),
         586. [T; rptd.: item 242]

[197]   Shelley, Percy Bysshe. "Continuation of the Shelley
         Papers. The Age of Pericles: With Critical Notices
         of the Sculpture in the Florence Gallery," *The Athenaeum*,
         No. 255 (September 15, 1832), 601-602. [T; rptd.:
         item 242]

[198]   Shelley, Percy Bysshe. "Continuation of the Shelley
         Papers. Critical Notices of the Sculptre [*sic*] in the
         Florence Gallery," *The Athenaeum*, No. 256 (September 22,
         1832), 617-618. [T; rptd.: item 242]

[199]   Shelley, Percy Bysshe. "Continuation of the Shelley
         Papers. Arch of Titus," *The Athenaeum*, No. 257 (Septem-
         ber 29, 1832), 633. [T; rptd.: item 242]

[200]   [Anonymous]. "Percy Bysshe Shelley.," *Tait's Edinburgh Maga-
         zine*, II, No. vii (October, 1832), 92-103. [C]

[201]   [Eagles, John]. "Hesiod. No. II.," *Blackwood's Edinburgh
         Magazine*, XXXII, No. cxcix, Part I (October, 1832), 505-
         518. [C; M: 511]

[202]   [Hogg, Thomas Jefferson]. "Percy Bysshe Shelley at Ox-
         ford," *The New Monthly Magazine*, XXXV, No. cxlii (October,
         1832), 321-330. [B; rptd.: items 216, 664, 1849]

[203]   Shelley, Percy Bysshe. "Continuation of the Shelley
         Papers.," *The Athenaeum*, No. 260 (October, 1832), 680.
         [T; rptd.: item 242]

[204] Shelley, Percy Bysshe. "Continuation of the Shelley
      Papers. Remarks on 'Mandeville' and Mr. Godwin,"
      The Athenaeum, No. 261 (October 27, 1832), 698-699.
      [T; rptd.: item 242]

[205] Shelley, Percy Bysshe. "Stanzas by Percy Bysshe Shelley.
      To ***** ['The Serpent Is Shut Out From Paradise'],"
      Fraser's Magazine, VI, Part II, No. xxxv (November,
      1832), 599-600. [T]

[206] [Anonymous]. "Reviews—The Masque of Anarchy; a Poem.,"
      The Athenaeum, No. 262 (November 3, 1832), 705-707. [R:
      item 220]

[207] [Anonymous]. " *The Beauties of Percy Bysshe Shelley; consisting
      of Miscellaneous Selections from his Poetical Works: the Whole
      of the Sensitive Plant, Adonais, Alastor, Julian and Maddalo,
      and Queen Mab free from the objectionable Passages. With a Bio-
      graphical Memoir*. Third Edition. 12mo., pp. 287. Lon-
      don, 1832. Lumley.," *The Literary Gazette*, No. 824 (No-
      vember 3, 1832), 692-693. [R]

[208] [Anonymous]. " *The Masque of Anarchy; a Poem.* By Percy Bysshe
      Shelley. Now first published; with a Preface by Leigh
      Hunt. London, 1832. Moxon.," *The Literary Gazette*, No.
      824 (November 3, 1832), 693-694. [C: extracts from
      "Preface.," item 220]

[209] Shelley, Percy Bysshe. "Continuation of the Shelley
      Papers. On 'Frankenstein,'" *The Athenaeum*, No. 263
      (November 10, 1832), 730. [T; rptd.: item 242]

[210] [Anonymous]. " *The Masque of Anarchy; a Poem.* By Percy Bysshe
      Shelley. Now first published; with a Preface by Leigh
      Hunt. London, 1832. Moxon.," *The Literary Gazette*, No.
      825 (November 10, 1832), 709. [R: item 220]

[211] Shelley, Percy Bysshe. "An Ariette for Music. To a Lady
      Singing to Her Accompaniment on the Guitar," *The Athen-
      aeum*, No. 264 (November 17, 1832), 746. [T; rptd.:
      item 242]

[212] Shelley, Percy Bysshe. "Continuation of the Shelley
      Papers. On the Revival of Literature," *The Athenaeum*,
      No. 265 (November 24, 1832), 761-762. [T; rptd.:
      item 242]

[213] [Anonymous]. "Art. XIV. — *The Masque of Anarchy*, a Poem, by
      Percy Bysshe Shelley. Now first published with a Pre-
      face. By Leigh Hunt. London: Moxon. 1832.," *The
      Monthly Review*, Fourth Series III [whole number CXXIX],
      No. iv (December, 1832), 580-585. [R: item 220]

[214] [Anonymous]. "Percy Bysshe Shelley.," *Tait's Edinburgh Magazine*, II, No. ix (December, 1832), 331-342. [C]

[215] [Hogg, Thomas Jefferson]. "Percy Bysshe Shelley at Oxford," *The New Monthly Magazine*, XXXV, No. cxliv (December, 1832), 505-513. [B; rptd.: items 664, 1849]

[216] [Hogg, Thomas Jefferson]. "Shelley.," *The Mirror, of Literature, Amusement, and Instruction*, XX, No. 581 (December 15, 1832), 407-408. [B; rptd. from item 202]

Books:

[217] [Ayton, William Edmondstoune]. *Poland, Homer, and Other Poems.* 117pp. London: Longman, Rees, Orme, Brown, Green, & Longman, 1832. [Contains: "A Lament for Percy Bysshe Shelley," 95-108]

[218] Brydges, [Samuel] Egerton. *The Lake of Geneva, A Poem, Moral and Descriptive, in Seven Books.* 2 vols. Geneva: A. Cherbuliez; London: Bossange and Co., 1832. [M: I, 40-41]

[219] [Forster, Thomas Ignatius Maria]. *Medicina Simplex; or, The Pilgrim's Waybook, Being an Inquiry into the Moral and Physical Conditions of Healthy Life and Happy Old Age. With Household Prescriptions. By a Physician.* xxxii+255 [misprinted for 259]pp. London: Keating and Brown, 1832. [M: 248]

[220] Hunt, Leigh. *The Masque of Anarchy. A Poem. By Percy Bysshe Shelley. Now First Published, with a Preface by Leigh Hunt.* xxx+47pp. London: Edward Moxon, 1832. [T, B, C]

[221] [Cancelled].

[222] Southey, Robert. *Essays, Moral and Political, by Robert Southey.* 2 vols. London: John Murray, 1832. [B: II, 196-205]

1833

Periodicals:

[223] [?Heraud, John Abraham]. "Œuvres de Platon. Traduites par Victor Cousin.," *Fraser's Magazine*, VII, No. xxxvii (January, 1833), 116-122. [M: 116]

[224] [Peabody, William Bourne Oliver]. "Art. VI. Lord Byron's
       Conversations on Religion. [/] *Conversations on Religion
       with Lord Byron and others.* By the Late James Kennedy, M.D.
       London. 1830.," *North American Review*, XXXVI. No. lxxviii
       (January, 1833), 152-188. [R; M: 176]

[225] Shelley, Percy Bysshe. "Poem, by Shelley. To A. B., with
       a Guitar. By Percy Bysshe Shelley.," *Fraser's Magazine*,
       VII, No. xxxvii (January, 1833), 79. [T]

[226] [Anonymous]. "English Poetry. Barry Cornwall, Motherwell,
       and Leigh Hunt.," *Fraser's Magazine*, VII, No. xxxviii
       (February, 1833), 198-222. [M throughout]

[227] [Anonymous]. "Horæ Germanicæ. No. II.," *The Knickerbacker*
       [*sic*]: *or, New-York Monthly Magazine*, I, No. 2 (February,
       1833), 77-87. [M: 84]

[228] [Anonymous]. "A Peep at the Pow-wow.," *The Knickerbacker* [*sic*]:
       or, New-York Monthly Magazine, I, No. iii (March, 1833),
       179-184. [C]

[229] [Anonymous]. "Cottage of Shelley, the Poet, at Great Mar-
       low, Bucks.," *The Mirror of Literature, Amusement and Instruc-
       tion*, XXI, No. 593 (March 2, 1833), [129]-130. [B]

[230] [Empson, William]. "Art. VI. — *Faust; a Dramatic Poem by
       Goethe. Translated into English Prose, with Remarks on Former
       Translations and Notes.* By the Translator of Savigny's
       'Of the Vocation of our Age for Legislation and Juris-
       prudence.' 8vo. London: 1833 [Running title: "Hay-
       ward's *Translation of Faust*"]," *Edinburgh Review*, LVII, No.
       cxv (April, 1833), 107-143. [R: item 240; M: 128]

*[231] [Fox, William Johnson]. " *Pauline; A Fragment of a Confession*,"
       The Monthly Repository [/] *and Review of Theology and General
       Literature*, New Series VII, No. 76 (April, 1833), 252-
       262. [R: item 238; M]

[232] Shelley, Percy Bysshe. "Continuation of the Shelley
       Papers. A System of Government by Juries," *The Athen-
       aeum*, No. 286 (April 20, 1833), 250. [T; rptd.: item
       242]

[233] [Hogg, Thomas Jefferson]. "The History of Percy Bysshe
       Shelley's Expulsion from Oxford," *The New Monthly Magazine*,
       XXXVIII, No. cxlix (May, 1833), 17-19. [B; rptd.:
       items 246, 664, 1849]

*[234] [Fox, William Johnson]. "Local Logic," *The Monthly Reposi-
       tory* [/] *and Review of Theology and General Literature*, New
       Series VII, No. 78 (June, 1833), 413-426. [M: 421]

[235]   F [?Sumner L. Fairfield]. "Poetical Portraits. Coleridge,
        Shelley, Bruce, Wolfe, Keats, Knowles.," *The North Ameri-
        can Magazine*, II, No. xi (September, 1833), 309-317.
        [C: 312-314]

[236]   Antiquus [pseud. of John Stuart Mill]. "The Two Kinds of
        Poetry," *The Monthly Repository* [/] *and Review of Theology and
        General Literature*, New Series VII, No. 82 (October,
        1833), 714-724. [C; rptd.: item 681]

[237]   Cunningham, Allan. "Biographical and Critical History of
        the Literature of the Last Fifty Years. By Allan Cun-
        ningham. British Poetry — Continued from No. 313, p.
        721.," *The Athenaeum*, No. 316 (November 16, 1833), 769-
        777. [B, C: 771-772; rptd.: item 255]

Books:

[238]   [Browning, Robert]. *Pauline; A Fragment of a Confession.* 71pp.
        London: Saunders and Otley, 1833. [M: 30ff and 70]

[239]   Bulwer, Edward Lytton [Baron Bulwer-Lytton]. *England and the
        English.* 2 vols. London: Richard Bentley, 1833. [C:
        II, 96-104]

*[240] [Hayward, Abraham, trans, and ed.]. *Faust: a Dramatic Poem
        by Goethe. Translated into English Prose, with remarks on Former
        Translations and Notes. By the Translator of Savigny's "Of the
        Vocation of Our Age for Legislation and Jurisprudence."* lxxxvii+
        [292]pp. London: [?], 1833. [C]

[241]   Madden, R[ichard] R[obert]. *The Infirmities of Genius* [/] *Illus-
        trated by Referring the Anomalies in the Literary Character, to
        the Habits and Constitutional Peculiarities of Men of Genius.*
        2 vols. Philadelphia: Carey, Lea, and Blanchard, 1833.
        [M: I, 5; II, 111-112]

[242]   Medwin, T[homas]. *The Shelley Papers* [/] *Memoir of Percy Bysshe
        Shelley* [/] *By T. Medwin, Esq. And Original Poems and Papers* [/]
        By Percy Bysshe Shelley. Now First Collected. vii+180pp.
        London: Whittaker, Treacher & Co., 1833. [B, T; rptd.
        from items 185, 186, 190, 192, 193, 194, 195, 196,
        197, 198, 199, 203, 204, 205, 209, 211, 212, 232]

                              1834

Periodicals:

[243]   [Signed "Egeria"]. "Character and Writings of Shelley,"

The Literary Journal, [/] and Weekly Register of Science and the
Arts [Providence, R.I.], I, No. 32 (January 11, 1834),
252-253. [C]

[244] [Anonymous]. "Shelley.," The Oxford University Magazine, I,
No. i (March, 1834), [3]-15. [C]

[245] [Anonymous]. "Conversations of Lord Byron, By the Countess
of Blessington.," The Gentleman's Magazine, New Series I
[CLV] (April, 1834), [347]-358. [R: item 253; M: 354-
355]

[246] [Hogg, Thomas Jefferson]. "Anecdote of Percy Bysshe Shel-
ley.," The New-York Mirror, [/] A Weekly Journal, Devoted to
Literature and the Fine Arts, XI, No. 44 (May 3, 1834), 346.
[B; rptd. from item 233]

[247] [Cunningham, Allan]. "Shelley.," The Literary Journal [Provi-
dence, R.I.], I, No. 52 (May 31, 1834), 409. [B, C;
rptd. from item 255]

*[248] [Anonymous]. "[Remarks on item 244]," The Calcutta Literary
Gazette, [?] (July 5, 1834), [?p]. [C]

[249] [Wilson, John]. "Noctes Ambrosianæ. No. LXVII," Blackwood's
Edinburgh Magazine, XXXVI, No. ccxxv (August, 1834), 258-
288. [M: 272-273; rptd.: items 388, 599, 621]

[250] Browne, James Hamilton. "Narrative of a Visit, in 1823, to
the Seat of the War in Greece," Blackwood's Edinburgh Magazine, XXXVI, No. ccxxvi (September, 1834), 392-407.
[M: 395]

[251] [Wilson, John]. "Spenser. No. II. The Fairy Queen.,"
Blackwood's Edinburgh Magazine, XXXVI, No. ccxxvi (September, 1834), 408-430. [M: 421]

[252] [Wilson, John]. "Coleridge's Poetical Works," Blackwood's
Edinburgh Magazine, XXXVI, No. ccxxvii (October, 1834),
542-570. [M: 557, 559]

Books:

[253] Blessington, [Marguerite Gardiner,] Countess of. Conversations of Lord Byron with the Countess of Blessington. iv+409pp.
London: Henry Colburn, 1834. [M: 75-76; rptd. from
item 189]

[254] Brydges, [Samuel] Egerton. The Autobiography, Times, Opinions,
and Contemporaries of Sir Egerton Brydges. 2 vols. London:
Cochrane and M'Crone, 1834. [M: I, 322, 329; II, 337]

[255]   Cunningham, Allan. *Biographical and Critical History of the*
        British Literature of the Last Fifty Years.   xv+348pp.
        Paris: Baudry's Foreign Library, 1834.   [B,C:
        "Shelley.," 101-102; rptd. from item 237]

[256]   Taylor, Henry. *Philip Van Artevelde; A Dramatic Romance.   In Two*
        Parts.   [Part I:] xxvi+287pp. + [Part II:] 306pp.
        London: Edward Moxon, 1834.   [C: xxi-xxvi]

                              1835

Periodicals:

[257]   [Anonymous].   "Sigourney's Poems," *American Monthly Magazine*
        [New York], IV, No. iv (January, 1835), 275-284.   [M:
        275]

[258]   [Wilson, John].   "Audubon's Ornithological Biography.,"
        Blackwood's Edinburgh Magazine, XXXVII, No. ccxxx (January,
        1835), 107-124.   [R; M: 116]

[259]   [Tuckerman, Henry Theodore].   "Art. VI.   —Italy. [/] *Italy:*
        with Sketches of Spain and Portugal. By the Author of Vathek.
        2 vols.   Philadelphia, 1834," *North American Review*, XL,
        No. lxxxvii (April, 1835), 417-447.   [R; M: 433]

[260]   [Wilson, John]. "Mant's British Months.," *Blackwood's Edin-*
        burgh Magazine, XXXVII, No. ccxxiv (April, 1835), 684-
        698.   [R; M: 687]

[261]   [Wilson, John].   "Stoddart's Art of Angling in Scotland.,"
        Blackwood's Edinburgh Magazine, XXXVIII, No. ccxxxvii (July,
        1835), 119-127.   [R; M: 121]

[262]   [Anonymous].   "Our Library Table," *The Athenaeum*, No. 408
        (August 22, 1835), 639-640.   [M: 640]

[263]   [Wilson, John].   "Clare's Rural Muse.," *Blackwood's Edinburgh*
        Magazine, XXXVIII, No. ccxxxviii (August, 1835), 231-
        247.   [R; M: 232]

[264]   [Anonymous].   "Art. I. — *Philip Van Artevelde; a Dramatic*
        Romance, in two parts. By Henry Taylor.   Cambridge and
        Boston.   2 vols.   12mo.   1835.," *American Quarterly Review*,
        XVIII, No. xxxv (September, 1835), 1-19.   [R; C: 5-7]

*[265]   [Mac-Carthy, Denis Florence].   "To the Memory of Percy
        Bysshe Shelley," *The Dublin Weekly Satirist*,   [?] (October
        10, 1835), [?p].   [A poem]

[266]   Driver, Henry Austen. *Harold de Burun. A Semi-Dramatic Poem;
        in Six Scenes.* xiii+153pp. London: Longman, Rees, Orme,
        Brown, Green, and Longman, 1835. [C: 'Percy' in Scene
        I is Shelley]

[267]   Slatter, Henry. "Note," 160-169 in Robert Montgomery,
        *Oxford. A Poem. . . Fourth Edition, Illustrated with Additional
        Notes and Biographical Recollections of Canning, Heber, Shelley,
        &c.* iii+185pp. Oxford: Henry Slatter, 1835. [B]

[268]   [Tuckerman, Henry Theodore]. *The Italian Sketchbook.* xii+
        216pp. Philadelphia: Key & Biddle, 1835. [C: 56-68]

[269]   Wade, Thomas. *Mundi et Cordis: De Rebus Sempiternis et Temporari-
        is: Carmina [/] Poems and Sonnets.* xvi+285pp. London: John
        Miller, 1835. [Contains three sonnets: "Shelley.,"
        120; "Shelley & Keats, & Their Reviewer.," 121; and
        "Julian and Maddalo.," 122]

                                1836

Periodicals:

[270]   [Anonymous]. "Art. II — *The School of Heart, and other Poems.
        By Henry Alford, Vicar of Wimewould, and late fellow
        Trinity College, Cambridge. Two vols. 12mo.* Cam-
        bridge: 1835.," *Edinburgh Review*, LXII, No. cxxvi (Janu-
        ary, 1836), 297-318. [R; C: 299-200]

[271]   [Anonymous]. "Shelley.," *The Lady's Book* [known as *Godey's
        Lady's Book*], XII (February, 1836), 84 [and portrait on
        unnumbered interleaf]. [B]

[272]   [Anonymous]. "Critical Notices. [/] Drake—Halleck.,"
        Southern Literary Messenger, II, No. v (April, 1836), 326-
        336. [R; C: 328, 332]

[273]   [Signed "D."]. "Art. III. The Poets of Our Age, Con-
        sidered As to Their Philosophic Tendencies [running
        title: "Wordsworth, Shelley and Coleridge."].," *The
        Westminster Review*, XXV, No. i (April, 1836), 60-71. [C]

[274]   [Anonymous]. "Art. I — *The Shelley Papers.* London. 1833.,"
        The American Quarterly Review, XIX, No. xxxviii (June,
        1836), 257-287. [R: item 242; C]

[275]   [Anonymous]. "Bust of Shelley.," *The Court Journal: Gazette
        of the Fashionable World*, No. 372 (June 11, 1836), 379.
        [B: on Marianne Hunt's portrait bust]

[276] Pemberton, Mr. [?pseud.]. "Reminiscences. Lord Byron and his Contemporaries, &c., by an intimate Friend of his Lordship. —No. III," *The Metropolitan Journal of Literature, Science, and the Fine Arts, &c.*, I, No. x (June 11, 1836), 151-154. [M: 153-154]

Books:

*[277] Hemans, Mrs. [Felicia Dorothea]. *Poetical Remains of the late Mrs. Hemans.* xxxii+321pp. Edinburgh: William Blackwood & Sons; London: T. Cadell, 1836. [Introductory C]

[278] [Kaye, John William]. *Jerningham, or The Inconsistent Man.* 3 vols. London: Smith, Elder & Co., 1836. [B: the character of Everand Sinclair is a fictionalized portrait of Shelley]

1837

Periodicals:

[279] Poe, [Edgar Allan]. "Editorial. [/] Critical Notices. [/] Bryant.," *Southern Literary Messenger*, III, No. i (January, 1837), 41-49. [R; M: 49]

[280] [Signed "D. L."]. "Art. 7. —Shelley and Pollok.," *The Western Messenger*, III, No. 1 (February, 1837), 474-478. [C]

[281] [Anonymous]. "Modern English Tragedy. Art. IX. — *Ion: a tragedy in five acts.* By Thomas Noon Talfourd. New York. 1837.," *The American Quarterly Review*, XXI, No. xli (March, 1837), 187-213. [M: 196-197]

[282] E. B. [Edward Lytton Bulwer, later Baron Bulwer-Lytton]. "*The Works of Thomas Grey.* Edited by the Rev. John Mitford. 4 vols. Pickering. London, 1837," *The London and Westminster Review*, XXVII, [New Series V], No. ii (July, 1837), [1]-16. [R; C: 14-15]

[283] [Anonymous]. "Art. III. — *Henrietta Temple, a Love Story.* By the Author of 'Vivian Grey.' 3 vols. 8vo. Second Edition. London: 1837. [/] *Venetia.* By the Author of 'Vivian Grey,' and 'Henrietta Temple.' 3 vols. 8vo. London: 1837 [running title: "D'Israeli's Novels"]," *Edinburgh Review*, LXVI, No. cxxxiii (October, 1837), 59-72. [R; M: 59, 68-72]

[284] North, Christopher [pseud. of John Wilson]. "Our Two
       Vases,"*Blackwood's Edinburgh Magazine*, XLII, No. cclxiv
       (October, 1837), 548-572. [C; M: 564]

Books:

[285] Chambers, Robert and Royal Robbins. *History of the English
       Language and Literature. By Robert Chambers. To Which Is Added
       A History of American Contributions to the English Language and
       Literature. By Royal Robbins*. vi+328pp. Hartford, Conn.:
       Edward Hopkins, 1837. [C: 219-220]

[286] [Beaconsfield, Benjamin Disraeli, 1st Earl of]. *Venetia*.
       3 vols. London: H. Colburn, [1837]. [B: the character
       of Marmion Herbert is a fictionalized portrait of Shel-
       ley]

                              1838

Periodicals:

*[287] Buchanan, Robert. "**On Shelley**," *The New Moral World*, IV,
        No. 14 (January 27, 1838), [?p]. [C]

[288]   [Anonymous]. "Present State of Poetry.," *The Monthly Chroni-
        cle*, I, [No. 4] (June, 1838), 307-316. [R; C: 310-311]

[289]   [?Medwin, Thomas]. "The Poetry of Shelley," *Fraser's Maga-
        zine*, XVII, No. cii (June, 1838), [653]-676. [C]

[290]   [Anonymous]. "Lines, Written on hearing of the Death of
        Louisa Missouri Miller.," *The American Monthly Magazine*
        [New York], XII (July, 1838], 63-64. [Quotation, 63]

*[291] [Norton, Andrews]. "The New School in Literature and Reli-
        gion," *The Boston Daily Advertiser*, XLIII, [?] (August 27,
        1838), 2. [C]

[292]   [Signed "W. H. C. H."]. "Funeral of Shelley," *The Knicker-
        bocker*, XII, No. 3 (September, 1838), 242. [A poem]

*[293] Clarke, James Freeman. "To the Editor of the Boston Daily
        Advertiser," *The Boston Daily Advertiser*, XLIII, [?] (Sep-
        tember 28, 1838), 2. [C]

*[294] [Norton, Andrews]. "Shelley and the Western Messenger,"
        The Boston Daily Advertiser, XLIII, [?] (October 5, 1838),
        2. [C]

[295]   [Clarke, James Freeman].   "The New School in Literature
        and Religion.," *The Western Messenger*, VI, No. 1 (Novem-
        ber, 1838), 42-47.   [M: 42-43]

[296]   [Anonymous].   "A Review of Modern Poets, and Illustrations
        of the Philosophy of Modern Poetry.   Article I.
        —Shelley.," *The New Moral World*, V, No. 6 (December 1,
        1838), 83-85.   [C]

[297]   [Anonymous].   "A Review of Modern Poets, and Illustrations
        of the Philosophy of Modern Poetry.," *The New Moral
        World*, V, No. 7 (December 8, 1838), 103.   [C]

[298]   [Anonymous].   "Modern Poets and Modern Poetry.   Article
        III.   Shelley's Prometheus.," *The New Moral World*, V,
        No. 9 (December 22, 1838), 134-136.   [C]

[299]   [?Hunt, Leigh].   "Personal Sketches of Eminent Men of the
        Present Day.   Chap. VIII.," *The Literary and Pictorial
        Repository; A Record of Historical, Biographical, Theological,
        Topographical, Philosophical, and General Knowledge.   Embracing
        Literature, Science, and Art*, I, No. 12 ([no month indi-
        cated], 1838), 179-182.   [M: 180-181]

[300]   [?Hunt, Leigh].   "Abstinence.," *The Literary and Pictorial
        Repository; A Record of Historical, Biographical, Theological,
        Topographical, Philosophical, and General Knowledge.   Embracing
        Literature, Science, and Art*, I, No. 18 ([no month indi-
        cated], 1838), 288.   [B]

Books:

[301]   Chorley, Henry F[othergill].   *The Authors of England.   A
        Series of Medallion Portraits of Modern Literary Characters,
        Engraved from the Works of British Artists, By Achille Collas.
        With Illustrative Notices by Henry F. Chorley.*   vi+93+12pp.
        London: Charles Tilt, 1838.   [B: 56-64]

*[302] [Hunt, Leigh].   "[Biographical Notice of Shelley]," [?pp]
        in: S[amuel] C[arter] Hall, ed., *The Book of Gems.
        The Poets and Artists of Great Britain.*   3 vols.   London:
        Whittaker and Co. [volume III], 1838.   [B: III, (?p)]

1839

Periodicals:

[303]   [Alexander, James Waddell, and Albert Baldwin].   "Art. III.
        —1. *Elements of Psychology, included in a Critical Examination*

*of Locke's Essay on the Human Understanding, with Additional
Pieces.* By Victor Cousin, Peer of France, Member of
the Royal Council of Public Instruction, Member of the
Institute, and Professor of the History of Ancient
Philosophy in the Faculty of Literature. Translated
from French, with an Introduction and Notes, by Rev.
C. S. Henry, D.D. Second Edition, prepared for the
use of Colleges. New York: Gould and Newman. 1838.
pp 423. 12mo. [/] 2. *Introduction to the History of Philo-
sophy.* By Victor Cousin, Professor of Philosophy of the
Faculty of Literature at Paris. Translated from the
French, by Henning Gottfried Linberg. Boston. 1832.
pp 458. 8vo. [/] 3. *An Address delivered before the Senior
Class in Divinity College, Cambridge, Sunday, 15th July, 1838.*
By Ralph Waldo Emerson. Boston. pp. 31. 8vo.,"
The Biblical Repertory and Princeton Review, XI, No. 1 (Janu-
ary, 1839), 37-101. [M: 77]

[304] [Anonymous]. "Modern English Poetry. —Byron, Shelley,
Wordsworth.," *The American Biblical Repository*, Second
Series I [whole number XIII], No. i [whole number
xxxiii] (January, 1839), 206-238. [C]

[305] [?Brownson, Orestes]. "Art. IV. — *The Evidence of the Genuine-
ness of the Four Gospels.* By Andrews Norton.," *The Boston
Quarterly Review*, II, No. i (January, 1839), 86-113.
[M: 113]

[306] [Anonymous]. "Modern Poets and Modern Poetry. Article IV.
Shelley's Prometheus.," *The New Moral World*, V, No. 11
(January 5, 1839), 166-168. [C]

[307] [Anonymous]. "Shelley's Poetical Works," *The Spectator*, XII,
No. 552 (January 26, 1839), 88-89. [R: item 345]

[308] [Anonymous]. "The Literary Examiner.," *The Examiner*, No.
1618 (February 3, 1839), 68-70. [R: vol. I of item
345]

[309] [Anonymous]. "Literature.," *The Court Journal: Gazette of the
Fashionable World*, [X], No.511 (February 9, 1839), 100-
101. [R: vol. I of item 345]

[310] [Anonymous]. "The Life of Shelley.," *The National: A Library
for the People*, [No vol. or issue] (February 9, 1839),
76-78. [B]

[311] [Anonymous]. "Modern Poets and Modern Poetry. Article V.
Shelley's Prometheus.," *The New Moral World*, V, No. 17
(February 16, 1839), 262-264. [C]

[312]   [Anonymous]. " *The Poetical Works of Percy Bysshe Shelley*. Edited
        by Mrs. Shelley. 4 vols. Moxon, Dover Street.," *The
        Cambridge University Magazine*, I, No. i (March, 1839), 78-
        79. [R: item 345]

[313]   Blessington, [Marguerite Gardiner,] Countess of. "Anecdote
        Gallery. Characteristic Anecdotes of Byron and Shel-
        ley.," *The Mirror*, XXXIII, No. 940 (March 16, 1839),
        175-176. [B; rptd. from item 339]

[314]   [Anonymous]. "Lord Byron at Pisa," *The Corsair, A Gazette of
        Literature, Art, Dramatic Criticism, Fashion and Novelty*, I,
        No. 3 (March 30, 1839), 46-47. [M]

[315]   [Anonymous]. "Shelley's Poems.," *The Monthly Chronicle*, III,
        [No. 4] ([April, 1839]), 340-348. [R: item 345]

[316]   [Signed "W. D. B."]. "The Cremation of Shelley, on the
        Coast of Tuscany, Under the Direction of Lord Byron.,"
        Bentley's Miscellany, V, [No. 4] (April, 1839), 415.
        [A forty-eight line poem]

[317]   O.C. [Otway Curry]. "Percy Bysshe Shelley," *The Hesperian*
        [Columbus, Ohio], II, No. vi (April, 1839), 440-447.
        [C]

[318]   [Wilson, John]. "Christopher in His Alcove.," *Blackwood's
        Edinburgh Magazine*, XLV, No. cclxxxii (April, 1839), 538-
        570. [C; M: 546]

[319]   Medwin, Thomas. "Hazlitt in Switzerland. A Conversation,"
        *The Corsair, A Gazette of Literature, Art, Dramatic Criticism,
        Fashion and Novelty*, I, No. 5 (April 13, 1839), 72-73.
        [M]

[320]   [Anonymous]. "Our Library Table. *The Poetical Works of P. B.
        Shelley*, edited by Mrs. Shelley. 4 vols. vol. 1 to
        3.," *The Athenaeum*, No. 600 (April 27, 1839), 313. [R:
        item 345]

[321]   [Anonymous]. "The Poets of England Who Have Died Young.
        No. II. —Percy Bysshe Shelley.," *The Cambridge University
        Magazine*, I, No. ii (May, 1839), 81-101. [C]

*[322] [Anonymous]. " [On Robert Owen and Shelley]," *The General
        Baptist Repository*, [?] (May, 1839), [?p]. [C]

[323]   [Anonymous]. "The Literary Examiner.," *The Examiner*,
        No. 1634 (May 26, 1839), 323-326. [323-324: R: item
        345]

[324]   [Anonymous]. "Review of Modern Poets and Poetry. Shelley's
        Revolt of Islam.," *The New Moral World*, V, No. 34 (June 15,
        1839), 533-535. [C]

[325] [Anonymous]. "Modern Poets. (Continued from page 525
       [*sic* for 535].) Shelley's Revolt of Islam. Act II.,"
       The New Moral World, V, No. 35 (June 22, 1839), 550-
       552. [C]

[326] [Anonymous]. "Art. VIII. —*The Poetical Works of Percy Bysshe
       Shelley*. Edited by Mrs. Shelley. 4 vols. 12mo. Lon-
       don: 1839.," *Edinburgh Review*, LXIX, No. cxl (July, 1839),
       503-527. [R: item 345]

[327] [Blessington, Marguerite Gardiner, Countess of]. "Byron
       and Shelley.," *The New-York Mirror, A Weekly Journal of Litera-
       ture and the Fine Arts*, XVII, No. 10 (August 31, 1839), 75.
       [B; rptd. from item 339]

[328] [Anonymous]. "The Taste for Poetry," *The United States Maga-
       zine and Democratic Review*, VI, No. xxi (September, 1839),
       219-222. [M: 222]

[329] [Anonymous]. "5. *The Poetical Works of Robert Southey, Collected
       by Himself. Ten Volumes in One.* New York: D. Appleton &
       Co., 1839. pp. 810, royal octavo.," *The American Biblical
       Repository* [later *The Biblical Repository and Classical Review*],
       Second Series II [whole number XIV], No. iv [whole
       number xxxvi] (October, 1839), 491-493. [M: 492]

[330] [Signed "G."]. "Thoughts and Reflections.," *The Southern
       Literary Messenger*, V, No. x (October, 1839), 706-707.
       [M: 707]

[331] [Signed "S.O."]. "Art. I. —1. *The Hunchback of Notre Dame.* By
       Victor Hugo. [/] 2. *Picciola, or, Captivity Captive.* By M.
       D. Saintaine. [running titles: "The Satanic School of
       Literature," and "The Satanic School of Literature and
       Its Reformers"]," *The Christian Examiner and General Review*,
       XXVII [Third Series IX], No. 11 (November, 1839),
       [145]-161. [C]

[332] [Anonymous]. "1. *Poems, written in Newfoundland. By Henrietta
       Prescott.* Saunders and Otley. London, 1839. [/] 2.
       Edgina: an Historical Poem. By John B. Worrell. Edward Bull.
       London, 1839. [/] 3. *Nothings. By E. Darby, Jun.* E. Chur-
       ton. London, 1839. [/] 4. *Melaia, and other Poems. By
       Eliza Cook.* Charles Tilt. London, 1839. [/] 5. *Goethe's
       Faust. Part II., with other Poems, Original and Translated. By
       Leopold J. Bernays, Scholar of St. John's College, Oxford.* S.
       Low. London, 1839. [/] 6. *The Poetical Works of Percy
       Bysshe Shelley.* Edward Moxon. London, 1839. [/] 7.
       *Reliques of Ancient Poetry. By Thomas Percy, D.D., Bishop of
       Dromore.* John Templeton. London, 1839.," *The Atlas, A
       General Newspaper and Journal of Literature* [London], XIV,
       No. 706 (November 23, 1839), 750-751. [R of item 346:
       751]

[333]   [Anonymous].   "Shelley's Complete Poetical Works," *The Spectator*, XII, No. 595 (November 23, 1839), 1118-1119.   [R: item 346]

*[334]   [Anonymous].   "Poetical Works of P. B. Shelley," *The London Weekly Observer*, [?] (November 27, 1839), [?p] [R: item 346]

[335]   [Anonymous].   "Reviews. *The Poetical Works of Percy Bysshe Shelley*. Edited by Mrs. Shelley. Moxon. [/] *Essays, Letters from Abroad, Translations, and Fragments*. By Percy Bysshe Shelley. Edited by Mrs. Shelley. Moxon.," *The Athenaeum*, No. 633 (December 14, 1839), 939-942. [R: items 344, 346]

[336]   [Anonymous].   "Shelley's Posthumous Prose," *The Spectator*, XII, No. 598 (December 14, 1839), 1186-1187.   [R: item 344]

[337]   [Anonymous].   " *Essays, Letters from Abroad, Translations and Fragments*. By Percy Bysshe Shelley. Edited by Mrs. Shelley. Two vols. Moxon.," *The Examiner*, No. 1663 (December 15, 1839), 788-789.   [R: item 344]

[338]   [Anonymous].   "*Essays, Letters from Abroad, Translations and Fragments*. By Percy Bysshe Shelley. Edited by Mrs. Shelley. [Second Notice] [brackets in original]," *The Athenaeum*, No. 635 (December 28, 1839), 982-985.   [R: item 344]

Books:

*[339]   Blessington, [Marguerite Gardiner,] Countess of.   *The Idler in Italy*.   3 vols.   London: Henry Colburn, 1839-1840. [B: ?]

[340]   Carlyle, Thomas.   "Characteristics," in volume IV of *Critical and Miscellaneous Essays of Thomas Carlyle*.   4 vols. New York: Scribner, Welford and Co., 1839.   [C; M: IV, 28; rptd. from item 173]

[341]   Δ[pseud. of Henry Dudley Ryder].   "On the Character and Poetry of Shelley.," 40-52 in [William Anderson, ed.,] *The Gift for All Seasons*.   v+354pp.   London: Smith, Elder & Co., 1839.   [C]

[342]   Dawes, Rufus.   *Geraldine, Athenia of Damascus, and Miscellaneous Poems*.   343pp.   New York: Samuel Colman, 1839.   [M: 34, 110; B: the character of Clifford in "Geraldine" is loosely based on Shelley]

[343] Lowell, James Russell. "Memoir of Shelley.," in volume I,
[13]-31, in *The Poetical Works of Shelley. Edited by Mrs.
Shelley. With a Memoir by James Russell Lowell*. 3 vols. New
York: James Miller, [1839]. [B]

[344] Shelley, Mrs. [Mary Wollstonecraft], ed. *Essays, Letters from
Abroad, Translations and Fragments, by Percy Bysshe Shelley*. 2
vols. London: Edward Moxon, 1840 [published in mid-
November, 1839, but bearing the date 1840 on the title
page]. [T; B,C: "Preface.," I, (v)-xxviii]

[345] Shelley, Mrs. [Mary Wollstonecraft], ed. *The Poetical Works of
Percy Bysshe Shelley*. 4 vols. London: Edward Moxon, 1839.
[T; B,C: "Preface.," I, (vii)-xvi; "Note on Queen Mab.,"
I, (96)-106; "Note on Alastor.," I, (139)-142; "Note on
the Revolt of Islam.," I, (375)-380; "Note on the Prometheus Unbound.," II, (129)-140; "Note on the Cenci.,"
II, (272)-280; "Note on Hellas.," II, (343)-347; "Note
on the Early Poems.," III, (15)-17; "Note on Poems of
1816.," III, (35)-36; "Note on Poems of 1817.," III,
(68)-72; "Note on Poems Written in 1818.," III, (159)-
164; "Note on Poems of 1819.," III, (205)-210; "Note on
Poems Written in 1820.," IV, (49)-54; "Note on Poems of
1821.," IV, (149)-154; "Note on Poems Written in 1822.,"
IV, (225)-236; "Preface to the Volume of Posthumous
Poems, Published in 1824.," IV, (237)-240.]

[346] Shelley, Mrs. [Mary Wollstonecraft], ed. *The Poetical Works of
Percy Bysshe Shelley*. xvi+363pp. London: Edward Moxon,
1840 [published in mid-November, 1839, but bearing the
date 1840 on the title page]. [T,B,C; a one volume edition of item 345]

[347] Shelley, Percy Bysshe. "Zastrozzi. [/] A Romance. [/] By
Percy Bysshe Shelley.," *The Romancist, And Novelist's Library*. No. 10 [1839], [145]-158. [T]

[348] Shelley, Percy Bysshe. "St. Irvyne; [/] or, The Rosicru-
cian. [/] A Romance. [/] By Percy Bysshe Shelley.,"
The Romancist, And Novelist's Library. No. 60 [1839], [113]-
126. [T]

1840

Periodicals:

[349] [Anonymous]. "Article IV. *The Poetical Works of P. B. Shelley*.
London: Moxon, 1839.," *The British and Foreign Review; or,
European Quarterly Journal*, X, No. xix (January, 1840),
98-127. [R: item 345]

[350] [Anonymous]. "Art. XXI. 1. *The Poetical Works of Percy Bysshe Shelley*. Edited by Mrs. Shelley. Moxon. [/] 2. *Essays, Letters from Abroad, Translations, and Fragments*. By P. B. Shelley. Edited by Mrs. Shelley. London: Moxon, 1840.," *The Monthly Review*, New Series I [whole number CLI], No. i (January, 1840), 125-130. [R: items 344, 346]

[351] [Anonymous]. "Shelley's Poetical Works," *Tait's Edinburgh Magazine*, New Series VIII, No. lxxiii (January, 1840), 56-59. [R: item 345]

[352] [Anonymous]. "Shelley's Complete Poetical Works," *The Corsair*, I, No. 44 (January 11, 1840), 698-699. [R: item 345]

[353] [Anonymous]. "Review of New Books.," *The Monthly Chronicle*, V, [No. 2] ([February, 1840]), 179-192. [R of item 344: 179-182]

[354] [Anonymous]. "Shelley.," *The Yale Literary Magazine*, No. 4 (February, 1840), 183-189. [C]

[355] [Ferrier, James F.]. "Poetical Translations of Faust," *Blackwood's Edinburgh Magazine*, XLVII, No. ccxcii (February, 1840), 223-240. [C; M: 229-231]

[356] [Anonymous]. "Shelley's Letters, Essays & Fragments.," *The Corsair*, I, No. 48 (February 8, 1840), 759-760. [R: item 344]

[357] [Anonymous]. "Extracts from Shelley's Letters from Italy," *The Corsair*, I, No. 49 (February 15, 1840), 783-784. [C; T: rptd. from item 344]

[358] [Anonymous]. "Art. VI. —1. *Speech of the Right Reverend the Lord Bishop of Exeter on Socialism*. London. 1840. [/] 2. *Weekly Tales and Tracts. Under the Sanction of the Lord Bishop of Ripon*. Edited by the Rev. W. F. Hook, D.D., Vicar of Leeds. London. 1839-1840. [running title: "Socialism"]," *The Quarterly Review*, LXV, No. cxxx (March, 1840), 484-527. [M: 516]

[359] [Anonymous]. "Shelley's Translation of 'The Banquet' of Plato.," *The Monthly Chronicle*, V, [No. 4] ([April, 1840]), 313-321. [T: rptd. from item 344]

[360] [Anonymous]. "Shelley's Paper Boats," *The Mirror, of Literature, Amusement, and Instruction*, XXXV, No. 1001 (April 18, 1840), 260. [B]

[361]   Tuckerman, H[enry] T[heodore]. "Shelley," *The Southern
        Literary Messenger*, VI, No. 6 (June, 1840), [393]-397.
        [C: rptd.: item 457]

[362]   [Anonymous]. "Shelley's Essays, &c.," *The Southern Literary
        Messenger*, VI, No. 6 (June, 1840), 470-471. [R: item
        344]

[363]   [Signed "Dahlia"]. "Chat in Boston Bookstores. —No. II.,"
        The Boston Quarterly Review, III, No. iii (July, 1840),
        323-331. [C: 331]

[364]   E[merson, Ralph Waldo]. "Thoughts on Modern Literature,"
        The Dial, I, No. 2 (October, 1840), [137]-158. [C;
        M: 149-150]

[365]   Smith, Seba. "Shelley.," *The Southern Literary Messenger*, VI,
        No. 11 (November, 1840), 717-720. [C, a letter in
        reply to item 361]

[366]   [Signed "A Fellow of St. John's College, Cambridge"].
        "Letters from the Continent.," *The Monthly Chronicle*,
        VI, [No. 6] (December, 1840), 505-531. [C: "Rome—
        Shelley's Grave—Shelley—Keats, &c.," 505-511]

[367]   [Signed "A Friend of Virtue"]. "Reply to Some Remarks on
        Shelley, [/] In the Southern Literary Messenger, for
        June 1840.," *The Southern Literary Messenger*, VI, No. 12
        (December, 1840), 826-828. [C, a letter in reply to
        item 361]

Books:

*[368] [Anonymous]. *Shelley's Genius, with a Sketch of His Life.* [?]pp.
        London: [?], 1840. [B]

*[369] [Signed "H.T.B."]. "Essay on Shelley," 69-93 in *The
        Silcoates Album; or, Original Contributions in Prose and Verse,
        Composed for the Bazaar to be held in Wakefield, July 1, 1840.*
        [?]pp. London: [?], 1840. [?C]

*[370] [Johnstone, (?)]. *The Table Talker or Brief Essays on Society and
        Literature.* 2 vols. London: William Pickering, 1840.
        [C: "Shelley's Essays" (?pp)]

[371]   Rowan, Archibald Hamilton. *Autobiography of Archibald Hamilton
        Rowan, Esq. With Additions and Illustrations by William Hamilton
        Drummond.* xvi+475pp. Dublin: Thomas Tegg and Co.,
        1840. [B, T: 388-389]

1841

[372]   [Signed "A Fellow of St. John's College, Cambridge"].
        "Letters from the Continent.," *The Monthly Chronicle*, VII,
        [No. 1] (January, 1841), 11-37. [M: 25]

[373]   [Signed "H."]. "Lord Byron," *The Southern Literary Messenger*,
        VII, No. 1 (January, 1841), 32. [M]

[374]   Tuckerman, H[enry] T[heodore]. "Shelley.," *The Southern
        Literary Messenger*, VII, No. 1 (January, 1841), 28-29.
        [C, in reply to item 367]

[375]   Medwin, Thomas. "Sydney. From the Memoranda of a Physi-
        cian," *Bentley's Miscellany*, IX, ([February, 1841]), 168-
        178. [B: the character of Sydney is a fictionalized
        portrait of Shelley]

[376]   Jones, William A. "The Culture of the Imagination,"
        Arcturus, A Journal of Books and Opinions, I, No. iv (March,
        1841), 236-243. [M: 237]

[377]   [Smith, William Henry]. "Wordsworth," *Blackwood's Edinburgh
        Magazine*, XLIX, No. cccv (March, 1841), 359-371. [C;
        M: 360, 369-371]

[378]   [Anonymous]. "Pencillings on Poetry," *The Southern Literary
        Messenger*, VII, No. 4 (April, 1841), 310-313. [C; M:
        312]

[379]   L[ewes], G[eorge] H[enry]. "Art. II —1. *The Poetical Works of*
        Percy Bysshe Shelley. Moxon, 1839. [/] 2. *Letters and Essays*
        from Abroad. By P. B. Shelley. Moxon, 1840. [/] 3. *Die*
        Cenci. Trauerspiel aus dem Englischen von Shelley über-
        setst von Felix Adolphie. Berlin, 1838. [/] 4. *Adone*.
        Nella Morte di Giovanni Keats. Elegia di P. B. Shelley. Tra-
        dotta da L. A. Damaso Pareto. Geneva, 1830. [running
        title: "Percy Bysshe Shelley]," *Westminster Review*, XXXV,
        No. lxix (April, 1841), 303-344. [R: items 344, 345;
        C]

[380]   M., M. [John M. Mackie]. "Shelley," *The Dial*, I, No. iv
        (April, 1841), 470-493. [R: item 344; rptd.: item 455]

[381]   [Merle, Gibbons]. "A Newspaper Editor's Reminiscences.
        Chap. IV. The Poetical Magazine—Tour of Dr. Syntax—
        Early History of Shelley—Visions of Dyspepsia, ETC.,"
        Fraser's Magazine, XXIII, No. cxxxviii (June, 1841), 699-
        710. [B]

[382]   [Anonymous].   "Courts of Law.   Court of Queen's Bench.
          Shelley's Works.   —The Queen *v.* Moxon.," *The Examiner*,
          No. 1743 (June 26, 1841), 412.   [C]

[383]   Pike, Albert.   "Shelley.," *The Ladies Companion: A Monthly Maga-
          zine Embracing Every Department of Literature, Embellished with
          Original Engravings, and Music Arranged for the Piano Forte, Harp
          and Guitar*, XV (July, 1841), 114.   [C]

[384]   [Anonymous].   "Art. X. —Speech for the Defendant in the
          Prosecution of the Queen *v.* Moxon, for the Publication
          of Shelley's Works.   By T. N. Talfourd, Sergeant at
          Law.   London: Moxon.," *The Monthly Review*, New Series II,
          No. iv [whole number clv] (August, 1841), 545-552.   [R:
          item 392]

[385]   [Blackie, John Stuart].   "Traits and Tendencies of German
          Literature.," *Blackwood's Edinburgh Magazine*, L, No. cccx
          (August, 1841), 143-160.   [C; M: 160]

[386]   [Anonymous].   "Talfourd's Defence of Moxon," *Arcturus, A
          Journal of Books and Opinion*, II, No. x (September, 1841),
          251-254.   [R: item 392]

[387]   P., H. S. [?Orestes Brownson].   "Art. I. —1. *The Poetical
          Works of Percy Bysshe Shelley*.   Edited by Mrs. Shelley.
          London: Edward Moxon.   1840.   [/] 2. *Essays, Letters from
          Abroad, Translations and Fragments, by Percy Bysshe Shelley*.
          Edited by Mrs. Shelley.   Philadelphia: Lea & Blanchard.
          1840.," *The Boston Quarterly Review*, IV, No. iv (October,
          1841), [393]-436.   [R: item 344, and American edition
          of item 345]

[388]   [Anonymous].   "Chapters on English Poetry.   Shelley.,"
          Tait's Edinburgh Magazine, New Series VIII, No. xcv (Novem-
          ber, 1841), [681]-685.   [C]

[389]   [Signed "L.D."].   "On the Recent Prosecution of the Publi-
          sher of 'Shelley's Poems,'" *Tait's Edinburgh Magazine*, New
          Series VIII, No. xcv (November, 1841), 727.   [C: a
          poem]

[390]   [Anonymous].   "*Speech for the Defendant in the Prosecution of The
          Queen v. Moxon, for the publication of Shelley's Works.   By T. N.
          Talfourd, Serjeant-at-Law*.   Moxon.," *The Athenaeum*, No. 733
          (November 13, 1841), 869.   [R: item 392]

Books:

[391]   [Lewes, George Henry].   "Shelley, Percy Bysshe," in volume
          XXI, 374-376, of *The Penny Cyclopedia of the Society for the*

Diffusion of Knowledge. 30 vols. London: Charles Knight and Co., 1832-1845 [Volume XXI: 1841]. [B, C]

[392] Talfourd, T[homas] N[oon]. *Speech for the Defendant, in the Prosecution of The Queen v. Moxon, for Publication of Shelley's Works. Delivered in the Court of Queen's Bench, June 23, 1841, and Revised. By T. N. Talfourd, Sergeant at Law.* 58pp. London: Edward Moxon, 1841. [C]

*[393] Tuckerman, Henry T[heodore]. *Rambles and Reveries.* vi+436pp. New York: James P. Giffing, 1841. [C: "Shelley," (?p)]

1842

Periodicals:

[394] [Anonymous]. "Shelley," *The New World [/] A Weekly Journal of Popular Literature, Science, Music and the Arts,* IV, No. 6 [whole number 88] (February, 1842), 84. [C: fourteen lines of blank verse]

[395] [Signed "E.D."]. "The 'Prometheus Unbound' of Shelley," *The Southern Literary Messenger,* VIII, No. 3 (March, 1842), 194-197. [C]

[396] [Poe, Edgar Allan]. "Review of New Books," *Graham's [Lady's and Gentleman's] Magazine* [Philadelphia], XX, No. 3 (March, 1842), [186]-192. [M: 189]

[397] [Anonymous]. "Art. II. — *Ahasuerus. A Poem. By a Virginian.* New York: Harper & Brothers, 82 Cliff-street. 1842. pp. 46. octavo.," *Southern Quarterly Review* [Charleston], II, No. 4 (October, 1842), 312-321. [R; M: 314]

*[398] An Admirer of Shelley [Denis Florence MacCarthy]. "[?]," *The Dublin Evening Post,* [?] (November 24, 1842), [?p]. [B]

[399] [Wilson, John]. "Lays of Ancient Rome.," *Blackwood's Edinburgh Magazine,* LII, No. cccxxvi (December, 1842), 802-824. [R; M: 803]

*[400] An Admirer of Shelley [Denis Florence MacCarthy]. "[?]," *The Dublin Evening Post,* [?] (December 6, 1842), [?p]. [B]

Periodicals:

[401] Shelley, Percy Bysshe. "The Creed of Pythagoras," *The Model
       Republic*, No. 2 (February 1, 1843), 32. [T: first pub-
       lished extract from "A Refutation of Deism"]

*[402] Shelley, Percy Bysshe. "[Extract from 'A Refutation of
       Deism'], *The Model Republic*, No. [?] (May 1, 1843), [?p].
       [T]

[403] [Whipple, Edwin Percy]. "Art. III. *Critical and Miscellaneous
       Writings of T. Noon Talfourd, Author of 'Ion.'* Philadelphia;
       Carey & Hart. 1842. 12mo. pp. 354.," *North American
       Review*, LVII, No. cxxi (October, 1843), 333-352. [R;
       M: 342-344]

[404] Godwin, Parke. "Prince's Poems," *The Present*, I, No. 3
       (November 15, 1843), 98-105. [M: 104]

[405] [Godwin, Parke]. "Percy Bysshe Shelley," *The United States
       Magazine and Democratic Review*, New Series XIII, No. lxvi
       (December, 1843), 603-623. [C; rptd.: item 837]

Books:

[406] Simmons, B[artholomew]. *Legends, Lyrics, and Other Poems.*
       ix+276pp. Edinburgh and London: William Blackwood and
       Sons, 1843. [C: "Lines written in the first blank leaf
       of Shelley's poems.," (112)-114, a forty-eight line
       poem]

*[407] Wilson, John. *The Noctoes Ambrosianæ of "Blackwood."* 4 vols.
       Philadelphia: Carey and Hart, 1843. [C: rptd. from
       items 37, 114, 249]

Periodicals:

[408] [Whipple, Edwin Percy]. "Art. I. — *The Poets and Poetry of
       America; with a Historical Introduction.* By Rufus W. Griswold.
       Philadelphia: Carey & Hart. 8vo. pp. xxvi. and 476.,"
       North American Review, LVIII, No. cxxii (January, 1844),
       1-39. [R; M: 26-27, 30]

[409] Chivers [misprinted Chivres], T[homas] H[olley]. "Shelley.
(Extract from a Lecture on the 'Genius of Shelley'),"
Southern Literary Messenger, X, No. 2 (February, 1844),
104-106. [C]

[410] C[hanning, William Henry]. "The Death of Shelley," *The Dial*,
IV, No. 4 (April, 1844), 471. [C: an eighteen line
poem]

[411] Hunter, James L. "Poetical Similarities.," *Southern Literary
Messenger*, X, No. 4 (April, 1844), 233-240. [C; Shelley: 234-238]

[412] [Anonymous]. "Art. II. —*Speeches and Forensic Arguments*. By
Daniel Webster. Boston: Tappan and Dennet, 1830-1843.
3 vols. 8vo.," *The North American Review*, LIX, No. 124
(July, 1844), 44-70. [R; M: 63]

[413] Lea, Henry C. "Remarks on Various Late Poets. No. I.
Leigh Hunt.," *Southern Literary Messenger*, X, No. 10
(October, 1844), 619-629 [misprinted 926]. [C; M:
620, 621, 620]

[414] [Whipple, Edwin Percy]. "Art. IV. — *The Complete Poetical Works
of William Wordsworth*. Philadelphia: James Kay, Jr. &.
Brother. 8vo. 1837.," *The North American Review*, LIX,
No. cxxv (October, 1844), 352-384. [R; M: throughout]

Books:

[415] [Signed "J.B.B."]. "Art. XIII. —Imitation of Shakespeare
by Shelley, in his Tragedy of 'The Cenci.,'" *The Shakespeare Society Papers*, I, (1844), 52-54. [C]

[416] Barrett, Elizabeth Barrett. *Poems*. 2 vols. London: Edward
Moxon, 1844. [C: "A Vision of Poets," (3)-59; M: 25]

[417] Chambers, Robert, ed. *Cyclopaedia of English Literature; A History, Critical and Biographical, of British Authors, from the
Earliest to the Present Times*. 2 vols. Edinburgh: William
and Robert Chambers, 1844. [B,C: "Percy Bysshe
Shelley.," II, 395-402; rptd. item 608]

[418] Hunt, Leigh. *Imagination and Fancy; or Selections from the English
Poets, Illustrative of Those First Requisites of Their Art; with
Markings of the Best Passages, Critical Notices of the Writers,
and an Essay in Answer to the Question "What is Poetry?"* xii+
345pp. London: Smith, Elder, and Co., 1844. [C,T:
"Shelley, Born, 1792,—Died, 1822.," (292)-311]

[419]   Paton, J[oseph] Noel. *Compositions From Shelley's Prometheus
         Unbound.* [unnumbered]pp. London: M.M. Holloway, [1844].
         [Twelve engravings illustrating passages from *Prometheus
         Unbound*]

                              1845

Periodicals:

[420]   [Lea, Henry C.]. "Remarks on Various Late Poets. . . .
         No. II [/] Barry Cornwall's Songs," *Southern Literary
         Messenger*, XI, No. 1 (January, 1845), 31-37. [C; M: 31-
         32]

[421]   [Whipple, Edwin Percy]. "Art. III. — *The Works of Lord Byron
         in Verse and Prose, including his Letters, Journals, &c., with a
         Sketch of his Life.* New York: A. V. Blake. 8vo. 1843.,"
         North American Review, LX, No. cxxvi (January, 1845), 64-
         86. [R; M: 67, 85]

[422]   [Anonymous]. "Art. VII. — *The Life of the Rev. Joseph Blanco
         White, written by Himself; with portions of his Correspondence.*
         Edited by John Hamilton Thom. In 3 vols. 8vo.
         London, 1845.," *The Quarterly Review*, LXXVI, No. cli
         (June, 1845), 164-203. [R; M: 201-202]

[423]   [Bowen, Francis]. "Art. VIII. —*The Poets and Poetry of Europe,
         with Introductions and Biographical Notices.* By Henry Longfel-
         low. Philadelphia: Carey & Hart. 1845. 8vo. pp
         779.," *North American Review*, LXI, No. cxxviii (July,
         1845), 199-231. [R; M: 216]

[424]   [Whipple, Edwin Percy]. "The Poets and Poetry of England,"
         The American Review: A Whig Journal, II, No. i (July, 1845),
         30-58. [R: item 435; C: 33-37; rptd.: items 492, 588]

[425]   L[ea, Henry C.]. "Remarks on Various Late Poets. . . .
         No. V. L.E.L. [Letitita Elizabeth Landon]," *Southern
         Literary Messenger*, XI, No. 8 (August, 1845), 468. [C; M]

*[426]   Poe, Edgar Allan. "Miss Barrett's 'A Drama of Exile and
         Other Poems,'" *The Broadway Journal*, II, No. [?] (August
         2, 1845), 1-2. [M; rptd.: item 1875]

[427]   [Whipple, Edwin Percy]. "Art. VII. —1. *Contributions to the
         Edinburgh Review.* By Francis Jeffrey, now one of the
         Judges of the Court of Sessions in Scotland. London:
         Londman & Co. 4 vols. 8vo. [/] 2. Wiley & Putnam's
         Library of Choice Reading: Characters of Shakespeare. By Wil-
         liam Hazlitt. New York. 16mo. [/] 3. *Imagination and*

                              [45]

Fancy. By Leigh Hunt. New York: Wiley & Putnam. 16mo.,"
North American Review, LXI, cxxix (October, 1845), 468-
497. [R; M: numerous]

[428] De Quincey, Thomas. "Notes on Gilfillan's 'Gallery of
Literary Portraits,'" *Tait's Edinburgh Magazine*, New
Series XII, No. cxliv (December, 1845), 756-761. [B,
C: 760-761; rptd.: items 441, 731]

*[429] [MacCarthy, Denis Florence]. "[?]," *The Nation*, [?] (December 20, 1845), [?p]. [C]

*[430] [MacCarthy, Denis Florence]. "[?]," *The Nation*, [?] (December 27, 1845), [?p]. [C]

Books:

[431] Craik, Geo[rge] L. *Sketches of the History of Literature and Learning in England. With Specimens of the Principal Writers.* [6
vols. in 2]. London: Charles Knight & Co., 1845. [C:
"Shelley.," VI, 188-192]

[432] Forster, Thomas Ignatius Maria. *Philosophia Musarum [/] containing the Song and Romances of the Pipers Wallet, Pan, The Harmonia
Musarum, and Other Miscellaneous Poems.* xxxxvii+285pp.
Bruges: sold at the Albion Library, Dyver, 1845. [M:
xxvii]

[433] Foster, G[eorge] G., ed. *The Poetical Works of Percy Bysshe
Shelley, First American Edition (Complete): with Some Remarks on
the Poetical Faculty, and Its Influence on Human Destiny, Embracing a Biographical and Critical Notice, by G. G. Foster.* 750pp.
New York: J. S. Redfield, 1845. [T; B, C: "Preface.,"
(1)-24]

[434] Gilfillan, George. *A Gallery of Literary Portraits.* [Later
designated "First Series."] 443pp. Edinburgh: William
Tait, 1845. [C: "Percy Bysshe Shelley.," 71-105;rptd.:61

[435] Griswold, Rufus W. *The Poets and Poetry of England, in the Nineteenth Century.* 504pp. Philadelphia: Carey & Hart, 1845.
[M: 6; C: "Percy Bysshe Shelley,: 270-272; T: 272-285]

*[436] Snow, Robert. *Memorials of a Tour on the Continent to Which Are
Added Miscellaneous Poems.* vii+311pp. London: William
Pickering, 1845. [C: a poem, "Spezia"]

Periodicals:

[437] [Anonymous]. "24. *The Poetical Works of Percy Bysshe Shelley.*
First American Edition (Complete): with some Remarks on the Poetical Faculty, and its Influence on Human Destiny, embracing a biographical and critical notice. By G. G. Foster. New York:
J. S. Redfield. 1845. pp. 750, 12mo.," *The Biblical
Repository and Classical Review*, Third Series II [whole number LXI], No. 1 (January, 1846), 185. [R: item 433]

[438] De Quincey, Thomas. "Notes on Gilfillan's 'Gallery of
Literary Portraits,'" *Tait's Edinburgh Magazine*, New
Series XIII, No. cxlv (January, 1846), 23-29. [C;
rptd.: item 443]

[439] [Anonymous]. "Review," *The Harbinger, Devoted to Social and Political Progress*, II, No. 5 (January 10, 1846), 74076. [R:
items 433, 434]

[440] [Anonymous]. "Review of New Books," *Graham's [American Monthly]
Magazine*, XXVIII, No. 2 (February, 1846), [92]-96. [R:
item 433: 96]

[441] De Quincey, Thomas. "Notes on Gilfillan's 'Gallery of
Literary Portraits,'" *The Eclectic Magazine*, VII, No. 2
(February, 1846), 221-236 [misprinted 336]. [B, C:
233-236; rptd. from item 428]

[442] L[ea, Henry C.]. "Remarks on Various Late Poets. . . .
No. VI. William Motherwell," *Southern Literary Messenger*,
XII, No. 3 (March, 1846), 153-158. [C; M: 158]

[443] De Quincey, Thomas. "Notes on Gilfillan's 'Gallery of
Literary Portraits,'" *The Eclectic Magazine*, VII, No. 4
(April, 1846), 520-529. [C; rptd. from item 438]

[444] [Anonymous]. "Shelley's Minor Poems.," *Hood's Magazine*, V,
No. v (May, 1846), 471-473. [R, C]

[445] [Anonymous]. "The Poetical Works of Percy Bysshe Shelley.
First American edition complete. Edited by G. G. Foster. New York: J. S. Redfield," *The American Review: A
Whig Journal*, III, No. vi (June, 1846), 673. [R: item
433]

[446] [Anonymous]. "*Pen-and-Ink Sketches of Poets, Preachers, and Politi-
cians*. Bogue.," *The Athenaeum*, No. 983 (August 29, 1846),
882-884. [R: item 452; M: 883]

[447] [Signed "Sylvan Southgate"]. "Shelley's Hampstead Adven-
       ture. August 3.," *The Athenaeum*, No. 984 (September 5,
       1846), 910-911. [B; refutation of item 446]

[448] [Anonymous]. "Review," *The Harbinger, Devoted to Social and Poli-
       tical Progress*, III, No. 16 (September 26, 1846), 249-
       252. [R: item 453; M: 251]

[449] [Anonymous]. "Modern English Poets," *The United States and
       Democratic Review*, New Series XIX, No. c (October, 1846),
       316-320 [an error in pagination creates two consecutive
       groups of pages so numbered; these are the first such
       group]. [R: item 453; C: throughout]

[450] [Anonymous]. "Shelley.," *The Southern and Western Literary Messen-
       ger and Review* [variant title for *Southern Literary Messenger*]
       XII, No. [12] (December, 1846), 737-742. [C]

[451] Shelley, Percy Bysshe. "Ode to the West Wind," *The Harbinger*,
       Devoted to Social and Political Progress, IV, No. 2 (December
       19, 1846), 26. [T]

Books:

[452] [Dix, John (later John Dix Ross)]. *Pen and Ink Sketches of
       Poets, Preachers, and Politicians*. xii+275pp. London:
       David Bogue, 1846. [B: "Personal Notices of Shelley
       and Hazlitt.," (140)-154]

[453] Fuller, S. Margaret. *Papers on Literature and Art*. vi+183pp.
       New York: Wiley and Putnam, 1846. [C: "Modern British
       Poets.," (58)-99; Shelley: 68-74]

[454] Gilfillan, George. *Sketches of Modern Literature, and Eminent
       Literary Men, (Being a Gallery of Literary Portraits,) By George
       Gilfillan. Reprinted entire from the London Edition. [Appleton's
       Literary Miscellany*, vols. 6 and 7] 2 vols. New York:
       D. Appleton & Co., 1846. [C: "Percy Bysshe Shelley,"
       I, 89-125; rptd. from item 434]

[455] M.M. [John M. Mackie]. "Shelley.," in volume I, (215)-243
       in *Characteristics of Men of Genius; A Series of Biographical,
       Historical, and Critical Essays, Selected, By Permission, Chiefly
       from the North American Review*. [Ed. John Chapman]. 2 vols.
       London: Chapman, Brothers, 1846. [R: item 344; rptd.
       from item 380]

[456] Titmarsh [pseud. of William Makepeace Thackeray]. *Notes of a
       Journey from Cornhill to Grand Cairo, by way of Lisbon, Athens,
       Constantinople, and Jerusalem: Performed in the steamers of the
       Peninsular and Oriental Company*. xiv+301pp. London: Chapman
       and Hall, 1846. [M: 293]

[457]   Tuckerman, Henry T[heodore].   *Thoughts on the Poets.*   318pp.
         New York: C. S. Francis & Co., 1846.   [C: "Shelley.,"
         (137)-153; rptd. from item 361]

                              1847

Periodicals:

[458]   [Bacon, R. H.].   "Gilfillan's Literary Portraits," *The Ameri-*
         can Review, V, No. iv (April, 1847), 386-396.   [R: item
         454; M: 392-393]

[459]   [Barrett, Joseph Hartwell].   "Characteristics of Shelley,"
         The American Review: A Whig Journal, V, No. v (May, 1847),
         534-537.   [C]

[460]   [Anonymous].   "Letter from Italy. Naples, April 17, 1847,"
         The Harbinger, Devoted to Social and Political Progress, V, No.
         4 (July 3, 1847), 49-50.   [M: 49]

[461]   [Signed "L.D."].   "Shelley's Cenci," *Theatrical Times*, II,
         No. 63 (July 17, 1847), 219-220.   [C]

[462]   Bedingfield, Richard.   "On Shelley's Tragedy of 'The
         Cenci.,'" *Hood's Magazine*, VIII, No. iii(September, 1847),
         247-249.   [C]

[463]   [Signed "R.B."; ?Richard Bedingfield].   "Modern Dramatists
         and Modern Actors," *Theatrical Times*, II, No. 71 (Septem-
         ber 11, 1847), 284.   [C]

[464]   [Heraud, John Abraham].   "Reviews [/] *The Life of Percy Bysshe*
         Shelley. By Thomas Medwin. 2 vols. Newby.," *The Athen-*
         aeum, No. 1038 (September 18, 1847), 971-973.   [R: item
         477]

[465]   [Heraud, John Abraham].   " *The Life of Percy Bysshe Shelley.* By
         Thomas Medwin. [Second Notice.] (brackets in origi-
         nal)," *The Athenaeum*, No. 1039 (September 25, 1847),
         1002-1004.   [R: item 477; C]

[466]   Bedingfield, Richard.   "On Shelley;s Tragedy of 'The
         Cenci.,'" *Hood's Magazine*, VIII, No. iv (October, 1847),
         350-355.   [C]

[467]   [Smith, Horace].   "A Graybeard's Gossip About His Literary
         Acquaintances. No. VIII," *The New Monthly Magazine*, LXXXI,
         No. cccxxii (October, 1847), 227-240.   [B: 235-240]

                              [49]

[468] [Anonymous]. "Medwin's Life of Shelley," *The Spectator*, XX,
       No. 1006 (October 9, 1847), 976-977. [R: item 477]

[469] [Anonymous]. "Medwin's Life of Shelley," *The New Monthly Maga-
       zine*, LXXXI, No. cccxxiii (November, 1847), 295-296.
       [R: item 477]

[470] [Anster, John Henry]. "Art. IX. —1. *The Poetical Works of
       Percy Bysshe Shelley*, edited by Mrs. Shelley. 3 vols.
       London, 1847. [/] 2. *Shelley at Oxford—Papers in the New
       Monthly Magazine*, vols. 36 and 37. [/] 3. *The Life of P. B.
       Shelley*. By Thomas Medwin. 2 vols. London, 1847. [/]
       4. *Gallery of Literary Portraits*. By George Gilfillan.
       Edinburgh, 1845. [/] 5. *An Address to the Irish People*.
       By Percy Bysshe Shelley. Dublin, 1812.," *The North
       British Review*, VIII, No. xv (November, 1847), 218-257.
       [R: 1847 edition of item 346; items 175, 176, 180, 184,
       202,215, 233; item 477; item 434. Rptd.: items 480,
       482]

[471] [Smith, Horace]. "A Graybeard's Gossip About His Literary
       Acquaintance. No. IX. Forsan et haec olim meminisse
       juvabit [/] Percy Bysshe Shelley, Continued and Con-
       cluded.," *The New Monthly Magazine*, LXXXI, No. cccxxiii
       (November, 1847), 288-294. [B]

[472] Gilfillan, George. "Female Authors. —No. III. —Mrs.
       Shelley," *Tait's Edinburgh Magazine*, New Series XIV,
       No. clxviii (December, 1847), 850-854. [B]

*[473] [Anonymous]. "Medwin's Life of Shelley," *The London and Paris
       Observer*, XXIII, [?] ([?], 1847), 445-447. [R: item
       477; rptd. from item ?]

*[474] [Heraud, John Abraham]. "Medwin's Life of Shelley," *The
       London and Paris Observer*, XXIII, [?] ([?], 1847), 644-
       647. [R: item 477; rptd. from item 465]

Books:

[475] Headley, J[oel] T[yler]. *Letters from Italy*. viii+224pp.
       New York: Wiley and Putnam, 1847. [M: 144]

[476] Howitt, William. *Homes and Haunts of the Most Eminent British
       Poets*. 2 vols. London: Richard Bentley, 1847. [B:
       "Percy Bysshe Shelley," I, (436)-466]

[477] Medwin, Thomas. *The Life of Percy Bysshe Shelley*. 2 vols.
       London: Thomas Cautley Newby, 1847. [B]

Periodicals:

[478] [Anonymous]. "5. *The Poetical Works of Lord Byron;* complete in
       one volume. Collected and arranged, with Illustrative
       Notes by Thomas Moore, Lord Jeffrey, Sir Walter Scott,
       Bishop Heber, Samuel Rogers, Professor Wilson, J. G.
       Lockhart, George Ellis, Thomas Campbell, Rev. H. H.
       Milman, &c. &c. With a Portrait and View of Newstead
       Abbey. New York: D. Appleton & Co. 1847.," *The Southern
       Quarterly Review*, XIII, No. 25 (January, 1848), 264-268.
       [M: 266]

[479] [Anonymous]. "2. The Life of Percy Bysshe Shelley. By
       Thomas Medwin. In 2 vols. London: T. C. Newby, 72,
       Mortimer Street, Cavendish Square. 1847.," *The West-
       minster Review*, XLVIII, No. ii (January, 1848), 568-577.
       [R: item 477]

[480] [Anster, John Henry]. "Life and Writings of Percy Bysshe
       Shelley," *The Eclectic Magazine*, XIII, No. 1 (January,
       1848), 1-23. [R: item 477; rptd. from item 470]

[481] Burr, C. Chauncey. "Poetic Character.," *The Nineteenth
       Century* [Philadelphia], II (January, 1848), 167-170.
       [C]

[482] [Anster, John Henry]. "1. *The Poetical Works of Percy Bysshe
       Shelley*, edited by Mrs. Shelley. 3 vols. London, 1847.
       [/] 2. *Shelley at Oxford—Papers in the New Monthly Magazine*,
       Vols. 36 and 37. [/] 3. *The Life of P. B. Shelley*. By
       Thomas Medwin. 2 vols. London, 1847. [/] 4. *Gallery
       of Literary Portraits*. By George Gilfillan. Edinburgh,
       1845. [/] 5. *An Address to the Irish People*. By Percy
       Bysshe Shelley. Dublin, 1812.," *Littell's Living Age*,
       XVI, No. cxci (January 8, 1848), [49]-66. [R: item
       477, etc.; rptd. from item 470]

[483] [Anonymous]. "Art. II. *The Life of Percy Bysshe Shelley.* By
       Thomas Medwin. In Two Volumes. London: Thomas Cautley
       Newby, Mortimer Street, Cavendish Square. 1847.,"
       The Eclectic Review, Fourth Series XXIII [whole number
       LXXXVII] (February, 1848), 149-171. [R: item 477]

[484] [Anonymous]. "Extracts from the Portfolio of a Man of the
       World," *The Gentleman's Magazine*, New Series XXIX [whole
       number CLXXXIII] (February, 1848), 149-157. [C: 150-
       152]

[485]   [Merle, William Henry]. "Shelley at Eton," *The Athenaeum*,
         No. 1062 (March 4, 1848), 244. [B]

[486]   [Bowen, Francis]. "Art. X. —*Poems*. By James Russell Lowell
         Second Series. Cambridge: George Nichols. 1848.
         12mo. pp. 184.," *North American Review*, LXVI, No. cxxxix
         (April, 1848), 458-482. [R; M: 459, 464]

[487]   A[mos], A[ndrew]. "Shelley and His Contemporaries at Eton,
         The Athenaeum, No. 1068 (April 15, 1848), 390-391. [B]

[488]   Curtis, George H. "Southern Italy," *The [Sartain's] Union Maga
         zine of Literature and Art*, III, No. i (July, 1848), 22-26
         [M: 23]

[489]   [Headley, Joel Tyler]. "The Grave of Shelley," *Pictorial
         National Library, A Monthly Miscellany of the Useful and Enter-
         taining in Science, Art and Literature*, I (October, 1848),
         179-180. [B; rptd. from item 475]

[490]   [Anonymous]. "Sale of Mr. Hodges's Collection of Auto-
         graphs," *The Athenaeum*, No. 1104 (December 23, 1848),
         1297-1298. [M]

Books:

*[491]   Richardson, David Lester. *Literary Chit-Chat with Miscellaneous
         Poems and an Appendix of Prose Papers*.   xi+xiv+[496]pp.
         London: J. Madden, 1848; Calcutta: P. S. d'Rozario and
         Co., 1848. [?C]

[492]   Whipple, Edwin P[ercy]. *Essays and Reviews*. 2 vols. New
         York: D. Appleton & Company, 1848-1849. [C: "English
         Poets of the Nineteenth Century," I, (285)-354; Shel-
         ley: 293-303; rptd. from item 424; 2nd ed.: item 588]

1849

Periodicals:

[493]   Burr, C. Chauncey. "Men of Genius.," *The Nineteenth Century*
         [Philadelphia], III (January, 1849), 115-129. [C]

[494]   Burr, C. Chauncey. "Men of Genius. Part II. —Heresy,
         Radicalism, Infidelity.," *The Nineteenth Century* [Philadel-
         phia], III (January, 1849), 233-253. [M: throughout]

[495]   [?Burr, C. Chauncey]. "Reviewer's Department. [/] Carlos
         D. Stuart.," *The Nineteenth Century* [Philadelphia], III
         (January, 1849), 305-310. [M]

[496] Stuart, Carlos D. "Shelley the Democrat," *The Nineteenth Century* [Philadelphia], III (January, 1849), 60-68. [C]

[497] Taylor, J. Bayard. "Ode to Shelley," *Graham's Magazine*, XXXIV, No. 1 (January, 1849), [61]. [C: sixty line poem]

[498] Robbins, E. W. "Shelley," *American Literary Magazine*, IV, No. 2 (February, 1849), 479-480. [C: a poem]

[499] [Anonymous]. "Art. IV. —Percy Bysshe Shelley.," *The Prospective Review; A Quarterly Journal of Theology and Literature* [London], V, No. xvii [or, "formerly," *The Christian Teacher*, XI, No. 43] ([April], 1849), 58-85. [R: item 477]

[500] [Signed "H.W.P."]. "The Death of Shelley—A Vision," *The American Review: A Whig Journal*, IX, No. xvii (May, 1849), 530-532. [B: fictionalized]

[501] Poe, Edgar Allan. "Marginalia.," *Southern Literary Messenger*, XV, No. v (May, 1849), 292-293. [M]

[502] [Mayo, Amory D.]. "The Poetry of Keats," *The Massachusetts Quarterly Review*, II, No. vii (September, 1849), 414-428. (C; M: throughout]

[503] [De Vere, Aubrey]. "Art. III. —1. *The Princess: a Medley*. Poems by Alfred Tennyson. Fifth Edition. London: 1848. [/] 2. *The Poetical Works of Percy Bysshe Shelley*. 3 vols. London: 1847. [/] 3. *Life, Letters, and Literary Remains of John Keats*. Edited by R. Monckton Milnes. 2 vols. London: 1848.," *Edinburgh Review*, XC, No. clxxxii (October, 1849), 388-433. [R of 1847 edition of item 346: 419-425; revised and rptd.: item 1363]

[504] Burr, C. Chauncey. "Men of Genius. Part III. Love.," *The Nineteenth Century*, IV ([no month], 1849), 5-23. [C]

Books:

*[505] [Clark, William George]. *A Score of Lyrics*. viii+[64]pp. London: William Pickering, 1849. [Contains a poem, "Cor Cordium"]

[506] [Hawtrey, Edward Craven]. *Sermons and Lectures Delivered in Eton College Chapel, in the Years 1848-9*. 114pp. Eton [printed by E. P. Williams], 1849. [B: 111-112]

[507] Shaw, Thomas B. *Outlines of English Literature*. xii+540pp. London: John Murray, 1849. [C: "Shelley," 450-457]

*[508] Thackeray, William Makepeace. *The History of Pendennis; His Fortunes and Misfortunes, His Friends and His Greatest Enemy*. 2 vols London: Bradbury and Evans, 1849-50. [M: Chap. XXXIV]

Periodicals:

[509]   [Anonymous]. "The Poetical Works of Percy Bysshe Shelley.
        With some Remarks on the Poetical Faculty, and its
        Influence on Human Destiny; embracing a Biographical
        and Critical Notice, by G. G. Foster. Third edition.
        J. S. Redfield, Clinton Hall, New York. 1850.," *The
        Spirit of the Age* [New York], II, No. 1 (January 5, 1850),
        15-16. [R of third edition of item 433]

[510]   Shelley, P. B. "The Warning.," *The Spirit of the Age* [New
        York], II, No. 2 (January 12, 1850), [17]. [T: four
        and a half stanza excerpt from *The Revolt of Islam*,
        Canto XI, 15-19]

[511]   Shelley, P. B. "Equality.," *The Spirit of the Age* [New York],
        II, No. 4 (January 26, 1850), [49]. [T: five stanza
        excerpt from *The Revolt of Islam*, Canto V, 2-6]

[512]   [Anonymous]. "Edgar Allan Poe.," *Southern Literary Messenger*,
        XVI, No. 3 [whole number clxxxiii] (March, 1850), 172-
        187. [M: 185]

[513]   [Signed "J.L."]. "Percy Bysshe Shelley. A Biographic
        Sketch," *The Truth-Seeker: or Present Age: a Catholic Review
        of Literature, Philosophy, and Religion* [London], II, [No. 4]
        ([?April], 1850), 137-144. [B]

[514]   Shelley, Percy Bysshe. "Prose Thinkings, from the Poet
        Shelley.," *Cooper's Journal: or, Unfettered Thinker and Plain
        Speaker for Truth, Freedom, and Progress* [London], I, No. 14
        (April 16, 1850), 215. [T]

[515]   Langford, John Alfred. "Sonnet. To Shelley.," *Cooper's
        Journal: or, Unfettered Thinker and Plain Speaker for Truth,
        Freedom, and Progress* [London], I, No. 21 (May 25, 1850),
        328. [C: a poem]

[516]   [Signed "P."]. "A Few Words about Tennyson," *The American Whig
        Review*, New Series VI [whole number XII], No. xxxii
        [whole number lxviii] (August, 1850), 176-181. [C:
        177-178]

[517]   Merriman, Josiah J. "The Maniac. A Tale from Shelley's
        Poem, Julian and Maddalo," *The National Instructor* [Lon-
        don], I, No. 20 (October 5, 1850), [305]-307. [Prose
        paraphrase and T]

[518]   [Anonymous]. "Leigh Hunt," *The United States Magazine and Demo-*
        cratic Review, New Series XXVII, No. cxlix (November,
        1850), 426-434. [R: item 522; M: 432-434]

[519]   [Anonymous]. "Shelley and Cowper," *Hogg's Instructor* [London],
        New Series IV ([no month], 1850), 257-259. [C]

Books:

[520]   [Anonymous]. *Life of Percy Bysshe Shelley* [/] *(From the Metropolitan*
        Literary Journal.) 16pp. Manchester: A. Heywood, [n.d.:
        ?1850]. [B]

[521]   Creasy, Edward S[hepherd]. *Memoirs of Eminent Etonians: with*
        Notices of the Early History of Eton College. xv+504pp.
        London: Richard Bentley, 1850. [B,C: "Percy Bysshe
        Shelley," (481)-497]

[522]   Hunt, Leigh. *The Autobiography of Leigh Hunt; with Reminiscences of*
        Friends and Contemporaries. 3 vols. London: Smith, Elder
        and Co., 1850. [B,C: II, 31-33, 153-154, 179-202; III,
        12-22, 307-322]

*[523] Ossoli, Margaret Fuller. *Art, Literature and the Drama.* [?]pp.
        New York: [?], 1850. [M: 78]

[524]   [Redding, Cyrus]. *Memoir of Percy Bysshe Shelley,* [/] *Author of*
        "Queen Mab," "Masque of Anarchy," etc. 15pp. London: Austin
        & Co., [n.d.: ?1850]. [B; rptd. from item 141]

[525]   Southey, Robert. *The Life and Correspondence of Robert Southey.*
        Edited by his son, the Rev. Charles Cuthbert Southey. 6 vols.
        London: Longman, Brown, Green, and Longmans, 1849-1850
        [I: 1849; II-VI: 1850]. [C: III, 323-326]

[526]   Whipple, Edwin P[ercy]. *Lectures on Subjects Connected with Liter-*
        ature and Life. 218pp. Boston: Ticknor, Reed and Fields,
        1850. [M: 112; rptd.: item 1169]

                              1851

Periodicals:

[527]   [Signed "B."]. "Shelley and Tennyson," *The United States Maga-*
        zine and Democratic Review, New Series XXVIII, No. cli
        (January, 1851), 49-54. [C]

[528]   [Anonymous]. "Mrs. Shelley.," *The Athenaeum*, No. 1216
        (February 15, 1851), 191. [C]

[529]   [Anonymous]. "Mary Wolstonecraft [*sic*] Shelley," *The Inter-*
        national Monthly Magazine, III, No. i (April, 1851), 16-
        18. [C]

[530]   [Donne, William Bedham]. "Art. III. *The Life and Correspondence*
        of Robert Southey. London: 150.," *Edinburgh Review*, XCIII,
        No. cxc (April, 1851), 370-402. [R: item 525; M: 381]

[531]   [Signed "J.S."]. "Death Verses: A Stroll through the
        Valley of the Shadow of Death with Tennyson, in Company
        with Shelley, Milton, Blair, Swift, Coleridge, Moore,
        and Others," *The American Whig Review*, New Series VII [whole
        number XIII], No. vi [whole number lxxviii] (June,
        1851), 534-544. [C; Shelley: 541-544]

[532]   [Signed "O.W.W."]. "William Wordsworth," *The American Whig*
        Review, XIV, No. lxxix (July, 1851), 68-80. [M: 70, 73]

[533]   [Signed "Philo."]. "9. Shelley's Children," *Notes and Queries*,
        IV, No. 90 (July 19, 1851), 40. [B]

[534]   [Anonymous]. "Mulchinock's Poems," *The American Whig Review*,
        XIV, No. lxxx (August, 1851), 115-121. [R; M: 119]

[535]   Brimley, George. "Wordsworth. Part II.," *Fraser's Magazine*,
        XLIV, No. cclx (August, 1851), 186-199. [C; M: 197]

[536]   [Anonymous]. "Wordsworth, Byron, Scott, and Shelley.,"
        Harper's New Monthly Magazine, III, No. xvi (September,
        1851), 502-505. [C]

[537]   [Signed "W.D."]. "Imagination and Fact," *The American Whig*
        Review, XIV, No. lxxxiii (November, 1851), 392-399. [C;
        M: 398-399]

[538]   [Smith, William Henry]. "The Dramas of Henry Taylor," *Black-*
        wood's Edinburgh Magazine, LXX, No. ccccxxxiii (November,
        1851), 505-521. [R; C: 505]

Books:

[539]   Beddoes, Thomas Lovell. *The Poems* [/] *Posthumous and Collected of*
        Thomas Lovelll Beddoes. 2 vols. London: William Pickering
        1851. [C: I, xxii-xxiv; xxviii-xxix; xxxv-xxxvi; liv;
        lvii; 163: "Lines (/) Written in a Blank Leaf of 'Pro-
        metheus Unbound.'"]

[540] Meredith, George. *Poems.* [160]pp. London: John Parker and
         Son, [1851]. [C: "The Poetry of Shelley" (a quatrain),
         (24)]

[541] Moir, D[avid] M[acbeth]. *Sketches of the Poetical Literature of
         the Past Half-Century in Six Lectures Delivered at the Edinburgh
         Philosophical Association.* viii+330pp. Edinburgh: William
         Blackwood and Sons, 1851. [C: 221-229]

[542] Wordsworth, Christopher. *Memoirs of William Wordsworth, Poet
         Laureate, D.C.L.* 2 vols. London: Edward Moxon, 1851.
         [C: II, 474]

                              1852

Periodicals:

[543] [Anonymous]. "Bayard Taylor's Poems," *The American Whig Review,*
         XV, No. lxxxv (January, 1852), 30-35. [M: 31, 35]

[544] [Anonymous]. "A Pair of Poets [i.e., Bayard Taylor and
         R. H. Stoddard," *Southern Literary Messenger,* XVIII, No. 1
         (January, 1852), 13-19. [C; Shelley: 16-17]

[545] [Anonymous]. "*Letters of Percy Bysshe Shelley. With an Introductory
         Essay.* By Robert Browning. Moxon.," *The Athenaeum,*
         No. 1269 (February 21, 1852), 214-215. [R: item 573]

[546] [Anonymous]. "*Letters of Percy Bysshe Shelley.* With an Introduc-
         tory Essay by Robert Browning. Moxon.," *The Examiner,*
         No. 2,299 (February 21, 1852), 117-118. [R: item 573;
         rptd.: item 563]

[547] [Anonymous]. "Reviews. [/] *Letters of Percy Bysshe Shelley; with
         an Introductory Essay* by Robert Browning. Moxon.," *The
         Literary Gazette,* No. 1831 (February 21, 1852), 173-175.
         [R: item 573]

[548] [Signed "Q."]. "Percy Bysshe Shelley's Letters," *The Literary
         Gazette,* No. 1832 (February 28, 1852), 205. [C, T]

[549] [Smith, William Henry]. "Miss Mitford's 'Recollections,'"
         Blackwood's Edinburgh Magazine, LXXI, No. ccccxxxvii (March,
         1852), 259-272. [R: item 578; C: 266-267]

[550] [Anonymous]. "Shelley's Letters," *The New Monthly Magazine,*
         XCIV, No. ccclxxv (March, 1852), 357-360. [R: item 573]

[551] [Signed "J.L."]. "Percy Bysshe Shelley," *The Biographical Magazine* [London], I (March, 1852), 105-119. [B; rptd. item 575, apparently a retitled reissue]

[552] [Anonymous]. "Literary Forgeries," *The Athenaeum*, No. 1271 (March 6, 1852), 278-279. [T; rptd.: item 566]

[553] [Anonymous]. "Literary Fraud," *The Literary Gazette*, No. 1833 (March 6, 1852), 230. [T]

[554] White, W[illiam]. "To Correspondents," *The Literary Gazette*, No. 1833 (March 6, 1852), 239. [T]

[555] Horne, R[ichard] H[engist]. "The Shelley Letter Fraud," *The Literary Gazette*, No. 1834 (March 13, 1852), 254. [T]

[556] [Anonymous]. "The Literary Forgeries.," *The Athenaeum*, No. 1273 (March 20, 1852), 325-326. [T]

[557] [Anonymous]. "The Shelley Letter Forgeries," *The Literary Gazette*, No. 1835 (March 20, 1852), 279-280. [T]

[558] [Anonymous]. "Our Weekly Gossip," *The Athenaeum*, No. 1274 (March 27, 1852), 355-356. [M: 355]

[559] [Anonymous]. "Notes of the Month [/] Literary Forgeries," *The Gentleman's Magazine*, New Series XXXVII [whole number CXCI] (April, 1852), 374-379. [M: 378-379]

[560] [Anonymous]. "Literature.," *Tait's Edinburgh Magazine*, New Series XIX, No. ccxx (April, 1852), 251-252. [R of item 573: 252]

[561] [Lewes, George H.]. "Art. V. Shelley and the Letters of Poets," *Westminster Review*, New Series I [whole number LVII], No. ii [whole number cxii] (April, 1852), 502-511. [R: item 573]

[562] [Anonymous]. "Our Weekly Gossip," *The Athenaeum*, No. 1275 (April 3, 1852), 381-382. [M]

[563] [Anonymous]. "*Letters of Percy Bysshe Shelley*. With an Introductory Essay by Robert Browning. Moxon.," *Littell's Living Age*, XXXIII, No. 411 (April 3, 1852), 45-46. [R: item 573; rptd. from item 546]

[564] Milnes, R[ichard] Monckton. "Our Weekly Gossip," *The Athenaeum*, No. 1277 (April 17, 1852), 431-432. [M: 431]

[565] Clements, H. H. "Fragments to Shelley," *The Southern Literary Messenger*, XVIII, No. 5 (May, 1852), 277-278. [C: an eighty line poem]

[566]   [Anonymous]. "Literary Forgeries," *Littell's Living Age*,
        XXXIII, No. 415 (May 1, 1852), 235-236. [T; rptd.
        from item 552]

[567]   [Signed "Bon Gualtier"]. "Tom Moore. —The Poet of Erin,"
        Graham's Magazine, XL, No. 6 (June, 1852), [593]-600.
        [M: 598]

[568]   Gilfillan, George. "Shelley. —Proofs of a God.," *Monthly
        Literary Miscellany [/] A Compendium of Literary, Philosophical
        and Religious Knowledge* [Detroit], VII, No. v (November,
        1852), 508-509. [C; (?rptd. from item 434?)]

Books:

[569]   Alastor [pseud. of James Orton]. *Alastor: or the New Ptolemy.
        A Dialogue.* 172pp. London: Saunders and Otley, 1852.
        [?C]

[570]   Alastor [pseud. of James Orton]. *"Excelsior" or the Realms of
        Poesie by Alastor.* xvi+148pp. London: William Pickering,
        1852. [?C]

[571]   Belfast, [Frederick Richard Chichester], The Earl of. *Poets
        and Poetry of the XIXth Century. A Course of Lectures by the Earl
        of Belfast.* xii+283pp. London: Longman, Brown, Green
        and Longmans, 1852. [C: "Shelley," 165-197]

[572]   [Bennett, Wilson Cox]. *Verdicts.* iv+70pp. London: Effingham
        Wilson, 1852. [?M]

[573]   Browning, Robert. *Letters of Percy Bysshe Shelley. With an Intro-
        ductory Essay, by Robert Browning.* viii+165pp. London:
        Edward Moxon, 1852. [C: "Introductory Essay," 1-44;
        rptd.: item 1414]

[574]   Dallas, E[neas] S[weetland]. *Poetics: An Essay on Poetry.*
        viii+294pp. London: Smith, Elder, and Co., 1852.
        [M: 10-11, 147, 263]

[575]   [Signed "J.L."]. *Lives of the Illustrious.* [?]pp. London:
        [?], 1852. [B: "Percy Bysshe Shelley," 105-119; rptd.
        from item 551, apparently a retitled reissue]

[576]   Langford, John Alfred. *The Drama of Life [/] and Aspiranda.*
        [?]pp. London and Birmingham: [?], 1852. [C: a poem
        to Shelley]

[577]   Mitford, Mary Russell. *Recollections of a Literary Life; or,
        Books, Places, People.* 3 vols. London: Richard Bentley,
        1852. [C: II, 183-188]

[578]   White, W[illiam]. *The Calumnies of the "Athenaeum" Journal Exposed*
        [/] Mr. White's Letter to Mr. Murray, on the Subject of the Byron,
        Shelley, and Keats MSS. 15pp. London: William White,
        1852. [T]

                              1853

Periodicals:

[579]   Ray, William Porter. "The Graves of Shelley and Keats,"
        Graham's Magazine, XLII, No. 5 (May, 1853), 542-543. [C]

[580]   [Signed "Uneda"]. "A Poem by Shelley, Not in His Works,"
        Notes and Queries, VIII, No. 195 (July 23, 1953), 71-72.
        [T]

[581]   Pinkerton, W. "Poem attributed to Shelley (Vol. VIII, p.
        71)," *Notes and Queries*, VIII, No. 199 (August 20,
        1853), 183-184. [T]

[582]   [Kingsley, Charles]. "Thoughts on Shelley and Byron,"
        Fraser's Magazine, XLVIII, No. cclxxxvii (November, 1853),
        568-576. [C; rptd.: item 590, 680, 1082]

Books:

*[583] Haydon, Benjamin Robert. *Life of Benjamin Robert Haydon, Histori-*
        cal Painter, from his Autobiography and Journals. Edited and
        Compiled by Tom Tayler. 3 vols. London: Longman,
        Brown, Green and Longmans, 1853. [B,C]

[584]   Hillard, George Stillman. *Six Months in Italy.* 2 vols.
        London: John Murray, 1853. [C: "Shelley," 333-338]

[585]   Landor, Walter Savage. *The Last Fruit Off an Old Tree.* x+520pp.
        London: Edward Moxon, 1853. [C: "CLXXIX. To the
        Nightingale," a sixteen line poem, 412]

[586]   Spalding, William. *The History of English Literature; with an*
        Outline of the Origin and Growth of the English Language: Illus
        trated by Extracts. For the Use of Schools and of Private
        Students. 414pp. Edinburgh: Oliver & Boyd, 1853.
        [C: 379-380]

[587]   Tuckerman, Henry T[heodore]. *A Month in England.* 243pp.
        New York: Redfield, 1853. [C: 148-149]

[588]   Whipple, Edwin [Percy]. *Essays and Reviews*. 2 vols. [Second
         edition]. Boston: Ticknor, Reed, and Fields, 1853.
         [C: "English Poets of the Nineteenth Century.," I,
         (299)-371; Shelley: 307-318; rptd. from item 424]

                                   1854

Periodicals:

[589]   Hayne, Paul H[amilton]. "Shelley," *The Southern Literary
         Messenger*, XX, No. i (January, 1854), 32. [C: a sonnet]

[590]   Kingsley, Charles. "Thoughts on Shelley and Byron," *The
         Eclectic Magazine*, XXXI, No. 1 (January, 1854), 82-89.
         [C; rptd. from item 582]

[591]   Warden, J. S. "Shelley's 'Prometheus Unbound,'" *Notes and
         Queries*, IX, No. 233 (April 14, 1854), 351-352. [C,T]

[592]   [Signed "F.C.H."]. "Shelley's 'Prometheus Unbound' (Vol.
         IX., p. 351)," *Notes and Queries*, IX, No. 238 (May 20,
         1854), 481. [C]

[593]   [Signed "Erica"]. "Shelley's 'Prometheus Unbound' (Vol.
         IX, 351, 481)," *Notes and Queries*, X, No. 245 (July 8,
         1854), 37. [C]

Books:

[594]   Blanchard, Edmund Forster. "Percy Bysshe Shelley," in
         Volume IV, 281-285 in *Johnson's Lives of the British Poets*
         [/] *Completed by William Hazlitt*. 4 vols. London: Nathaniel
         Cooke, The National Illustrated Library, 1854. [B,C]

[595]   Gilfillan, George. *A Third Gallery of Literary Portraits*.
         viii+536pp. Edinburgh: James Hogg, 1854. [C:
         "Æschylus; Prometheus Bound and Unbound," 488-500;
         rptd.: item 617]

[596]   Patmore, P[eter] G[eorge]. *My Friends and Acquaintance: Being
         Memorials, Mind-Portraits, and Personal Recollections of Deceased
         Celebrities of the Nineteenth Century: with selections from their
         unpublished letters*. 3 vols. London: Saunders and Otley,
         1854. [C: III, 133-138]

[597]   [Redding, Cyrus]. *A Brief Sketch of* [/] *The Life of Percy Bysshe
         Shelley*. 15pp. London: Published for James Watson,
         By Holyoake and Co., 1854. [B; ?rptd. from item 141]

*[598]   Talfourd, T[homas] N[oon].   *Supplement to "Vacation Rambles,"*
         consisting of a tour through France, to Italy, and Homeward
         by Switzerland, in the vacation of 1846.   x+266pp.   London:
         Edward Moxon, 1854.   [M]

[599]   Wilson, John, W[illiam] Maginn, J[ohn] G[ibson] Lockhart,
         James Hogg, "etc."   *Noctes Ambrosianæ.*   Edited by R.
         Shelton Mackenzie.   5 vols.   New York: Redfield, 1854.
         [M: I, 145, 199, 220, 262; III, 197; V, 9, 289; vols.
         III and V rptd. from items 37, 114, 249]

                              1855

Periodicals:

[600]   [Signed "A Fellow of St. John's College"].   "A Visit to the
         Grave of Shelley.   By a Fellow of St. John's College,
         Cambridge.,"   *The London Investigator: A Monthly Journal of
         Secularism,* II, No. 13 (April, 1855), [1]-3.   [C]

[601]   Reed, P[eter] Fishe.   "The Principles of Poetry. —No. 1.,
         *The Genius of the West. An Original Magazine of Western Litera-
         ture* [Cincinnati], IV, No. 5 (May, 1855), [135]-137.
         [C; Shelley: 137]

[602]   Massey, Gerald.   "The Poetry of Alfred Tennyson.,"   *The
         Eclectic Magazine,* XXXVI, No. v (September, 1855), 616-
         628.   [C; M: 621]

[603]   Reed, P[eter] Fishe.   "Principles of Poetry. —No. III.,"
         The Genius of the West, A Monthly Magazine of Western Literature
         [Cincinnati], IV, No. 9 [September, 1855], [268]-270.
         [C]

[604]   [Signed "A Desultory Reader"].   "Shelley's 'Queen Mab.,'"
         Notes and Queries, XIII, No. 305 (September 1, 1855), 165
         [T]

[605]   [Anonymous].   "Review of New Books," *Graham's Magazine,* XLVII
         No. 4 (October, 1855), 371-373.   [M: 372]

[606]   Blessington, [Marguerite Gardiner], Countess of. "Byron an
         Shelley.,"   *The London Investigator: A Monthly Journal of
         Secularism,* II, No. 19 (October, 1855), 100-101.   [B;
         rptd. from item 339]

Books:

[607]   Browning, Robert.   *Men and Women.*   2 vols.   London: Chapman

                              [62]

and Hall, 1855. [C: "Memorabilia.," I, 259-260;
*"Popularity.," II, (?pp)]

[608]   Chambers, Robert, ed. *Cyclopaedia of English Literature: A
Selection of the Choicest Productions of English Authors, from the
Earliest to the Present Time, Connected by a Critical and Bio-
graphical History* [/] *Elegantly Illustrated.* 2 vols. Boston:
Gould and Lincoln, 1855. [C: "Percy Bysshe Shelley.,"
II, 395-402; rptd. from item 417; rptd.: item 698]

[609]   Reed, Henry. *Lectures on English Poetry, from Chaucer to Tennyson.*
xxiii+411pp. Philadelphia: Parry & McMillan, 1855.
[C: 292-294, 321-323]

                          1856

Periodicals:

[610]   Tlepolemus [pseud. of George Charles Swayne]. "War and
Woodcraft. Letter to Irenaeus," *Blackwood's Edinburgh
Magazine*, LXXIX, No. cccclxxxvi (April, 1856), 388-403.
[M: 392-393]

[611]   [Anonymous]. "Art. II —1. *Tragedies; to which are added a few
Sonnets and Verses.* By Sir T. N. Talfourd, D.C.L. London,
Edward Moxon. [/] 2. *Vacation Rambles: comprising the
Recollections of Rome, Continental Tours, &c.* By Sir T. N.
Talfourd, D.C.L. Third Edition. London, Edward Moxon.
[/] 3. *Critical and Miscellaneous Writings of T. N. Talfourd.
Author of "Ion."* In one Volume. Philadelphia, Carey &
Hart, 1842.," *The North British Review*, XXV, No. xlix
(May, 1856), 47-78. [M: 70-71]

[612]   Bungay, George W. "The Skylark," *Graham's Magazine*, XLVIII,
No. 5 (May, 1856), 432. [C: twelve line poem]

[613]   [Campbell, Lewis]. "Prometheus," *The Oxford and Cambridge
Magazine*, I, No. 5 (May, 1856), 259-264. [C]

[614]   [Bagehot, Walter]. "Art. IV. —Percy Bysshe Shelley. [/]
The Poetical Works of Percy Bysshe Shelley. Edited by Mrs.
Shelley. 1853. [/] *Essays, Letters from Abroad, Transla-
tions, and Fragments.* By Percy Bysshe Shelley. Edited by
Mrs. Shelley. 1854. [/] *The Life of Percy Bysshe Shelley.*
By Captain Thomas Medwin. 1847.," *The National Review*,
III, No. vi (October, 1856), 342-379. [C; rptd.: items
663, 1048]

[615]   'I.' [Charles Bradlaugh]. "Percy Bysshe Shelley," *Half-
Hours with the Freethinkers*, [I], No. 4 (November 15, 1856),
[25]-32. [C; rptd.: items 627, 2068]

[616]   Ingleby, C. Mansfield. "Queries on Shelley," *Notes and Queries*, Second Series II, No. 46 (November 15, 1856), 388. [T]

Books:

[617]   Gilfillan, George. *Galleries of Literary Portraits*. 2 vols. Edinburgh: James Hogg, 1856-1857 [I: 1856; II: 1857]. [C: "Æschylus; Prometheus Bound and Unbound.," I, (1)-8, rptd. from item 595; "Percy Bysshe Shelley.," 94-110, rptd. from item 434]

[618]   Parkes, Bessie Rayner. *Gabriel*. ix+110pp. London: John Chapman, 1856. [B: fictionalized poetic portrait of Shelley as Gabriel]

*[619] Richardson, J[ohn]. *Recollections Political, Literary, Dramatic and Miscellaneous of the Last Half-Century [/] Containing Anecdotes and Notes of Persons of Various Ranks, Prominent in Their Vocations, with Whom the Writer Was Personally Acquainted*. 2 vols. London: C. Mitchell, 1856. [M]

[620]   Rogers, Samuel. *Recollections of the Table-Talk of Samuel Rogers. To Which Is Added Porsoniana*. [ed. A. Dyce]. viii+355pp. London: Edward Moxon, 1856. [C: 235-236]

[621]   Wilson, John. *Noctes Ambrosianæ*. 4 vols. Edinburgh and London: William Blackwood and Sons, 1855-1856 [I+II: 1855; III+IV: 1856]. [M: II, 144-145, rptd. from item 114; IV, 109-110, rptd. from item 249]

1857

Periodicals:

[622]   [Anonymous]. "[?]," *The United States Magazine and Democratic Review*, XXXIX, No. [?] (March, 1857), 219-224. [?]

[623]   [Signed "E.N.V."]. "Shelley," *The Knickerbocker* [New York], XLIX, No. 3 (March, 1857), [219]-224. [C; plagiarized from item 503]

[624]   Landor, Walter Savage. "Byron and Shelley.," *The Investigator; A Monthly Journal of Secularism*, IV, No. 38 (May, 1857) 31. [B; rptd. from item 117]

[64]

[625] Shelley, Percy Bysshe. "Desolation," *Graham's Illustrated Magazine*, L, No. 5 (May, 1857), 399. [T]

[626] De Vere, Aubrey. "Lines Composed near Shelley's House at Lerici.," *Fraser's Magazine*, LVI, No. cccxxxv (November, 1857), 547-550. [Poem; rptd.: item 1200]

Books:

[627] [Bradlaugh, Charles]. *Half-Hours with the Freethinkers* [/] *Edited by J. Watts, 'Iconoclast,' and A. Collins. Containing a Sketch of the Life and Philosophy of Des Cartes, Volney, Lord Bolingbroke, Shelley.* 192pp. London: Holyoake and Co., 1857. [B, C: "Percy Bysshe Shelley," (25)-32; rptd. from item 615; rptd.: item 2068]

[628] Buckle, Henry Thomas. *History of Civilization in England.* 2 vols. London: John W. Parker and Son, 1857. [C: II, 504-505]

[629] Gilfillan, George, ed. *The Poetical Works of Richard Crashaw and Quarles' Emblems. With Memoirs and Critical Dissertations, By the Rev. George Gilfillan.* Edinburgh: James Nichol, 1857. [C: viii, xiii]

1858

Periodicals:

[630] [Anonymous]. "Art. IV. Shelley.," *Westminster Review*, New Series XIII [whole number LXIX], No. i [whole number cxxxv] (January, 1858), 97-131. [C; R of two editions in 1853, and items 242, 477]

[631] [Anonymous]. " *Shelley and his Writings.* By Charles S. Middleton. 2 vols. Newby.," *The Athenaeum*, No. 1580 (February 6, 1858), 174-176. [R: item 665]

[632] [Signed "A.X."]. "Shelley's 'Letters,'" *Notes and Queries*, Second Series V, No. 110 (February 6, 1858), 112. [T]

[633] Oxenford, J[ohn]. "Our Weekly Gossip," *The Athenaeum*, No. 1581 (February 13, 1858), 211. [T]

[634] Middleton, C[harles] S. "Our Weekly Gossip," *The Athenaeum*, No. 1582 (February 20, 1858), 243. [T]

[635]   [Anonymous]. " *Recollections of the Last Days of Shelley and Byron*
        By E. J. Trelawny. (Moxon.)," *The Athenaeum*, No. 1583
        (February 27, 1858), 267-269. [R: item 669]

[636]   [Anonymous]. "Reviews [/] Shelley.," *The Saturday Review*, V,
        No. 122 (February 27, 1858), 215-217. [R: items 665,
        669]

[637]   [Anonymous]. "Trelawny's Last Days of Shelley and Byron,"
        The Spectator, XXXI, No. 1548 (February 27, 1858), 236-
        237. [R: item 669; rptd.: item 643]

[638]   [Anonymous]. "Shelley and His Writings," *Chambers's Journal*,
        Third Series IX [whole number XXIX], No. 218 (March 6,
        1858), 148-151. [R: item 665]

[639]   [Anonymous]. "Art. II. —Percy Bysshe Shelley.," *The
        Eclectic Review*, Sixth Series III [whole number CVII]
        (April, 1858), 319-352. [R: items 665, 669]

[640]   [Anonymous]. "Art. II. —Recollections of Shelley and
        Byron," *Westminster Review*, New Series XIII [whole number
        LXIX], No. ii [whole number cxxxvi] (April, 1858), 350-
        369. [R: item 669; rptd.: items 648, 651]

[641]   [Anonymous]. " *The Life of Percy Bysshe Shelley*. By Thomas
        Jefferson Hogg. 4 vols. Vols. I. and II. (Moxon.),"
        The Athenaeum, No. 1590 (April 17, 1858), 492-495. [R:
        item 664]

[642]   [Anonymous]. " *The Life of Percy Bysshe Shelley*. By Thomas
        Jefferson Hogg. Vols. I. and II. [Second Notice.]
        (brackets in original)," *The Athenaeum*, No. 1591 (April
        24, 1858), 524-526. [R: item 664]

[643]   [Anonymous]. "Trelawny's Last Days of Shelley and Byron,"
        Littell's Living Age, LVII, No. 726 (April 24, 1858),
        266-268. [R: item 669; rptd. from item 637]

[644]   [Anonymous]. "The Last Days of Byron and Shelley,"
        Chambers's Journal, Third Series IX [whole number XXIX],
        No. 226 (May, 1858), 276-278. [R: item 669]

[645]   [Anonymous]. "Memorials of Shelley: Middleton and
        Trelawny," *The New Monthly Magazine*, CXIII, No. ccccxlix
        (May, 1858), 91-95. [R: items 665, 668]

[646]   [Anonymous]. " *Shelley and his Writings*. By Charles S. Middle-
        ton. 2 vols. London: Newby, 1858. [/] *The Life of Percy
        Bysshe Shelley*. By Thomas Jefferson Hogg. Vols. I. and
        II. London: Moxon, 1858. [/] *Recollections of the Last Days
        of Shelley and Byron*. By E. J. Trelawny. London: Moxon,
        1858.," *The New Quarterly Review*, VII, No. xxvi ([May],
        1858), 166-174. [R: items 664, 665, 669]

[647]   [Signed "C.R.S."]. "Mr. Jefferson Hogg's Life of Percy
        Bysshe Shelley," *Notes and Queries*, Second Series V,
        No. 123 (May 8, 1858), 373-374. [T,B]

[648]   [Anonymous]. "Recollections of Shelley and Byron,"
        Littell's Living Age, LVII, No. 730 (May 22, 1858), 580-
        591. [R: item 669; rptd. from item 640]

[649]   [Signed "E.D.B."]. "Shelley's Marriage (2nd S. V. 373.),"
        Notes and Queries, Second Series V, No. 126 (May 29,
        1858), 443. [B]

*[650] [Anonymous]. "Percy Bysshe Shelley," *The Cosmopolitan Art
        Journal, A Record of Art, Biography, and General Literature*,
        II (March and June, 1858), 84-86. [B,C]

[651]   [Anonymous]. "Recollections of Shelley and Byron,"
        Eclectic Magazine, XLIV, No. ii (June, 1858), 164-175.
        [R: item 669; rptd. from item 640]

[652]   [Anonymous]. "Hogg's Life of Shelley.," *The Spectator*
        [: *Spectator Supplement*, dated May 1, 1858, and paginated
        to follow the regular issue of that date], XXXI, No.
        1557 (May 1, 1858), 477-478. [R: item 664; rptd.:
        item 655]

[653]   Peacock, Thomas Love. "Memoirs of Percy Bysshe Shelley,"
        Fraser's Magazine, LVII, No. cccxlii (June, 1858), [643]-
        659. [B; R: items 664, 665, 669; rptd.: items 935,
        1973]

[654]   M'Carthy [*sic*], D[enis] F[lorence]. "Crashaw and Shelley,"
        Notes and Queries, Second Series V, No. 127 (June 5,
        1858), 449-452. [C]

[655]   [Anonymous]. "Hogg's Life of Shelley," *Littell's Living Age*,
        LVII, No. 735 (June 26, 1858), 1008-1012. [R: item
        664; rptd. from item 652]

[656]   [Signed "A.A.W."]. "Crashaw and Shelley, and Their Poeti-
        cal Coincidences with Each Other. (2nd S. v. 449.),"
        Notes and Queries, Second Series V, No. 130 (June 26,
        1858), 516-518. [C]

[657]   [Signed "A.B."]. "[Untitled, following item 656]," *Notes
        and Queries*, Second Series V, No. 130 (June 26, 1858),
        518. [C]

[658]   [Anonymous]. "Art. X. —Literary Reviews.," *Meliora: A
        Quarterly Review of Social Science in Its Ethical, Economical,
        Political, and Ameliorative Aspects*, I, No. 2 ([July, 1858]),
        196-200. [R of item 664: 199]

[659] [Anonymous]. "Hogg's Life of Shelley," *The New Monthly Magazine*, CXIII, No. ccccli (July, 1858), 337-343. [R: item 664]

[660] Turnbull, W. B. "Crashaw and Shelley (2nd S. V. 449, 516.)," *Notes and Queries*, Second Series VI, No. 133 (July 17, 1858), 54. [No M]

[661] M'Carthy [*sic*], D[enis] F[lorence]. "Crashaw and Shelley (2nd S. V. 449. 516.; VI. 54.)," *Notes and Queries*, Second Series VI, No. 135 (July 31, 1858), 94-96. [C,T]

[662] Howard, Philip H. "Inedited Letters of Shelley," *Notes and Queries*, Second Series VI, No. 151 (November 20, 1858), 405-406. [T]

Books:

[663] Bagehot, Walter. *Estimates of Some Englishmen and Scotchmen, A Series of Articles Reprinted by Permission Principally from the National Review.* 453pp. London: Chapman and Hall, 1858. [C: "Percy Bysshe Shelley," (274)-329; rptd. from item 614]

[664] Hogg, Thomas Jefferson. *The Life of Percy Bysshe Shelley.* 2 vols. London: Edward Moxon, 1858. [B; I, 48-135, 213-236, rptd. from items 175, 176, 180, 184, 202, 215, 233; rptd.: items 1849, 2620]

[665] Middleton, Charles S. *Shelley and His Writings.* 2 vols. London: T. C. Newby, 1858. [B,C]

[666] Redding, Cyrus. *Fifty Years' Recollections, Literary and Personal, with Observations on Men and Things.* 3 vols. London: Charles J. Skeet, 1858. [C: II, 363-366]

*[667] Robertson, Frederick W[illiam]. *Lectures and Addresses on Literary and Social Topics.* xxxviii+308pp. London: Smith, Elder and Co., 1858. [C]

[668] Simeon, John. *Miscellanies of the Philobiblon Society.* Volume IV. 8+44+108+72+28+136pp. London: Philobiblon Society [printed by Charles Whittingham], 1857-1858. [C: "Contemporaneous Narrative of the Trial and Execution of the Cenci.," 72pp.; Shelley: 7-14]

[669] Trelawny, E[dward] J[ohn]. *Recollections of the Last Days of Shelley and Byron.* viii+304pp. London: Edward Moxon, 1858. [B; revised as item 669]

Periodicals:

[670]   [Anonymous].   " *Shelley Memorials: from Authentic Sources.* Edited
           by Lady Shelley. To which is added an Essay on Chris-
           tianity, by Percy Bysshe Shelley: now first printed.
           (Smith, Elder & Co.)," *The Athenaeum*, No. 1657 (July 30,
           1859), 139-141. [R: item 683]

[671]   [Anonymous]. "Shelley Memorials," *The Spectator*, XXXII,
           No. 1623 (August 6, 1859), 813-814. [R: item 683]

[672]   [Anonymous]. "*Shelley Memorials.* Edited by Lady Shelley.
           (Smith & Elder.)," *The Literary Gazette*, New Series III,
           No. 59 (August 13, 1859), 157-159. [R: item 683;
           rptd.: item 678]

[673]   Hunt, Leigh. "The Occasional. By Leigh Hunt. No. XV.
           A Word or Two Respecting the 'Shelley Memorials.'
           Shelley not a man to be judged by ordinary rules.
           Question of the attempted assassination in Wales; of
           morbid visions; and of his character for veracity.
           Caution against forged letters. A complete biography
           of Shelley not to be looked for at present.," *The
           Spectator*, XXXII, No. 1624 (August 13, 1859), 834-835.
           [R: item 683; B]

[674]   Hunt, Leigh. "The Occasional. By Leigh Hunt. No. XVI.
           Corrections of Last Week's Occasional. Cause of its
           need of them, and its incompleteness—Opinions respec-
           ting madness and wickedness—Danger of confounding the
           occasional morbid impression of ill health on great
           minds with subjections of their intellect.," *The
           Spectator*, XXXII, No. 1625 (August 20, 1859), 859. [B]

[675]   [Anonymous]. "Art. III. — *Shelley Memorials.* Edited by Lady
           Shelley. London: Smith, Elder and Co. 1859.," *The
           British Quarterly Review*, XXX, No. lx (October, 1859),
           360-391. [R: item 683; C]

*[676]   [Anonymous]. "[?]," *The Universal Review*, [?] (October,
           1859), [?p]. [?R: item 683?]

[677]   [Stirling, James Hutchinson]. "Art. III. —1. *Tennyson's
           Poems.* Eleventh edition. [/] 2. *Tennyson's Princess: a
           Medley.* Seventh edition. [/] 3. *In Memoriam.* Seventh
           edition. [/] 4. *Tennyson's Maud; and other Poems.* Second
           edition. [/] 5. *Tennyson's Idylls of the King.* London:
           Edward Moxon and Co. 1859.," *Meliora: A Quarterly Review
           of Social Science in Its Ethical, Economical, Political, and
           Ameliorative Aspects*, II, No. 7 ([October, 1859]), 225-
           248. [R; C: 226-229, 244-247; rptd.: item 801]

[678]   [Anonymous]. "Shelley Memorials. Edited by Lady Shelley.
         Smith and Elder.," *Littell's Living Age*, LXIII, No. 801
         (October 1, 1859), 43-46. [R: item 683; rptd. from
         item 672]

Books:

*[679]   Garnett, Richard. *Io in Egypt, and Other Poems.* viii+152pp.
         London: Bell and Daldy, 1859. [C: "To the Memory of
         Shelley," a sonnet]

[680]   Kingsley, Charles. *Miscellanies.* 2 vols. London: John W.
         Parker and Son, 1859. [C: "Thoughts on Shelley and
         Byron," I, (304)-324; rptd. from item 582]

[681]   Mill, John Stuart. *Dissertations and Discussions [/] Political,*
         Philosophical, and Historical [/] Reprinted Chiefly from the
         Edinburgh and Westminster Reviews. 2 vols. London: John W.
         Parker and Son, 1859. [C: "Thoughts on Poetry and Its
         Varieties.," (63)-94; 77-94 rptd. from item 236]

[682]   Ossoli, Margaret Fuller. *Life Without and Life Within; or,*
         Reviews, Narratives, Essays, and Poems. Edited by Arthur B.
         Fuller. 422pp. Boston: Brown, Taggard and Chase,
         1859. [R of item 433: "Shelley's Poems," 149-152]

[683]   Shelley, Lady [Jane], ed. *Shelley Memorials: From Authentic*
         Sources. Edited by Lady Shelley. To Which Is Added An Essay
         on Christianity, By Percy Bysshe Shelley: Now First Printed.
         vi+290pp. London: Smith, Elder and Co., 1859. [B,T]

                              1860

Periodicals:

[684]   Peacock, Thomas Love. "Memoirs of Percy Bysshe Shelley.
         Part II.," *Fraser's Magazine*, LXI, No. ccclxi (January,
         1860), 92-109. [B; rptd.: items 935, 1973]

*[685]   [Anonymous]. "Editor's Table," *Russell's Magazine*, [?] (Febru-
         ary, 1860), 469-472. [R]

*[686]   [Anonymous]. "[?]," *The Prebyterian Quarterly Review* [Philadel-
         phia], IX, No. [?] (February, 1860), [?p]. [?C]

[687]   Peacock, Thomas Love. "Unpublished Letters of Percy Bysshe
         Shelley. From Italy —1818 to 1822.," *Fraser's Magazine*,
         LXI, No. ccclxiii (March, 1860), [301]-319. [T; rptd.:
         items 935, 1973, 2620]

[688]   Peacock, Thomas Love. "Postscript to the Shelley Letters,"
        Fraser's Magazine, LXI, No. ccclxv (May, 1860), 738. [C;
        rptd.: items 935, 1973, 2620]

[689]   Garnett, Richard. "Shelley in Pall Mall," *Macmillan's Maga-
        zine*, II, No. 8 (June, 1860), 100-110. [T, B]

[690]   [Anonymous]. "Reviews.," *The National Reformer*, I, No. 4
        (June 9, 1860), 7. [R; M]

[691]   [Dowe, W.]. "More Words about Shelley," *The Atlantic Monthly*,
        VI, No. xxxiii (July, 1860), 59-60. [C]

[692]   [Bradlaugh, Charles]. "Reviews.," *The National Reformer*, I,
        No. 12 (August 4, 1860), 6. [R; M]

[693]   "B.V." [pseud. of James "B.V." Thomson]. "Open Column.,"
        The National Reformer, I, No. 15 (August 25, 1860), 8.
        [C; rptd.: items 1205, 1695]

[694]   Masson, David. "The Life and Poetry of Shelley," *Macmillan's
        Magazine*, II, No. 11 (September, 1860), 338-350. [C;
        rptd.: item 913]

[695]   [Anonymous]. "Reviews.," *The National Reformer*, I, No. 17
        (September 8, 1860), 7. [R: item 694]

[696]   [Anonymous]. "Art. IV. —(1.) *Heinrich von Kleist's ausgewählte
        Schriften*. Heraus-gegeben von Ludwig Tieck. Berlin.
        1846. Vorrede von L. Tieck. [/] (2.) *Heinrich von Kleist's
        'Leben und Briefe.'* Mit einem Anhänge. Heraus-gegeben von
        Eduard von Bülow. Berlin. 1848. [/] (3.) *Poëtes Mo-
        dernes de l'Allemagne*. Henri de Kleist. Saint-Réné Taill-
        andier. 1859.," *The British Quarterly Review*, XXXII, No.
        lxiv (October, 1860), 367-389. [M: 369, 388]

[697]   "B.V." [pseud. of James "B.V." Thomson]. "Open Column.
        Shelley,"*The National Reformer*, I, No. 32 (December 22,
        1860), 6-7. [C; rptd.: items 1205, 1617, 1695]

Books:

[698]   Chambers, Robert, ed. *Cyclopaedia of English Literature* [/] *A
        History, Critical and Biographical, of British Authors from the
        Earliest to the Present Times.* 2 vols. Philadelphia:
        J. B. Lippincott, [1860]. [B, C: "Percy Bysshe Shel-
        ley.," II, 355-363; rptd. from item 608]

[699]   Giraldus [pseud. of William Allingham], ed. *Nightingale
        Valley, a collection including a great number of the choicest
        Lyrics and Short Poems in the English Language.* xvi+288pp
        London: Bell and Daldy, 1860. [T]

*[700]   Hayne, Paul Hamilton. *Arvolio*. 244pp. Boston: Ticknor
          and Fields, 1860. [M: introduction?]

[701]   Langford, John Alfred. *Shelley: The Death of St. Polycarp, and
          Other Poems*. viii+149pp. London: Smith, Elder and Co.,
          1860. [C: "Shelley.," 1-57, a nine hundred and sixty-
          three line poem]

[703]   M'D., G. [George Macdonald]. "SHELLEY, Percy Bysshe.," in
          Volume XX, 100-104 in *The Encyclopædia Britannica, or
          Dictionary of Arts, Sciences, and General Literature*. Eighth
          edition. Edinburgh: Adam and Charles Black, 1860.
          [B,C]

                            1861

Periodicals:

[704]   [Signed "By and Old School-Fellow."]. "Recollections of
          Keats.," *The Atlantic Monthly*, VII, No. xxxix (January,
          1861), 86-100. [B: 98-99]

[705]   [Burbidge, Thomas]. "Art. II. —1. *Shelley and his Writings*.
          By C. S. Middleton. [/] 2. *Trelawney's* [*sic*] *Recollections
          of the Last Days of Shelley and Byron*. [/] 3. *Life of P. B.
          Shelley*. By Thomas Jefferson Hogg. London, 1858. Vols
          I and II. [/] 4. *Shelley Memorials from Authentic Sources*.
          Edited by Lady Shelley. London, 1859," *The North British
          Review*, XXXIV, No. lxvii (February, 1861), 33-64. [R:
          items 664, 665, 669, 683]

[706]   [Signed "Γ."]. "Shelley, the Poet and 'Erotica Biblion'
          of Mirabeau," *Notes and Queries*, Second Series XI,
          No. 280 (May 11, 1861), 367-368. [T]

[707]   Bates, William. "Shelley, the Poet, and the 'Erotika[*sic*]
          Biblion' of Mirabeau. (2nd S. xi. 367)," *Notes and
          Queries*, Second Series XI, No. 283 (June 1, 1861), 429.
          [T]

[708]   [Signed "Jaydee"]. "[Untitled, following item 707]," *Notes
          and Queries*, Second Series XI, No. 283 (June 1, 1861),
          429-430. [T]

[709]   [Signed "Γ."]. "Shelley and 'Erotika Biblion.' (2nd S. xi
          367. 429.)," *Notes and Queries*, Second Series XI, No. 28
          (June 15, 1861), 471-473. [T]

[710] [Signed "Jaydee"]. "Shelley and 'Erotika Biblion' (2nd S. xi. 367, 429, 471.)," *Notes and Queries*, Second Series XII, No. 289 (July 13, 1861), 36. [T]

[711] [Kinnear, Alexander S.]. "Art. I. —1. *The Works of Percy Bysshe Shelley*. Edited by Mrs. Shelley. One Volume. London, 1854. [/] 2. *Life of P. B. Shelley*. By Thomas Jefferson Hogg. London, 1858. Vols. I and II. [/] 3. *Shelley Memorials from Authentic Sources*. Edited by Lady Shelley. London, 1858. [/] 4. *Recollections of the Last Days of Shelley and Byron*. By E. J. Trelawney [*sic*]. London, 1858. [/] 5. *Fraser's Magazine*, Nos. 342 and 361, *Memoir of Percy Bysshe Shelley*. By T. L. Peacock.," *The Quarterly Review*, CX, No. 220 (October, 1861), 289-328. [R of 1854 edition of item 346 and items 664, 669, 683, 687, 688; rptd.: item 715]

[712] [Anonymous]. "On the Life and Poetry of Percy Bysshe Shelley," *Temple Bar*, III (November, 1861), 538-551. [B,C]

[713] Peacock, Edward. "Queen of My Heart," *Notes and Queries*, Second Series XII, No. 306 (November 9, 1861), 368. [T]

[714] [Signed "R.R."]. "'The Queen of My Heart' (2nd S. xii. 368)," *Notes and Queries*, Second Series XII, No. 309 (November 30, 1861), 442-443. [T]

[715] [Kinnear, Alexander S.]. "1. *The Works of Percy Bysshe Shelley*. Edited by Mrs. Shelley. One Volume. London, 1854. [/] 2. *Life of P. B. Shelley*. By Thomas Jefferson Hogg. London, 1858. Vols. I. and II. [/] 3. *Shelley Memorials from Authentic Sources*. Edited by Lady Shelley. London, 1859. [/] 4. *Recollections of the Last Days of Shelley and Byron*. By E. J. Trelawney [*sic*]. London, 1858. [/] 5. *Fraser's Magazine*, Nos. 342 and 361, *Memoir of Percy Bysshe Shelley*. By T. L. Peacock.," *Littell's Living Age*, LXXI, No. 914 (December 7, 1861), 443-465. [R of 1854 edition of item 346 and items 664, 669, 683, 687, 688; rptd. from item 711]

Books:

*[716] [Anonymous]. *The Poetic Magazine*. iv+188pp. London: Farrah and Dunbar, 1861. [M]

[717] Craik, George L. *A Compendious History of English Literature, and of the English Language, from the Norman Conquest. With Numerous Specimens*. 2 vols. London: Griffin, Bohn, and Company, 1861. [C,T: "Shelley.," II, 496-502]

[718]   Holmes, Oliver Wendell. *Songs in Many Keys.*   x+308pp.
        Boston: Ticknor and Fields, 1861. [C: "After a
        Lecture on Shelley. (Composed 1853)," 106-107; a
        thirty-six line poem; rptd.: item 1606]

[719]   L[eadbetter], J.   *A Pilgrimage to the Shrines of Buckinghamshire.*
        [140]pp. London: Hall, Virtue, & Co., [1861]. [B:
        "Shelley. Great Marlow.," 113-118]

*[720] [Paton, Joseph Noel].   *Poems, by a Painter.* viii+159pp.
        Edinburgh and London: W. Blackwood and Sons, 1861.
        [C; contains a poem on Shelley]

                            1862

Periodicals:

[721]   Peacock, Thomas Love. "Percy Bysshe Shelley. A Supplemen-
        tary Notice.," *Fraser's Magazine*, LXV, No. ccclxxxvii
        (March, 1862), 343-346. [B; rptd.: items 935, 1973]

[722]   MacCarthy, D[enis] F[lorence]. "Shelley's 'Laon and
        Cythna' and 'Revolt of Islam.,'" *Notes and Queries*, Third
        Series I, No. 15 (April 12, 1862), 283-285. [T]

[723]   [Signed "A.B."]. "Shelley's 'Laon and Cythna' (3rd S. i.
        283.)," *Notes and Queries*, Third Series I, No. 18 (May 3,
        1862), 355. [C]

[724]   Garnett, R[ichard]. "Shelley's 'Laon and Cythna' (3rd S.
        i. 283, 355)," *Notes and Queries*, Third Series I, No. 21
        (May 24, 1862), 419. [C]

[725]   Shelley, Percy Bysshe. "Lines Written in the Bay of
        Lerici," [ed. Richard Garnett], *Macmillan's Magazine*, VI,
        No. 32 (June, 1862), 122-123. [T]

[726]   [Palgrave, Francis Turner]. "Art. V. —English Poetry from
        Dryden to Cowper," *The Quarterly Review*, CXII, No. 223
        (July, 1862), 146-179. [C; M: 164-165]

[727]   [Anonymous]. " *Relics of Shelley.* Edited by Richard Garnett.
        (Moxon & Co.)," *The Athenaeum*, No. 1810 (July 5, 1862),
        9-12. [R: item 734]

[728]   [Anonymous]. "Relics of Shelley," *Littell's Living Age*, LXXV,
        No. 960 (October 25, 1862), 178-180. [R: item 734]

[729]   Grenfell, J. G. "Shelley and Tennyson," *The Athenaeum*,
        No. 1829 (November 15, 1862), 629. [C]

Books:

[730] Collier, William Francis. *A History of English Literature. In a Series of Biographical Sketches.* viii+538pp. London: T. Nelson and Sons, 1862. [B: "Percy Bysshe Shelley," 418-419]

[731] DeQuincey, Thomas. *Dr. Samuel Parr of Whiggism in Its Relations to Literature [/] And Other Writings. DeQuincey's Works.* Volume V. Edinburgh: Adam and Charles Black, 1862. [C: "Percy Bysshe Shelley.," (1)-29; rptd. from item 428]

[732] Farrar, Adam Storey. *A Critical History of Free Thought in Reference to the Christian Religion. Eight Lectures Preached before the University of Oxford, in the Year M.DCCC.LXII. On the Foundation of the Late Rev. John Bampton, M.A. Canon of Salisbury.* lix+684pp. London: John Murray, 1862. [C: 285-291]

[733] [Frothingham, Washington]. *Atheos; or, The Tragedies of Unbelief.* 331pp. New York: Sheldon & Company, 1862. [B,C: "The Reformer.," (151)-208]

[734] Garnett, Richard, ed. *Relics of Shelley.* xvi+191pp. London: Edward Moxon & Co., 1862. [T,C]

[735] Gray, David. *The Luggie and Other Poems. By David Gray. With a Memoir by James Hedderwick, and a Prefatory Notice by R. M. Milnes.* xlviii+151pp. Cambridge and London: Macmillan and Company, 1862. [M (by Hedderwick): viii]

[736] Gronow, R[ees] H[owell]. *Reminiscences of Captain Gronow, Formerly of the Grenadier Guards, and M.P. for Stafford: Being Anecdotes of the Camp, the Court, and the Clubs, at the Close of the Last War with France. Related by Himself.* x+245pp. London: Smith, Elder and Co., 1862. [B: "Shelley," 212-215]

[737] Shirley [pseud. of John Skelton]. *Nuggæ Criticæ [/] Occasional Papers Written at the Seaside.* 492pp. Edinburgh: Edmonston and Douglas, 1862. [M: 266, 268, 333]

1863

Periodicals:

[738] [Hutton, Richard Holt]. "Art. IV—Shelley's Poetical Mysticism. [/] *Relics of Shelley.* Edited by Richard Garnett. Moxon, 1862. [/] *Memorials of Shelley.* By Lady

Shelley. Moxon, 1859. [/] *Recollections of the Last Days of Shelley and Byron.* By E. J. Trelawny. Moxon, 1858. [/] *The Life of Percy Bysshe Shelley.* By Thomas Jefferson Hogg. Vols. I and II. Moxon, 1858.," *The National Review,* XVI, No. xxxi (January, 1863), 62-87. [R: items 664, 669, 683, 734; rptd.: item 860]

[739] Hunt, Thornton. "Shelley. By One Who Knew Him.," *The Atlantic Monthly,* XI, No. lxiv (February, 1863), 184-204. [B; rptd.: item 2395]

[740] White, William. "The Suicide of Mrs. Shelley," *Weldon's Register of Facts and Occurrences Relating to Literature, the Sciences, and the Arts* (June, 1863), 429-432. [R: items 683, 734, 739]

[741] [Worsley, Philip Stanhope]. "Translations of Horace," *Blackwood's Edinburgh Magazine,* XCIV, No. dlxxiv (August, 1863), 184-198. [M: 185]

Books:

[742] Chambers, R[obert], ed. *The Book of Days* [/] *A Miscellany of Popular Antiquities in Connection with the Calendar Including Anecdotes, Biography, & History* [/] *Curiosities of Literature and Oddities of Human Life and Character.* 2 vols. Edinburgh: W. & R. Chambers, Ltd., [1863]. [B: "Shelley.," II, 172-174]

*[743] Kenealy, Edward Vaughan [Hyde]. *A New Pantomime.* iv+570pp. London: Reeves and Turner, 1863. [?]

*[744] Parkes, Bessie Rayner. *Ballads and Songs by Bessie Rayner Parkes.* viii+216pp. London: Bell and Daldy, 1863. [C: contains a poem on Shelley's grave]

1864

Periodicals:

*[745] Ellis, Sumner. "Atheism and Its Exponents," *The Universalist Quarterly* [Boston], New Series I [whole number XXI], No. 1 (January, 1864), 80-93. [C]

[746] [Signed "Polyprag."]. "Shelley's Sonnets on the Pyramids," *Notes and Queries,* Third Series V, No. 120 (April 16, 1864), 322. [M]

[747]   [Signed "Athor"].   "Shelley and Moore," *Notes and Queries*,
        Third Series VI, No. 150 (November 12, 1864), 386.   [C]

Books:

[748]   Kenealy, Edward Vaughan [Hyde].   *Poems and Translations.*
        xiv+460pp.   London: Reeves and Turner, 1864.   [C:
        "Shelley.," 234-235, a twenty line poem]

[749]   Knight, Charles.   *Passages of a Working Life During Half a Century:
        with a Prelude of Early Reminiscences.*   3 vols.   London:
        Bradbury & Evans, 1864.   [B: I, 44, 101-102]

                          1865

Periodicals:

[750]   Kebbel, T[homas] E[dward].   "English Love of Latin Poetry,"
        Fortnightly Review, I, [No. v] (July 15, 1865), [605]-611.
        [M: 610-611]

*[751] [Anonymous].   "[?]," *The Reader* [London], II, [No. ?] ([?],
        1865), 66.   [?C]

Books:

*[752] [Anonymous].   *Catalogue of the Special Exhibition of Portrait Mini-
        atures on Loan at South Kensington Museum, June, 1865.   Science
        and Art Department of the Committee of Council on Education.*
        xxii+[341]pp.   London: Whittingham and Wilkins, 1865.
        [B?]

[753]   Arnold, Matthew.   *Essays in Criticism.*   [Later designated
        "First Series"].   xix+302pp.   London: Macmillan and
        Co., 1865.   [M: 108-109]

[754]   Gronow, R[ees] H[owell].   *Celebrities of London and Paris; Being
        a Third Series of Reminiscences and Anecdotes of the Camp, the
        Court, and the Clubs: Containing a Correct Account of the Coup
        D'Etat.*   vii+234pp.   London: Smith, Elder & Co., 1865.
        [B: "Shelley's Fight at Eton," 99-101]

*[755] [?Norton, Charles Eliot; alternately ascribed to James
         Russell Lowell]. *The Poetical Works of Percy Bysshe Shelley.
         With a Memoir.* [?]pp.   Boston: Little, Brown and
         Company, 1865. [B,C: "Memoir," (?p)]

*[756] Young England [unidentified]. *Pessimus: A Rhapsody, and a
         Paradox.* By Young England. [Oxford: T. and G. Shrimpton]
         x+62pp. London: Williams and Norgate, 1865. [C]

                              1866

Periodicals:

[757]   [Anonymous]. "Cor Cordium," *Temple Bar*, XVI (January, 1866),
         206-208. [C: a poem]

[758]   [Signed "A.B."]. "A Ramble—to a Tomb," *Temple Bar*, XVI
         (February, 1866), 450-454. [C]

[759]   [Anonymous]. "Percy Bysshe Shelley—His Life and Charac-
         ter," *Dublin University Magazine*, LXVII, No. cccxcix
         (March, 1866), 292-309. [B; rptd.: item 760]

[760]   [Anonymous]. "Percy Bysshe Shelley. His Life and Charac-
         ter," *Littell's Living Age*, LXXXIX, No. 1142 (April 21,
         1866), 135-149. [B; rptd. from item 759]

[761]   [Signed "C.W.M."]. "P. B. Shelley's 'Adonais.,'" *Notes and
         Queries*, Third Series X, No. 260 (December 22, 1866),
         494. [T]

Books:

[762]   Chanter, John Roberts. *Sketches of the Literary History of
         Barnstaple, Being the Substance of a Series of Papers Read at
         the Literary Institution, Barnstaple, by John Roberts Chanter,
         to Which Is Appended the Diary of Philip Wyot, Town Clerk of
         Barnstaple, From 1586 to 1608.* 129pp. Barnstaple:
         E. J. Arnold, [1866]. [B: 55-56, 82]

*[763] Grant, Charles [also known as Charles Grant Glenelg].
         The Last Hundred Years of English Literature. viii+220pp.
         London: Williams & Norgate, 1866. [C]

[764]   Tuckerman, Henry T[heodore]. *The Criterion; or the Test of
         Talk about Familiar Things. A Series of Essays.* New York:
         Hurd and Houghton, 1866. [C: "Authors.," (43)-76;
         Shelley: 44, 47, 62-63, 73]

                              [78]

Periodicals:

[765]   [Signed "J.W.W."]. "Shelley's 'Adonais' (3rd S. x. 494.),"
        Notes and Queries, Third Series XI, No. 263 (January 12,
        1867), 44. [T]

[766]   Bouchier, Jonathan. "[Untitled, following item 765],"
        Notes and Queries, Third Series XI, No. 263 (January 12,
        1867), 44. [T]

[767]   Bouchier, Jonathan. "Shelley's 'Adonais' (3rd S. xi.
        44.)," *Notes and Queries*, Third Series XI, No. 266
        (February 2, 1867), 106. [T]

[768]   [Signed "W.S.J."]. "Shelley's 'Adonais' (3rd S. x. 494;
        xi. 44.)," *Notes and Queries*, Third Series XI, No. 269
        (February 23, 1867), 163. [T]

[769]   [Signed "C.W.B."]. "Shelley's 'Adonais' (3rd S. x. 494;
        xi. 45 [*sic* for 44].)," *Notes and Queries*, Third Series
        XI, No. 274 (March 30, 1867), 265-266. [T]

[770]   [Signed "G.R.K."]. "Reading in Shelley's 'Cloud.,'" *Notes
        and Queries*, Third Series XI, No. 277 (April 20, 1867),
        311-312. [T]

[771]   Robertson, John. "Shelley's 'Adonais' (3rd S. xi. 106.),"
        Notes and Queries, Third Series XI, No. 278 (April 27,
        1867), 343-344. [C]

[772]   Jackson, S. "Shelley's 'Sensitive Plant.,'" *Notes and
        Queries*, Third Series XI, No. 281 (May 18, 1867), 397.
        [T]

[773]   Bouchier, Jonathan. "Reading in Shelley's 'Cloud' (3rd S.
        xi. 311.)," *Notes and Queries*, Third Series XI, No. 282
        (May 25, 1867), 428. [T]

[774]   [Signed "J.W.W."]. "Shelley's 'Sensitive Plant' (3rd S.
        xi. 397)," *Notes and Queries*, Third Series XI, No. 284
        (June 8, 1867), 469. [T]

[775]   [Signed "O.T.D."]. "Emendation of Shelley.," *Notes and
        Queries*, Third Series XII, No. 307 (November 16, 1867),
        389. [T]

[776]   [Signed "O.T.D."]. "Emendation of Shelley. (3rd S. xii.
        389.)," *Notes and Queries*, Third Series XII, No. 310
        (December 7, 1867), 466-467. [T]

[777] [Signed "C.A.W."]. "[Untitled, following item 776],"
      Notes and Queries, Third Series XII, No. 310 (December 7,
      1867), 467. [T]

[778] L'Estrange, Thomas. "Emendation of Shelley. (3rd S. xii.
      289, 466.)," *Notes and Queries*, Third Series XII, No.
      313 (December 28, 1867), 527-528. [T]

[779] Westwood, T. "[Untitled, following item 778]," *Notes and
      Queries*, Third Series XII, No. 313 (December 28, 1867),
      528. [T]

[780] [Signed "F.C.H."]. "Shelley's 'Tall Flower' (3rd S. xii.
      466.)," *Notes and Queries*, Third Series XII, No. 313
      (December 28, 1867), 535. [T]

Books:

[781] Alger, William Rounseville. *The Solitudes of Nature and of Man;
      or, The Loneliness of Human Life.* xii+412pp. Boston:
      Roberts Brothers, 1867. [C: "Shelley.," 272-276]

[782] [Anonymous]. *Prometheus in Atlantis; A Prophecy of the Extinction
      of the Christian Civilization.* 318pp. New York: G. W.
      Carleton & Co., Publishers, 1867. [M: 84-85]

                              1868

Periodicals:

[783] Dixon, James Henry. "Emendation of Shelley. (3rd S. xii.
      389, 466, 527, 535.)," *Notes and Queries*, Fourth Series
      I, No. 4 (January 25, 1868), 79-81. [T]

[784] Westwood, T. "[Untitled, following item 783]," *Notes and
      Queries*, Fourth Series I, No. 4 (January 25, 1868), 81.
      [T]

[785] [Signed "O.T.D."]. "Emendations of Shelley. (3rd S. xii.
      467.)," *Notes and Queries*, Fourth Series I, No. 7 (Febru-
      ary 15, 1868), 151-152. [T]

[786] [Signed "A Cobbler"]. "[Untitled, following item 785],"
      Notes and Queries, Fourth Series I, No. 7 (February 15,
      1868), 152. [T]

[787] [Signed "Fitzhopkins"]. "Shelley's 'Queen Mab.,'" *Notes and
      Queries*, Fourth Series I, No. 13 [*sic* for 12] (March 21,
      1868), 266. [T]

[788]   [Signed "Harfra"]. "Shelley's 'Epipsychidion.'" *Notes and Queries*, Fourth Series I, No. 13 (March 28, 1868), 296-297. [C]

[789]   Rossetti, W[illiam] M[ichael]. "Emendations of Shelley. (3rd S. xii. 389, 466, 527, 535; 4th S. i. 79.)," *Notes and Queries*, Fourth Series I, No. 13 (March 28, 1868), 301-302. [T]

[790]   Rossetti, W[illiam] M[ichael]. "Notes and Emendations on Shelley," *Notes and Queries*, Fourth Series I, No. 15 (April 11, 1868), 333-336. [T]

[791]   Rossetti, W[illiam] M[ichael]. "Notes and Emendations on Shelley," *Notes and Queries*, Fourth Series I, No. 16 (April 18, 1868), 357-360. [T]

[792]   Rossetii, W[illiam] M[ichael]. "Notes and Emendations on Shelley," *Notes and Queries*, Fourth Series I, No. 17 (April 25, 1868), 384-387. [T]

[793]   Bouchier, Jonathan. "Shelley: Three Sons of Light," *Notes and Queries*, Fourth Series I, No. 18 (May 2, 1868), 411. [T]

[794]   [Signed "A.H."]. "Passage in Shelley. (4th S. i. 386.)," *Notes and Queries*, Fourth Series I, No. 22 (May 30, 1868), 516. [T]

[795]   [Elmes, John James]. "Some Notes on Othello.," *The Cornhill Magazine*, XVIII, No. 106 (October, 1868), 419-440. [C: 430-433]

[796]   [Signed "J.M."]. "Percy Bysshe Shelley," *Temple Bar*, XXIV (November, 1868), 457-472. [B]

[797]   Bede, Cuthbert [pseud. of Edward Bradley]. "Olphar Hamst's 'Handbook of Fictitious Names' (4th S. i. 407, 475, 513.)," *Notes and Queries*, Fourth Series II, No. 49 (December 5, 1868), 545. [M]

Books:

*[798]   [Anonymous]. *Catalogue of the Third and Concluding Exhibition of National Portraits Commencing with the Fortieth Year of the Reign of George the Third and Ending with the Year MDCCCLXVII on Loan to the South Kensington Museum. April 13, 1868. Science and Art Department of the Committee of Council on Education.* x+209pp. London: Strangeways and Walden, [1868]. [B]

[799]   [Anonymous]. "Shelley.," in Volume VIII, 668-669, in
        Chambers's Encyclopedia [/] *A Dictionary of Universal Knowledge*.
        London: W. and R. Chambers, 1868.   [B]

[800]   Cunningham, George Godfrey. *The English Nation; or A History
        of England in the Lives of Englishmen*.   5 vols.   Edinburgh:
        A. Fullarton & Co., [1863-1868; vol. V: 1868].   [B:
        "Percy Bysshe Shelley.," V, 528-535]

[801]   Stirling, James Hutchinson. *Jerrold, Tennyson and Macaulay with
        Other Critical Essays*.   [vii]+243pp.   Edinburgh: Edmonston
        & Douglas, 1868.   [C; "Alfred Tennyson.," (51)-111;
        Shelley: 53-60, 102-110; rptd. from item 677]

                              1869

Periodicals:

[802]   Swinburne, Algernon Charles.   "Notes on the Text of
        Shelley," *Fortnightly Review*, New Series V [whole number
        XI], No. xxix (May 1, 1869), 539-561.   [T,C: rptd.:
        item 938]

[803]   Lamb, James, J.   "'The Liberal,'" *Notes and Queries*, Fourth
        Series III, No. 71 (May 8, 1869), 429.   [M]

[804]   Prowett, C. G.   "Shelley's 'Ode to Liberty,'" *Notes and
        Queries*, Fourth Series III, No. 73 (May 22, 1869),
        475-476.   [T,C]

[805]   [Fane, Julian Henry Charles].   "Art. VII.—*The Ring and the
        Book*. By Robert Browning, M.A.   4 vols.   London:
        1869.," *Edinburgh Review*, CXXX, No. cclxv (July, 1869),
        164-186.   [R; M: 165]

[806]   MacCarthy, D[enis] F[lorence].   "Shelley's 'Laon and
        Cythna' and 'Revolt of Islam,'" *The American Bibliopolist*,
        I, No. 12 (December, 1869), 359-361.   [T]

Books:

[807]   Clough, Arthur Hugh.   *The Poems and Prose Remains of Arthur Hugh
        Clough with a Selection from His Letters and Memoir Edited by His
        Wife*.   2 vols.   London: Macmillan and Co., 1869.   [M:
        I, 314, 380-381; II, 40].

[808]   [Friswell, James Hain]. *Essays on English Writers, By the*
         Author of "The Gentle Life." viii+360pp. London: Sampson
         Low, Marston, Searle, and Rivington, 1869. [C:
         "Chapter XXVIII. Poets of the Present Century.
         Shelley, Keats, Landor, Barry Cornwall, Crabbe, and
         Thomas Hood.," (383)-349]

[809]   Lamb, Charles. *The Works of Charles Lamb. Comprising His Most*
         Interesting Letters. —Essays of Elia. The Last Essays of Elia.
         —Rosamund Gray.—Poems.—Sonnets. Translations, and Final
         Memorials. Collected and Edited, with a Sketch of His Life, By
         Sir Thomas Noon Talfourd. A New Edition. iv+648pp. London:
         Bell and Daldy, 1869. [M: 136]

[810]   Robinson, Henry Crabb. *Diary [/] Reminiscences, and Correspon-*
         dence of Henry Crabb Robinson, Barrister-at-Law, F.S.A. [Edited
         by Thomas Sadler]. 3 vols. London: Macmillan and Co.,
         1869. [M: II, 67-68, 387, 390, 456; III, 84]

                                1870

Periodicals:

[811]   [Anonymous]. " *The Poetical Works of Percy Bysshe Shelley.* A
         Revised Text, with Notes and a Memoir by W. M. Ros-
         setti. 2 vols. (Moxon.)," *The Athenaeum*, No. 2205
         (January 29, 1870), 154-156. [R: item 839]

[812]   Rossetti, W[illiam] M[ichael]. "The New Edition of
         Shelley: Emendations," *Notes and Queries*, Fourth Series
         V, No. 111 (February 12, 1870), 167-168. [T]

[813]   Pierson, Helen. "Concerning Shelley," *Lippincott's Magazine*,
         V (March, 1870), 318-322. [B,C]

[814]   [Signed "A London Bookseller"]. "Shelley's 'Queen Mab'
         and 'Declaration of Rights.,'" *Notes and Queries*, Fourth
         Series V, No. 114 (March 5, 1870), 246. [T]

[815]   [Signed "E.L.S."]. "Dr. Keate (4th S. v. 167.)," *Notes and*
         Queries, Fourth Series V, No. 117 (March 26, 1870), 328.
         [B,T]

[816]   Rossetti, W[illiam] M[ichael]. "Shelley's 'Queen Mab' and
         'Declaration of Rights.' (4th S. v. 246.)," *Notes and*
         Queries, Fourth Series V, No. 116 (March 19, 1870),
         301-302. [T]

[817]   Symonds, J[ohn] A[ddington].   "*The Poetical Works of Percy Bysshe Shelley.* —The Text carefully revised with Notes and a Memoir, by W. M. Rossetti. 2 vols. London. Moxon, 1870.," *The Academy*, I, No. [8] (April 9, 1870), 172-173. [R: item 839]

[818]   Rossetti, W[illiam] M[ichael]. "Doctor Keate: Shelley (4th S. v. 167, 328)," *Notes and Queries*, Fourth Series V, No. 122 (April 30, 1870), 437. [T]

[819]   [Signed "J.J.M."]. "Responsio Shelleiana," *Fraser's Magazine*, New Series I, No. v (May, 1870), 657. [C: a poem]

[820]   S[hepherd], R[ichard] H[erne]. "Mr. Rossetti's Edition of Shelley.," *Notes and Queries*, Fourth Series V, No. 123 (May 7, 1870), 445. [T]

[821]   [Signed "Lumen."]. "Shelley.," *Notes and Queries*, Fourth Series V, No. 125 (May 21, 1870), 490. [T]

[822]   L[ocock], C[harles] D[ealtry]. "Shelley's 'Daemon of the World,'" *Notes and Queries*, Fourth Series V, No. 127 (June 4, 1870), 534-535. [T]

[823]   Smith, W. J. Bernhard. "Shelley (4th S. v. 490.)," *Notes and Queries*, Fourth Series V, No. 128 (June 11, 1870), 569. [T]

[824]   Blinde,Mathilde. "Art. V. Shelley," *Wesminster Review*, New Series XXXVIII [whole number XCIV], No. i [whole number clxxxv] (July, 1870), 75-97. [R: item 839]

[825]   Hodgkin, John Eliot. "Shelley's 'Daemon of the World.' (4th S. v. 534.)," *Notes and Queries*, Fourth Series VI, No. 138 (August 20, 1870), 159-160. [T]

[826]   Kerr, J. A. "Shelley: 'And That Tall Flower,' Etc. (4th S. v. 490, 569)," *Notes and Queries*, Fourth Series VI, No. 139 (August 27, 1870), 183. [T]

[827]   [Anonymous]. "Sale of the Poet Shelley's Estates," *Notes and Queries*, Fourth Series VI, No. 139 (August 27, 1870), 186. [M]

[828]   [Simcox, George Augustus]. "The Poems of Shelley.," *The North British Review*, LIII, No. cv (October, 1870), [30]-58. [C: rptd.: item 842]

[829]   [Signed "P.P."]. "Shelley: 'And That Tall Flower,' Etc. (4th S. v. 490, 569; vi. 183.)," *Notes and Queries*, Fourth Series VI, No. 145 (October 8, 1870), 308.   [T]

[830] Dixon, James Henry. "[Untitled, following item 829]," *Notes and Queries*, Fourth Series VI, No. 145 (October 8, 1870), 308. [T]

[831] Horne, R[ichard] H[engist]. "On the Drowning of Shelley," *Fraser's Magazine*, New Series II, No. ix (November, 1870), 618-625. [B]

[832] Roscoe, Edward. "Shelley," *The Victoria Magazine*, XVI (November, 1870), 52-65. [B, C]

[833] [Morley, John]. "Byron," *Fortnightly Review*, New Series VIII [whole number XIV], No. xlviii (December, 1870), 650-673. [C; rptd.: item 861]

[834] Ellis, A[*(sic)* Frederick] S[tartridge]. "Shelley and Byron.," *Notes and Queries*, Fourth Series VI, No. 153 (December 3, 1870), 473. [B]

Books:

[835] Allibone, S. Austin. *A Critical Dictionary of English Literature and British and American Authors Living and Deceased From the Earliest Accounts to the Latter Half of the Nineteenth Century.* 2 vols. Philadelphia: [Volume I,] Childs & Peterson, 1859, [Volume II,] J. B. Lippincott, 1870. [B,C: "Shelley, Percy Bysshe," II, 2068-2071]

[836] Blind, Mathilde. *Shelley. A lecture delivered to the Church of Progress, in St. George's Hall, Langham Place, London, W., on Sunday evnening, January 9th, 1870, by Miss Mathilde Blind.* 8pp. London: Taylor & Co., [1870]. [C]

[837] Godwin, Parke. *Out of the Past: (Critical and Literary Papers.)* 461pp. New York: G. P. Putnam & Sons, 1870. [C: "Percy Bysshe Shelley.," (111)-144; rptd. from item 405]

*[838] Griffin, Gilderoy Wells. *Studies in Literature.* iii+158pp. Baltimore: Henry Turnbull, Jr., 1870. [C]

[839] Rossetti, William Michael, ed. *The Poetical Works of Percy Bysshe Shelley: Including Various Additional Pieces [/] From MS. and Other Sources. The Text carefully revised, with Notes and [/] A Memoir.* 2 vols. London: E. Moxon, Son & Co., 1870. [T,C,B,; revised edition: item 1033]

*[840] Rossetti, William Michael. *Memoir of Shelley.* [?]pp. London: E. Moxon, Son & Co., 1870. [C,B; rptd. from item 839]

*[841]   [Worsley, F.] *The Feast of Famine: An Irish Banquet. With
         Other Poems. By the Author of "The Lost Thane, A National
         Tragedy."* 103pp. London: Chapman and Hall, 1870.
         [Contains a poem on Shelley]

                              1871

Periodicals:

[842]   [Simcox, George Augustus]. "The Poems of Shelley,"
         Littell's Living Age, CVIII, No. 1387 (January 1, 1871),
         3-18. [C; rptd. from item 828]

[843]   Rossetti, W[illiam] M[ichael]. "Shelley in 1812-13: An
         unpublished poem, and other particulars.," *Fortnightly
         Review*, New Series IX [whole number XV], No. xlix
         (January, 1871), 67-85. [T]

[844]   Rossetti, W[illiam] M[ichael]. "Shelley's 'Daemon of the
         World' (4th S. v. 534; vi. 159.)," *Notes and Queries*,
         Fourth Series VII, No. 158 (January 7, 1871), 24. [T]

[845]   Rossetti, W[illia]m M[ichael]. "Shelley's Heart.," *The
         Dark Blue*, I, No. I (March, 1871), 35. [B: a sonnet]

*[846]   [Thomson, James "B.V."]. "[On Moxon's cheap edition of
         Shelley]," *The National Reformer*, [?] (?March, 1871),
         [?p]. [R; rptd.: item 1205]

[847]   [Oliphant, Margaret]. "New Books," *Blackwood's Edinburgh
         Magazine*, CIX, No. dclxvi (April, 1871), 440-464. [R of
         item 860: 440-450; Shelley: 448-449]

[848]   [Baynes, Thomas Spencer]. "Art. V. —*The Poetical Works of
         Percy Bysshe Shelley, including various Additional Pieces from
         MS. and other sources.* The Text carefully Revised, with
         Notes and a Memoir. By William Michael Rossetti.
         2 vols. London: 1870.," *Edinburgh Review*, CXXXIII,
         No. cclxxii (April, 1871), 426-459. [R: item 839]

[849]   Mallock, W[illiam] H[urrell]. "Prophets and Poets.,"
         The Dark Blue, I, No. II (April, 1871), 152-162. [C;
         Shelley: 153-156]

[850]   [Signed "J.A.K."]. "Passages in Shelley," *Notes and Queries*,
         Fourth Series VII, No. 178 (May 27, 1871), 455-456.
         [T]

[851]   Bouchier, Jonathan. "Sonnet Queries.," *Notes and Queries*,
        Fourth Series VII, No. 178 (May 27, 1871), 456. [T]

[852]   Rossetti, W[illiam] M[ichael]. "Passages in Shelley
        (4th S. vii. 455.)," *Notes and Queries*, Fourth Series
        VIII, No 183 (July 1, 1871), 14. [T]

[853]   [Signed "Silurian"]. "Passages in Shelley (4th S. vii.
        455; viii. 14.)," *Notes and Queries*, Fourth Series VIII,
        No. 187 (July 29, 1871), 97. [T]

[854]   [Grant, Alexander]. "Art. I- —*The Dialogues of Plato. Trans-
        lated into English with Analyses and Introductions.* By B.
        Jowett, M.A., Master of Balliol College, Regius
        Professor of Greek in the University of Oxford. In
        4 vols. Oxford: at the Clarendon Press. 1871.,"
        Edinburgh Review, CXXXIV, No. cclxxiv (October, 1871),
        [303]-342. [M: 305, 308-309]

[855]   Noel, Roden. "A Study of Walt Whitman, The Poet of Modern
        Democracy.," *The Dark Blue*, II, No. VIII (October, 1871),
        241-253. [C; M: 245, 247, 252]

[856]   West, E. Dickinson. "Browning as a Preacher.," *The Dark
        Blue*, II, No. VIII (October, 1871), 171-184. [C;
        M: 183; rptd.: item 858]

[857]   [Anonymous]. "Byron and Shelley," *Temple Bar*, XXXIV (Decem-
        ber, 1871), 30-49. [C]

[858]   [West, E. Dickinson]. "Browning as a Preacher.," *Littell's
        Living Age*, Fourth Series XXIII [whole number CXI],
        No. 1437 (December 23, 1871), 707-723. [C; M: 714-
        715; rptd. from item 856]

[859]   [Signed "O.T.D."]. "Shelley.," *Notes and Queries*, Fourth
        Series X, No. 261 (December 28, 1871), 517-518. [T]

Books:

[860]   Hutton, Richard Holt. *Essays Theological and Literary*. 2 vols.
        London: Strahan & Co., 1871. [C; II: "III. Shelley's
        Poetical Mysticism.," (147)-189; rptd. from item 738]

[861]   Morley, John. *Critical Miscellanies.* xii+375pp. London:
        Chapman and Hall, 1871. [C: "Byron.," (249)-290;
        rptd. from item 833]

[862]   Swinburne, Algernon Charles. *Songs Before Sunrise.* viii+
        287pp. London: F. S. Ellis, 1871. [C: "Cor Cordium,"
        205, a sonnet]

[863]   Taine, H[ippolyte] A[dolphe].   *History of English Literature.*
        Translated by H. van Laun. 2 vols. Edinburgh:
        Edmonston and Douglas, 1871.   [C: II, 265-269; original
        French edition: Paris, 1863]

                                1872

Periodicals:

[864]   [Oliphant, Margaret]. "A Century of Great Poets, from 1750
        Downwards. No. VI. —Percy Bysshe Shelley," *Blackwood's
        Edinburgh Magazine*, CXI, No. dclxxviii (April, 1872), 415-
        440. [C; rptd.: items 865, 868]

[865]   [Oliphant, Margaret]. "A Century of Great Poets, From 1750
        Downwards. No. VI. —Percy Bysshe Shelley.," *Littell's
        Living Age*, CXIII, No. 1458 (May 18, 1872), 387-405.
        [C; rptd. from item 864]

[866]   [Anonymous]. "Art. V. — *The Poetical Works of Percy Bysshe
        Shelley: including various Additional Pieces from MS. and other
        Sources.* The Text carefully revised, with Notes and a
        Memoir, by W. M. Rossetti. Two vols. London. E.
        Moxon, Son, and Co. 1870.," *The London Quarterly Review*,
        XXXVIII, No. lxxv (April, 1872), 124-149. [R: item
        839; C]

[867]   Cordery, A. "Shelley's Metaphysics," *The Dark Blue*, III,
        No. xvi (June, 1872), 478-488. [C]

[868]   [Oliphant, Margaret]. "Percy Bysshe Shelley," *The Eclectic
        Magazine*, LXXIX [New Series XVI], No. i (July, 1872),
        17-37. [C; rptd. from item 864]

[869]   [Signed "Pelagius"]. "Line in Shelley.," *Notes and Queries*,
        Fourth Series X, No. 238, No. 238 (July, 1872), 49.
        [T]

[870]   Dalby, John Watson. "'The Cenci,'" *Notes and Queries*,
        Fourth Series X, No. 242 (August 17, 1872), 126.   [T]

[871]   Cocke, W. Archer. "Byron and Shelley," *The Southern Magazine*
        [Baltimore], XI [New Series IV], No. 4 (October, 1872),
        496-506. [C]

[872]   Phelps, Egbert. "The Shelley and the Dialect Schools in
        English Literature," *The Lakeside Monthly*, VIII, No. 47
        (November, 1872), 331-339. [C]

[873]   [Anonymous]. "*Shelley's Early Life, from Original Sources*. By
        Denis Florence MacCarthy. (Hotten.)," *The Athenaeum*,
        No. 2350 (November 9, 1872), 592-593. [R: item 876]

[874]   [Anonymous]. "*Shelley's Early Life, from Original Sources*. By
        Denis Florence Mac-Carthy [*sic*]. (Hotten.)," *Notes and
        Queries*, Fourth Series X, No. 256 (November 23, 1872),
        423-424. [R: item 876]

[875]   Rossetti, W[illiam] M[ichael]. "*Shelley's Early Life; from
        Original Sources*. With Curious Incidents, Letters, and
        Writings, now first published or collected. By Denis
        Florence MacCarthy, M.R.I.A. Hotten.," *The Academy*, III,
        No. 61 (December 1, 1872), 441-443. [R: item 876]

Books:

[876]   Mac-Carthy, Denis Florence [*sic*]. *Shelley's Early Life from
        Original Sources. With Curious Incidents, Letters, and Writings,
        Now First Published or Collected*. xxiv+408pp. London:
        John Camden Hotten, [1872]. [B]

[877]   Graduate of Oxford, A [pseud. of John Ruskin]. *Modern
        Painters*. 5 vols. [Third Edition:] New York: John
        Wiley & Son, 1872. [C; M: I, xxxiv, 218, 353n; II,
        90, 164, 192, 194-195, 195n, 198, 203; III: 272, 276,
        291, 294, 301, 302, 303, 312; V, 367. Editions after
        1883 contain "Epilogue of 1883" in vol. II; Shelley:
        ¶7]

                              1873

Periodicals:

[878]   Rossetti, W[illiam] M[ichael]. "Shelley (4th S. x. 517.),"
        Notes and Queries, Fourth Series XI, No. 265 (January 25,
        1873), 80. [T]

[879]   Hall, H. "Jean Paul Marat: Percy Bysshe Shelley.," *Notes
        and Queries*, Fourth Series XI, No. 268 (February 15,
        1873), 136. [B]

[880]   [Signed "Maureen"]. "Percy B. Shelley (4th S. xi. 136.),"
        Notes and Queries, Fourth Series XI, No. 270 (March 1,
        1873), 188. [B]

[881]   Shaw, S[amue]l. "[Untitled, following item 880," *Notes and
        Queries*, Fourth Series XI, No. 270 (March 1, 1873), 186.
        [B]

[882]   [Anonymous]. "III. General Literature. [/] *Shelley's
        Early Life, from Original Sources.* With Curious Incidents,
        Letters, and Writings, now First Published or Collec-
        ted. By Dennis Florence MacCarthy, M.R.I.A.," *The London
        Quarterly Review,* XL, No. lxxix (April, 1873), 239-241.
        [R: item 876]

[883]   Searle, January. "Some Passages in Shelley's Early His-
        tory," *Lippincott's Magazine,* XII (July, 1873), 113-116.
        [B]

[884]   Campkin, Henry. "Shelley's Poem of 'The Sensitive Plant.,'"
        Notes and Queries, Fourth Series XII, No. 289 (July 12,
        1873), 25. [T]

[885]   Bouchier, Jonathan. "Keats.," *Notes and Queries,* Fourth
        Series XII, No. 296 (August 30, 1873), 169. [T]

[886]   [Burroughs, John]. "The Birds of the Poets," *Scribner's
        Monthly,* VI, No. 5 (September, 1873), 565-574. [M:
        568]

[887]   Oakley, J. H. I. "Keats (4th S. xii. 169.)," *Notes and
        Queries,* 215. [T]

[888]   [Signed "R.T.O."]. "Shelley's 'Cenci.,'" *Notes and Queries,*
        Fourth Series XII, No. 304 (October 25, 1873), 328.
        [C]

[889]   [Signed "W.A.C."]. "Shelley's 'Cenci' (4th S. xii. 328.),"
        Notes and Queries, Fourth Series XII, No. 307 (November
        15, 1873), 395. [C]

[890]   Jackson, Stephen. "Shelley's 'Cenci' (4th S. xii. 328,
        395.)," *Notes and Queries,* Fourth Series XII, No. 312
        (December 20, 1873), 504. [C]

Books:

*[891] Arnold, Frederick. *Oxford and Cambridge: Their Colleges,
        Memories, and Associations.* viii+400pp. London: The
        Religious Tract Society, [1873]. [?B]

[892]   Devey, J[oseph]. *A Comparative Estimate of Modern English Poets.*
        vii+421pp. London: E. Moxon, Son, and Co., 1873.
        [C: 239-262]

[893]   Greg, W[illiam] R[athbone]. *Literary and Social Judgments.*
        352pp. Boston: James T. Osgood and Company, 1873.
        [C: "Kingsley and Carlyle," (115)-145; Shelley: 131-
        135]

Periodicals:

[894] [Palgrave, Francis Turner]. "Art. VI. — *Autobiography.* By
       John Stuart Mill. London, 1873," *The Quarterly Review,*
       CXXXVI, No. 271 (January, 1874), 150-179. [R; M: 157-
       158]

[895] [Anonymous]. "Shelley. [/] *The Poetical Works of Percy Bysshe
       Shelley.* Now First Printed from the Author's Original
       Editions. Second Series. Edited by the Author of
       'Tennysoniana.' (Chatto & Windus)," *The Athenaeum,*
       No. 2414 (January 31, 1874), 154-155. [R: item 937,
       vol. II]

[896] [Brown, James Bucham]. "Scepticism and Modern Poetry,"
       Blackwood's Edinburgh Magazine, CXV, No. dcc (February,
       1874), 223-231. [C; Shelley: 227-229; rptd.: item
       1035]

[897] [Anonymous]. "The Cycle of English Song. [/] Conclusion.,"
       Temple Bar, XL (March, 1874), 478-494. [C]

[898] Jackson, Stephen. "Parallel Passages, &c.," *Notes and
       Queries,* Fifth Series I, No. 13 (March 28, 1874),
       246-247. [C,T]

[899] Clive, Arthur [pseud. of Standish O'Grady]. "Shelley's
       'Prometheus Unbound,'" *The Gentleman's Magazine,* New
       Series XII [whole number CXXXVI], No. lxxi (April,
       1874), [421]-437. [C]

[900] [Anonymous]. "Shelley," *Notes and Queries,* Fifth Series I,
       No. 21 (May 23, 1874), 403. [T]

[901] D[ennis], J[ohn]. "English Lyrical Poetry.," *The Cornhill
       Magazine,* XXIX, No. 74 (June, 1874), 698-719. [C;
       Shelley: 713-715; rptd.: items 906, 962]

[902] [Signed "N."]. "Shelley's Titles to Poems," *Notes and
       Queries,* Fifth Series I, No. 23 (June 6, 1874), 445. [T]

[903] Norgate, Fr. "Shelley's Title to Poems (5th S. i. 445.),"
       Notes and Queries, Fifth Series I, No. 25 (June 20,
       1874), 494. [T]

[904] Jerram, C. S. "[Untitled, following item 903]," *Notes and
       Queries,* Fifth Series I, No. 25 (June 20, 1874), 494.
       [T]

[905] Skipton, H. S. "Edward King, of 'Lycidas': Portrait of
         Shelley," *Notes and Queries*, Fifth Series II, No. 29
         (July 18, 1874), 47-48. [M: 48]

[906] D[ennis], J[ohn]. "English Lyrical Poetry.," *Littell's
         Living Age*, Fifth Series VII [whole number CXXII],
         No. 1572 (July 25, 1874), 195-208. [C; Shelley:
         204-206; rptd. from item 901; rptd.: item 962]

[907] [Signed "N."]. "Balzac and Shelley," *Notes and Queries*,
         Fifth Series II, No. 32 (August 8, 1874), 106. [C]

[908] [Anonymous]. "Disraeli on Shelley and Byron," *The American
         Bibliopolist*, VI, Nos. 69 and 70 (September and October,
         1874), 138. [B]

[909] Ward, C[harles] A. "Shelley," *Notes and Queries*, Fifth Series
         II, No. 44 (October 31, 1874), 347. [T]

[910] Rossetti, W[illiam] M[ichael]. "Correspondence. [/]
         Shelley and Peter Finnerty," *The Academy*, VI, No. 137
         (December 19, 1874), 658. [T,B]

Books:

*[911] Blackie, John Stuart. *Horae Hellenicae: Essays and Discussions
         on some important points of Greek Philology and Antiquity.* xii+
         394pp. London: Macmillan and Co., 1874. [C: an essay
         on the *Prometheus Bound* of Aeschylus, containing refer-
         ences to Shelley begins on p. 60]

[912] Calvert, George H. *Brief Essays and Brevities.* 282pp.
         Boston: Lee and Shepard, 1874. [C: "Shelley.," (129)-
         139; 217-218]

[913] Masson, David. *Wordsworth, Shelley, Keats, and Other Essays.*
         305pp. London: Macmillan and Co., 1874. [B,C: "The
         Life and Poetry of Shelley.," (105)-142; rptd. from
         item 694]

*[914] Poe, Edgar Allan. *The Works of Edgar Allan Poe.* Edited by
         John H. Ingram. 4 vols. Edinburgh: [?], 1874. [C:
         Shelley and His Imitators," IV, 86-87]

1875

Periodicals:

[915] [Anonymous]. " *Shelley Memorials.* From Authentic Sources.

Edited by Lady Shelley. With, now first Printed, an
Essay on Christianity. Third Edition. (H. S. King &
Co.)," *Notes and Queries*, Fifth Series III, No. 53 (Janu-
ary 2, 1875), 18-19. [R: 3rd edition of item 683]

[916]   [Smith, George Barnett]. "Shelley's Earlier Years," *The
Cornhill Magazine*, XXXI, No. 182 (February, 1875), 184-
206. [B; rptd.: item 1011]

[917]   [Smith, George Barnett]. "Shelley: Politician, Atheist,
Philanthropist," *The Cornhill Magazine*, XXXI, No. 183
(March, 1875), 345-365. [B,C; rptd.: item 1011]

[918]   [Signed "S.D.L."]. "Shelley's 'Queen Mab.,'" *Notes and
Queries*, Fifth Series III, No. 65 (March 27, 1875),
248. [T]

[919]   [Anonymous]. "Our Library Table," *The American Bibliopolist*,
VII, No. 74 (April, 1875), 71-77. [R: 3rd edition of
item 683]

[920]   Buchanan, Robert. "Thomas Love Peacock: A Personal
Reminiscence," *The New Quarterly Magazine*, IV (April, 1875),
(238)-255. [M: 247-249]

[921]   Dixon, James Henry. "Shelley Memorials. (5th S. iii.
18.)," *Notes and Queries*, Fifth Series III, No. 69
(April, 1875), 329-330. [C]

[922]   Dixon, James Henry. "Shelley's Beatrice Cenci," *The American Bibliopolist*, VII, No. 75 (June, 1875), 165-167. [C]

[923]   Dixon, James Henry. "Shelley Memorials (5th S. iii. 18,
329.)," *Notes and Queries*, Fifth Series IV, No. 82
(July 24, 1875), 74. [C]

[924]   [Hasell, Elizabeth J.]. "Elegies," *Blackwood's Edinburgh
Magazine*, CXVIII, No. dccix (September, 1875), 345-366.
[C: 352-357]

[925]   Sotheran, Charles. "Percy Bysshe Shelley as a Philosopher
and Reformer. [/] A Paper Read before the New York
Liberal Club [Aug. 6, 1875] (brackets in original),"
The New Era, V, No. 10 (October, 1875), [597]-612.
[C; first of three parts; rptd.: item 968]

[926]   Sotheran, Charles. "Percy Bysshe Shelley as a Philosopher
and Reformer. [/] A Paper Read before the New York
Liberal Club [Aug. 6, 1875] (brackets in original),"
The New Era, V, No. 11 (November, 1875), [693]-708. [C;
second of three parts; rptd.: item 968]

[927] Sotheran, Charles. "Percy Bysshe Shelley as a Philsopher and Reformer. [/] A Paper Read before the New York Liberal Club [Aug. 6, 1875] (brackets in original)," *The New Era*, V, No. 12 (December, 1875), [736]-755. [C; third of three parts; rptd.: item 968]

[928] [Story, William Wetmore]. "In a Studio. Conversation No. IV," *Blackwood's Edinburgh Magazine*, CXVIII, No. dccxxii (December, 1875), 674-695. [C: 685-687]

[929] Rossetti, W[illiam] M[ichael]. "The Death of Shelley.," *The Times* [London], No. 28,487 (December 1, 1875), 11, column 6. [B]

[930] [Signed "W.T.M."]. "The Death of Shelley," *Notes and Queries*, Fifth Series IV, No. 101 (December 4, 1875), 459-460. [B]

[931] [Anonymous]. "The Death of Shelley.," *The Times* [London], No. 28,507 (December 24, 1875), 10, column 6. [B; rptd. from item 932]

[932] [Anonymous]. "The Death of Shelley," *The Athenaeum*, No. 2513 (December 25, 1875), 880. [B; rptd.: item 931]

Books:

[933] Clive, Arthur [pseud. of Standish O'Grady], ed. *Scintilla Shelleiana. [/] Shelley's Attitude Towards Religion, Explained and Defended by Himself.* 27pp. Dublin: William McGee, 1875. [C,T]

[934] Dilke, Charles Wentworth. *The Papers of a Critic. Selected from the Writings of the Late Charles Wentworth Dilke. With a Biographical Sketch by his Grandson, Sir Charles Wentworth Dilke, Bart., M.P.* 2 vols. London: John Murray, 1875. [M: I, 11]

[935] Peacock, Thomas Love. *The Works of Thomas Love Peacock, Including His Novels, Poems, Fugitive Pieces, Criticisms, Etc., with a Preface by the Right Hon. Lord Houghton, A Biographical Notice by His Grand-Daughter, Edith Nicolls, and a Portrait.* Edited by Henry Cole. 3 vols. London: Richard Bentley and Son, 1875. [B,C,T,: III, 385-479; rptd. from items 653, 684, 687, 688, 721; rptd.: item 2620]

[936] Rennie, John. *Autobiography of Sir John Rennie, F.R.S., . . . Comprising the History of His Professional Life, Together with Reminiscences Dating from the Commencement of the Century to the Present Time.* viii+464pp. London: E. & F. N. Spon, 1875. [B: 2]

[937]   [Shepherd, Richard Herne, ed.]. *The Poetical Works of Percy
        Bysshe Shelley. Now First Given from the Author's Original
        Editions. With Some Hitherto Inedited Pieces.* ["The Golden
        Library"]. 4 vols. Volume I, London: John Camden
        Hotten, [1871]; volume II: London: Chatto and Windus
        Publishers, 1873; volummes III, IV [titled *The Works
        of Percy Bysshe Shelley*], London: Chatto and Windus Pub-
        lishers, 1875. [T,C,B; the volumes are designated on
        their title pages as Series I, Series II, etc., in
        lieu of Volume I, Volume II, etc.]

[938]   Swinburne, Algernon Charles. *Essays and Studies.* xii+380pp.
        London: Chatto and Windus, 1875. [T: "Notes on the
        Text of Shelley.," 184-237; rptd. from item 802]

                              1876

Periodicals:

[939]   Trelawny, E[dward] J[ohn]. "The Death of Shelley.," *The
        Times* [London], No. 28,515 (January 3, 1876), 6, column
        3. [B]

[940]   E[yre], V[incent]. "The Death of Shelley.," *The Times*
        [London], No. 28,516 (January 4, 1876), 8, column 2.
        [B]

[941]   [Signed "R.K.D."]. "Shelley.," *Notes and Queries*, Fifth
        Series V, No. 106 (January 8, 1876), 29. [T]

[942]   F[orman], H[arry] B[uxton]. "'St. Irvyne; or, the Rosicru-
        cian" (5th S. v. 29.)," *Notes and Queries*, Fifth Series
        V, No. 108 (January 22, 1876), 76. [T]

[943]   Holland, R. A. "The Soul of Shelley.," *The Western: A Journal
        of Literature, Education, and Art* [St. Louis], New Series II,
        No. 3 (March, 1876), [129]-161. [C]

[944]   Mayer, S. R. Townshend. "Shelley's Sonnet 'To the Nile,'"
        The American Bibliopolist, VIII, No. 80 (April, 1876), 31.
        [T]

[945]   [Signed "J.S.S."]. "Shelley.," *Notes and Queries*, Fifth
        Series V, No. 118 (April 1, 1876), 269. [T]

[946]   Mayer, S. R. Townshend. "Shelley's Sonnet 'To the Nile,'"
        Notes and Queries, Fifth Series V, No. 121 (April 22,
        1876), 326. [T]

[947]   [Signed "J.W.E."]. "Shelley: His 'Sensitive Plant' (5th S
        v. 269.)," *Notes and Queries*, Fifth Series V, No. 124
        (May 13, 1876), 392. [C,T]

[948]   Kinsley, William W. "Was Shelley Consistent?—I.," *The Penn*
        Monthly [Philadelphia], VII (June, 1876), 444-461. [C;
        rptd.: item 1106]

[949]   Kinsley, William W. "Was Shelley Consistent?—II.," *The Penn*
        Monthly [Philadelphia], VII (July, 1876), 513-527. [C;
        rptd.: item 1106]

[950]   Forman, H[arry] Buxton. "Shelley.," *Notes and Queries*, Fifth
        Series VI, No. 131 (July 1, 1876), 8. [T]

[951]   Kinglake, Arthur. "Shelley's Family.," *Notes and Queries*,
        Fifth Series VI, No. 132 (July 8, 1876), 39. [B]

[952]   [Signed "P.P."]. "Shelley's 'Sensitive Plant' (5th S. v.
        269, 392.)," *Notes and Queries*, Fifth Series VI, No.
        138 (August 19, 1876), 156. [T]

[953]   Legis, R. H. "Shakspeare [*sic*] and Shelley.," *Notes and*
        Queries, Fifth Series VI, No. 148 (October 28, 1876),
        341-342. [C; first of two parts]

[954]   Legis, R. H. "Shakspeare [*sic*] and Shelley. (Concluded
        from p. 342.)," *Notes and Queries*, Fifth Series VI,
        No. 149 (November 4, 1876), 361-362. [C; second of
        two parts]

[955]   [Signed "Jabez."]. "Shakspeare [*sic*] and Shelley: 'The
        Two Noble Kinsmen' (5th S. vi. 341, 361.)," *Notes and*
        Queries, Fifth Series VI, No. 150 (November 11, 1876),
        392. [C]

[956]   Ward, C[harles] A. "[Untitled, following item 955]," *Notes*
        and Queries, Fifth Series VI, No. 150 (November 11,
        1876), 392-393. [C]

[957]   [Signed "C.D."]. "Shakspeare [*sic*] and Shelley: 'The Two
        Noble Kinsmen' (5th S. vi. 341, 361, 392.)," *Notes and*
        Queries, Fifth Series VI, No. 154 (December 9, 1876),
        478. [C]

[958]   Gosse, Edmund W. "Shelleiana," *The Athenaeum*, No. 2565
        (December 23, 1876), 835. [C]

[959]   [Signed "Lupus."]. "Shakspeare [*sic*] and Shelley: 'The Two
        Noble Kinsmen' (5th S. vi. 341, 361, 392, 478.)," *Notes*
        and Queries, Fifth Series VI, No. 156 (December 23,
        1876), 517. [C]

Books:

[960]   [Anonymous]. *The Eton Portrait Gallery, Consisting of Short*
        Memoirs of the More Eminent Eton Men; by a Barrister of the
        Inner Temple. xiv+581pp. Eton College: Williams &
        Son, 1876. [B: "Percy Bysshe Shelley," 530-534]

[961]   Bennett, D[e Robigne] M[ortimer]. *The World's Sages, Infidels,*
        and Thinkers, Being Biographical Sketches of Leading Philosophers,
        Teachers, Reformers, Innovators, Founders of New Schools of
        Thought, Eminent Scientists, Etc. x+1048pp. New York:
        D. M. Bennett, 1876. [C: "Shelley.," 719-725]

*[962] Dennis, John. *Studies in English Literature.* [?]pp. London:
        [?], 1876. [C; rptd. from item 901]

[963]   Forster, John. *Walter Savage Landor [/] A Biography* [Volume I
        of *The Works and Life of Walter Savage Landor*]. xii+560pp.
        London: Chapman and Hall, 1876. [M: 54, 62, 304]

[964]   Hall, S[amuel] C[arter]. *A Book of Memories of Great Men and*
        Women of the Age, from Personal Acquaintance. xiv+495pp.
        London: Virtue and Company, 1876. [B: 247]

[965]   Haydon, Benjamin Robert. *Benjamin Robert Haydon: Correspondence*
        and Table Talk. With a Memoir by his son, Frederic Wordsworth
        Haydon. 2 vols. London: Chatto and Windus, 1876.
        [M: I, 111, 316, 318; II, 72n, 79, 268, 290-291, 383]

[966]   Moultrie, John. *Poems by John Moultrie. New Edition. With Memoir*
        by the Rev. Prebendary Coleridge. 2 vols. London: Macmillan
        and Co., 1876. [C: "Musae Etonensis.," a poem, 370-
        379; Shelley: 376-379]

[967]   Paul, C[harles] Kegan. *William Godwin: His Friends and Contempor-*
        aries. 2 vols. London: Henry S. King & Co., 1876.
        [C,B: I, 201-290]

[968]   Sotheran, Charles. *Percy Bysshe Shelley as a Philosopher and*
        Reformer. ["Including an Original Sonnet by Charles
        W. Frederickson..."]. 51pp. New York: Charles P.
        Somerby, 1876. [C; rptd. from items 925, 926, 927]

                                1877

Periodicals:

[969]   [Anonymous]. " *The Poetical Works of Percy Bysshe Shelley.* Edited
        by Harry Buxton Forman. Vol. II. (Reeves & Turner.),"
        Notes and Queries, Fifth Series VII, No. 159 (January 13,
        1877), 39. [R: item 1008]

[970]   Bright, Henry A. "Shelley's 'Oedipus' (5th S. vi. 39.),"
         Notes and Queries, Fifth Series VII, No. 161 (January 27,
         1877), 78.   [T]

[971]   Welford, Charles. "Shelley," *Scribner's Monthly*, XIII, No. 4
         (February, 1877), 570-571.   [R: item 1012]

[972]   Bouchier, Jonathan. "Shelley's Place in English Literature.
         (5th S. vi. 341, 361, 392, 478, 517.)," *Notes and Queries*,
         Fifth Series VII, No. 167 (March 10, 1877), 189-190.
         [C]

[973]   Kemble, Fanny [Frances Anne]. "Old Woman's Gossip. XXI.,"
         The Atlantic Monthly, XXIX, No. ccxxxiv (April, 1877),
         432-445.   [M: 436-437]

[974]   [Paul, Charles Kegan]. "Shelley's Second Marriage—The
         Honeymoon," *The Eclectic Magazine*, LXXXVIII [New Series
         XXV], No. 4 (April, 1877), 512.   [B; excerpted from
         item 967]

[975]   Blake, Robert. "Essays on Shelley's Works. Queen Mab,"
         The Poet's Magazine, II (April, 1877), 146-149.   [C]

[976]   [Signed "Jabez."]. " *Posthumous Fragments of Margaret Nicholson*,"
         Notes and Queries, Fifth Series VII, No. 171 (April 7,
         1877), 269.   [C]

[977]   Forman, H[arry] Buxton. "Authors of Books Wanted (5th S.
         vii. 269.)," *Notes and Queries*, Fifth Series VII, No. 172
         (April 14, 1877), 299.   [C]

[978]   Leicester-Warren, J. [*sic* for J. Leicester Warren]. "[Un-
         titled, following item 978]," *Notes and Queries*, Fifth
         Series VII, No. 172 (April 14, 1877), 299.   [C]

[979]   [Signed "J.O."]. "Authors of Books Wanted (5th S. vii. 269,
         299.)," *Notes and Queries*, Fifth Series VII, No. 174
         (April 28, 1877), 339.   [T]

[980]   [Signed "Prester John"]. "Shelley's Queen Mab and Prome-
         theus Unbound," *Dublin University Magazine*, LXXXIX, No.
         dxxxiv (June, 1877), 773-779.   [C]

[981]   MacCarthy, D[enis] F[lorence]. "Shelley's 'Scenes from
         Calderon.,'" *Notes and Queries*, Fifth Series VII, No. 179
         (June 2, 1877), 421-422.   [T]

[982]   [Signed "H.B.C."]. "Authors of Books Wanted (5th S. vii.
         269, 299, 339.)," *Notes and Queries*, Fifth Series VII,
         No. 180 (June 9, 1877), 459.   [C]

[983] Forman, H[arry] Buxton. "Shelley's 'Scenes from Calderon'
       (5th S. vii. 421.)," *Notes and Queries*, Fifth Series VII,
       No. 180 (June 9, 1877), 458. [T]

[984] Dowden, Edward. "The Transcendental Movement and Litera-
       ture.," *The Contemporary Review*, XXX (July, 1877), [297]-
       318. [C; Shelley: 300-301, 306-308]

[985] [?Dowden, Edward]. "A Group of Memoirs," *The Contemporary
       Review*, XXX (July, 1877), 336-347. [R of item 967:
       341-345]

[986] [Anonymous]. "Art. V. *The Poetical Works of Percy Bysshe Shelley*.
       Edited by Harry Buxton Forman. In Four Volumes.
       Reeves and Turner.," *The London Quarterly Review*, XLVIII,
       No. xcvi (July, 1877), 376-403. [R: item 1008]

[987] Warren, J. Leicester. "Byron and Shelley in the Environs of
       Geneva during the Summer of 1816.," *Notes and Queries*,
       Fifth Series VIII, No. 184 (July 7, 1877), 1-2. [B]

[988] Warren, J. Leicester. "Byron and Shelley in the Environs of
       Geneva during the Summer of 1816. [/] (Concluded from
       p. 2.)," *Notes and Queries*, Fifth Series VIII, No. 185
       (July 14, 1877), 23-24. [B]

[989] Walker, J. L. "Casa Magni (5th S. vii. 422.)," *Notes and
       Queries*, Fifth Series VIII, No. 187 (July 28, 1877),
       77. [B]

[990] [Anonymous]. "The Text of Shelley's Poems," *The Contemporary
       Review*, XXX (August, 1877), 514-515. [T]

[991] [Signed "Thus."]. "Byron and Shelley in the Environs of
       Geneva, 1816 (5th S. viii. 1, 23.)," *Notes and Queries*,
       Fifth Series VIII, No. 189 (August 11, 1877), 115. [B]

[992] Elwes, Dudley Cary. "[Untitled, following item 991]," *Notes
       and Queries*, Fifth Series VIII, No. 189 (August 11,
       1877), 115. [B]

[993] Morse, F. Louise. "The Poetry of Shelley," *The Canadian
       Monthly and National Review*, XII, No. 3 (September, 1877),
       247-257. [C]

[994] [Signed "E.B."]. "Shelley.," *Notes and Queries*, Fifth Series
       VIII, No. 195 (September 22, 1877), 228. [C]

[995] [Anonymous]. "*The Poetical Works of Percy Bysshe Shelley*. Edited
       by Harry Buxton Forman. 4 vols. (Reeves & Turner),"
       The Athenaeum, No. 2605 (September 29, 1877), 396-400.
       [R: item 1008]

[996] Dalby, John Watson. "Percy Bysshe Shelley," *Notes and Queries*,
       Fifth Series VIII, No. 196 (September 29, 1877), 242-
       244. [R: item 1008, vols. III and IV]

[997] Forman, H[arry] Buxton. "Mr. Browning on Shelley (5th S.
       viii. 228.)," *Notes and Queries*, Fifth Series VIII,
       No. 197 (October 6, 1877), 277. [C]

[998] Rossetti, W[illiam] M[ichael]. "*The Poetical Works of Percy
       Bysshe Shelley*. Edited by Harry Buxton Forman. In Four
       Volumes. London: Reeves & Turner. 1876-1877.," *The
       Academy*, II, No. 284 (October 13, 1877), 356-357. [R:
       item 1008]

[999] Forman, H[arry] Buxton. "Mr. Forman's Shelley," *The Athen-
       aeum*, No. 2607 (October 13, 1877), 468. [C,T]

[1000] [Anonymous]. "Mr. Barnett Smith's Biography of Shelley,"
       The Contemporary Review, XXX (November, 1877), 1103-1104.
       [R: item 1011]

[1001] [Anonymous]. "Literature [/] *Shelley: a Critical Biography*.
       By George Barnett Smith. (Edinburgh, Douglas,)," *The
       Athenaeum*, No. 2612 (November 17, 1877), 621-622. [R:
       item 1011]

[1002] [Signed "Horatio."]. "Percy Bysshe Shelley: The Name
       Bysshe.," *Notes and Queries*, Fifth Series VIII, No. 206
       (December 8, 1877), 441-442. [B]

Books:

[1003] [Anonymous]. *Catalogue of the Library of Geo. A. Avery, Esq.,
       Containing an Extraordinary Collection of Shelleyana; An unusual
       Collection of the Works of William Godwin, Mary Wollstonecraft,
       Geo. H. Lewes, John Stuart Mill, Etc.* 54pp. New York:
       The Messrs. Leavitt, Auctioneers., 1877. [T: 27-35]

[1004] Armstrong, Edmund J[ohn]. *Essays and Sketches of Edmund J.
       Armstrong*. Edited by George Francis Armstrong. vii+
       306pp. London: Longmans and Co., 1877. [C: "Shelley,
       127-175]

[1005] Bradlaugh, Charles. *Jesus, Shelley, and Malthus; or, Pious
       Poverty and Heterodox Happiness*. 16pp. London: Freethought
       Publishing Company, [1877]. [C]

[1006] Browning, Elizabeth Barrett. *Letters of Elizabeth Barrett
       Browning Addressed to Richard Hengist Horne, Author of "Orion,"*

"*Gregory VII.*," "*Cosimo De' Medici,*" *Etc. With Comments on Con-temporaries.* Edited by S. R. Townshend Mayer. 2 vols. London: Richard Bentley and Son, 1877. [C: I, 188; II, 107-108]

[1007]   Doyle, Francis Hastings. *Lectures on Poetry.* ["Second Series."] viii+291pp. London: Smith, Elder, & Co., 1877. [M: 73-76]

[1008]   Forman, Harry Buxton, ed. *The Poetical Works of Percy Bysshe Shelley.* 4 vols. London: Reeves and Turner, 1876-1877. [T,C,B,; rptd.: item 1081; revised editions: items 1137,1605]

[1009]   Melbrook, Geoffrey [pseud. of George Milner], Morgan Brierly, J. E. Smith, Felix Folio [pseud. of John Page], Charles Potter, R. Gray, West Morland [pseud. of J. H. Nodal], W. E. A. Axon. "Shelley and the Sky-lark," *Papers of the Manchester Literary Club, III* [vi+ 308pp. Manchester: Abel Heywood and Sons], [121]-140. [C; rptd.: item 1010]

[1010]   Milner, George, Morgan Brierly, John Page, Charles Potter, J. H. Nodal, W. E. A. Axon, and others [i.e., J. E. Smith, R. Gray]. *Shelley and the Skylark.* 22pp. Man-chester: Abel Heywood, 1877. [C; rptd. from item 1009]

[1011]   Smith, George Barnett. *Shelley* [/] *A Critical Biography.* x+ 249pp. Edinburgh: David Douglas, 1877. [B,C; revised and expanded from items 916, 917]

[1012]   Stoddard, Richard Henry. *Anecdote Biography of Percy Bysshe Shelley.* ["Sans Souci Series."] xxii+290pp. New York: Scribner, Armstrong and Company, 1877. [B]

1878

Periodicals:

[1013]   Rossetti, W[illiam] M[ichael]. "*Shelley: a Critical Biography.* By. George Barnett Smith. (Edinburgh: Douglas, 1877.)," *The Academy*, XIII, No. 298 (January 19, 1878), 48-49. [R: item 1011]

[1014]   Rossetti, William Michael. "Shelley's Life and Writings. Two Lectures. By William Michael Rossetti. Lecture I.," *Dublin University Magazine*, XCI [New Series I] (Febru-ary, 1878), 138-155. [C,B]

[1015]   Rossetti, William Michael. "Shelley's Life and Writings.
         Two Lectures, By William Michael Rossetti. Lecture
         II.," *Dublin University Magazine*, XCI [New Series I]
         (March, 1878), 262-277. [C]

[1016]   Gosse, Edmund W[illiam]. "*The Complete Poetical Works of
         Percy Bysshe Shelley.* The Text Carefully revised, with
         Notes and a Memoir by William Michael Rossetti. 3
         volumes. (London: E. Moxon & Sons, 1878)," *The
         Academy*, XIII, No. 308 (March 30, 1878), 273. [R:
         item 1033]

[1017]   [Thomson, James "B.V."]. "The Smoke Room Table. [/] *The
         Complete Poetical Works of Percy Bysshe Shelley. The Text care-
         fully revised, with Notes and a Memoir, by William Michael Ros-
         setti. In three volumes.* London: E. Moxon, Son, and Co.,
         1878.," *Cope's Tobacco Plant. A Monthly Periodical, Interestin*
         to the Manufacturer, the Dealer, and the Smoker., II, No. 97
         (April, 1878), 166. [R: item 1033; rptd.: item 1205]

[1018]   Forman, H[arry] Buxton. "Shelley's 'Oedipus Tyrannus, or
         Swellfoot the Tyrant.,'" *Notes and Queries*, Fifth Series
         IX, No. 229 (May 18, 1878), 381. [T,C]

[1019]   Bouchier, Jonathan. "Shelley's Place in Literature (5th S
         vi. 341, 361, 392, 478, 517; vii. 189.)," *Notes and
         Queries*, Fifth Series IX, No. 230 (May 25, 1878), 415-
         416. [C]

[1020]   Garnett, Richard. "Shelley's Last Days," *The Fortnightly
         Review*, New Series XXIII [whole number XXIX], No.
         cxxxviii (June 1, 1878), 850-866. [R: item 1037; T]

[1021]   Trelawny, E[dward] J[ohn]. "Shelley's Last Days. (A
         Reply to R. Garnett's Article in the 'Fortnightly.'),"
         The Athenaeum, No. 2649 (August 3, 1878), 144. [C;
         rptd.: item 1023]

[1022]   [Anonymous]. "Notes," *The Nation*, XXVII, No. 686 (August
         22, 1878), 115-117. [M: 117]

[1023]   Trelawny, J. W. [*sic* for Edward John]. "Shelley's Last
         Days," *The Eclectic Magazine*, XCI [New Series XXVIII],
         No. 5 (October, 1878), 511-512. [C; rptd. from item
         1021]

[1024]   [Anonymous]. "Literature. [/] *Shelley*. By John Addington
         Symonds. *English Men of Letters*. (Macmillan & Co.)," *The
         Athenaeum*, No. 2662 (November 2, 1878), 553. [R: item
         1036]

[1025]   Gosse, Edmund W[illiam]. "*Shelley*. By John Addington
          Symonds. English Men of Letters. Macmillan and Co.,"
          The Academy, XIV, No. 342 (November 23, 1878), 488-489.
          [R: item 1036]

[1026]   Townsend, Walter. "Shelley," [*Rose Belford's*] *Canadian Monthly
          and National Review*, XIV [New Series I] (December, 1878),
          673-688. [C]

[1027]   Bayne, Thomas. "English Men of Letters. Shelley.," *The
          St. James Magazine*, XXXIV [*sic*, though given as "43" in
          all other citations, and so listed in Poole] (December,
          1878), 1111-1118. [R: item 1036]

[1028]   [Woodberry, George Edward]. "Percy Bysshe Shelley," *The
          Nation*, XXVII, No. 704 (December 26, 1878), 401-402.
          [R: item 1036; rptd.: items 1511, 1768]

Books:

[1029]   Clarke, Charles, and Mary Cowden Clarke. *Recollections of
          Writers*. viii+347pp. London: Sampson Low, Marston,
          Searle & Rivington, 1878. [M: 19, 25-26, 28, 150-153,
          195-196]

[1030]   Dowden, Edward. *Studies in Literature* [/] *1789-1877*. viii+
          523pp. London: C. Kegan Paul & Co., 1878. [C: 28-35,
          60-66, 101-103, 112-115]

[1031]   Kemble, Frances Anne. *Records of a Girlhood*. 3 vols. London:
          Richard Bentley and Son, 1878. [C: II, 325-326; III,
          172, 175]

[1032]   Rossetti, William Michael. *Lives of Famous Poets*. xii+406pp.
          London: E. Moxon, Son, & Co., 1878. [B: "Percy
          Bysshe Shelley," (309)-328]

[1033]   Rossetti, William Michael, ed. *The Complete Poetical Works of
          Percy Bysshe Shelley*. *The Text carefully revised with Notes and*
          [/] *A Memoir*. 3 vols. London: E. Moxon, Son, and Co.,
          1878. [T,C,B; revised edition of item 839]

[1034]   Scott, R. Pickett. *The Place of Shelley Among the English Poets
          of His Time*. 63pp. Cambridge, Eng.: Deighton, Bell, and
          Co., 1878. [C]

[1035]   Selkirk, J. B. [pseud. of James Bucham Brown]. *Ethics and
          Aesthetics of Modern Poetry*. 237pp. London: Smith, Elder,
          & Co., 1878. [C: 15-18, 182-187; rptd. from item 896]

[1036]   Symonds, John Addington. *Shelley*. ["English Men of
          Letters" Series]. viii+188pp. London: Macmillan
          and Co., 1878. [B; revised edition: item 1382]

[1037]   Trelawny, Edward John. *Records of Shelley, Byron and the Author*
          2 vols. London: Basil Montagu Pickering. [B]

[1038]   Walpole, Spencer. *A History of England from the Conclusion of the
          Great War in 1815*. 2 vols. London: Longmans, Green, and
          Co., 1878. [C: 364-368]

                              1879

Periodicals:

[1039]   [Signed "Nisus." and "Ed. Nation."]. "Shelley's Religion.
          [letter to the editor and reply]," *The Nation*, XXVIII,
          No. 706 (January 9, 1879), 30-31. [C]

[1040]   [Anonymous]. "Shelley," *The Literary World*, X, No. 4 (Febru-
          ary 15, 1879), 52. [R: item 1036, and an edition of
          the minor poems]

[1041]   Stephen, Leslie. "Hours in a Library. No. XX.—Godwin
          and Shelley," *Cornhill Magazine*, XXXIX, No. 231 (March,
          1879), 281-302. [C; rptd.: items 1043, 1044, 1045,
          1854]

[1042]   White, W[illiam] Hale. "Notes on Shelley's Birthplace,"
          Macmillan's Magazine, XXXIX, No. 233 (March, 1879), 461-
          465. [B; rptd.: items 2042, 2092]

[1043]   Stephen, Leslie. "Godwin and Shelley," *Appleton's Journal*,
          XXI [New Series VI], No. 34 (April, 1879), 344-356.
          [C; rptd. from item 1041]

[1044]   Stephen, Leslie. "Godwin and Shelley," *Littell's Living Age*,
          CXLI, No. 1817 (April 12, 1879), 67-80. [C; rptd.
          from item 1041]

[1045]   Stephen, Leslie. "Godwin and Shelley," *The Eclectic Magazine*
          XCII, [New Series XXIX], No. 5 (May, 1879), 532-547.
          [C; rptd. from item 1041]

[1046]   Shairp, J[ohn] C[ampbell]. "Shelley as a Lyric Poet,"
          Fraser's Magazine, New Series [whole number C], No. cxv
          [whole number dxcv] (July, 1879), 38-53. [C; rptd.:
          item 1107]

[1047]   Shirley [pseud. of John Skelton].   "Bibliomania in 1879;
         A Chat About Rare Books," *Fraser's Magazine*, New Series
         XX [whole number C], No. cxv [whole number dxcv]
         (July, 1879), 71-88.   [T,C: 81-87]

Books:

[1048]   Bagehot, Walter.   *Literary Studies* [/] *By the Late Walter Bagehot.*
         [/] With a Prefatory Memoir [/] Edited by Richard Holt
         Hutton.   2 vols.   London: Longmans, Green, and Co.,
         1879.   [C: "Percy Bysshe Shelley. [/] (1856.)," I,
         75-125; rptd. from item 614]

[1049]   Carr, J. Comyns.   *Essays on Art.*   253pp.   London: Smith,
         Elder, & Co., 1879.   [C: "The Artistic Spirit in Modern
         English Poetry.," (3)-34; Shelley: 12-19; rptd. from
         item 3254]

[1050]   Forman, Harry Buxton, ed.   *Notes on Sculpture in Rome and Florence*
         [/] *Together with a Lucianic Fragment and a Criticism of Peacock's*
         Poem "Rhododaphne" by Percy Bysshe Shelley.   Edited by Harry
         Buxton Forman.   viii+61pp.   London: printed for private
         distribution, 1879.   [T]

[1051]   Jones, Ebenezer.   *Studies of Sensation and Event* [/] *Poems* [/] by
         Ebenezer Jones [/] Edited Prefaced and Annotated by
         Richard Herne Shepherd with Memorial Notices of the
         Author by Sumner Jones and William James Linton.
         lxxxiv+207pp.   London: Pickering and Co., 1879.   [M:
         xxx, xliv]

[1052]   Vita, Victor M.   *Poems of the Future.*   viii+192pp.   London:
         Arthur H. Moxon, 1879.   [Fictionalized biographical
         poem, "Kindred Spirits"]

                              1880

Periodicals:

[1053]   Forman, H[arry] Buxton.   "The Improvvisatore Sgricci in
         Relation to Shelley," *The Gentleman's Magazine*, New
         Series XXIV [whole number CCXLVIII; misprinted on
         title page as CCXLVI], No. 1789 (January, 1880),
         115-123.   [B,C]

[1054]   Blind, Mathilde.   "Trelawny on Byron and Shelley.," *The*
         Whitehall Review, [?] (January, 1880), [?p].   [?R]

[1055]　[Thomson, James "B.V."].　"Our Smoke Room Table. [/]
　　　　English Men of Letters. Edited by John Morley. London:
　　　　Macmillan and Co. 1878-1879. [/] IX. Shelley, by
　　　　John Addington Symonds. (1878.)," *Cope's Tobacco Plant*,
　　　　II, No. 119 (February, 1880), 444. [R: item 1036;
　　　　rptd.: 1205, 1695]

[1056]　Myers, Frederic W[illiam] H[enry].　"Stanzas on Shelley,"
　　　　Macmillan's Magazine, XLI, No. 245 (March, 1880), 391-
　　　　392. [C: Fifty-six line poem]

[1057]　[Signed "A.B."].　"M. Schoeré's Articles on Shelley,"
　　　　Notes and Queries, Sixth Series I, No. 13 (March 27,
　　　　1880), 255. [M; the articles which "A.B." seeks to
　　　　identify are: Édouard Schuré, "Le Poète Panthéiste de
　　　　L'Angleterre," *Revue des Deux Mondes*, Troisième Période,
　　　　Tome XIX, 3e livraison (3rd S. XIX. No. 3) (February,
　　　　1877), (537)-569; and, Édouard Schuré, "Le Poète
　　　　Panthéiste de L'Angleterre (II.)," *Revue des Deux Mondes*,
　　　　Troisième Période, Tome XIX, 4e livraison (3rd S.
　　　　XIX. No. 4) (March, 1877), (745)-779]

[1058]　Forman, H[arry] B[uxton].　"M. Schoeré's Articles on
　　　　Shelley (6th S. i. 255.)," *Notes and Queries*, Sixth
　　　　Series I, No. 15 (April 10, 1880), 307. [M: gives
　　　　location of articles as above in item 1057]

[1059]　Forman, Harry Buxton.　"Shelley's Life near Spezzia, His
　　　　Death and Burials," *Macmillan's Magazine*, XLII, No. 247
　　　　(May, 1880), 43-58. [B]

[1060]　Royce, Josiah.　"Shelley and the Revolution," *The Californian*
　　　　I, No. 6 (June, 1880), 543-553. [C]

[1061]　Brooke, Stopford A[ugustus].　"Some Thoughts on Shelley,"
　　　　Macmillan's Magazine, XLII, No. 248 (June, 1880), 124-
　　　　135. [C; rptd.: items 1064, 1065]

[1062]　Platt, William.　"M. Schoeré's Articles on Shelley. (6th
　　　　S. i. 255, 307).," *Notes and Queries*, Sixth Series I,
　　　　No. 25 (June 19, 1880), 505. [M]

[1063]　[Brownell, W. C.].　"Notes," *The Nation*, XXXI, No. 783
　　　　(July 1, 1880), 11-14. [M: 12]

[1064]　Brooke, Stopford A[ugustus].　"Some Thoughts on Shelley,"
　　　　Appleton's Journal, XXIV [New Series IX], No. 50 (August
　　　　1880), 119-127. [C; rptd. from item 1061]

[1065]　Brooke, Stopford A[ugustus].　"Some Thoughts on Shelley,"
　　　　The Eclectic Magazine, XCV [New Series XXXII], No. 2
　　　　(August, 1880), 217-227. [C; rptd. from item 1061]

[1066]   [Anonymous]. "A Study of Shelley," *The Saturday Review of
         Politics, Literature, Science, and Art*, 50, No. 1,294
         (August 14, 1880), 208-209. [R: item 1084]

[1067]   [Anonymous]. "'A Study of Shelley,'" *The Pall Mall Gazette*,
         XXXII, No. 4835 (August 21, 1880), 11-12. [R: item
         1084]

[1068]   Ruskin, John. "Fiction—Fair and Foul. III. [Byron.]
         (brackets in original)," *The Nineteenth Century*, VIII,
         No. xliii (September, 1880), 394-410. [C; M: 395,
         407; rptd.: item 1528]

[1069]   [Anonymous]. " *The Prose Works of Percy Bysshe Shelley*. Edited
         by Henry Buxton Forman. 4 vols. (Reeves & Turner.),"
         The Athenaeum, No. 2758 (September 4, 1880), 297-299.
         [R: item 1079]

[1070]   [Anonymous]. "News and Notes," *The Literary World*, XI,
         No. 19 (September 11, 1880), 313-314. [R of item
         1079: 314; excerpted from item 1069]

[1071]   Bower, George Spencer. "The Philosophical Element in
         Shelley," *The Journal of Speculative Philosophy*, XIV,
         No. 4 (October, 1880), 421-454. [C]

*[1072] Vecchi, A[ugusto] V[ittorio]. "The Eagle's Nest of the
         Italian Navy, Spezzia," *Minerva* [Rome], No. II
         (October, 1880), 447-458. [M]

[1073]   [Anonymous]. "Literary Gossip.," *The Athenaeum*, No. 2768
         (November 13, 1880), 643. [T]

[1074]   Forman, H[arry] Buxton. "A Copy of 'Queen Mab.," *The
         Athenaeum*, No. 2769 (November 20, 1880), 675. [T]

[1075]   Forman, H[arry] Buxton. "A Copy of 'Queen Mab.," *The
         Athenaeum*, No. 2771 (December 4, 1880), 745. [T]

[1076]   [Woodberry, George Edward]. "*Coleridge, Shelley, Goethe.*
         Biographic aesthetic studies. By George H. Calvert.
         (Boston: Lee & Shepard.)," *The Nation*, XXXI, No. 808
         (December 23, 1880), 450. [R: item 1078]

Books:

[1077]   Brooke, Stopford [Augustus]. *English Literature*. vi+[210]pp.
         London: Macmillan and Co., 1880. [C: 178-181]

[1078]   Calvert, George H. *Coleridge, Shelley, Goethe.* 297pp.
          Boston: Lee and Shepard, 1880. [C: "Shelley.,"
          (125)-255]

[1079]   Forman, Harry Buxton, ed. *The Prose Works of Percy Bysshe
          Shelley.* 4 vols. London: Reeves and Turner, 1880.
          [T,C; rptd.: item 1081]

[1080]   [Forman, Harry Buxton, ed.]. *Shelley Pedigree. From the
          Records of the College of Arms.* 8pp. London: privately
          printed [Mitchell and Hughes], 1880. [B]

[1081]   Forman, Harry Buxton, ed. *The Works of Percy Bysshe Shelley
          in Verse and Prose. Edited, with Prefaces, Notes, and Appen-
          dices, by Harry Buxton Forman.* 8 vols. London: Reeves
          and Turner, 1880. [T,C,B; rptd. from items 1008,
          1079]

[1082]   Kingsley, Charles. *The Works of Charles Kingsley. Volume XX.
          Literary and General Lectures and Essays.* x+420pp. London:
          Macmillan and Co., 1880. [C: "Thoughts on Shelley
          and Byron.," (35)-58; rptd. from item 582]

[1083]   Myers, Frederic W[illiam] H[enry]. *The English Poets* [Edited
          by Thomas Humphry Ward] *Selections* [/] *With Critical Intro-
          ductions* [/] *By Various Writers* [/] *And a General Introduction
          by Matthew Arnold.* 4 vols. London: Macmillan and Co.,
          1880. [C: Frederic William Henry Myers, "Percy Bysshe
          Shelley.," IV, (348)-356; M: Matthew Arnold, "Intro-
          duction," (xvii)-xlvii; rptd.: item 1412]

[1084]   Todhunter, John. *A Study of Shelley.* vi+293pp. London:
          C. Kegan Paul & Co., 1880. [C]

                              1881

Periodicals:

[1085]   Forman, H[arry] Buxton. "Indentures Relating to the
          Shelley Family," *Notes and Queries*, Sixth Series III,
          No. 54 (January 8, 1881), 24-25. [B]

[1086]   [Anonymous]. "The Pedigree of Shelley," *The Antiquary*, III
          (February, 1881), 53-55. [R: item 1081]

[1087]   Seaton, R[obert] C[ooper]. "Shelley," *Temple Bar*, LXI
          (February, 1881), 218-240. [C]

                             [108]

[1088]   Marshall, George W.   "Correspondence.   [/]   The Pedigree
         of Shelley," *The Antiquary*, III (March, 1881), 141.   [B]

[1089]   [Anonymous].   "The Contributor's Club," *The Atlantic Monthly*,
         XLVII, No. cclxxxi (March, 1881), 433-446.   [C: 441-
         442]

[1090]   Arnold, Matthew.   "Byron.," *Macmillan's Magazine*, XLIII,
         No. 257 (March, 1881), 367-377.   [C: 367, 377; rptd: 1412]

[1091]   Rossetti, William M[ichael].   "The Wives of Poets," *The
         Atlantic Monthly*, XLVII, No. cclxxxii (April, 1881),
         518-525.   [B: 521-522]

[1092]   Drury, B. P.   "Shelley.," *The Western* [St. Louis], New
         Series VII, No. 3 (May, 1881), 215-218.   [C]

[1093]   I[ngleby], C[lement] M[ansfield].   "Shelley's Place in
         English Literature (5th S. vi. 341, 361, 392, 478,
         517; vii. 189; ix. 415).," *Notes and Queries*, Sixth
         Series IV, No. 89 (September 10, 1881), 211.   [C]

[1094]   Thomson, James ('B.V.').   "Notes on the Structure of
         Shelley's 'Prometheus Unound.' I.," *The Athenaeum*,
         No. 2812 (September 17, 1881), 370-371.   [C; rptd.:
         item 1205]

[1095]   Thomson, James ('B.V.').   "Notes on the Structure of
         Shelley's 'Prometheus Unbound.' II.," *The Athenaeum*,
         No. 2813 (September 24, 1881), 400-401.   [C; rptd.:
         item 1205]

[1096]   I[ngleby], C[lement] M[ansfield].   "Shelley and Schumann:
         a Parallel," *Notes and Queries*, Sixth Series IV, No. 91
         (September 24, 1881), 246.   [C]

[1097]   Parkes, Kineton.   "Shelley's Essays," *The Institute Magazine*,
         Part XLII (October, 1881), [18]-20.   [C]

[1098]   Thomson, James ('B.V.').   "Notes on the Structure of
         Shelley's 'Prometheus Unbound.' III.," *The Athenaeum*,
         No. 2815 (October 8, 1881), 464-465.   [C; rptd.:
         item 1205]

[1099]   I[ngleby], C[lement] M[ansfield].   "A Passage in Shelley's
         'Prometheus Unbound," Act II. Sc. IV.   (1st S. ix.
         351, 481; x. 37).,   *Notes and Queries*, Sixth Series IV,
         No. 96 (October 29, 1881), 345-346.   [C]

[1100]   [Signed "H.E.W."].   "Edward John Trelawny," *Temple Bar*,
         LXIII (November, 1881), 325-342.   [B]

[1101]   Thomson, James ('B.V.'). "Notes on the Structure of
          Shelley's 'Prometheus Unbound.' IV.," *The Athenaeum*,
          No. 2819 (November 5, 1881), 597-598. [C; rptd.:
          item 1205]

[1102]   Thomson, James ('B.V.'). "Notes on the Structure of
          Shelley's 'Prometheus Unbound.' (Conclusion.),"
          The Athenaeum, No. 2821 (November 19, 1881), 666-
          667. [C; rptd.: item 1205]

Books:

[1103]   Arnold, Matthew. *Poetry of Byron.* xxxvi+276pp. London:
          Macmillan and Co., 1881. [C:"Preface," (vii)-xxxi;
          M: (vii)-viii, xxxi]

[1104]   Carlyle, Thomas. *Reminscences.* Edited by James Anthony
          Froude. viii+352pp. New York: Harper & Brothers,
          1881. [M: 329]

[1105]   Fields, James T. *Biographical Notes and Personal Sketches* [/]
          *with Unpublished Fragments and Tributes from Men and Women
          of Letters.* v+275pp. Boston: Houghton, Mifflin and
          Company, 1881. [B: 64-65]

[1106]   Kinsley, William W. *Views on Vexed Questions.* 380pp.
          Philadelphia: J. B. Lippincott & Co., 1881. [C:
          "Shelley.," 255-302; rptd. from items 949, 950]

[1107]   Shairp, John Campbell. *Aspects of Poetry* [/] *Being Lectures
          Delivered at Oxford.* xi+464pp. Oxford: At the Clarendon
          Press, 1881. [C: "Shelley as a Lyric Poet.," (227)-
          255; rptd. from item 1046]

[1108]   Southey, Robert. *The Correspondence of Robert Southey with
          Caroline Bowles. To Which Are Added: Correspondence with
          Shelley, and Southey's Dreams.* Edited with an Introduc-
          tion by Edward Dowden. xxxii+385pp. Dublin: Hodges,
          Figgis, & Co., 1881 [M: 27-28, 72, 76, 136; T:
          "Correspondence with Shelley.," (357)-366]

[1109]   Wilde, Oscar. *Poems.* ix+236pp. London: David Bogue,
          1881. [C: "The Grave of Shelley.," a sonnet, 161]

1882

Periodicals:

[1110]   [Anonymous]. "Mrs. Shelley at Pisa," *Temple Bar*, LXIV

(January, 1882), 58-65. [B; rptd.: item 1113]

[1111] O'Conor, William A. "The Prometheus of Æschylus and of
        Shelley," *The Manchester Quarterly*, I, No. i (January,
        1882), 29-45. [C; rptd.: items 1141, 1473]

[1112] Shelley, Jane [Gibson, Lady]. "A Letter to the Editor.
        II.," *Temple Bar*, LXIV, (February, 1882), 319-320.
        [B]

[1113] [Anonymous]. "Mrs. Shelley at Pisa," *Littell's Living Age*,
        CLII, No. 1964 (February 11, 1882), 374-378. [B;
        rptd. from item 1110]

[1114] [Shairp, John Campbell]. "Art. III. —*The English Poets:
        Selections, with Critical Introductions by various Writers,
        and a General Introduction by Matthew Arnold*. Edited by
        Thomas Humphry Ward, M.A., late Fellow of Brasenose
        College, Oxford. 4 vols. London, 1880.," *The Quarterly
        Review*, CLIII, No. 306 (April, 1882), 431-463. [R:
        item 1083; Shelley: 457-459]

[1115] Austin, Alfred. "Shelley's House at Sant'Erenzo," *The
        Athenaeum*, No. 2444 (April 29, 1882), 538. [B]

[1116] Greene, George A. "Shelley's House at San Terenzo,"*The
        Athenaeum*, No. 2447 (May 20, 1882), 635. [B]

[1117] Cesaresco, Evelyn Martinengo. "[Untitled, following item
        1116]," *The Athenaeum*, No. 2447 (May 20, 1882), 635.
        [B]

[1118] Cesaresco, Evelyn Martinengo. "Shelley's House at San
        Terenzo," *The Athenaeum*, No. 2449 (June 3, 1882), 699.
        [B]

[1119] Edgcumbe, Richard. "Shelley's Ode to Mont Blanc," *Notes
        and Queries*, Sixth Series V, No. 128 (June 10, 1882),
        443. [T]

[1120] Enthoven, Arthur L. "Shelley's House at San Terenzio,"
        The Athenaeum, No. 2451 (June 27, 1882), 765. [B]

[1121] Greene, George A. "Shelley's House at San Terenzo,"
        The Athenaeum, No. 2452 (June 24, 1882), 796. [B]

[1122] Rossetti, W[illiam] M[ichael]. "Talks with Trelawny.,"
        The Athenaeum, No. 2855 (July 15, 1882), 78-79. [B;
        first of three parts]

[1123]   Rossetti, W[illiam] M[ichael].   "Talks with Trelawny. II.,
          The Athenaeum, No. 2857 (July 29, 1882), 144-145.   [B;
          second of three parts]

[1124]   Rossetti, W[illiam] M[ichael].   "Talks with Trelawny.
          III.," *The Athenaeum*, No. 2858 (August 5, 1882), 176-
          177.   [B; third of three parts]

[1125]   [Signed "Consideratis Considerandis"].   "Shelley's 'Mont
          Blanc' (6th S. v. 443).," *Notes and Queries*, Sixth Serie
          VI, No. 136 (August 5, 1882), 112.   [T]

[1126]   Edgcumbe, Richard.   "Shelley's 'Mont Blanc' (6th S. v.
          443; vi. 112).," *Notes and Queries*, Sixth Series VI,
          No. 137 (August 12, 1882), 139.   [T]

[1127]   Caine, T[homas] Hall.   "*The Poetical Works of Percy Bysshe
          Shelley*. Edited by Harry Buxton Forman.   In 2 vols.
          (Reeves & Turner.)," *The Academy*, XXII, No. 542
          (September 23, 1882), 213-214.   [R: item 1137; rptd.:
          item 1164]

[1128]   [Reeve, Henry].   "Art. VI. —*Shelley and Mary*.   A Collection
          of Letters and Documents of Biographical Character,
          in the possession of Sir Percy and Lady Shelley, for
          private circulation only.   3 vols.   8vo.   1882.,"
          Edinburgh Review, CLVI, No. cccxx (October, 1882), 472-
          507.   [R: item 1145; rptd.: item 1130]

[1129]   Salt, Henry S[tephens].   "Shelley as a Teacher," *Temple
          Bar*, LXVI (November, 1882), 365-377.   [C; rptd.:
          item 1426]

[1130]   [Reeve, Henry].   "Shelley and Mary," *Littell's Living Age*,
          CLV, No. 2004 (November 18, 1882), 387-406.   [R:
          item 1145; rptd. from item 1128]

[1131]   [Anonymous].   "The Select Letters of Shelley," *The Spectator*,
          LV, No. 2839 (November 25, 1882), 1510-1511.   [R:
          item 1138]

[1132]   Minto, William.   "*Select Letters of Percy Bysshe Shelley*, ed.
          Richard Garnett.   (Kegan Paul, Trench & Co.)," *The
          Academy*, XXII, No. 554 (December 16, 1882), 426.   [R:
          item 1138]

[1133]   [Anonymous].   "Shelley's Letters," *The Saturday Review*, LIV,
          No. 1,418 (December 30, 1882), 862-863.   [R: item
          1138]

Books:

[1134] Austin, Alfred. *Soliloquies in Song.* xii+158pp. London: Macmillan and Co., 1882. [Sixty-three line poem: "Shelley's Death," 142-145]

[1135] Cotterill, Henry Bernard. *An Introduction to the Study of Poetry.* viii+328pp. London: K. Paul, Trench and Co., 1882. [C: 298-328]

[1136] Edgcumbe, Richard. *Edward Trelawny,* [/] *A Biographical Sketch.* 36pp. Plymouth: W. H. Luke, 1882. [B]

[1137] Forman, Harry Buxton, ed. *The Poetical Works of Percy Bysshe Shelley* [/] *Given from His Own Editions and Other Authentic Sources* [/] *Collated with many Manuscripts and with all Editions of Authority* [/] *Together with Prefaces and Notes* [/] *His Poetical Translations and Fragments* [/] *and an Appendix of Juvenilia.* 2 vols. London: Reeves and Turner, 1882. [T,C; revised edition of item 1008]

[1138] Garnett, Richard, ed. *Select Letters of Percy Bysshe Shelley* [/] Edited with an Introduction by Richard Garnett. xix+ 255pp. London: Kegan Paul, Trench, & Co., 1882. [T, C]

[1139] Macdonald, George. *Orts.* vi+312pp. London: Sampson Low, Marston, Searle, & Rivington, 1882. [C: "Shelley.," (264)-281; published with the title *The Imagination, and Other Essays,* Boston and New York, 1883]

*[1140] Markley, John T. *Songs of Humanity and Progress: a Collection of Lyrics, Contributed to Various Publications.* [?]pp. Eastbourne: H. Holloway, 1882. [C: "Shelley and Longfellow," a prose study]

*[1141] O'Conor, William A. "The Prometheus of Æschylus and of Shelley," *Papers of the Manchester Literary Club* [Manchester: Abel Heywood & Son], VIII (1882), [C; rptd. from item 1111]

[1142] Oliphant, [Margaret O. W.]. *The Literary History of England* [/] *In the End of the Eighteenth Century and Beginning of the Nineteenth Century.* 3 vols. London: Macmillan and Co., 1882. [C: "Byron—Shelley.," III, 44-94; "Shelley— Byron.," III, 95-132]

[1143] Pfeiffer, Emily [Jane]. *Under the Aspens* [/] *Lyrical and Dramatic.* x+311pp. London: Kegan Paul, Trench & Co., 1882. [C: two sonnets, "Shelley.," 115-116]

[1144]   Scherr, J. *A History of English Literature*. Translated from the
         German by M. V. viii+312pp. London: Sampson Low,
         Marston, Searle, & Rivington, 1882. [C: "Shelley,"
         244-254]

[1145]   Shelley, Jane [Gibson, Lady], and [Sir] Percy Florence
         Shelley, eds. *Shelley and Mary*. 4 vols. [London:]
         for private circulation only, [1882]. [T,B]

                              1883

Periodicals:

[1146]   [Anonymous]. "Art. I.—Shelley: his Friends and Critics.
         [/] 1. *Records of Shelley, Byron, and the Author*. By Edward
         John Trelawny. London: Basil Montague Pickering.
         1878. [/] 2. *Aspects of Poetry; being Lectures delivered at
         Oxford*. By John Campbell Shairp, LL.D. Oxford: Claren-
         don Press. 1881.," *The Westminster Review*, CXIX [New
         Series LXIII], No. ccxxxv [New Series i] (January,
         1883), [1]-54. [R: items 1037, 1107]

[1147]   Salt, Henry S[tephens]. "On Certain Lyric Poets, and their
         Critics," *Temple Bar*, LXVII (January, 1883), 53-59. [C]

[1148]   [Anonymous]. "New English Books," *The Literary World*, XIV,
         No. 3 (February 10, 1883), 47. [M]

[1149]   [Anonymous]. "Shelley's Poetical Works," *The Saturday Review*,
         LV, No. 1,425 (February 17, 1883), 217-218. [R: item
         1137]

[1150]   [Anonymous]. "Selected Letters of Shelley," *The Literary
         World*, XIV, No. 7 (April 7, 1883), 103-104. [R: item
         1138]

[1151]   [Signed "C.H."]. "Adonais.," *New Church Magazine*, II, No. 17
         (May, 1883), 224-233. [C]

[1152]   [Anonymous]. "Keats and Shelley," *To-Day: A Monthly Gathering
         of Bold Thoughts*, I, No. 2 (June, 1883), 188-206. [C]

[1153]   [Abraham, Hayward]. "Art. III. —*The Real Lord Byron: New
         Views of the Poet's Life*. By John Cordy Jeaffreson....
         2 vols. London, 1883.," *The Quarterly Review*, CLVI,
         No. 311 (July, 1883), 90-131. [R: item 1167; Shelley:
         115-116]

                              [114]

[1154] Froude, J[ames] A[nthony]. "A Leaf from the Real Life of
        Lord Byron," *The Nineteenth Century*, XIV, No. 78 (August,
        1883), 228-242. [B]

[1155] [Woodberry, George Edward]. "Shelley's Select Letters,"
        The Nation, XXXVII, No. 944 (August 2, 1883), 100-101.
        [R: item 1137; revised and rptd.: items 1511, 1768]

[1156] Walford, E. "An Essay by Shelley," *Notes and Queries*, Sixth
        Series VIII, No. 188 (August 4, 1883), 85. [T,C]

[1157] Jeaffreson, John Cordy. "Jane Clermont and the Shelleys.,"
        The Athenaeum, No. 2914 (September 1, 1883), 273. [B]

[1158] Jeaffreson, John Cordy. "The Other Side of Mr. Froude's
        'Leaf from the Real Life of Byron,' I.," *The Athenaeum*,
        No. 2914 (September 1, 1883), 273-275. [B]

[1159] Prideaux, W. F. "Shelley: a Poliad.," *Notes and Queries*,
        Sixth Series VIII, No. 194 (September 15, 1883), 205.
        [C]

[1160] Jeaffreson, John Cordy. "The Other Side of Mr. Froude's
        'Leaf from the Real Life of Byron.' II.," *The Athenaeum*,
        No. 2917 (September 22, 1883), 366. [B]

[1161] [Signed "W.W."]. "Essay by Shelley (6th S. viii. 85).,"
        Notes and Queries, Sixth Series VIII, No. 195 (September
        22, 1883), 237. [T]

[1162] Forman, H[arry] Buxton. "[Untitled, following item 1161],"
        Notes and Queries, Sixth Series VIII, No. 195 (September
        22, 1883), 237. [T]

[1163] Hughes, T. Cann. "Vegetarianism.," *Notes and Queries*, Sixth
        Series VIII, No. 208 (December 22, 1883), 496. [M]

Books:

[1164] Caine, T[homas] Hall. *Cobwebs of Criticism. A Review of the
        First Reviewers of the 'Lake,' 'Satanic,' and 'Cockney' Schools.*
        xxiv+266pp. London: Elliot Stock, 1883. [C: "Shel-
        ley.," (191)-231; rptd. from item 1127]

[1165] Dennis, John. *Heroes of English Literature.* [/] *English Poets.*
        [/] *A Book for Young Readers.* vii+406pp. London: Society
        for Promoting Christian Knowledge, 1883. [C: 373-387]

[1166] Houstoun, Mrs. [Matilda C.]. *A Woman's Memories of World-Known
        Men.* 2 vols. London: F. V. White and Co., 1883. [B:
        I, 98-108]

[1167]   Jeaffreson, John Cordy.   *The Real Lord Byron* [/] *New Views of the*
         Poet's Life.   2 vols.   London: Hurst and Blackett, 1883.
         [B: II, 4-211]

[1168]   Lanier, Sidney.   *The English Novel and the Principle of Its*
         Development.   293pp.   New York: Charles Scribner's Sons,
         1883.   [C; 95-106]

[1169]   Whipple, Edwin P[ercy].   *Literature and Life.*   344pp.   Boston
         Houghton, Mifflin and Company.   [M: 112; rptd. from
         item 526]

*[1170] Williams, Howard.   *The Ethics of Diet. A Catena of Authorities*
         Deprecatory of the Practice of Flesh-Eating.   xiii+336pp.
         London: I. Pitman, John Heywood, 1883.   [?M]

                              1884

Periodicals:

[1171]   Axon, William E.   "Vegetarianism.   (6th S. viii. 496.),"
         Notes and Queries, Sixth Series IX, No. 211 (January 12,
         1884), 30.   [M]

[1172]   Ward, C[harles] A.   "[Untitled, following item 1171]," *Note*
         and Queries, Sixth Series IX, No. 211 (January 12, 1884)
         30-31.   [M]

[1173]   Buckley, W. E.   "[Untitled, following item 1172]," *Notes an*
         Queries, Sixth Series IX, No. 211 (January 12, 1884),
         31.   [M]

[1174]   Forman, H[arry] Buxton.   "[Untitled, following item 1173],
         Notes and Queries, Sixth Series IX, No. 211 (January 12,
         1884), 31.   [M]

[1175]   Scherren, H.   "[Untitled, following item 1174]," *Notes and*
         Queries, Sixth Series IX, No. 211 (January 12, 1884),
         31.   [M]

[1176]   Hibbert, James.   "[Untitled, following item 1175]," *Notes*
         and Queries, Sixth Series IX, No. 211 (January 12, 1884)
         31.   [M]

[1177]   Peet, W[illia]m H.   "[Untitled, following item 1176]," *Note*
         and Queries, Sixth Series IX, No. 211 (January 12, 1884)
         31-32.   [M]

[1178]   Marshall, Edward H.   "[Untitled, following item 1177],"
         Notes and Queries,   Sixth Series IX, No. 122 (January 12,
         1884), 32.   [M]

[1179] Slater, Walter B. "[Untitled, following item 1178]," *Notes and Queries*, Sixth Series IX, No. 122 (January 12, 1884), 32. [M]

[1180] Forman, H[arry] Buxton. "Campe's Edition of 'Queen Mab' (6th S. ix. 32).," *Notes and Queries*, Sixth Series IX, No. 212 (January 19, 1884), 52. [T]

[1181] Slater, J [*sic* for T]. "Shelley and the 'Prometheus Unbound,'" *The Month*, L [Third Series XXXI], No. 236 (February, 1884), [181]-193. [C; first of two parts]

[1182] Thomson, James ['B.V.']. "A Note on Shelley," *Progress*, III (February, 1884), [113]-117. [C; rptd.: item 1205]

[1183] Slater, T. "Shelley and the 'Prometheus Unbound,'" *The Month*, L [Third Series XXXI], No. 237 (March, 1884), [383]-395. [C; second of two parts]

[1184] Swinburne, Algernon Charles. "Wordsworth and Byron," *The Nineteenth Century*, XV, No. 86 (April, 1884), 583-609. [C; first of two parts; rptd.: item 1307]

[1185] Swinburne, Algernon Charles. "Wordsworth and Byron," *The Nineteenth Century*, XV, No. 87 (May, 1884), 764-791. [C; second of two parts; rptd.: item 1307]

[1186] Birrell, Augustine. "Shelley.," *The Athenaeum*, No. 2949 (May 3, 1884), 567-568. [B]

[1187] I[ngleby], C[lement] M[ansfield]. "Essays by Shelley (6th S. iv. 345; viii. 85, 237.)," *Notes and Queries*, Sixth Series IX, No. 227 (May 3, 1884), 359. [M]

[1188] [Anonymous]. " *The Poetical Works of Percy Bysshe Shelley*. Edited, with an Introductory Memoir, by William B. Scott. (George Routledge & Sons.)," *The Athenaeum*, No. 2955 (June 14, 1884), 755-756. [R]

[1189] Didier, Eugene L. "The Graves of Keats and Shelley," *The Literary World*, XV, No. 12 (June 14, 1884), 196-197. [M]

[1190] [Heron, Robert Matthew]. "Art. VI. —1. *Lycidas*. By John Milton. 1637. [/] 2. *Adonais*. By Percy Bysshe Shelley. 1821. [/] 3. *In Memoriam*. By Alfred Tennyson. 1850.," *The Quarterly Review*, CLVIII, No. 315 (July, 1884), 162-183. [C]

[1191] Dowden, Edward. "Some Early Writings of Shelley," *Contemporary Review*, XLVI (September, 1884), [383]-396. [T,C]

[1192]   [Anonymous]. "Shelley," *The Literary World*, XV, No. 18
          (September 6, 1884), 292-293. [C]

[1193]   Baron, B. J. "Portrait of the Poet Shelley by Severn.,"
          Notes and Queries, Sixth Series X, No. 247 (September 20,
          1884), 227. [B]

[1194]   Graves, Algernon. "Portrait of Shelley by Severn (6th S.
          X. 227).," *Notes and Queries*, Sixth Series X, No. 248
          (September 27, 1884), 251. [B]

[1195]   Forman, H[arry] Buxton. "[Untitled, following item 1194],
          Notes and Queries, Sixth Series X, No. 248 (September 27,
          1884), 251-252. [B]

[1196]   Robertson, John [Mackinnon]. "Shelley and Poetry.," *Our
          Corner*, IV, No. 4 (October, 1884), 212-218. [C; first
          of three parts; rptd.: item 1715]

[1197]   Robertson, John [Mackinnon]. "Shelley and Poetry.," *Our
          Corner*, IV, No. 5 (November, 1884), 269-275. [C; secon
          of three parts; rptd.: item 1715]

[1198]   Robertson, John [Mackinnon]. "Shelley and Poetry.," *Our
          Corner*, IV, No. 6 (December, 1884), 339-350. [C; third
          of three parts; rptd.: item 1715]

Books:

[1199]   Andrews, Samuel. *Our Great Writers; or, Popular Chapters on Some
          Leading Authors.* iv+275pp. London: Elliot Stock, 1884.
          [C: "Shelley.," (226)-251]

[1200]   De Vere, Aubrey. *The Poetical Works of Aubrey De Vere.*   3 vols.
          London: Kegan Paul, Trench & Co., 1884. [Poem:
          "Lines Composed Near Shelley's House at Lerici, on
          All Souls' Day, 1856.," III, 357-362; rptd. from item
          626]

[1201]   Hoffman, Frederick A. *Poetry [/] Its Origin, Nature, and History*
          [/] *Being [/] A General Sketch of Poetic and Dramatic Literature.*
          [/] *Comprehending Critical, Historical and Biographical Notices,*
          with Specimens, of [/] The Most Distinguished Writers from the
          Earliest Period [/] To the Middle of the Present Century; to
          Which [/] Is Added (Separately Bound) [/] A Compendium of the
          Works of the Poets of All Times and Countries, with Explanatory
          Notes, Synoptical Tables, [/] A Chronological Digest [/] And A
          Copious Index. 2 vols. London: Thurgate & Sons, 1884.
          [C: "Shelley," I, 466-483; M: 61, 65, 871]

*[1202]   Little, James Stanley. *What Is Art?*   181pp. London:
          W. Swan Sonnenschein and Co., 1884. [M]

[1203]   Skipsey, Joseph, ed. *The Lyrics and Minor Poems of Percy Bysshe
          Shelley. With a Prefatory Notice, Biographical and Critical.*
          viii+288pp. London: Walter Scott, 1884. [C: "Prefa-
          tory Notice.," (9)-32]

*[1204]   Stapylton, Henry Edward Chetwynd.   *The Eton School Lists from
          1791 to 1877, with Notes and Index.* xiv+451pp.   Eton:
          R. Ingalton Drake, 1884.   [B]

[1205]   Thomson, James ('B.V.').   *Shelley, a Poem: with other Writings
          relating to Shelley, by the late James Thomson ('B.V.'): to
          which is added an Essay on The Poems of William Blake by the
          same Author.* Edited by Bertram Dobell. xii+128pp.
          London: printed for private circulation [Charles
          Whittingham and Co. at the Chiswick Press], 1884.
          [Poem; C: rptd. from items 693, 697, 846, 1017, 1055,
          1094, 1095, 1098, 1101, 1102, 1182]

                                  1885

Periodicals:

[1206]   [De Vere, Aubrey].   "Art. V. — *The Works of Edmund Spenser.*
          Edited by the Rev. Dr. Grosart. In 8 vols. London:
          1883.," *The Edinburgh Review*, CLXI, No. cccxxix (January,
          1885), 142-176. [R; M: 176; rptd.: item 1363]

[1207]   Dobell, Bertram. "Shelleyana.," *The Athenaeum*, No. 2993
          (March 7, 1885), 313. [C]

[1208]   Courthope, William John. "The Liberal Movement in English
          Literature. IV. The Revival of Romance: Scott, Byron,
          Shelley.," *The National Review*, V, No. 26 (April, 1885),
          220-237. [C; rptd.: item 1238]

[1209]   Dobell, Bertram. "Shelleyana. II.," *The Athenaeum*, No. 3002
          (May 9, 1885), 597-598. [C]

[1210]   [Anonymous].   " *The Real Shelley: New Views of the Poet's Life.*
          By John Cordy Jeaffreson. 2 vols. (Hurst & Blackett.)
          [/] (First Notice.)," *The Athenaeum*, No. 3005 (May 30,
          1885), 687-689. [R: item 1239]

[1211]   [Anonymous]. "Jeaffreson's 'Shelley,'" *The Pall Mall Gazette*,
          XLI, No. 6305 (May 30, 1885), 5. [R: item 1239; rptd.:
          item 1221]

[1212]   [Anonymous].   " *The Real Shelley: New Views of the Poet's Life.*
          By John Cordy Jeaffreson. 2 vols. (Hurst & Blackett.)
          [/] (Second Notice.)," *The Athenaeum*, No. 3006 (June 6,
          1885), 720-722. [R: item 1239]

[1213] Dowden, Edward. "*The Real Shelley:* New Views of the Poet's
        Life. By John Cordy Jeaffreson. In 2 vols. (Hurst &
        Blackett.)," *The Academy*, XXVII, No. 683 (June 6,
        1885), 393-395. [R: item 1239]

[1214] Jeaffreson, John Cordy. "Correspondence. [/] 'The Real
        Shelley.,'" *The Academy*, XXVII, No. 684 (June 13, 1885),
        420-422. [B]

[1215] Jeaffreson, John Cordy. "The Expulsion of Shelley and
        Hogg.," *The Athenaeum*, No. 3007 (June 13, 1885), 761.
        [B]

[1216] [Anonymous]. "'The Real Shelley," *The Graphic*, XXXI, No. 811
        (June 13, 1885), 614. [R: item 1239]

[1217] Dowden, Edward. "Correspondence. [/] The Expulsion of
        Shelley from University College, Oxford.," *The Academy*,
        XXVII, No. 685 (June 20, 1885), 438. [B]

[1218] [Anonymous]. "Reviews. [/] The Real Shelley," *The Saturday
        Review*, LIX, No. 1,547 (June 20, 1885), 827-828. [R:
        item 1239]

[1219] Saunders, T. B. "Shelley's Expulsion from University
        College, Oxford.," *The Academy*, XXVII, No. 686 (June 27,
        1885), 456-457. [B]

[1220] Bicknell, A. S. "'The Cor Cordium.,'" *The Athenaeum*,
        No. 3009 (June 27, 1885), 823. [B]

[1221] [Anonymous]. "An Inordinately Long Book," *The Critic*, New
        Series III [whole number VI], No. 78 (June 27, 1885),
        310-311. [R: item 1239; rptd. from item 1211]

[1222] [Signed "M.A.W."]. "French Views on English Writers,"
        The Critic, New Series IV [whole number VII], No. 80
        (July 11, 1885), 19-21. [C; first of two parts]

[1223] [Anonymous]. "Jeaffreson's Shelley," *The Critic*, New Series
        IV [whole number VII], No. 80 (July 11, 1885), 22-23.
        [R: item 1239; excerpted from item 1218]

[1224] [Signed "M.A.W."]. "French Views on English Writers,"
        The Critic, New Series IV [whole number VII], No. 81
        (July 18, 1885), 32-34. [C; second of two parts]

*[1225] Lang, Andrew. "Letters to Eminent Authors. III. ──To
        Percy Bysshe Shelley," *The St. James Budget*, [?] (August
        15, 1885), 8. [C; rptd.: item   ]

[1226] Harrison, James A. "Two Views of Shelley," *The Critic*, New
        Series IV [whole number VII], No. 87 (August 29, 1885),
        97-98. [C]

[1227]   Thomson, James ['B.V.']. "Shelley," *The Critic*, New Series
         IV [whole number VII], No. 88 (September 5, 1885),
         118. [Poem; excerpted from item 1205]

[1228]   [Signed "G.F.R.B."]. "Shelley's Schooldays," *Notes and
         Queries*, Sixth Series XII, No. 297 (September 5, 1885),
         186. [B]

[1229]   Noel, Roden [Berkeley Wriothesley]. "Art. II. —The
         Poetry of Shelley," *The British Quarterly Review*, LXXXII,
         No. clxiv (October, 1885), 277-287. [C; revised and
         rptd.: item 1290]

[1230]   [Signed "Bat's-Eyes"]. "Shelley's 'Sensitive Plant.,'"
         Notes and Queries, Sixth Series XII, No. 303 (October 17,
         1885), 309. [T]

[1231]   Forman, H[arry] Buxton. "Shelley's 'Sensitive Plant'
         (6th S. xii. 309).," *Notes and Queries*, Sixth Series
         XII, No. 306 (November 7, 1885), 376. [T]

[1232]   [Signed "W.S."]. "[Untitled, following item 1231],"
         Notes and Queries, Sixth Series XII, No. 306 (November 7,
         1885), 376. [T]

[1233]   [Signed "A.J.M."]. "[Untitled, following item 1232],"
         Notes and Queries, Sixth Series XII, No. 306 (November 7,
         1885), 376-377. [T]

[1234]   Marshall, Edward H. "[Untitled, following item 1233],"
         Notes and Queries, Sixth Series XII, No. 306 (November 7,
         1885), 376. [T]

[1235]   [Signed "P.P."]. "Shelley's 'Sensitive Plant' (6th S. xii.
         309, 376, 411).," *Notes and Queries*, Sixth Series XII,
         No. 311 (December 12, 1885), 475. [T]

Books:

[1236]   Appleton, Thomas Gold. *Life and Letters of Thomas Gold Appleton*.
         Prepared by Susan Hale. 348pp. New York: D. Appleton
         and Company, 1885. [M: 194]

*[1237] Brodie, E[rasmus] H[enry]. *Sonnets*. xvi+154pp. London:
         George Bell and Sons, 1885. [?poem]

[1238]   Courthope, William John. *The Liberal Movement in English
         Literature*. xiv+240pp. London: John Murray, 1885. [C:
         "The Revival of Romance: Scott, Byron, Shelley.,"
         (109)-156; rptd. from item 1208]

[1239] Jeaffreson, John Cordy. *The Real Shelley. New Views of the Poet's Life*. 2 vols. London: Hurst and Blackett, Publishers, 1885. [B]

[1240] Maginn, William. *Miscellanies: Prose and Verse*. Edited by R. W. Montagu. 2 vols. London: Sampson Low, Marston, Searle, & Rivington, 1885 [C: "Remarks on Shelley's Adonais.," II, (300)-311]

[1241] Mason, Edward T. *Personal Traits of British Authors*. 4 vols. New York: Charles Scribner's Sons, 1885. [B: "Percy Bysshe Shelley.," I, (73)-140]

1886

Periodicals:

[1242] Davey, Richard. "Beatrice Cenci.," *The Antiquary*, XIII, No. 74 (February, 1886), 67-71. [M]

[1243] Symons, Arthur. "The Shelley Society.," *Time: A Monthly Magazine of Current Topics, Literature & Art*, New Series III [whole number XIV] (February, 1886), [182]-184. [M]

*[1244] Dobell, Bertram. "The 'Ode to the Death of Summer.,'" *The Athenaeum*, No. 3041 (February 6, 1886), [?p]. [T]

[1245] Jeaffreson, John Cordy. "The 'Ode to the Death of Summer' and the 'Poetical Essay on the Existing State of Things.,'" *The Athenaeum*, No. 3043 (February 20, 1886), 263. [T]

[1246] [Anonymous]. "Three Americans and Three Englishmen," *The Critic*, New Series V [whole number VIII], No. 113 (February 27, 1886), 104. [R: item 1286]

[1247] Dobell, B[ertram]. "The 'Ode to the Death of Summer.,'" *The Athenaeum*, No. 3044 (February 27, 1886), 296. [T]

[1248] James, S. B. "Shelley," *The Whitgift Magazine* [Croydon], IV, No. 2 (March, 1886), [18]-22. [C]

*[1249] [Anonymous]. "[Article on the Shelley Society Meeting]," *The Pall Mall Gazette*, [?] (March 11, 1886), [?p]. [M]

*[1250] Brooke, S[topford] A[ugustus]· and F[rederick] J[ames] Furnivall. "Mr. Matthew Arnold and the Philistines.," *The Pall Mall Gazette*, [?] (March 12, 1886), [?p]. [C]

[1251]   [Lang, Andrew]. "The Shelley Society.," *The Saturday Review*,
           LXVI, No. 1,585 (March 13, 1886), 354. [Poem; rptd.:
           item 1288]

*[1252]   [Signed "The Writer of the Note."]. "Mr. Furnivall and
           the Philistines.," *The Pall Mall Gazette*, [?] (March 13,
           1886), [?p]. [M]

[1253]   [Anonymous]. "Shelley and Vegetarianism," *Book-Lore: A
           Monthly Magazine of Bibliography*, III, No. 17 (April, 1886),
           [121]-132. [T,M; includes rpt. of item 17]

*[1254]   Aveling, Edward. "The Cenci," *Progress*, VI (June, 1886),
           260-265. [C]

[1255]   [Anonymous]. " *Shelley Society Publications*. —Series II.
           Nos. 1-4. Series IV. Nos 1-3. (Shelley Society).),"
           The Athenaeum, No. 3058 (June 5, 1886), 743-744. [R]

[1256]   [Prothero, Rowland]. "Art. II. —The Prose Works of Percy
           Bysshe Shelley. Edited by H. Buxton Forman. 4 vols.
           London: 1880.," *Edinburgh Review*, CLXIV, No. cccxxxv
           (July, 1886), 42-72. [R: item 1079]

[1257]   Butler, A. J. "Two Unpublished Letters of Shelley,"
           The Academy, XXX, No. 743 (July 31, 1886), 72-73. [T]

[1258]   [Anonymous]. "Mary Wollstonecraft Shelley," *The Dial*, VII,
           No. 77 (September, 1886), 106-108. [R: item 1289]

[1259]   Baker, W. T. "Sir Walter Scott and Tennyson (7th S. ii.
           128, 214.," *Notes and Queries*, Seventh Series II, No.
           40 (October 2, 1886), 276. [B]

[1260]   Bouchier, Jonathan. "Sir Walter Scott and Tennyson (7th S.
           ii. 128, 214, 276).," *Notes and Queries*, Seventh Series
           II, No. 43 (October 23, 1886), 338. [T]

[1261]   Dowden, Edward. "Shelley's *Philosophical View of Reform*,"
           The Fortnightly Review, New Series XL [whole number XLVI],
           No. ccxxxix (November, 1886), 543-562. [C,T: rptd.:
           item   ]

[1262]   [Anonymous]. "The Shelley Society. *Shelley Society's Publica-
           tions*. —Series II. No. 3 and No. 5. [/] *The Inaugural
           Address to the Shelley Society*. By the Rev. Stopford A.
           Brooke M.A. (Privately printed.) [/] *Notes on the First
           Performance of Shelley's Cenci*. Edited by Sydney E. Preston.
           (Privately printed.) [/] *Shelley's Beatrice Cenci and her
           First Interpreter*. (Privately printed.) [/] *The Camelot
           Classics*. —Essays and Letters by Percy Bysshe Shelley. Edited,
           with Introductory Notes, by Ernest Rhys. (Scott.) [/]
           The Fortnightly Review, November, 1886. (Chapman & Hall).,"
           The Athenaeum, No. 3081 (November 13, 1886), 629-630.

[R: items 1281, 1291, 1298, and a minor edition of
Shelley prose]

[1263]   [Anonymous]. "The Morality of 'Epipsychidion,'" *The
        St. James's Gazette*, XIII, No. 2011 (November 13, 1886),
        5-6. [C]

[1264]   [Anonymous]. "The Subjection of 'Hellas,'" *The St. James's
        Gazette*, XIII, No. 2014 (November 17, 1886), 5-6. [C]

*[1265] Robertson, John. "Shelley in Oratorio.," *The National
        Reformer*, [?] (November 28, 1886), [?p]. [M]

[1266]   Verschoyle, John. "The Character of Shelley," *The Fort-
        nightly Review*, New Series XL [whole number XLVI],
        No. ccxl (December, 1886), [766]-775. [R: item 1283
        rptd.: item 1320]

[1267]   [Anonymous]. "The Authorized Shelley. [First Notice.]
        (brackets in original)," *The Pall Mall Budget*, XXXIV,
        No. 949 (December 2, 1886), 28-29. [R: item 1283]

[1268]   [Patmore, Coventry]. "What Shelley Was," *The St. James's
        Gazette*, XIII, No. 2027 (December 2, 1886), 6-7.
        [R: item 1283; rptd.: item 1506]

[1269]   Caine, T[homas] Hall. "Literature [/] *The Life of Percy
        Bysshe Shelley*. By Edward Dowden. In 2 vols. (Kegan
        Paul, Trench & Co.)," *The Academy*, XXX, No. 761
        (December 2, 1886), 371-374. [R: item 1283]

[1270]   [Anonymous]. "The Authorized Shelley. [Second Notice.]
        (brackets in original)," *The Pall Mall Budget*, XXXIV,
        950 (December 9, 1886), 27-28. [R: item 1283]

[1271]   [Anonymous]. "*The Life of Percy Bysshe Shelley*. By Edward
        Dowden, LL.D. 2 vols. (Kegan Paul, Trench &Co.),"
        The Athenaeum, No. 3085 (December 11, 1886), 775-776.
        [R: item 1283]

[1272]   [Anonymous]. "Professor Dowden's Life of Shelley. [First
        Notice] (brackets in original)," *The Spectator*, LIX,
        No. 3050 (December 11, 1886), 1661-1662. [R: item
        1283]

[1273]   B[aker], W. T. "Sir Walter Scott and Tennyson (7th S.
        ii. 128, 214, 276, 338).," *Notes and Queries*, Seventh
        Series II, No. 50 (December 11, 1886), 471-472. [C]

[1274]   Dowden, Edward. "Correspondence. [/] 'A Noticeable Man
        with Large Grey Eyes,'" *The Academy*, XXX, No. 762
        (December 11, 1886), 395-396. [B]

[1275] L.B. [L. B. Walford]. "Mr. Gosse's Lectures on Shelley,"
        The Critic, New Series VI [whole number IX], No. 154
        (December 11, 1886), 292-293. [C]

[1276] [Anonymous]. "Percy Bysshe Shelley," *The Saturday Review*,
        LXII, No. 1,625 (December 18, 1886), 820-821. [R:
        item 1283]

[1277] [Anonymous]. "Professor Dowden's Life of Shelley.
        [Second Notice] (brackets in original," *The Spectator*,
        LIX, No. 3051 (December 18, 1886), 1711-1713. [R:
        item 1283]

[1278] [Signed "H.B."]. "London Letter," *The Critic*, New Series
        VI [whole number IX], No. 155 (December 18, 1886),
        308-309. [R of item 1283: 309]

[1279] Caine, T[homas] Hall, and W. J. Newcomb. "Correspondence.
        [/] 'A Noticeable Man with Large Grey Eyes,'" *The
        Academy*, XXX, No. 763 (December 18, 1886), 412. [B]

Books:

[1280] Blind, Mathilde. *Shelley's View of Nature Contrasted with
        Darwin's*. 22pp. London: privately printed, 1886.
        [C; rptd.: item 1431]

[1281] Brooke, Stopford Augustus. *The Inaugural Address to the Shelley
        Society*. 22pp. London: privately printed, 1886. [C;
        rptd.: items 1431, 1913]

[1282] Dawson, W[illiam] J[ames]. *Quest and Vision [/] Essays in Life
        and Literature*. 248pp. London: E. Stock, 1886. [C:
        "Shelley," 1-44]

[1283] Dowden, Edward. *The Life of Percy Bysshe Shelley*. 2 vols.
        London: Kegan Paul, Trench & Co., 1886. [B; revised
        edition, one vol.: item 1692]

[1284] Forman, Alfred. *Sonnets*. 50pp. London: privately printed
        [Chiswick Press], 1886. [Poems: "Shelley. (The
        Inaugural Meeting of the Shelley Society, March 10th,
        1886)," 47; "Shelley. (First Performance of 'The
        Cenci,' May 7th, 1886)," 48]

[1285] Forman, H[arry] Buxton. *The Shelley Library [/] An Essay in
        Bibliography [/] By H. Buxton Forman [/] Shelley's own Books,
        Pamphlets & Broadsides [/] Posthumous Separate Issues and Post-
        humous Books wholly [/] Or mainly by [/] Him*. The Shelley
        Society Publications. Fourth Series. Miscellaneous.
        No. 1. 127pp. London: Reeves and Turner, 1886. [T]

*[1286]   Johnson, Charles F[rederick].   *Three Americans and Three*
          Englishmen.   vii+245pp.   New York: T. Whittaker, 1886.
          [B: "Shelley.," 92- (?)]

 [1287]   Lang, Andrew.   *Letters to Dead Authors.*   x+234pp.   London:
          Longmans, Green, and Co., 1886.   [C:"To Percy Bysshe
          Shelley.," 173-183; rptd. from item 1225]

 [1288]   Lang, Andrew.   *Lines on the Inaugural Meeting of the Shelley*
          Society.   26pp.   London: privately printed, 1886.
          [Poem; rptd. from item 1251]

 [1289]   Moore, Helen.   *Mary Wollstonecraft Shelley.*   346pp.   Philadel-
          phia: J. B. Lippincott Company, 1886.   [B]

 [1290]   Noel, Roden [Berkeley Wriothesley].   *Essays on Poetry and*
          Poets.   viii+356pp. London: Kegan Paul, Trench & Co.,
          1886.   [C: "Shelley.," 114-131; rptd. from item 1229]

 [1291]   Preston, Sydney E., ed.   *The Cenci [/] Five Act Tragedy [/] By*
          Percy Bysshe Shelley [/] Extracts from Reviews of the First
          Performance 7th May 1886 [/] With a Preface by Sydney E. Preston.
          32pp.   London: privately printed, 1886.   [C]

*[1292]   Preston, Sydney E.   *Notes on the First Performance of Shelley's*
          Cenci.   [?]pp.   London: privately printed, 1886.   [C]

 [1293]   Rossetti, William Michael.   *A Memoir of Shelley [/] (With a Fresh*
          Preface).   [Shelley Society Publications.   Fourth Series
          No. 2].   viii+154pp.   London: Richard Clay & Sons,
          1886.   [B; revised edition of item 840]

 [1294]   Rossetti, William Michael.   *Memoir of Percy Bysshe Shelley [/]*
          (With New Preface).   [Shelley Society Publications.
          Fourth Series.   No. 2].   viii+162pp.   London: John
          Slark, 1886.   [B; rptd. from item 1293, with added
          index]

 [1295]   Rossetti, William M[ichael].   *Shelley's Prometheus Unbound.*
          A Study of its Meaning and Personages.   29pp.   London:
          privately printed, 1886.   [C; rptd.: 1431]

 [1296]   R[ossetti], W[illiam] M[ichael].   "Shelley," in Volume
          XXI,   789-794 in *The Encyclopaedia Britannica.* Ninth
          Edition.   Edinburgh: Adam and Charles Black, 1875-
          1889 [Vol. XXI: 1886].   [B, C; revised: eleventh ed.
          (1911), XXIV, 827-832]

 [1297]   Ruskin, John.   *Praeterita. Outlines of Scenes and Thoughts*
          perhaps worthy of Memory in my past Life.   Volume I.
          [vii+432pp.]   New York: J. Wiley & Sons, 1886.   [M:
          336, 337, 404, 405; rptd. from volume one of the Eng-
          lish edition, Orpington: G. Allen, 1885-1900]

[1298]   [Signed "M.S.S."].   *Shelley's Beatrice Cenci and Her First
         Interpreter.*   15pp.   London: privately printed, 1886.
         [C]

[1299]   Sharp, William.   *Sonnets of this Century [/] Edited and arranged
         with a Critical Introduction on the Sonnet.*   lxxxi+324pp.
         London: Walter Scott, 1886.   [T: 202; C: 291-292, 312]

*[1300] Shelley, Jane [Gibson], Lady.   *Memoir of Percy Bysshe Shelley.*
         [?]pp.   London: privately printed, 1886.   [B; rptd.
         from item 683]

[1301]   Shelley, Percy Bysshe.   *Alastor; or, The Spirit of Solitude:
         and Other Poems.   By Percy Bysshe Shelley.   A Facsimile Reprint
         of the Original Edition, First Published in 1816.*   viii+vi+
         101pp.   London: Reeves and Turner and B. Dobell, 1886.
         [Shelley Society Publications, Second Series, No. 3;
         T]

[1302]   Shelley, Percy Bysshe.   *The Cenci [/] A Tragedy in Five Acts by
         Percy Bysshe Shelley [/] Given from the Poet's Own Editions [/]
         with an Introduction by Alfred Forman and H. Buxton Forman [/]
         and a Prologue by John Todhunter.*   xv+107pp.   London: Reeves
         and Turner, 1886.   [Shelley Society Publications,
         Fourth Series, No. 3; T]

[1303]   Shelley, Percy Bysshe.   *Essays and Letters by Percy Bysshe
         Shelley.*   Edited, with an introductory note, by Ernest
         Rhys.   xxiv+392pp.   London: Walter Scott, 1886.   [T,C]

[1304]   Shelley, Percy Bysshe.   *Hellas [/] A Lyrical Drama by Percy
         Bysshe Shelley.   A Reprint of the Original Edition Published in
         1822 with the Author's Prologue and Notes by Various Hands.
         Edited by Thomas J. Wise.*   lviii+xl+60pp.   London: Reeves
         and Turner, 1886.   [Shelley Society Publications,
         Second Series, No. 5; T]

[1305]   Shelley, Percy Bysshe.   *Hellas [/] A Lyrical Drama by Percy
         Bysshe Shelley.   Reprinted from the original edition of 1822.
         Edited by Thomas J. Wise.*   viii+xi+60pp.   London: Reeves
         and Turner, 1886.   [T]

[1306]   Shelley, Percy Bysshe.   *Review of Hogg's Memoirs of Prince
         Alexey Haimatoff by Percy Bysshe Shelley [/] Together with an
         Extract from Some Early Writings of Shelley by Prof. E. Dowden
         [/] Edited with an Introductory Note by Thomas J. Wise.   Revised
         Edition.*   54pp.   London: Reeves and Turner, 1886.
         [Shelley Society Publications, Second Series, No. 2; T]

[1307]   Swinburne, Algernon Charles.   *Miscellanies.*   x+390pp.   Lon-
         don: Chatto & Windus, 1886.   [C: "Wordsworth and Byron,"
         63-156, rptd. from items 1184, 1185; "Sir Henry Taylor
         on Shelley," 371-372]

1887

Periodicals:

[1308]   [Anonymous]. " *The Life of Percy Bysshe Shelley*. By Edward
         Dowden, LL.D. In two volumes. Lond: Kegan Paul,
         Trench & Co. 1886.," *Illustrations*, [II] (January,
         1887), 117-119. [R: item 1283]

[1309]   Courthope, William John. "Thoughts on Dowden's 'Life of
         Shelley.,'" *The National Review*, VIII, No. 47 (January,
         1887), 618-633. [R: item 1283]

[1310]   [Oliphant, Margaret]. "In Maga's Library: The Old
         Saloon," *Blackwood's Edinburgh Magazine*, CXLI, No. dccclv
         (January, 1887), 126-153. [R of item 1283: 131-137]

[1311]   Payne, William Morton. "Cor Cordium," *The Dial*, VII,
         No. 81 (January, 1887), [215]-219. [R: item 1283]

[1312]   Bouchier, Jonathan. "Shelley's 'Prometheus Unbound.,'"
         Notes and Queries, Seventh Series III, No. 53 (January 1,
         1887), 10. [T]

[1313]   Carman, Bliss. "Shelley," *The Literary World*, XVIII, No. 1
         (January 8, 1887), 8. [C: a sixty line poem]

[1314]   [Anonymous]. "Dowden's Life of Shelley," *The Literary World*,
         XVIII, No. 2 (January 22, 1887), 19-20. [R: item
         1283]

[1315]   Ellis, F[rederick] S[tartridge]. "Shelley's 'Mask of
         Anarchy,'" *The Athenaeum*, No. 3091 (January 22, 1887),
         129. [T]

[1316]   [Ellis, Frederick Startridge]. "Shelley's Jottings.," *The
         Academy*, XXXI, No. 769 (January 29, 1887), 76. [T]

[1317]   [Signed "I.S.A."]. "Alastor," *The Institute Magazine* [Birming-
         ham], Part XXXVIII (February, 1887), 89-94. [C]

[1318]   [Anonymous]. "Review. [/] Percy Bysshe Shelley.," *The
         Congregational Review*, I (February, 1887), 185-190. [R:
         item 1283]

[1319]   Emery, Alfred. "Shelley Worship," *Illustrations*, [II]
         (February, 1887), 158-159. [C]

[1320]   Verschoyle, John. "The Character of Shelley," *The Eclectic
         Magazine*, CVIII [New Series XLV], No. 2 (February, 1887)
         178-184. [R: item 1283; rptd. from item 1266]

[1321]   Harrison, James A.   "A Few Words About Shelley," *The Critic*,
         New Series VII [whole number X], No. 163 (February 12,
         1887), 73-74.   [C; rptd.: item 1329]

*[1322]   [Anonymous].   "Crabbe and Shelley.," *The St. James's Gazette*,
         [?] (February 16, 1887), 6.   [C]

[1323]   [Woodberry, George Edward].   "Dowden's Shelley," *The Nation*,
         XLIV, No. 1129 (February 17, 1887), 146-147.   [R:
         item 1283]

[1324]   Steggall, Robert.   "Shelley's 'Prometheus Unbound' (7th S.
         iii. 10).," *Notes and Queries*, Seventh Series III, No. 61
         (February 26, 1887), 173.   [T]

[1325]   Forman, H[arry] Buxton.   "Shelley, 'Peterloo,' and 'The
         Mask of Anarchy,'" *The Gentleman's Magazine*, New Series
         XXXVIII [whole number CCLXII], No. 1875 (March, 1875),
         235-252.   [C; rptd.: item 1365, 1431]

[1326]   Cavan, Lewis.   "The Shelley Forgeries," *Notes and Queries*,
         Seventh Series III, No. 62 (March 5, 1887), 187.   [T]

[1327]   Foote, G. W.   "Infidel Homes.," *The Freethinker*, VII, No. 12
         (March 20, 1887), [89]-90.   [R: item 1384; M: 90]

[1328]   Salt, H[enry] S[tephens].   "Shelley's 'Julian and Mad-
         dalo.,'" *The Academy*, XXXI, No. 777 (March 26, 1887),
         220-221.   [C; rptd.: item 1427]

[1329]   Harrison, James A.   "A Few Words About Shelley," *Book-Lore*,
         V, No. 29 (April, 1887), 146-148.   [C; rptd. from item
         1321]

*[1330]   Salt, Henry S[tephens].   "Shelley's Religious Opinions,"
         Progress, VIII (April, 1887), [?p].   [C; rptd.: item
         1427]

[1331]   Symonds, John Addington.   "Correspondence. [/] Shelley's
         Separation from His First Wife," *The Fortnightly Review*,
         New Series XLI [whole number XLVII], No. ccxliv (April,
         1887), [613]-615.   [B]

[1332]   [Prothero, Rowland].   "Art. I— *The Life of Percy Bysshe Shelley*.
         By Edward Dowden, LL.D., Professor of English Litera-
         ture in the University of Dublin. 2 vols. London,
         1886.," *The Quarterly Review*, CLXIV, No. 328 (April,
         1887), [285]-321.   [R: item 1283; running title: "The
         Character of Shelley"]

[1333]   [Woodberry, George Edward].   "Some Remarks on Shelley's
         Life," *The Atlantic Monthly*, LIX, No. cccliv (April,

1887), 559-567. [R: item 1283; revised and rptd.:
items 1511, 1768]

[1334] [Anonymous]. "Shelley's 'Wandering Jew.,'" *Volunteer
Service Gazette*, XXVIII, No. 1,431 (April 2, 1887),
336. [R: item 1380]

[1335] Dowden, Edward. "Shelley's 'Julian and Maddalo,'" *The
Academy*, XXXI, No. 778 (April 2, 1887), 237. [C]

[1336] [Signed "Este."]. "The Shelley Forgeries (7th S. iii.
187).," *Notes and Queries*, Seventh Series III, No. 66
(April 2, 1887), 277-278. [T]

[1337] Peacock, Edward· "[Untitled, following item 1336]," *Notes
and Queries*, Seventh Series III, No. 66 (April 2,
1887), 278. [T]

[1338] Coleman, Everard Home. "[Untitled, following item 1337],"
Notes and Queries, Seventh Series III, No. 66 (April 2,
1887), 278. [T]

[1339] [Anonymous]. "Our Library Table," *The Athenaeum*, No. 3102
(April 9, 1887), 477-478. [R: item 1374: 477]

*[1340] [Signed "𝕿."]. "Shelley on Coercion,." *The St. James's
Gazette*, [?] (April 13, 1887), 5. [C]

[1341] [Anonymous]. "Percy Bysshe Shelley," *The American*, XIV,
No. 351 (April 30, 1887), 23-24. [R: item 1283]

[1342] [Anonymous]. "The New Shelley," *The Critic*, New Series
VII (whole number X], No. 174 (April 30, 1887), 214.
[R: item 1283]

[1343] Forman, H[arry] Buxton. "The Hermit of Marlow: A Chapter
in the History of Reform," *The Gentleman's Magazine*, New
Series XXXVIII [whole number CCLXII], No. 1877 (May,
1887), 483-497. [C; rptd.: items 1364, 1431]

*[1344] [Anonymous]. "The Wandering Jew.," *The Saturday Review*, (May
14, 1887), [?p]. [R: item 1380]

[1345] Dowden, Edward. "The Quarterly Review and Shelley," *The
Athenaeum*, No. 3107 (May 14, 1887), 641 [B]

[1346] Traill, H[enry] D[uff]. "'Chatter about Shelley.' [/]
(An Academical Dialogue.)" *Macmillan's Magazine*, LVI,
No. 33 (July, 1887), 174-181. [B]

[1347] [Anonymous]. "The Hermit of Marlow: A Chapter in the
History of Reform. (Reeves & Turner)," *The Athenaeum*,
No. 3120 (August 13, 1887), 211. [R: item 1364]

[1348]　King, Alice. "Percy Bysshe Shelley," *The Argosy*, XLIV
　　　　(September, 1887), 230-235. [B]

[1349]　Frederickson, C[harles] W. "The Hermit of Marlow," *The
　　　　Athenaeum*, No. 3124 (September 10, 1887), 341. [T]

[1350]　[Anonymous]. " *Shelley: sa Vie et ses Œuvres.* Par Felix
　　　　Rabbe. (Paris, Savine.)," *The Athenaeum*, No. 3125
　　　　(September 17, 1887), 368. [R]

[1351]　[Anonymous]. "Shelley and the Shelley Society," *The Church
　　　　Quarterly Review*, XXV, No. xlix (October, 1887), 51-77.
　　　　[R: item 1283 and the publications of the Shelley
　　　　Society]

[1352]　Dowden, Edward. "Last Words on Shelley," *The Fortnightly
　　　　Review*, New Series XLII [whole number XLVIII], No. ccl
　　　　(October, 1887), [461]-481. [C; rptd.: item 1416]

[1353]　Johnson, Charles F[rederick]. "Shelley," *Temple Bar*, LXXXI
　　　　(October, 1887), 242-263. [C]

[1354]　Shore, Arabella. "Shelley's 'Julian and Maddalo,'" *The
　　　　Gentleman's Magazine*, New Series XXXIX [whole number
　　　　CCLXIII], No. 1882 (October, 1887), 329-342. [C,B]

*[1355]　[Anonymous]. "The Mask of Anarchy.," *The Saturday Review*,
　　　　[?] (October 1, 1887), 462-463. [R: item 1379]

[1356]　[Anonymous]. "The Wandering Jew. [/] *The Shelley Society's
　　　　Publications.* Second Series, No. 12. *The Wandering Jew:
　　　　a Poem.* By Percy Bysshe Shelley. Edited by Bertram
　　　　Dobell. (Reeves & Turner.)," *The Athenaeum*, No. 3129
　　　　(October 15, 1887), 496-497. [R: item 1380; T]

[1357]　Warner, Charles Dudley. "Shelley," *The New Princeton Review*,
　　　　IV, No. 6 (November, 1887), [289]-305. [C]

[1358]　Scarlett, B. F. "Shelley Family," *Notes and Queries*, Seventh
　　　　Series IV, No. 101 (December 3, 1887), 446-447. [B]

[1359]　[Anonymous]. "Our Library Table," *The Athenaeum*, No. 3140
　　　　(December 31, 1887), 892-893. [R: item 1379]

*[1360]　Salt, H[enry] S[tephens]. "Books of To-Day," *To-Day*, New
　　　　Series VII, ([?], 1887), 62-64. [R]

Books:

[1361]　[Anonymous]. *An Interview with Miss Alma Murray* [/] *Her opinions
　　　　of "The Cenci"* [/] *From the "Evening News" of 26th July, 1887.*
　　　　7pp. London: Reeves and Turner, 1887. [C]

[1362] Buchanan, Robert. *A Look Round Literature*. xi+386pp.
London: Ward and Downey, 1887. [C: 347-358; M:
1-53]

[1363] De Vere, Aubrey. *Essays Chiefly on Poetry*. 2 vols. London:
Macmillan and Co., 1887. [C: *"Spenser as a Philo-
sophic Poet," I, [?p]; "The Two Chief Schools of
English Poetry. Poetic Versatility [/] Shelley and
Keats," II, (100)-142, adapted from item 503]

[1364] Forman, H[arry] Buxton. *The Hermit of Marlow* [/] *A Chapter
in the History of Reform*. 28pp. London: privately printed
[Reeves and Turner], 1887. [C; rptd. from item 1343]

[1365] Forman, H[arry] Buxton. *Shelley* [/] *"Peterloo" and "The Mask
of Anarchy."* 29pp. London: privately printed, 1887.
[C; rptd. from item 1315]

[1366] Forman, H[arry] Buxton. *The Vicissitudes of Shelley's Queen Mab
[/] A Chapter in the History of Reform*. 23pp. London:
privately printed, 1887. [C; rptd.: item 1431]

[1367] Garnett, Richard. *Shelley and Lord Beaconsfield*. 23pp.
London: privately printed, 1887. [B; rptd.: items 143?
1782]

[1368] Griswold, Hattie Tyng. *Home Life of Great Authors*. Chicago:
A. C. McClurg and Company, 1887. [B: "Shelley.," (102)-
111]

[1369] Hodgkins, Louise Manning. *A Guide to the Study of Nineteenth
Century Authors*. vi+101+56pp. Boston: D. C. Heath &
Co., 1887. [C: "Percy Bysshe Shelley, 1792-1822.,"
26-30]

[1370] Longfellow, Henry Wadsworth. *Henry Wadsworth Longfellow*.
Edited by Samuel Longfellow. vi+447pp. Boston:
Ticknor and Company, 1887. [M: 288]

[1371] Mosely, B. L. *Miss Alma Murray As Beatrice Cenci*. 24pp.
London: Reeves and Turner, 1887. [C]

[1372] Pearson, Howard S. *The Religious Beliefs of Shelley*. 15pp.
Birmingham: privately printed, 1887. [C]

[1373] [Preston, Sydney E., and James Little Stanley, eds.]
Notebook of the Shelley Society [/] *The Shelley Society's
Note-Book. Part I*. 213pp. [London: Reeves and Turner,
1886-1887]. [C,T,B; an alternate version exits with
an additional page at 157, consequently containing
214pp; this item was issued in numbers through 1886
and 1887, and reissued as a bound whole in 1887 without date, and apparently again in 1888 with date;

[1374]   Rossetti, William Michael. *Shelley's Prometheus Unbound Con-
         sidered as a Poem.* 20pp. London: privately printed
         [Richard Clay and Sons], 1887. [C; rptd.: item 1431]

[1375]   Salt, H[enry] S[tephens]. *A Shelley Primer.* 128pp. London:
         Reeves and Turner, 1887. [C; Shelley Society Publica-
         tions, Fourth Series, No. 4]

*[1376] Salt, Henry S[tephens]. "Shelley's Vegetarianism," *The
         Vegetarian Annual,* [?] (1887), [?p]. [B; rptd.: item
         1427]

[1377]   Sharp, William. *Life of Percy Bysshe Shelley.* 201+xxviipp.
         London: Walter Scott, 1887. [B; with appended
         bibliography of editions and criticism, by John P.
         Anderson of the British Museum]

*[1378] Shelley, Percy Bysshe. *Epipsychidion by Percy Bysshe Shelley.
         A Type-Facsimile Reprint of the Original Edition First Published
         in 1821. With an Introduction by the Rev. Stopford A. Brooke,
         M.A., and a Note by Algernon Charles Swinburne. Edited by Robert
         Alfred Potts.* lxvi+31pp. London: Reeves and Turner,
         1887. [T,C; Shelley Society Publications, Second
         Series, No. 7; introduction rptd.: item 1913]

*[1379] Shelley, Percy Bysshe. *The Mask of Anarchy* [/] *Written on the
         Occasion of the Massacre at Manchester* [/] *By Percy Bysshe
         Shelley. Fac-simile of the Holograph Manuscript* [/] *With an
         Introduction by H. Buxton Forman.* 52+[25]pp. London:
         Reeves and Turner, 1887. [T,C; Shelley Society
         Publication, Extra Series, No. 4]

*[1380] Shelley, Percy Bysshe. *The Wandering Jew. A Poem by Percy
         Bysshe Shelley.* Edited by Bertram Dobell. xxxiii+115pp.
         London: Reeves and Turner, 1887. [T,C; Shelley Society
         Publications, Second Series, No. 12]

[1381]   Southey, Robert. *Robert Southey* [/] *The Story of His Life Written
         in His Letters.* Edited by John Dennis. 443pp. Boston:
         D. Lothrop Company, [1887]. [B: 238-239]

[1382]   Symonds, John Addington. *Shelley.* A New Edition. x+197pp.
         London: Macmillan and Co., 1887. [B; revised and
         rptd. from item 1036]

[1383]   Todhunter, John. *Notes on Shelley's Unfinished Poem "The Triumph
         of Life."* 21pp. London: privately printed, 1887.
         [C; rptd.: item 1431]

*[1384] Watkinson, William L. *The Influence of Scepticism on Character.*
         162pp. London: T. Woolmer, 1887. [?B?C]

[1385]   Welsh, Alfred H.   *English Masterpiece Course.*   xxxii+205pp.
          Boston: Silver, Burdett & Co., 1887. [C: bibliograph
          of criticism, 133-136]

                              1888

Periodicals:

[1386]   Arnold, Matthew. "Shelley," *The Nineteenth Century*, XXIII,
          No. 131 (January, 1888), 23-29. [R: item 1283; rptd.:
          items 1392, 1393, 1412]

[1387]   Gannett, A. M. "Shelley's Morality," *The North American
          Review*, CXLVI, No. 374 (January, 1888), 104-105. [C]

[1388]   Salt, H[enry] S[tephens]. "Shelley and the Quarterly
          Review," *To-Day*, New Series IX, No. 50 (January,
          1888), 5-11 [misprinted as 1]. [C; rptd.: item 1427]

*[1389]   [Anonymous]. "'Common Sense' About Shelley.," *The Pall Mall
          Gazette*, [?] (January 2, 1888), 11. [R: item 1386]

*[1390]   Shorter, Clement K. "Shelley and His Critics.,"*The Pall
          Mall Gazette*, [?] (January 5, 1888), 6.   [R: item 1386]

[1391]   [Anonymous]. "Epipsychidion," *The Saturday Review*, LXV,
          No. 1,680. (January 7, 1888), 20-21. [R: item 1378]

[1392]   Arnold, Matthew. "Shelley," *Littell's Living Age*, CLXXVI,
          No. 2276 (February 11, 1888), 323-333. [R: item 1283;
          rptd. from item 1386]

[1393]   Arnold, Matthew. "Shelley," *The Eclectic Magazine*, CX [New
          Series XLVII], No. 3 (March, 1888), 402-413. [R:
          item 1283; rptd. from item 1386]

[1394]   [Anonymous]. "Shelley and Smollett," *The Literary World*,
          XIX, No. 5 (March 3, 1888), 70. [R: item 1377 and
          Hannay's *Life of Smollett*]

[1395]   [Anonymous]. "Sharp's Shelley," *The Critic*, New Series IX
          [whole number XII], No. 222 (March 31, 1888), 151.
          [R: item 1377]

[1396]   Aveling, Edward, and Eleanor Marx Aveling. "Shelley and
          Socialism. Part I.," *To-Day*, New Series IX, No. 53
          [misprinted 52 on cover] (April, 1888), 103-116.
          [C; rptd.: item 1413]

[1397]   Buckley, W. E. "Shelley's 'Address to the People on the

Death of the Princess Charlotte.,'" *Notes and Queries*,
Seventh Series V, No. 119 (April 7, 1888), 265-266.
[T]

[1398] Marshall, Julian [*sic*, not Mrs. Julian Marshall]. "Shelley's Address to the People on the Death of the Princess Charlotte (7th S. v. 265).," *Notes and Queries*,
Seventh Series V, No. 122 (April 28, 1888), 336. [T]

[1399] Austin, Alfred. "Matthew Arnold," *The National Review*, XI,
No. 63 (May, 1888), 415-419. [M: 416]

*[1400] [Anonymous]. "'Poet's' Prize Competition.," *Wit and Wisdom*,
[?] (May 5, 1888), [?p]. [M]

[1401] [Anonymous]. "Cheap Shelley Literature. [/] *Life of Percy
Bysshe Shelley*. By William Sharp. "Great Writers."
(Scott.) [/] *Shelley*. By John Addington Symonds.
New Edition. "English Men of Letters." (Macmillan
& Co.) [/] *The Banquet of Plato, and Other Pieces, Translated
and Original*. By Percy Bysshe Shelley. "Cassell's
National Library." (Cassell & Co.) [/] *Prometheus
Unbound, with Adonais, The Cloud, Hymn to Intellectual Beauty,
and An Exhortation*. By Percy Bysshe Shelley. "Cassell's
National Library." (Same publishers.)," *The Athenaeum*,
No. 3165 (June 23, 1888), 793. [R: items 1377, 1382,
1427, and two popular editions of selections]

[1402] Harney, Geo[rge] Julian. "Byron, Shelley, and Keats,"
Notes and Queries, Seventh Series VI, No. 135 (July 28,
1888), 64. [M]

[1403] Axon, William E. A. "Dr. Thomas Forster and Shelley,"
Notes and Queries, Seventh Series VI, No. 140 (September
1, 1888), 161-162. [B]

[1404] Sanborne, Alvan F. "Shelley's Atheism," *The Open Court*
[Chicago], II, No. 28 (September 6, 1888), 1189-1192.
[C]

[1405] Fells, W. "Shelley's 'Adonais.,'" *Notes and Queries*, Seventh
Series VI, No. 149 (November 3, 1888), 347. [T]

[1406] [Signed "C.C.B."]. "Shelley's 'Adonais' (7th S. vi. 347.,"
Notes and Queries, Seventh Series VI, No. 153 (December 1,
1888), 431. [T]

[1407] Buckley, W. E. "[Untitled, following item 1406]," *Notes and
Queries*, Seventh Series VI, No. 153 (December 1, 1888),
431. [T]

[1408] Sympson, E. Mansel. "[Untitled, following item 1407],"
Notes and Queries, Seventh Series VI, No. 153 (December 1,
1888), 431. [T]

[1409] Bouchier, Jonathan. "[Untitled, following item 1408],"
        Notes and Queries, Seventh Series VI, No. 153 (December 1
        1888), 431. [T]

[1410] [Woodberry, George Edward, ed.]. "Shelley's Skylark, a
        Facsimile of the Original Manuscript, with a Note on
        Other Manuscripts of Shelley, in Harvard College
        Library.," *Library of Harvard University. Bibliographical
        Contributions*, II, No. 30 (1888), [facsimile: 6pp;
        "Editorial Note:" 1p.]. [T]

[1411] [Anonymous]. "The Byron Forgeries," *The Archivist*, I,
        ([?], 1888), 2-7. [T]

Books:

[1412] Arnold, Matthew. *Essays in Criticism* [/] *Second Series*.   vii+
        331pp. London: Macmillan and Co., 1888. [C: "The
        Study of Poetry," (1)-55, rptd. from item 1083;
        "Byron," (163)-204, rptd. from item 1090; "Shelley,"
        (205)-252, rptd. from item 1386]

[1413] Aveling, Edward, and Eleanor Marx Aveling. *Shelley's
        Socialism. Two Lectures*. 30pp. London: privately printed
        1888. [C; first lecture rptd. from item 1396; the
        whole rptd.: items 1529, 3131]

[1414] Browning, Robert. *An Essay on Percy Bysshe Shelley*. Edited
        by W. Tyas Harden. 27pp. London: Reeves and Turner,
        1888. [C; Shelley Society Publication, Series Four,
        No. 8; rptd. from item 573]

[1415] Dillon, Arthur. *Shelley's Philosophy of Love*. 17pp. London:
        privately printed, 1888. [C; rptd.: item 1529]

[1416] Dowden, Edward. *Transcripts and Studies*.   525pp. London:
        Kegal Paul, Trench & Co., 1888. [C: "Shelley's
        'Philosophical View of Reform.,'" (41)-74, rptd. from
        item 1261; "Last Words on Shelley," (75)-111, rptd.
        from item 1352]

*[1417] Ellis, Frederick S[tartridge]. *An Alphabetical Table of
        Contents to Shelley's Poetical Works* [/] *Adapted to the Edition
        in 3 vols. Edited by W. M. Rossetti, Esq.* [/] *The 2 volume
        Edition of H. B. Forman, Esq.* [/] *The 4 volume Edition of H. B.
        Forman, Esq.* 20pp. London: Reeves and Turner, 1888.
        [T; Shelley Society Publication, Series Four, No. 6]

[1418] Forman, H[arry] Buxton. *Rosalind and Helen* [/] *A Lecture*.
        27pp. London: privately printed, 1888. [C; rptd.:
        item 1529]

[1419]   Hamilton, Walter, ed. *Parodies of the Works of English and American Authors*. 6 vols. London: Reeves & Turner, 1884-1889 [Volume V: 1888]. [C: "Percy Bysshe Shelley," V, 233-236]

[1420]   Hime, H[enry] W[illiam] L[ovett]. *The Greek Materials of Shelley's 'Adonais' [/] With Remarks on the Three Great English Elegies*. 16pp. London: Dulau & Co., 1888. [C]

[1421]   James, Henry. *The Aspern Papers [/] Louisa Pallant [/] The Modern Warning*. 2 vols. London: Macmillan and Co., 1888. [B; *The Aspern Papers* is fictionalized account of Claire and Shelley papers in her possession]

[1422]   Mayor, Joseph Bickersteth. *A Classification of Shelley's Metres*. 48pp. London: privately printed, 1888. [C; rptd.: item 1529]

[1423]   Parkes, Kineton. *Shelley's "Revolt of Islam," and Mr. Herbert Spencer's "Ecclesiastical Institutions."* ["A Paper Read before the Birmingham Branch of the Shelley Society, November 8th, 1887"]. 15pp. Birmingham: William Downing, 1888. [C]

[1424]   Parkes, Kineton. *Shelley's Faith. Its Development and Relativity*. 22pp. London: privately printed, 1888. [C; rptd.: items 1529, 1543, 1562]

[1425]   Rabbe, Felix. *Shelley: The Man and the Poet*. 2 vols. London: Ward and Downey, 1888. [B; translated from the French, *Shelley: sa Vie et ses Œuvres* (Paris: Savine, 1887)]

[1426]   Salt, H[enry] S[tephens]. *Literary Sketches*. 235pp. London: Swan Sonnenschein, Lowrey & Co., 1888. [C: "Shelley as a Teacher," (14)-38; rptd. from item 1129]

[1427]   Salt, H[enry] S[tephens]. *Percy Bysshe Shelley [/] A Monograph*. viii+277pp. London: Swan Sonnenschein, Lowrey & Co., 1888. [C; an appendix (237-277) rptd. from items 1328, 1330, 1376, 1388; revised and rptd.: item 1694]

*[1428]   Salt, H[enry] S[tephens], and Henry T. Wharton. *A Study of Shelley's "Julian and Maddalo," To Which Is Added A Note on the Identification of "The Aziola," by Henry T. Wharton*. 32pp. London: privately printed, 1888. [C; Salt's essay is rptd. from item 1328; both are rptd.: item 1529]

[1429]   Sharpe, Charles Kirkpatrick. *Letters From and To Charles Kirkpatrick Sharpe, Esq*. Edited by Alexander Allardyce. With a Memoir by the Rev. W. K. R. Bedford. 2 vols. Edinburgh: William Blackwood and Sons, 1888. [B: II, 204-205]

*[1430] Shelley, Percy Bysshe. *Rosalind and Helen* [/] *A Modern Eclogue*
         [/] *With Other Poems by Percy Bysshe Shelley. A Type Fac-simile*
         of the Original Edition of MDCCCXIX. Edited by H. Buxton Forman.
         xxiv+vi+92pp. London: Reeves and Turner, 1888. [T,C;
         Shelley Society Publications, Second Series, No. 17]

[1431]   The Shelley Society's Publications. First Series. No. I.
         The Shelley Society's Papers. Part I. Being the First Part
         of the First Volume. 179+30pp. London: Reeves and
         Turner, 1888. [C; rptd. from items 1280, 1281, 1295,
         1325, 1343, 1366, 1367, 1374, 1383; additional thirty
         page appendix of society reports and news]

[1432]   Sweet, Henry. *Shelley's Nature Poetry.* 56pp. London:
         privately printed, 1888. [C; rptd.: item 1529]

*[1433] Taylor, Henry. *Correspondence of Henry Taylor.* Edited by
         Edward Dowden. xix+421pp. London: Longmans, Green
         and Co., 1888. [M]

[1434]   Trench, Richard Chevenix. *Richard Chevenix Trench* [/] *Archbisho*
         [/] *Letters and Memorials.* Edited by Miss M. Trench.
         2 vols. London: Kegan Paul, Trench & Co., 1888. [M:
         I, 42-43, 49-50, 52-53]

                              1889

Periodicals:

[1435]   Bensly, Edward. "A Forged Letter of Shelley," *The Athenaeum*,
         No. 3195 (January 12, 1889), 51. [T]

[1436]   Brunton, William. "Shelley," *The Open Court* [Chicago], II,
         No. 50 [whole number 76] (February 7, 1889), 1460.
         [C: a sonnet]

[1437]   Schuyler, Eugene. "Shelley with Byron," *The Nation*, XLVIII,
         No. 1232 (February 7, 1889), 113-116. [B]

[1438]   [Signed "F.H."]. "The Spurious Shelley Letters," *The Nation*
         XLVIII, No. 1233 (February 14, 1889), 138. [T]

[1439]   Anderson, Melville B. "Shelley's Latest Biographer,"
         Modern Language Notes, IV, No. 3 (March, 1889), 79-81.
         [R: item 1425; rptd.: item 1444]

[1440]   Short, R. A. "Wordsworth and Shelley," *Notes and Queries*,
         Seventh Series VII, No. 167 (March 9, 1889), 188. [T]

[1441]   Edgcumbe, Richard. "Shelley Pedigree," *Notes and Queries*,
         Seventh Series VII, No. 170 (March 30, 1889), 248.
         [B]

[1442]   [Signed "C.C.B."]. "Wordsworth and Shelley (7th S. vii.
         188.)," *Notes and Queries*, Seventh Series VII, No. 170
         (March 30, 1889), 258.   [T]

[1443]   Marshall, Edward H. "[Untitled, following item 1442],"
         Notes and Queries, Seventh Series VII, No. 170 (March 30,
         1889), 258.   [T]

[1444]   [Anderson, Melville B.]. "The Library," *Poet-Lore*, I,
         No. 4 (April, 1889), 196-201. [R: item 1425; rptd.
         from item 1439]

[1445]   Shelley, C. Percy. "Shelley's Lyrics," *The Central Literary
         Magazine* [Birmingham], IX, No. 2 (April, 1889), 56-64.
         [C]

[1446]   Buckley, W. E. "Wordsworth and Shelley (7th S. vii. 188,
         258,)," *Notes and Queries*, Seventh Series VII, No. 174
         (April 27, 1889), 338.   [T]

[1447]   Prideaux, W. F. "Shelley's 'Lines to an Indian Air,'"
         Notes and Queries, Seventh Series VII, No. 175 (May 4,
         1889), 349.   [T]

[1448]   [Signed "H.W."]. "Shelley Pedigree (7th S. vii. 248.),"
         Notes and Queries, Seventh Series VII, No. 175 (May 4,
         1889), 358.   [B]

[1449]   Morris, J. B. "[Untitled, following item 1448]," *Notes and
         Queries*, Seventh Series VII, No. 175 (May 4, 1889),
         358.   [B]

[1450]   Russell, Constance. "[Untitled, following item 1450],"
         Notes and Queries, Seventh Series VII, No. 175 (May 4,
         1889), 358.   [B]

[1451]   [Signed "C.M."]. "Wordsworth and Shelley (7th S. vii.
         188, 258, 338).," *Notes and Queries*, Seventh Series VII,
         No. 178 (May 25, 1889), 417.   [T]

[1452]   Marshall, Edward H. "Shelley's 'Lines to an Indian Air'
         (7th S. vii. 349).," *Notes and Queries*, Seventh Series
         VII, No. 179 (June 1, 1889), 435.   [T]

[1453]   Webb, Alfred. "Harriet Shelley and Catherine Nugent.—I.,"
         The Nation, XLVIII, No. 1249 (June 6, 1889), 464-467.
         [T,B]

[1454] Webb, Alfred. "Harriet Shelley and Catherine Nugent.
        —II.," *The Nation*, XLVIII, No. 1250 (June 13, 1889),
        484-486. [T,B]

[1455] [Anonymous]. "Harriet Shelley's Letters," *The Athenaeum*,
        No. 3220 (July 6, 1889), 35. [M]

[1456] Salt, H[enry] S[tephens]. "Shelley and the Superior
        Person.," *The International Review*, II, No. 3 (September,
        1889), 100-112. [B]

[1457] [Anonymous]. "Still More Chatter," *The Saturday Review*,
        LXVIII, No. 1,768 (September 14, 1889), 289-290. [B]

[1458] Malleson, W. T. "Shelley and Wordsworth.," *The Spectator*,
        LXIII, No. 3,194 (September 14, 1889), 334. [C]

[1459] Woodberry, George Edward. "Notes on the MS. Volume of
        Shelley's Poems in the Library of Harvard College.,"
        Library of Harvard University. Bibliographical Contributions,
        II, No. 35 ([October,] 1889), [3]-[12]. [T]

[1460] Wotherspoon, G. "Zoroaster," *Notes and Queries*, Seventh
        Series VIII, No. 203 (November 16, 1889), 388. [C]

[1461] [Anonymous]. "Mary Wollstonecraft Shelley," *The Saturday
        Review*, LXVIII, No. 1,777 (November 16, 1899), 565-566.
        [R: item 1472]

[1462] [Anonymous]. "The Life and Letters of Mary Wollstonecraft
        Shelley. 2 vols. (Bentley & Son)," *The Athenaeum*,
        No. 3239 (November 23, 1889), 699-701. [R: item 1472]

[1463] Bentley, George. "Mrs. Shelley's Letters," *The Athenaeum*,
        No. 3240 (November 30, 1889), 744. [M]

[1464] Monroe, Harriet. "With a Copy of Shelley," *Century Magazine*,
        XXXIX, No. 2 (December, 1889), 313. [C: a sonnet]

[1465] [Anonymous]. "Notes and News," *Poet-Lore*, I, No. 12
        (December, 1889), 583-592. [M: 592]

[1466] [Anonymous]. "The Shelley Manuscript Volume in the
        Harvard Library," *The Athenaeum*, No. 3241 (December 7,
        1889), 780-781. [R: item 1459]

[1467] [Signed "J.J.M."]. "Shelley's 'Prometheus.,'" *Notes and
        Queries*, Seventh Series VIII, No. 207 (December 14,
        1889), 469. [T]

[1468] [Anonymous]. "Notes," *The Critic*, New Series XII, No. 311
        (December 21, 1889), 306. [M]

[1469] Hope, Henry Gerald. "Zoroaster (7th S. viii. 388).," *Notes and Queries*, Seventh Series VIII, No. 208 (December 21, 1889), 498-499. [C]

[1470] [Anonymous]. "The Life of Mary Shelley," *The Spectator*, LXIII, No. 3,209 (December 28, 1889), 923-924. [R: item 1472]

Books:

*[1471] Antaeus [pseud. of William Joseph Ibbett]. *Poems by Antaeus*. 136pp. London: [?], 1889. [C: contains a poem on Shelley's *Prometheus Unbound*]

[1472] Marshall, Mrs. Julian. *The Life and Letters of Mary Wollstone-craft Shelley*. 2 vols. London: Richard Bentley & Son, 1889. [B]

*[1473] O'Conor, William Anderson. *Essays in Literature and Ethics*. Edited with a Biographical Introduction by William E. A. Axon. xvii+254pp. Manchester: J. E. Cornish, 1889. [C: "The Prometheus of Æschylus and of Shelley," (?p); rptd. from item 1111]

[1474] Salt, H[enry] S[tephens]. *An Examination of Hogg's "Life of Shelley."* 23pp. London: privately printed, 1889. [B; rptd.: item 1529]

[1475] Todhunter, John. *Shelley and The Marriage Question*. 19pp. London: privately printed, 1889. [C; rptd.: item 1529]

[1476] [Wise, Thomas James, and Harry Buxton Forman, eds.]. *Letters from Percy Bysshe Shelley to Jane Clairmont*. viii+104pp. London: privately printed, 1889. [T]

1890

Periodicals:

[1477] Wotherspoon, G. "Zoroaster (7th S. viii. 388, 498).," *Notes and Queries*, Seventh Series IX, No. 210 (January 4, 1890), 17. [T]

[1478] Scott, Ernest. "'The Cremation of Shelley.,'" *Notes and Queries*, Seventh Series IX, No. 213 (January 25, 1890), 66. [B]

[1479] [Anonymous]. "Browning Memorial Notes," *Poet-Lore*, II, No. 2 (February, 1890), 100-111. [C: 107-108]

[1480]   Herford, C[harles] H[arold]. "Shelley's Welsh Haunts,"
         Lippincott's Magazine, XLV (February, 1890), 254-257.   [B

[1481]   Gulliver, Julia H[enrietta]. "Article VI. —Shelley—The
         Poet," *New Englander and Yale Review*, New Series XVI [whol
         number LII], No. ccxxxix (February, 1890), 138-146.
         [C]

[1482]   Ouida [pseud. of Louise de la Ramée]. "A New View of
         Shelley," *The North American Review*, CL, No. 399 (February
         1890), [246]-262.   [C; rptd.: item 1679]

[1483]   Simpson, Jane H. "Shelley at Essex Hall, London.," *Poet-
         Lore*, II, No. 2 (February, 1890), 78-81.   [C]

[1484]   Yardley, E. "Shelley's 'Prometheus Unbound' (7th S. viii.
         469).," *Notes and Queries*, Seventh Series IX, No. 214
         (February 1, 1890), 96.   [T]

[1485]   Pickford, John. "The Cremation of Shelley (7th S. ix.
         66).," *Notes and Queries*, Seventh Series IX, No. 217
         (February 22, 1890), 151-152. [B]

[1486]   Austin, Alfred. "At Shelley's House at Lerici.," *The New
         Review*, II, No. 10 (March, 1890), [193]-198.   [B: a
         one hundred and thirty line poem]

*[1487]   [Anonymous].   "[?]," *Poet-Lore*,   II, No. 3 (March, 1890),
         131.   [?]

*[1488]   Wood, G. "Shelley's Plagiarism.," *The Times* [London], [?]
         (March 1, 1890), 4, col. 6. [T]

*[1489]   Dowden, Edward. "Shelley's Plagiarism.," *The Times* [London]
         [?] (March 6, 1890), 10, col. 6.   [T]

[1490]   [Signed "J.A.J."]. "Shelley's 'Cloud.,'" *Notes and Queries*,
         Seventh Series IX, No. 220 (March 15, 1890), 207.   [T]

[1491]   [Signed "Este"]. "Cremation of Shelley (7th S. ix. 66,
         151.)," *Notes and Queries*, Seventh Series IX, No. 221
         (March 22, 1890), 236.   [B]

[1492]   Herford, C[harles] H[arold]. "Mary Wollstonecraft Shelley,
         Lippincott's Magazine, XLV (April, 1890), 596-607.   [B]

[1493]   [Anonymous].   " *The Life and Letters of Mary Wollstonecraft Shelley*
         By Mrs. Julian Marshall. 2 vols. London: Richard
         Bentley & Son," *The Nation*, L, No. 1294 (April 17,
         1890), 320-321. [R: item 1472]

[1494]   [Rawnsley, Hardwicke Drummond]. "The Last of the Cal-
         verts," *The Cornhill Magazine*, New Series XIV, No. 83

(May, 1890), 494-520. [B: 501]

[1495] Fleay, F. G. "The Story of Shelley's Life in his 'Epi-
        psychidion,'" *Poet-Lore*, II, No. 5 (May, 1890), [225]-
        233. [C,B]

[1496] [Anonymous]. "Mrs. Shelley," *The Saturday Review*, LXIX,
        No. 1,801 (May 3, 1890), 540-541. [R: item 1508]

*[1497] [Anonymous]. "Nativity of P. B. Shelley, Poet &c.,"
        Fate and Fortune, I (July, 1890), 14-15. [?B]

[1498] [Anonymous]. "M. E. M. ('Essays on Shelley's Poems').,"
        Notes and Queries, Seventh Series X, No. 244 (August 30,
        1890), 180. [C]

[1499] [Signed "M.E.M."]. "Shelley.," *Notes and Queries*, Seventh
        Series X, No. 246 (September 13, 1890), 207. [C]

[1500] Smith, C. Ernest. "Shelley (7th S. x. 207).," *Notes and
        Queries*, Seventh Series X, No. 250 (October 11, 1890),
        292. [C]

[1501] Yardley, E. "Byron.," *Notes and Queries*, Seventh Series X,
        No. 260 (December 20, 1890), 485. [C]

[1502] Bouchier, Jonathan. "Shelley's 'Cloud' (7th S. ix. 207).,"
        Notes and Queries, Seventh Series X, No. 261 (December 27,
        1890), 511. [T]

Books:

[1503] Brooks, Sarah Warner. *English Poetry and Poets*. x+506pp.
        Boston: Estes and Lauriat, 1890. [C: "Shelley,"
        456-470]

[1504] Dawson, W[illiam] J[ames]. *The Makers of Modern English. A
        Popular Handbook to the Greater Poets of the Century*. viii+
        375pp. New York: Thomas Whittaker, 1890. [C:
        "Shelley.," (36)-47]

[1505] Lowell, James Russell. *Literary Essays*. [Volume II of *The
        Writings of James Russell Lowell (/) In Ten Volumes*]. Cam-
        bridge, Mass.: Houghton Mifflin, The Riverside Press,
        1890. [M: 145-146, 229]

[1506] Patmore, Coventry. *Principle in Art [/] Etc*. Second edition.
        London: George Bell and Sons, 1890. [C: "What Shelley
        Was," (87)-96; rptd. from item 1268]

[1507]   Reid, T. Wemyss. *The Life, Letters, and Friendships of Richard
         Monckton Milnes, First Lord Houghton.* Second edition. 2
         vols. London: Cassell & Company, 1890. [M: I, 73-83,
         116, 435-436; II, 162-163]

[1508]   Rossetti, Lucy Madox.   *Mrs. Shelley.* [Eminent Women Series,
         edited by John H. Ingram]. viii+238pp. London:
         W. H. Allen, 1890.   [B]

[1509]   Saintsbury, George. *Essays in English Literature* [/] *1780-1860.*
         xxix+451pp. London: Percival and Co., 1890.   [B:
         "Peacock," (234)-269]

[1510]   [Wise, Thomas James, and Harry Buxton Forman, eds.]. *Letters
         from Percy Bysshe Shelley to Elizabeth Hitchener.*   2 vols.
         London: privately printed, 1890. [T]

[1511]   Woodberry, George Edward.   *Studies in Letters and Life.* 296pp.
         Boston and New York: Houghton Mifflin and Company
         [Cambridge, Mass.: The Riverside Press], 1890.   [C:
         "Remarks on Shelley: I. His Career.," (124)-133,
         revised and rptd. from item 1028; "II. His Acquaint-
         ances.," 133-155, revised and rptd. from item 1333;
         "III. His Italian Letters.," 156-166, revised and
         rptd. from item 1155; all rptd.: item 1768]

                              1891

Periodicals:

[1512]   [Anonymous]. "Poetry and Verse," *The Critic,* New Series XV,
         No. 371 (February 7, 1891), 68. [R: item 1526]

[1513]   Ward, C[harles] A. "Shelley's 'Cloud' (7th S. ix. 207; x.
         511).," *Notes and Queries,* Seventh Series XI, No. 270
         (February 28, 1891), 170-171. [T]

[1514]   Kingsland, William G. "London Literaria," *Poet-Lore,* III,
         No. 3 (March, 1891), 154-158. [B]

[1515]   MacQueary, Howard. "Shelley, the Sceptic," *Arena,* III,
         No. xvi (March, 1891), 421-437. [C]

[1516]   [Signed "H. de B. H."]. "Arethusa and Alpheus," *Notes and
         Queries,* Seventh Series XI, No. 272 (March 14, 1891),
         203. [C]

[1517]   Watts, T. G. "Shelley's 'Cloud' (7th S. ix. 207; x. 511;
         xi. 170).," *Notes and Queries,* Seventh Series XI, No.
         274 (March 28, 1891), 254. [T]

[1518] [Anonymous]. "Mr. Land on a Lark," *The Critic*, New Series
        XV, No. 386 (May 23, 1891), 281. [C]

[1519] Ireland, Annie E. "On Some Extracts from Harriet Shelley's
        Letters," *The Gentleman's Magazine*, New Series XLVII
        [whole number CCLXXI], No. 1929 (September, 1891),
        232-245. [B; rptd.: item 1521]

[1520] Ross, Janet. "Byron at Pisa," *The Nineteenth Century*, XXX,
        No. 177 (November, 1891), 753-763. [B]

[1521] Ireland, Annie E. "On Some Extracts from Harriet Shelley's
        Letters," *Littell's Living Age*, CXCI, No. 2472 (November
        14, 1891), 430-437. [B; rptd. from item 1519]

[1522] [Signed "W."]. "Sister of a Great Poet," *Notes and Queries*,
        Seventh Series XII, No. 310 (December 5, 1891), 447.
        [T]

[1523] [Anonymous]. "Minor Notices," *The Critic*, New Series XVI,
        No. 416 (December 19, 1891), 348-350. [R of item
        1525: 349]

Books:

[1524] Axon, William E. A. *Shelley's Vegetarianism*. 13pp. London:
        [The Vegetarian Society], [1891]. [B]

[1525] Cook, Albert S., ed. *A Defense of Poetry*. Edited with
        Introduction and Notes by Albert S. Cook. xxv+86pp.
        Boston: Ginn & Company, 1891. [C: "Introduction,"
        vii-xxv; "Notes," (63)-80; "Analysis," (83)-86]

[1526] Dowden, Edward. *The Poetical Works of Percy Bysshe Shelley*.
        xliv+708pp. London: Macmillan and Co., 1891. [C,T]

[1527] Rossetti, William Michael, ed. *Shelley [/] Adonais*. viii+
        154pp. Oxford: At the Clarendon Press, 1891. [T; C:
        (1)-66, (95)-148]

[1528] Ruskin, John. *The Ethics of the Dust [/] Fiction, Fair and Foul
        [/] The Elements of Drawing*. *The Complete Works of John Ruskin*,
        volume XVI]. 413pp. Philadelphia: Reuwee, Wattley &
        Walsh, 1891. [M: 199, 215; rptd. from item 1068]

[1529] The Shelley Society. *The Shelley Society's Publications*. *First
        Series*. *No. I*. *The Shelley Society's Papers*. *Part II*. 177-
        396pp. London: Reeves and Turner, 1891. [C; rptd.
        from items 1413, 1415, 1418, 1422, 1424, 1428, 1432,
        1474, 1475]

[1530] Wines, Emma Stansbury. *The Moral Teaching of Shelley's Poems*.
24pp. Washington, D.C.: Judd & Detweiller, 1891. [C]

[1531] [Wise, Thomas James, and Harry Buxton Forman, eds.]. *Letters
from Percy Bysshe Shelley to William Godwin*. 2 vols. London:
privately printed, 1891. [T]

1892

Periodicals:

[1532] [Anonymous]. "Briefs on New Books," *The Dial*, XII, No. 142
(February, 1892), 361-365. [R of item 1525: 364]

[1533] Edgcumbe, Richard. "Shelley the Atheist.," *Notes and Queries*,
Eighth Series I, No. 8 (February 20, 1892), 142-144.
[B]

[1534] Clarke, Helen Archibald. "A Sketch of the Prometheus Myth
in Poetry," *Poet-Lore*, IV, No. 3 (March, 1892), 135-144.
[C: 142-143]

[1535] [Anonymous]. "The Shelley Memorial," *The Athenaeum*, No. 3358
(March 5, 1892), 314-315. [B; excerpt rptd.: item
1538]

[1536] Biagi, Guido. "The Last Days of Percy Bysshe Shelley. [/]
(With New Documents.)," *Harper's New Monthly Magazine*,
LXXXIV, No. 503 (April, 1892), 782-795. [B; revised
as item 1735]

[1537] Ward, C[harles] A. "Shelley the Atheist (8th S. i. 142).,"
Notes and Queries, Eighth Series I, No. 15 (April 9,
1892), 304. [B]

[1538] [Anonymous]. "The Shelley Monument," *The Critic*, New Series
XVII [whole number XX], No. 531 (April 23, 1892), 246.
[B; excerpted from item 1535]

[1539] Ellis, F[rederick] S[tartridge]. "Shelley's Nightingale
Heresies," *The Athenaeum*, No. 3368 (May 14, 1892), 634.
[C]

[1540] [Anonymous]. "The Shelley Concordance," *The Saturday Review*,
LXXIII, No. 1,907 (May 14, 1892), 580. [R: item 1603]

[1541] [Signed "Este"]. "Shelley the Atheist (8th S. i. 142,
304).," *Notes and Queries*, Eighth Series I, No. 20
(May 14, 1892), 404. [B]

[1542]   Bayne, Thomas.   "[Untitled, following item 1541]," *Notes and Queries*, Eighth Series I, No. 20 (May 14, 1892), 404. [B]

[1543]   Parkes, Kineton.   "Shelley's Faith: I. Its Development and Relativity," *Poet-Lore*, IV, Nos. 6 and 7 (June-July, 1892), [289]-304.   [C; rptd. from the first half of item 1424]

[1544]   Kingsland, William G.   "Shelley's Letters to Elizabeth Hitchener," *Poet-Lore*, IV, Nos. 6 and 7 (June-July, 1892), 304-314.   [B]

[1545]   Bouchier, Jonathan.   "Shelley the Atheist (8th S. i. 142, 304, 404).," *Notes and Queries*, Eighth Series I, No. 24 (June 11, 1892), 484-485.   [No M, despite title]

[1546]   Edgcumbe, Richard.   "[Untitled, following item 1545]," *Notes and Queries*, Eighth Series I, No. 24 (June 11, 1892), 485.   [B]

[1547]   Bayne, Thomas.   "[Untitled, following item 1546]," *Notes and Queries*, Eighth Series I, No. 24 (June 11, 1892), 485. [No M, despite title]

[1548]   Harting, J. E.   "Shelley's 'Night-Raven,'" *The Athenaeum*, No. 3372 (June 11, 1892), 763.   [C]

[1549]   Scudder, Vida D.   "The Prometheus Unbound of Shelley: I. The Drama and the Time," *The Atlantic Monthly*, LXX, No. ccccxvii (July, 1892), 106-115.   [C; rptd.: item 1613]

[1550]   Salt, H[enry] S[tephens].   "Shelley's Gospel of Nature," *The Hygienic Review*, No. 19 (July, 1892), 185-187.   [C]

[1551]   Bayne, Thomas, and [Signed "C.C.B." and "Este"].   "Shelley the Atheist (8th S. i. 142, 304, 404, 484).," *Notes and Queries*, Eighth Series II, No. 29 (July 16, 1892), 54-55.   [No M, despite title]

[1552]   Swinburne, Algernon Charles.   "The Centenary of Shelley," *The Athenaeum*, No. 3379 (July 30, 1892), 159.   [A poem]

[1553]   Watson, William.   "Shelley's Centenary," *The Spectator*, LXIX, No. 3,344 (July 30, 1892), 162.   [A one hundred and eight line poem; rptd.: items 1581, 1618, 1879]

[1554]   Adams, Francis.   "Shelley," *The Fortnightly Review*, New Series LII [whole number LVIII], No. cccviii (August, 1892), [217]-223.   [C; rptd.: items 1588, 1747]

[1555]   Alger, G. W.   "In Memoriam, Shelley.   1792-1892.," *Poet-Lore*,
         IV, Nos. 8 and 9 (August-September, 1892), 315-318.
         [C]

*[1556]   [Anonymous].   "The Shelley Centenary," *The Library Review*,
         I (August, 1892), 383-390.   [C]

[1557]   [Anonymous].   "Mary Wollstonecraft Shelley," *Temple Bar*,
         XCV (August, 1892), 457-477.   [B]

*[1558]   Aylward, F. Graham.   "Review of Shelley Concordance," *The
         Library Review*, I (August, 1892), 390-393.   [R: item
         1603]

*[1559]   Britton, J. J.   "For the Shelley Centenary," *The Library
         Review*, I (August, 1892), 337.   [A sonnet]

*[1560]   Kingsland, William G.   "Shelley's Letters to Elizabeth
         Hitchener," *Poet-Lore*, IV, Nos. 8 and 9 (August-Septem-
         ber, 1892), 378.   [?B]

[1561]   Malone, John.   "A Search for Shelley's American Ancestor,"
         Century Magazine, XLIV, No. 4 (August, 1892), 634-636.
         [B]

[1562]   Parkes, Kineton.   "Shelley's Faith: II. Its Prophecy,"
         Poet-Lore, IV, Nos. 8 and 9 (August-September, 1892),
         397-408.   [C; rptd. from the second half of item 1424]

[1563]   Scudder, Vida D.   "The Prometheus Unbound of Shelley: II.
         The Myth of the Drama," *The Atlantic Monthly*, LXX, No.
         ccccxviii (August, 1892), 261-272.   [C; rptd.: item
         1613]

[1564]   Stedman, Edmund Clarence.   "Ariel," *The Atlantic Monthly*,
         LXX, No. ccccxviii (August, 1892), [145]-147.   [Poem;
         rptd.: items 1572, 1717]

[1565]   Woodberry, George E[dward].   "Shelley's Work," *Century
         Magazine*, XLIV, No. 4 (August, 1892), 622-629.   [C;
         rptd.: items 1768, 2189; excerpted in item 1572]

[1566]   Carman, Bliss.   "The White Gull.   [/] For the Centenary of
         the Birth of Shelley, Aug. 4th, 1892.," *The Independent*
         [New York], XLIV, No. 2279 (August 4, 1892), 9-10 [also
         continuously numbered as (1081)-(1082)].   [A one
         hundred and ninety-eight line poem]

[1567]   Tabb, John B.   "To Shelley.   [/] Born August 4th, 1792;
         Died July 8th, 1822.," *The Independent* [New York], XLIV,
         No. 2279 (August 4, 1892), [1] [also continuously
         numbered as (1073)].   [A twelve line poem]

[1568]   West, Kenyon. "The Centenary of Percy Bysshe Shelley.
          Born at Field Place, Sussex, England, August 4th, 1792.
          Drowned in the Gulf of Spezzia, Italy, July 8th,
          1822.," *The Independent* [New York], XLIV, No. 2279
          (August 4, 1892), 10-11 [also continuously numbered
          as (1082)-(1083)]. [C]

*[1569]   [Anonymous]. "Shelley and the Philistines," *The Pall Mall
          Gazette*, [?] (August [?], 1892), [?p]. [R: item 1612;
          rptd.: item 1571]

[1570]   [Anonymous]. "The Shelley Centenary," *The Christian Union*,
          XLVI, No. 6 (August 6, 1892), 236-237. [C; rptd.:
          item 1573]

[1571]   [Anonymous]. "'Shelley's Principles,'" *The Critic*, New
          Series XVIII [whole number XXI], No. 546 (August 6,
          1892), 63. [R: item 1612]

[1572]   [Anonymous]. "The Shelley Centenary," *The Critic*, New Series
          XVIII [whole number XXI], No. 546 (August 6, 1892),
          72-73. [C and M, in part rptd. from items 1564, 1565]

[1573]   [Anonymous]. "The Shelley Centenary," *The Critic*, New Series
          XVIII [whole number XXI], No. 547 (August 13, 1892),
          82-83. [A sonnet by Theodore Watts, and item rptd.
          from item 1570]

[1574]   West, Kenyon. "Percy Bysshe Shelley. 1792-1892," *The
          Literary World*, XXIII, No. 17 (August 13, 1892), 276-277.
          [C]

[1575]   [Anonymous]. "The Shelley Centenary [/] The Horsham
          Memorial," *The Critic*, New Series XVIII [whole number
          XXI], No. 549 (August 27, 1892), 111. [M]

[1576]   [Signed "W.C.B."]. "Shelley.," *Notes and Queries*, Eighth
          Series II, No. 35 (August 27, 1892), 163. [C]

*[1577]   Gosse, Edmund. "The Shelley Centenary," *The Library Review*,
          I (September, 1892), 473-476. [?C]

[1578]   Scudder, Vida D. "The Prometheus Unbound of Shelley: III.
          The Drama as a Work of Art," *The Atlantic Monthly*, LXX,
          No. ccccxix (September, 1892), 391-401. [C; rptd.:
          item 1613]

[1579]   Shaw, George Bernard. "Shaming the Devil about Shelley,"
          The Albemarle, II, No. 3 (September, 1892), 91-98. [C;
          rptd.: item 2583]

[1580] Sylvanus Urban [pseud. of Henry Charles Beeching]. "Table
        Talk," *The Gentleman's Magazine*, New Series XLIX [whole
        number CCLXXIII], No. 1941 (September, 1892), 319-324.
        [M; R of item 1603: 323-324]

[1581] Watson, William. "Shelley's Centenary," *The Eclectic Magazine*,
        New Series LVI [whole number CXIX], No. 3 (September,
        1892), 388-390. [A poem; rptd. from item 1563]

[1582] [Anonymous]. "A Century of Shelley," *The Dial*, XIII,
        No. 149 (September 1, 1892), 129-130. [C]

[1583] [Anonymous]. "Chronicle and Comment," *The Dial*, XIII,
        No. 149 (September 1, 1892), 131. [M]

[1584] McMahan, Anna B[enneson]. "Communications. Emerson's
        Obtuseness to Shelley," *The Dial*, XIII, No. 149 (September
        1, 1892), 130. [C]

[1585] [Signed "W.R.P."]. "Death of Shelley," *The Dial*, XIII,
        No. 149 (September 1, 1892), 130. [A sonnet]

[1586] Stedman, Edmund C[larence], and Richard Watson Gilder.
        "The Shelley Memorial Subscription," *The Dial*, XIII,
        No. 150 (September 16, 1892), 194. [M]

[1587] Stedman, Edmund C[larence], and Richard Watson Gilder.
        "The Shelley Memorial," *The Critic*, New Series XVIII
        [whole number XXI], No. 552 (September 17, 1892), 156.
        [M]

[1588] Adams, Francis. "Shelley," *The Eclectic Magazine*, New Series
        LVI [whole number CXIX], No. 4 (October, 1892), 500-
        504. [C; rptd. from item 1554]

[1589] Armitt, Annie. "Art. II. —The Story of Mary Shelley,"
        The Scottish Review, XX (October, 1892), 254-275. [B]

[1590] Kingsland, William G. "Notes and News," *Poet-Lore*, IV,
        No. 10 (October, 1892), 527. [M]

[1591] Waller, W. F. "Shelley.," *Notes and Queries*, Eighth Series
        II, No. 42 (October 15, 1892), 305. [C]

[1592] [Signed "Q.V."]. "Shelley (8th S. ii. 305).," *Notes and
        Queries*, Eighth Series II, No. 46 (November 12, 1892),
        396. [C]

[1593] Channing, Grace Ellery. "At Shelley's Grave," *The Califor-
        nian Illustrated Magazine*, III, No. 1 (December, 1892),
        123. [A twenty-eight line poem]

[1594]   Channing, Grace Ellery. "A Passionate Pilgrim," *The Califor-*
          nian Illustrated Magazine, III, No. 1 (December, 1892),
          125-131. [C]

[1595]   West, Kenyon. "Percy Bysshe Shelley. A Study of His
          General Characteristics," *The Andover Review*, XVIII,
          No. cviii (December, 1892), 573-591. [C]

[1596]   Waller, W. F. "Shelley (8th S. ii. 305, 396).," *Notes and*
          Queries, Eighth Series II, No. 50 (December 10, 1892),
          472. [C]

[1597]   Aldrich, T. B., R[ichard] W[atson] Gilder, and E[dmund]
          C[larence] Stedman. "The Shelley Memorial Subscrip-
          tion," *The Dial*, XIII, No. 156 (December 16, 1892),
          381. [M]

[1598]   [Anonymous]. "Mr. Woodberry's 'Centenary' Shelley," *The*
          Critic, New Series XVIII [whole number XXI], No. 565
          (December 24, 1892), 353. [R: item 1620]

Books:

[1599]   Callow, Alice M. "Essay on 'Epipsychidion.,'" [27]-33 in
          Byron-Shelley-Keats [/] *In Memoriam* [/] *Endowed Yearly Prizes for*
          the Best Essay in English, Written by a Woman of Any Nation.
          Each Writer is responsible for her own essay. *Prize*
          Essays [/] *Third Set.* With "Gossip" by Rose Mary Crawshay
          [editor]. 35pp. Cathedine, Bwlch, Breconshire:
          privately printed, [1892]. [C]

[1600]   Corson, Hiram. *A Primer of English Verse* [/] *Chiefly in Its*
          Aesthetic and Organic Character. iv+232pp. Boston: Ginn &
          Company, 1892. [C: 111-120, 139-141]

*[1601]   Crosse, Mrs. Andrew [Cornelia A. H.]. *Red Letters Days of My*
          Life. 2 vols. London: Richard Bentley & Son, 1892.
          [M]

[1602]   Dowden, Edward. "Shelley," 386-388 in Volume IX in
          Chambers's Encyclopedia [/] *A Dictionary of Universal Knowledge.*
          London: Willia & Robert Chambers, Limited, 1892. [B,C]

[1603]   Ellis, F[rederick] S[tartridge]. *A Lexical Concordance to the*
          Poetical Works of Percy Bysshe Shelley [/] *An Attempt to Classify*
          Every Word Found Therein According to Its Signification. xi+
          818pp. London: Bernard Quaritch, 1892. [T]

[1603]   Forman, H[arry] Buxton. *A Memoir of Percy Bysshe Shelley.*
          lxvipp. London: privately printed [Chiswick Press],
          1892. [B; revised and rptd.: item 1605]

[1605]   Forman, H[arry] Buxton, ed. *The Poetical Works of Percy Bysshe Shelley* [/] *Edited with a Memoir by H. Buxton Forman*. ["The Aldine Edition of the British Poets"]. 5 vols. London: George Bell & Sons, 1892. [T,B,C]

[1606]   Holmes, Oliver Wendell. *The Writings of Oliver Wendell Holmes*. 14 vols. Boston: Houghton Mifflin and Company, 1892. [M: II, 239-240; X, 18; XIV, 244, 253, 258, 309, 337; "After a Lecture on Shelley," a poem, XII, 227-229, rptd. from item 718]

[1607]   Hughson, Shirley Carter, ed. *The Best Letters of Percy Bysshe Shelley*. vi+328pp. Chicago: A. C. McClurg and Company, 1892. [T]

[1608]   Kingsland, William G. *Shelley: A Tribute*. 2pp. [London: privately printed, 1892]. [A poem]

[1609]   Middleton, Charles S. *Centenary Ode Written in Commemoration of Percy Bysshe Shelley, Born August 4th, 1792*. 4pp. [London: privately printed, 1892]. [A poem]

[1610]   Roberts, Charles G[eorge] D[ouglas]. *Ave: An Ode for the Centenary of the Birth of Percy Bysshe Shelley, August 4, 1792*. 27pp. Toronto: Williamson Book Company, 1892. [A poem]

[1611]   Royce, Josiah. *The Spirit of Modern Philosophy. An Essay in the Form of Lectures*. xv+519pp. Boston: Houghton Mifflin Company, 1892. [M: 226]

[1612]   Salt, Henry S[tephens]. *Shelley's Principles, Has Time Refuted or Confirmed Them. A Retrospect and Forecast*. viii+82pp. London: William Reeves, [1892]. [C]

[1613]   Scudder, Vida D. *Prometheus Unbound* [/] *A Lyrical Drama*. Edited by Vida D. Scudder. lviii+171pp. Boston: D. C. Heath & Co., 1892. [T; C: "Introduction," ix-lviii, rptd. from item 1549, 1563, 1578; "Suggestions. . . ," 121-144; "Notes," 145-169; "Bibliography," 171]

[1614]   Sharp, William. *The Life and Letters of Joseph Severn*. xix+308pp New York: Charles Scribner's Sons, 1892. [M: 33, 43, 63, 96, 115-124, 126, 127, 129, 130, 135, 250, 262-264]

[1615]   Stedman, Edmund Clarence. *The Nature and Elements of Poetry*. xx+338pp. Boston: Houghton, Mifflin and Company, 1892. [M: 25, 69, 89, 90, 117-118, 123-124, 132, 143, 169, 173, 179, 208, 218-219, 251, 266, 290]

[1616]   Swanwick, Anna. *Poets the Interpreters of Their Age*. x+392pp. London: George Bell & Sons, 1892. [C: "Percy Bysshe Shelley.," (300)-311]

[1617]   Thomson, James ["B.V."].   *Poems, Essays and Fragments.* xiv+
          267pp. London: Bertram Dobell, 1892. [C: "Shelley,"
          95-110; rptd. from item 697]

[1618]   Watson, William. *Shelley Centenary. (August 4th, 1892.)* 18pp.
          London: privately printed, 1892. [A poem; rptd. from
          item 1553]

[1619]   Wise, Thomas J[ames]. *The Shelley Centenary 1892.[/] Performance of
          the "Cenci."*   4pp. [London:] privately printed, 1892.
          [C]

[1620]   Woodberry, George Edward, ed.   *The Complete Poetical Works of
          Percy Bysshe Shelley [/] The Text newly collated and revised [/]
          and Edited with a Memoir and Notes [/] Centenary Edition.*
          4 vols. Boston: The Houghton Mifflin Company, 1892.
          [T,C,B; revised edition: item 1786]

                            1893

Periodicals:

[1621]   West, Kenyon.   "Percy Bysshe Shelley," *The Chautauquan,* New
          Series VII [whole number XVI], No. 4 (January, 1893),
          422-430.   [C]

[1622]   McDaniels, J. H.   "Woodberry's Shelley. —I.," *The Nation,*
          LVI, No. 1439 (January 26, 1893), 68-70. [R: item
          1620]

[1623]   Cook, Albert S.   "Dewy-Feathered," *MLN,* VIII, No. 2 (Febru-
          ary, 1893), 59-60.   [C]

[1624]   McDaniels, J. H.   "Woodberry's Shelley. —II.," *The Nation,*
          LVI, No. 1440 (February 2, 1893), 86. [R: item 1620]

[1625]   [Anonymous].   "Interpretation of Shelley's Prometheus
          Unbound," *The Dial,* XIV, No. 161 (March 1, 1893),
          150-151. [R: item 1613]

[1626]   [Anonymous].   "Woodberry's Shelley," *The Literary World,*
          XXIV, No. 5 (March 11, 1893), 69-70. [R: item 1620]

[1627]   [Anonymous].   "Minor Notices," *The Literary World,* XXIV,
          No. 5 (March 11, 1893), 75-76. [R: item 1613]

[1628]   [Anonymous].   "Educational Literature," *The Critic,* New
          Series XIX [whole number XXII], No. 580 (April 1,
          1893), 197-198. [R: item 1613]

[1629]   Anderson, Melville B.   "The Centenary Edition of Shelley,"
         The Dial, XIV, No. 164 (April 16, 1893), 244-246.   [R:
         item 1620]

[1630]   Aldrich, T. B., R[ichard] W[atson] Gilder and E[dmund]
         C[larence] Stedman.   "The Shelley Memorial Fund,"
         The Dial, XIV, No. 166 (May 16, 1893), 302.   [M]

[1631]   [Anonymous].   "The Contributor's Club [/] A Shelley Haunt,"
         The Atlantic Monthly, LXXI, No. ccccxxviii (June, 1893),
         855-856.   [B]

[1632]   [Hutton, Richard Holt].   "Shelley as Prophet," *The Spectator*,
         LXX. No. 3,391 (June 24, 1893), 846-847.   [C; rptd.:
         item 1891]

*[1633] Smyser, William E.   "Shelley's Revolutionary Ideal and Its
         Influence on His Poetry," *The Methodist Review*, LIII (July,
         1893), 538-553.   [C]

[1634]   [?Jeaffreson, John Cordy].   " *The Poetical Works of Percy Bysshe
         Shelley*. Edited, with a Memoir, by H. Buxton Forman.
         5 vols.   "The Aldine Edition" (Bell & Sons.) [/] (First
         Notice.).," *The Athenaeum*, No. 3428 (July 8, 1893), 55-57.
         [R: item 1605]

[1635]   Waugh, Arthur.   "London Letter," *The Critic*, New Series XX
         [whole number XXIII], No. 594 (July 8, 1893), 29.   [M]

[1636]   [?Jeaffreson, John Cordy].   "*The Poetical Works of Percy Bysshe
         Shelley*. Edited with a Memoir, by J. Buxton Forman.
         5 vols.   "The Aldine Edition." (Bell & Sons.) [/]
         (Second Notice).," *The Athenaeum*, No. 3429 (July 15,
         1893), 90-91.   [R: item 1605]

[1637]   [Anonymous].   "Shelley in the City.   [/] A Chat with Mr.
         Wise on the Guildhall Exhibition.," *The Westminster
         Gazette*, II, No. 141 (July 17, 1893), [1]-2.   [M]

[1638]   Edgcumbe, Richard.   "Sir Byssh [*sic*] Shelley," *Notes and
         Queries*, Eighth Series IV, No. 91 (September 23, 1893),
         245.   [B]

[1639]   Yardley, E.   "Shelley.," *Notes and Queries*, Eighth Series IV,
         No. 93 (October 7, 1893), 285.   [C]

[1640]   Graham, William.   "Chats with Jane Clermont," *The Nineteenth
         Century*, XXXIV, No. 201 (November, 1893), 753-769.   [B;
         first of two parts; rptd.: item 1737]

*[1641] [?Anonymous].   "[?]," *Poet-Lore*, V ([?],1893), 578.   [?M]

Books:

[1642] Allingham, William. *Varieties in Prose.* 3 vols. London:
        Longmans, Green and Co., 1893. [C: "Some Curiosities
        of Criticism," III, (313)-331; M: 329]

*[1643] Brooke, Stopford A. *The Development of Theology as Illustrated in
        English Poetry from 1780 to 1830.* [?pp]. London: [?],
        1893. [C]

[1644] Gosse, Edmund. *Questions at Issue.* xii+333pp. London:
        William Heinemann, 1893. [C: "Shelley in 1892," (199)-
        215]

[1645] Thompson, Maurice. *The Ethics of Literary Art* [/] *The Carew
        Lectures* [/] *For 1893* [/] *Hartford Theological Seminary.* 89pp.
        Hartford, Conn.: Hartford Seminary Press, 1893. [M;
        10-11, 74-75]

                              1894

Periodicals:

[1646] Graham, William. "Chats with Jane Clermont (concluded),"
        The Nineteenth Century, XXXV, No. 203 (January, 1894), 76-
        90. [B; second of two parts; rptd.: item 1737]

[1647] Harrison, Frederic. "English Literature of the Victorian
        Age.," *The Forum,* XVI (February, 1894), [703]-714. [C:
        710-711]

[1648] West, Kenyon. "Shelley and Vegetarianism.," *The Writer,* VII,
        No. 3 (March, 1894), 34-38. [B]

[1649] [Signed "D.J."]. "Shelley and Stacey.," *Notes and Queries,*
        Eighth Series V, No. 120 (April 14, 1894), 287. [B]

[1650] [Signed "C.C.B."]. "Shelley: 'The Question.,'" *Notes and
        Queries,* Eighth Series V, No. 121 (April 21, 1894),
        307. [T]

[1651] Marshall, Edward H. "Shelley: 'The Question' (8th S. v.
        307).," *Notes and Queries,* Eighth Series V, No. 126 (May
        26, 1894), 417. [T]

[1652] Platt, Isaac Hull. "The Cosmic Sense as Manifested in
        Shelley and Whitman," *The Conservator* [Philadelphia],
        V, No. 4 (June, 1894), 54-55. [C]

[1653]   Price, Thomas R.   "III. —King Lear: A Study of Shake-
         spere's Dramatic Method.," *PMLA*, IX, No. 2 (June,
         1894), 165-181.   [M: 165]

[1654]   Garnett, F. Brooksbank.   "Shelley and Stacey (8th S. v.
         287).," *Notes and Queries*, Eighth Series V, No. 129
         (June 16, 1894),471-472.   [B]

[1655]   Waller, W. F.   "[Untitled, following item 1654]," *Notes and
         Queries*, Eighth Series V, No. 129 (June 16, 1894), 472.
         [B]

[1656]   Twain, Mark [pseud. of Samuel Langhorne Clemens].   "In
         Defense of Harriet Shelley. —I," *The North American
         Review*, CLIX, No. 452 (July, 1894), [108]-119.   [B;
         rptd.: item 1720]

*[1657] Wheeler, D. H.   "Shelley's Place in English Poetry," *The
         Methodist Review*, LIV (July-August, 1894), 574-583.   [C]

[1658]   Twain, Mark [pseud. of Samuel Langhorne Clemens].   "In
         Defense of Harriet Shelley. —II," *The North American
         Review*, CLIX, No. 453 (August, 1894), [240]-251.   [B;
         rptd.: item 1720]

[1659]   Twain, Mark [pseud. of Samuel Langhorne Clemens].   "In
         Defense of Harriet Shelley. —III," *The North American
         Review*, CLIX, No. 454 (September, 1894), [353]-368.
         [B; rptd.: item 1720]

[1660]   Cappon, James.   "Shelley and Browning.," *Queen's Quarterly*,
         II, No. 2 (October, 1894), [168]-173.   [C]

[1661]   [Anonymous].   "Notes," *The Critic*, New Series XXII [whole
         number XXV], No. 660 (October 13, 1894), 249.   [M]

[1662]   [Anonymous].   "The Shelley Memorial at Viareggio," *The
         Critic*, New Series XXII [whole number XXV], No. 662
         (October 27, 1894), 279.   [B]

[1663]   Garnett, Richard.   "Shelley in Italy," *The English Illustrated
         Magazine*, XII, No. 135 (December, 1894), [143]-149.   [B]

*[1664] [Anonymous].   "Percy Bysshe Shelley and Mrs. Shelley,"
         Pratt Institute Library School [/] *Lectures on General Literature*
         [Brooklyn, New York], No. 60 (1893-1894), 557-561.' [T]

Books:

[1665]   Elton, Charles I[saac].   *An Account of Shelley's Visits to France,*

*Switzerland, and Savoy, in the Years 1814 and 1816, with
Extracts from "The History of a Six Weeks' Tour" and "Letters
Descriptive of a Sail Round the Lake of Geneva and of the
Glaciers of Chamouni," First Published in the Year 1817.*
viii+200pp. London: Bliss, Sands, & Foster, 1894. [B]

[1666] Lowell, James Russell. *Letters of James Russell Lowell.* Edited
by Charles Eliot Norton. 2 vols. New York: Harper &
Brothers, 1894. [M: II, 191]

[1667] Rossetti, W[illia]m M[ichael]. "Shelley at Cwm Elan and
Nantgwilt.," [17]-35 in R. Eustace Tickell, *The Vale
of Nantgwilt [/] A Submerged Valley [/] Illustrative and Descriptive of the Elan and Claerwen Valleys in Radnorshire [/] Shortly
to Be Submerged by the Reservoirs for the Water Supply of Birmingham.* 40pp. London: J. S. Virtue & Co., 1894. [B]

[1668] Swinburne, Algernon Charles. *Studies in Prose and Poetry.*
298pp. London: Chatto & Windus, 1894. [C: "Les
Cenci. 1883.," 146-157]

[1669] Tabb, John B. *Poems.* xi+172pp. London: John Lane, 1894.
[C: "To Shelley.," a poem, 114]

[1670] Wise, Thomas J[ames]. *Letters from Percy Bysshe Shelley to J. H.
Leigh Hunt.* 2 vols. [only Volume I printed]. London:
privately printed, 1894. [T]

1895

Periodicals:

[1671] Converse, Florence. "Shelley's Influence on Browning,"
Poet-Lore, VII, No. 1 (January, 1895), 18-28. [C]

[1672] Bouchier, Jonathan. "Poetic Parallel: Spenser, Shelley.,"
Notes and Queries, Eighth Series VIII, No. 199 (October
19, 1895), 304. [C]

[1673] Axson, Stockton. "Shelley's 'The Triumph of Life,'" *The
Citizen*, I, No. 9 (November, 1895), 209-212. [C]

[1674] Hurst, John L. "The Graves of Shelley and Trelawney [*sic*],"
The Critic, New Series XXIV [whole number XXVII], No. 715
(November 2, 1895), 285. [B]

[1675] Price, Charlotte A. "Famous Poets. VII—Percy Bysshe
Shelley," *Belgravia*, LXXXVIII (December, 1895), [399]-
430. [B]

[1676]   [Signed "E.M.S."]. "Percy Bysshe Shelley and the Sid-
          neys.," *Notes and Queries*, Eight Series VIII, No. 209
          (December 28, 1895), 505. [B]

*[1677]   [?Anonymous]. "[?]," *Poet-Lore*, VII ([?], 1895), 483.   [?M]

Books:

*[1678]   Browning, Robert. *Letters from Robert Browning to Various Corre-
          spondents.* [Browning Society Edition]. 2 vols. London
          privately printed, 1895. [M: I, (?p)]

[1679]   Ouida [pseud. of Louise de la Ramée]. *Views and Opinions.*
          [iii]+399pp. London: Methuen & Co., 1895. [C; rptd.
          from item 1482]

[1680]   Nicoll, W. Robertson, and Thomas J[ames] Wise, eds.
          *Literary Anecdotes of the Nineteenth Century: Contributions
          Towards A Literary History of the Period.* 2 vols. London:
          Hodder & Stoughton, [volume I] 1895 and [volume II]
          1896. [M: I, 26; T: "A Bundle of Letters from Shelley
          to Leight Hunt.," I, (319)-358; M: II, 107, 366 (mis-
          printed "66"]; B: "Jane Clairmont.," II, 459-461]

[1681]   Payne, William Morton. *Little Leaders.* x+278pp. Chicago:
          Way & Williams, 1895. [C: "Literature on the Stage.,"
          (13)-22; Shelley: 18-20]

[1682]   Scudder, Vida D. *The Life of the Spirit in the Modern English
          Poets.* v+349pp. Boston: Houghton, Mifflin and Company
          1895. [C: "Ideals of Redemption, Mediæval and Modern,
          (96)-144; and numerous M]

[1683]   Whittaker, Thomas. *Essays and Notices [/] Philosophical and Psy-
          chological.* xi+370pp. London: T. Fisher Unwin, 1895.
          [C: "The Musical and the Picturesque Elements in
          Poetry.," 95-110; Shelley: 103-109]

                              1896

Periodicals:

[1684]   Scarlett, B. Florence. "Percy Bysshe Shelley and the
          Sidneys (8th S. viii. 505).," *Notes and Queries*, Eighth
          Series IX, No. 211 (January 11, 1896), 37. [B]

[1685]   Platt, Isaac Hull. "Shelley and Whitman: A Comparison an a Contrast," *Poet-Lore*, VIII, No. 6 (June, 1896), 332-342. [C]

[1686] Fisher, Charles. "A Triad of Elegies," *Temple Bar*, CVIII (July, 1896), 388-396. [C]

[1687] Wilson, Alice L. "Shelley and Verlaine," *Poet-Lore*, VIII, No. 7 (July, 1896), 406-420. [C]

[1688] Colby, C. W. *"Percy Bysshe Shelley:* Poet and Pioneer. A Biographical Study. By Henry S. Salt. London: William Reeves; New York: Charles Scribner's Sons. 1896.," *The Nation*, LXIII, No. 1619 (July 9, 1896), 36. [R: item 1694]

[1689] [Anonymous]. "Shelley—Salted!," *The Literary World*, XXVII, No. 16 (August 8, 1896), 244-245. [R: item 1694]

[1690] [Anonymous]. "New Books and New Editions," *The Critic*, XXVI [whole number XXIX], No. 764 (October 10, 1896), 211-212. [R of item 1694: 212]

[1691] [Benson, Arthur Christopher]. "Shelley at Tremadoc," *Macmillan's Magazine*, LXXV, No. 446 (December, 1896), 126-132. [B]

Books:

[1692] Dowden, Edward. *The Life of Percy Bysshe Shelley*. viii+602pp. London: Kegan Paul, Trench, Trübner & Co., Ltd., 1896. [B; revised condensation of item 1283; rptd.: item 2416]

[1693] Saintsbury, George. *A History of Nineteenth Century Literature (1780-1895)*. xii+477pp. London: Macmillan and Co., 1896. [C: 81-88]

[1694] Salt, Henry S[tephens]. *Percy Bysshe Shelley* [/] *Poet and Pioneer* [/] *A Biographical Study*. xii+191pp. London: William Reeves. [B; revised and rptd. from item 1427]

[1695] Thomson, James ["B.V."]. *Biographical and Critical Studies*. Edited by Bertram Dobell. ix+483pp. London: Reeves and Turner and Bertram Dobell, 1896. [C: "Shelley," 270-283, rptd. from item 697; "Shelley's Religious Opinions," 283-288, rptd. from item 693; "Notice of 'The Life of Shelley' By John Addington Symonds ('English Men of Letters' Series)," 289-297, rptd. from item 1055]

[1696] Traill, H[enry] D[uff], ed. *Social England* [/] *A Record of the Progress of the People* [/] *In Religion Laws Learning Arts Industry*

*Commerce Science Literature and Manners from the Earliest Times
to the Present Day*.   6 vols.   London: Cassell and Company
1896.   [C: "Shelley's Early Work.," V, 586]

1897

Periodicals:

[1697]   Reynolds-Ball, E. A.   "Shelley's Italian Villa, Casa Magni
         and Its Neighbourhood," *The English Illustrated Magazine*,
         XVII, No. 164 (May, 1897), 121-124.   [B]

[1698]   [Anonymous].   "Academy Portraits.   XXVIII.—Percy Bysshe
         Shelley.," *The Academy*, LI, No. 1307 (May 22, 1897),
         548-559.   [C]

[1699]   North, Ernest Dressel.   "Some Unpublished Letters of
         Shelley.   With Notes on the Library of Their Late
         Owner C. W. Frederickson.   Part I.," *The Independent* [New
         York], XLIX, No. 2532 (June 10, 1897), [1]-3 [also
         continuously numbered as (737)-739].   [T]

[1700]   North, Ernest Dressel.   "Some Unpublished Letters of
         Shelley.   Part I.—Continued.," *The Independent* [New
         York], XLIX, No. 2533 (June 17, 1897), 7-8 [also
         continuously numbered as 775-776].   [T]

[1701]   North, Ernest Dressel.   "Some Unpublished Letters of
         Shelley.   Part II.," *The Independent* [New York], XLIX,
         No. 2536 (July 6, 1897), 5-6 [also continuously num-
         bered as 869-870].   [T]

[1702]   North, Ernest Dressel.   "Some Unpublished Letters of
         Shelley.   Part II. —Continued.,"*The Independent* [New
         York], XLIX, No. 2537 (July 15, 1897), 6 [also continu-
         ously numbered as 902].   [T]

[1703]   North, Ernest Dressel.   "Some Unpublished Letters of
         Shelley.   Part III.," *The Independent* [New York], XLIX,
         No. 2538 (July 22, 1897), 3-4 [also continuously num-
         bered as 931-932].   [No M, despite title]

[1704]   North, Ernest Dressel.   "Some Unpublished Letters of
         Shelley.   Part III. —Concluded.," *The Independent* [New
         York], XLIX, No. 2541 (August 12, 1897), 5-6 [also
         continuously numbered as 1037-1038].   [No M, despite
         title]

[1705]   [Anonymous].   "Mary Shelley.   A Local Reminiscence.   (From
         a Correspondent.),"*The Dundee Advertiser*, No. 11,382
         (September 7, 1897), 3.   [B]

[1706]   The Editors [Helen A. Clarke and Charlotte Porter].
          "School of Literature. New Ideas in Teaching English
          Literature. II. A Suggestion as to Required English.,"
          Poet-Lore, IX, No. 4 (October, November, December,
          1897), 585-606. [C]

Books:

[1707]   Cuthrie, W[illia]m Norman. *Modern Poet Prophets [/] Essays
          Critical and Interpretive.* viii+349pp. Cincinnati: The
          Robert Clarke Company, 1897. [C: "The Prometheus Un-
          bound of Shelley—A Drama of Human Destiny.," 146-
          202; "Appendices," 336-341]

[1708]   Dowden, Edward. *The French Revolution and English Literature.*
          vi+285pp. London: Kegan Paul, Trench, Trübner & Co.,
          Ltd., 1897. [C: "Renewed Revolutionary Advance:
          Moore, Landor, Byron, Shelley.," (243)-285]

[1709]   G[arnett], R[ichard]. "Shelley, Percy Bysshe," 31-40 in
          Volume LII of *The Dictionary of National Biography.* Edited
          by Sidney Lee. 63 vols. London: Smith, Elder & Co.,
          1897. [B; rptd.: item 1976]

[1710]   Herford, C[harles] H[arold]. *The Age of Wordsworth.* xxix+
          315pp. London: George Bell and Sons, 1897. [C:
          "The Shelley Group.," 216-284]

[1711]   Higginson, Thomas Wentworth. *Book and Heart [/] Essays on
          Literature and Life.* iv+237pp. New York: Harper &
          Brothers, 1897. [T: "A Shelley Manuscript," (22)-27]

[1712]   Lodge, Henry Cabot. *Certain Accepted Heroes [/] and Other Essays
          in Literature and Politics.* 269pp. New York: Harper &
          Brothers, 1897. [M: 130]

[1713]   Mitchell, Donald G[rant]. *English Lands Letters and Kings*
          [Volume IV:] *The Late Georges to Victoria.* xiii+294pp.
          New York: Charles Scribner's Sons, 1897. [C: 216-237]

[1714]   Palgrave, Francis T[urner]. *Landscape in Poetry from Homer to
          Tennyson.* xi+297pp. London: Macmillan and Co., Limited,
          1897. [C: 218-228]

[1715]   Robertson, John Mackinnon. *New Essays towards a Critical Method.*
          ix+[379]pp. London: John Lane, 1897. [C: "Shelley
          and Poetry (1884)," 191-235; rptd. from items 1196,
          1197, 1198]

[1716]   Rossetti, W[illiam] M[ichael], and H[arry] Buxton Forman,
          eds. *Letters from Percy Bysshe Shelley to Thomas Jefferson Hogg.*
          2 vols. [only Volume I printed]. London: privately

printed, 1897. [T]

[1717] Stedman, Edmund Clarence. *Poems* [/] *Now First Collected.*
        x+210pp. Boston: Houghton, Mifflin and Company, 1897.
        [A poem: "Ariel (/) In Memory of Percy Bysshe Shelley
        Born on the Fourth of August, A.D., 1792," (199)-206;
        rptd. from item 1564]

[1718] Strong, Augustus Hopkins. *The Great Poets and Their Theology.*
        xvii+531pp. Philadelphia: American Baptist Publication
        Society, 1897. [M: 3, 338, 416, 521]

[1719] Tennyson, Hallam. *Alfred Lord Tennyson* [/] *A Memoir* [/] *By His
        Son.* 2 vols. New York: The Macmillan Company, 1897.
        [M: I, 141; II, 70, 285, 287, 499]

[1720] Twain, Mark [pseud. of Samuel Langhorne Clemens]. *How to
        Tell a Story And Other Essays.* 233pp. New York: Harper &
        Brothers, 1897. [B: "In Defence of Harriet Shelley,"
        (13)-90; rptd. from items 1656, 1658, 1659]

1898

Periodicals:

[1721] Crewe, Earl of. "Among my Books. A Leaf from an Inn
        Album," *Literature*, I, No. 11 (January 1, 1898), 336-
        337. [B]

[1722] Garnett, R[ichard]. "'To Constantia.,'" *The Athenaeum*,
        No. 3664 (January 15, 1898), 88. [T]

[1723] Hebb, John. "Byron and Shelley at Pisa," *Notes and Queries*,
        Ninth Series I, No. 8 (February 19, 1898), 142-143.
        [B]

[1724] Kuhns, [Levi] Oscar. "Dante's Influence on Shelley," *MLN*,
        XIII, No. 6 (June, 1898), 161-165. [C; rptd.: item
        1851]

[1725] [Signed "V.L."]. "Note on Shelley's 'Ode to Liberty,'
        Stanza 13; also on 'Passage of the Apennines.,'"
        The Athenaeum, No. 3687 (June 25, 1898), 822-823. [C,T]

[1726] Kingsland, William G. "Shelley and Godwin.," *Poet-Lore*, X,
        No. 3 (July, August, September, 1898), 389-397. [B,T]

[1727] Taylor, I[da] A. "On Friendships," *Blackwood's Edinburgh Maga-
        zine*, CLXIV, No. dccccxcv (September, 1898), 364-373.
        [B: 367]

[1728] Caldwell, Mary Grace. "A Study of Sense Epithets in
Shelley and Keats. Wellesley College Psychological
Studies.," *Poet-Lore*, X, No. 4 (October, November,
December, 1898), 573-579. [C]

[1729] [Anonymous]. "A Shelley Discovery," *The Academy*, LV,
No. 1379 (October, 1898), 42-43. [T]

[1730] Q[uiller-] C[ouch], A[rthur] T. "A Literary Causerie.
Victor and Cazire," *The Speaker*, XVIII (October 15,
1898), 462-463. [R: item 1740; rptd.: items 1732,
1743]

[1731] [Anonymous]. "Shelley's Poor Beginnings," *The Academy*, LV,
No. 1381 (October 22, 1898), 113. [R: item 1740]

[1732] Quiller-Couch, A[rthur] T. "Victor and Cazire," *Littell's
Living Age*, CCXIX, No. 2838 (November 26, 1898), 595-
598. [R: item 1740; rptd. from item 1730]

[1733] Wise, Thomas J[ames]. "The Lost Shelley," *The Bookman* [New
York], VIII, No. 4 (December, 1898), 371-373. [R:
item 1740; T]

[1734] [Anonymous]. "The Sunset of Shelley," *The Academy*, LV,
No. 1390 (December 24, 1898), 512-513. [R: item
1735]

Books:

[1735] Biagi, Guido. *The Last Days of Percy Bysshe Shelley. New Details
from Unpublished Documents.* [Translated from the Italian
Gli Ultimi Giorni di P. B. Shelley (Con Nuovi Documenti),
Florence, 1892]. viii+167pp. London: T. Fisher
Unwin, 1898. [B; revised version of item 1536]

[1736] Forster, Joseph. *Great Teachers.* 347pp. London: George
Redway, 1898. [C: "Shelley," (65)-100]

[1737] Graham, William. *Last Links with Byron, Shelley, and Keats.*
xx+121pp. London: Leonard Smithers & Co., 1898. [B:
"Chats with Jane Clermont," 1-34, rptd. from item 1640;
"Chats with Jane Clermont—continued," 35-63, rptd.
from item 1646]

[1738] Lilley, A. L. "Shelley," 33-61 in *Prophets of the Century.*
Edited by Arthur Rickett. vii+337pp. London: Ward
Lock and Co. Limited, 1898. [C]

[1739] Scudder, Vida D. *Social Ideals in English Letters.* 329pp.
Boston: Houghton, Mifflin and Company, 1898. [M: 87,
114, 119, 120, 144, 162, 187, 194, 227, 278]

[1740]   [Shelley, Percy Bysshe, and Elizabeth Shelley]. *Original Poetry by Victor and Cazire*. Edited by Richard Garnett. xxvii+66pp. London: John Lane, 1898. [C,T]

[1741]   Smith, Elizabeth Grant. *Memoirs of a Highland Lady* [/] *The Autobiography of Elizabeth Grant of Rothiemurchus Afterwards Mrs Smith of Baltiboys* [/] *1797-1830*. Edited by Lady Strachey. xix+495pp. London: John Murray, 1898. [B: 128-129]

[1742]   Turner, Fred. *Brentford: Literary and Historical Sketches*. 81pp. London: Elliot Stock, 1898. [B: "Memorable Brentford Houses. Percy Bysshe Shelley at Syon House Academy.," (25)-32; "Shelley (Percy Bysshe).," 60]

                                  1899

Periodicals:

[1743]   Quiller-Couch, A[rthur] T. "Victor and Cazire," *The Eclectic Magazine*, New Series I [whole number CXXXII], No. 1 (January, 1899), 74-77. [R: item 1740; rptd. from item 1730]

[1744]   Bradley, A[ndrew] C[ecil]. "Shelley and Brunetto Latini," *The Athenaeum*, No. 3729 (April 15, 1899), 469. [C]

[1745]   Marshall, Edward H. "Shelley at Oxford.," *Notes and Queries*, Ninth Series IV, No. 79 (July 1, 1899), 7. [B]

[1746]   Bowen, Edwin W. "Catullus and Shelley," *The Sewanee Review*, VII, No. 3 (July, 1899), [335]-341. [C]

Books:

[1747]   Adams, Francis. *Essays in Modernity* [/] *Criticisms and Dialogues By Francis Adams*. 253pp. London: John Lane, 1899. [C: "Shelley," (167)-183; rptd. from item 1554]

[1748]   Beavan, Arthur H. *James and Horace Smith* [/] *Joint Authors of 'Rejected Addresses'* [/] *A Family Narrative Based upon Hitherto Unpublished Private Diaries, Letters, and Other Documents*. xii+312pp. London: Hurst and Blackett, Limited., 1899 [B: 136-139, 149-152, 154-156, 161-163, 167-177]

[1749]   Browning, Robert, and Elizabeth Barrett Barrett. *The Letters of Robert Browning and Elizabeth Barrett Barrett* [/] *1845-1846*. 2 vols. New York: Harper & Brothers, 1899. [M: I, 38, 57, 65, 96, 116, 185, 196, 214, 215, 226, 228, 322, 326, 476, 562; II, 79, 151, 153, 254, 313]

[1750] Edgar, Pelham. *A Study of Shelley with Special Reference to His Nature Poetry*. ["Dissertation Presented to the Board of University Studies of the Johns Hopkins University for the Degree of Doctor of Philosophy"]. 155pp. Toronto: William Briggs, 1899. [C]

[1751] Hale, Edward Everett. *James Russell Lowell and His Friends*. x+303pp. Boston: Houghton, Mifflin and Company, 1899. [M: 23]

[1752] Hancock, Albert Elmer. *The French Revolution and the English Poets [/] A Study in Historical Criticism*. xvi+197pp. New York: Henry Holt and Company, 1899. [C: "Shelley.," 50-77]

[1753] Trent, William P[eterfield]. *The Authority of Criticism and Other Essays*. ix+291pp. New York: Charles Scribner's Sons, 1899. [C: "Apropos of Shelley," 35-96]

1900

Periodicals:

[1754] [Signed "Sigma Tau"]. "Shelley Bibliography.," *Notes and Queries*, Ninth Series V, No. 109 (January 27, 1900), 67-68. [T]

[1755] Roberts, W. "Shelley's Mother.," *Notes and Queries*, Ninth Series V, No. 114 (March 3, 1900), 169. [B]

[1756] [Anonymous]. "About Shelley's Edinburgh Marriage. A Discovery.," *Chambers's Journal*, Sixth Series III [whole number LXXVII], No. 122 (March 31, 1900), [273]-277. [B]

[1757] Larminie, William. "Carlyle and Shelley. A Parallel and a Contrast," *Contemporary Review*, LXXVII (May, 1900), [728]-741. [C]

[1758] Harris-Bickford, E. L. T. "Shelly [*sic*].," *The Book-Lover* [San Francisco], I, No. 4 (Summer [June, July, August], 1900), 457. [A sonnet]

[1759] [Mallock, William Hurrell]. "Art. VIII. —The Conditions of Great Poetry.," *The Quarterly Review*, XCII, No. 383 (July, 1900), 156-182. [C; Shelley: 158-170]

[1760] Garnett, Richard. "Shelley's Views on Art," *The Anglo-Saxon Review*, VI (September, 1900), 120-132. [C; rptd.: item 1760]

[1761]   Livingston, Luther S[amuel]. "First Books of Some Englis▌
         Authors. VI. Percy Bysshe Shelley," *The Bookman* [New
         York], XII, No. 4 (December, 1900), [379]-383. [C]

Books:

[1762]   Baddeley, [Welbore] St. Clair. *Autographs of Cloud and Sunbea▌
         in England and Italy.* vii+123pp. [Edinburgh]: privately
         printed [at the Ballantyne Press], 1900. [A poem:
         "Thermae Antoninianae," 43]

[1763]   Champneys, Basil. *Memoirs and Correspondence of Coventry Patmore*
         2 vols. London: George Bell and Sons, 1900. [M: I,
         44, 53, 55, 387; II, 97, 121, 222, 340, 435]

[1764]   Farnham, Charles Haight. *A Life of Francis Parkman.* xv+394p▌
         Boston: Little, Brown, and Company, 1900. [M: 346,
         348]

[1765]   Lamb, Charles. *The Life and Works of Charles Lamb.* Edited by
         Alfred Ainger. 12 vols. London: Macmillan and Co.,
         1899-1900. [M: XI (separately titled *The Letters of
         Charles Lamb Newly Arranged, with Additions,* Volume III),
         154, 241, 252]

[1766]   Saintsbury, George. *A History of Criticism and Literary Taste
         in Europe from the Earliest Texts to the Present Day.* 3 vols.
         Edinburgh: William Blackwood and Sons, 1900-1904. [M▌
         I, 199, 215; II, 87, 426; III: 232, 244, 260, 274-275▐
         376, 387, 501]

[1767]   Sharp, R[obert] Farquharson. *Architects of English Literature
         [/] Biographical Sketches of Great Writers from Shakespeare to
         Tennyson.* 326pp. New York: E. P. Dutton & Co., 1900.
         [B: "Shelley.," 202-217]

[1768]   Woodberry, George Edward. *Makers of Literature [/] Being Essa▐
         on Shelley, Landor, Browning [/] Byron, Arnold, Coleridge, Lowel▌
         [/] Whittier, and Others.* viii+440pp. New York: The Mac-
         millan Company, 1900. [C: "Shelley's Poetry: A
         Sketch.," 51-62; "Remarks on Shelley.," 186-228, rptd▐
         from item 1511 (in turn revised and rptd. from items
         1028, 1333, 1155); "Shelley's Work.," 405-440, rptd.
         from item 1565]

1901

Periodicals:

[1769]   Nettleton, Charles P. "Shelley.," *The Book-Lover* [San

Francisco], II, No. 6 (Winter [January, February, March], 1901), 112. [Four line poem]

*[1770] Forman, H. Buxton. "The Death of Shelley.," *The Daily News* [London], [?] (June [?16, ?17], 1901), [?p]. [B]

*[1771] Nicholson, E. W. B. "Shelley's Death.," *The Daily News* [London, [?] (June 19, 1901), [?p]. [B; reply to item 1770]

*[1772] [Anonymous]. "Shelley's Death.," *The Daily News* [London], [?] (June [?23, ?24], 1901), [?p]. [B; reply to item 1771]

*[1773] Nicholson, E. W. B. "Shelley's Death.," *The Daily News* [London], [?] (June [?24, ?25, ?or later], 1901), [?p]. [B; in reply to items 1771, 1772]

[1774] Simpson, Lucie. "The Radicalism of Shelley," *The Humanitarian Review*, XIX (August, 1901), 119-125. [C]

[1775] Garnett, Richard. "Portraits of Shelley at the National Portrait Gallery," *The Magazine of Art*, XXV, Part 251 (September, 1901), 492-495. [B]

[1776] Chesterton, G[ilbert] K[eith]. "A Grammar of Shelley.," *The Daily News* [London], [?] (September 12, 1901), 6, columns 1 and 2. [C]

[1777] Church, F. "Shelley's Cottage at Lynmouth, Devon.," *Notes and Queries*, Ninth Series VIII, No. 209 (December 28, 1901), 523. [B]

Books:

[1778] Beers, Henry A[ugustin]. *A History of English Romanticism in the Nineteenth Century.* viii+424pp. New York: Henry Holt and Co., 1901. [C: 101-102, 232-235]

[1779] Carmichael, Montgomery. *In Tuscany [/] Tuscan Towns, Tuscan Types and the Tuscan Tongue.* xvii+355pp. London: John Murray, 1901. [M: 128-130]

[1780] Collins, John Churton. *Ephemera Critica [/] or Plain Truths about Current Literature.* 379pp. Westminster [London]: Archibald Constable and Co. Ltd., 1901. [R: "English Literature at the Universities [/] II. Text Books," 76-83, Rossetti's edition of *Adonais* (Oxford: at the Clarendon Press, 1891)]

[1781] Fitzgerald, Edward. *More Letters of Edward Fitzgerald.* 295pp. London: Macmillan and Co., 1901. [M: 200]

[1782] Garnett, Richard. *Essays of an Ex-Librarian*. viii+359pp.
         New York: Dodd, Mead & Company, 1901. [C: "Shelley
         and Lord Beaconsfield," (99)-125, rptd. from item
         1367; "Shelley's Views on Art," (329)-359, rptd. from
         item 1760]

*[1783] Hales, John W. "Shelley's Adonais," *The Hampstead Annual* [/]
         1901 [London: C. Mayle], 87-100. [C; rptd.: item 1799]

[1784] Schuyler, Eugene. *Italian Influences*. vi+435pp. London:
         Sampson Low, Marston & Company, 1901. [C: "Shelley
         with Byron," 135-155]

[1785] Sweet, H[enry]. "A Source of Shelley's *Alastor*," 430-435
         in *An English Miscellany* [/] *Presented to Dr. Furnivall in Honour
         of His Seventy-Fifth Birthday*. x+500pp. Oxford: At the
         Clarendon Press, 1901. [C]

[1786] Woodberry, George Edward, ed. *The Complete Poetical Works of
         Shelley*. ["The Cambridge Edition of the Poets"]. xliii+
         651pp. Boston: The Houghton Mifflin Company, 1901.
         [T,C,B; one volume revised edition of item 1620]

*[1787] Young, John Russell. *Men and Memories* [/] *Personal Reminiscences*
         Edited by May D. Russell. 2 vols. New York: F.
         Tennyson Neely, [1901]. [M: ?p]

                            1902

Periodicals:

[1788] Salt, Henry S[tephens]. "Shelley as a Pioneer," *The Humane
         Review*, [II, No. 8 (January, 1902)], [354]-366. [C;
         rptd.: item 1807]

[1789] Bayley, A. R. "Shelley's Cottage at Lynmouth, Devon (9th
         S. viii. 523).," *Notes and Queries*, Ninth Series IX,
         No. 213 (January 25, 1902), 74. [B]

[1790] Chesterton, G[ilbert] K[eith]. "Shelley, Mr. Salt and
         Humanity.," *The Daily News* [London], [?] (February 4,
         1902), 6, column 1. [R: item 1788]

*[1791] [Anonymous]. "Who Was the 'Brave and Gentle' Friend?"
         The Daily News [London], [?] (February 27, 1902), [?p]
         [B]

[1792] Whiting, Mary Bradford. "The Love of Antigone," *Temple Bar*,
         CXXV (April, 1902), 473-480. [B]

[1793]   Burns, Edward F.   "Shelley.," *The Book-Lover* [San Francisco],
          III, No. 12 (May, June, 1902), 176.   [A sixty-eight
          line poem]

[1794]   Edgar, Pelham.   "The Nature-Poetry of Byron and Shelley,"
          The Canadian Magazine, XIX, No. 2 (May, 1902), 18-24.   [C]

[1795]   [Harris, J. H.].   "2. The Prometheus of Æschylus and the
          Prometheus of Shelley, by Principal J. H. Harris,
          Michigan Military Academy.," *The School Review*, X, No. 5
          [whole number 95] (May, 1902), 376-378.   [C]

[1796]   Bayley, A. R.   "Shelley's Ancestry.," *Notes and Queries*, Ninth
          Series IX, No. 229 (May 17, 1902), 381-382.   [B]

[1797]   Edgcumbe, Richard.   "Shelley's Ancestry (9th S. ix. 381.),"
          Notes and Queries, Ninth Series IX, No. 235 (June 28,
          1902), 509-510.   [B]

[1798]   Dixon, Ronald.   "[Untitled, following item 1797]," *Notes
          and Queries*, Ninth Series IX, No. 235 (June 28, 1902),
          510.   [B]

[1799]   Hales, John W.   "Shelley's 'Adonais.,'" *The Modern Language
          Quarterly* [London], V, No. 2 (July, 1902), [61]-65.
          [C; rptd. from item 1783]

[1800]   Bayley, A. R.   "[Untitled, third entry under the title
          'Shelley's Ancestry.'(9th S. ix. 381, 509.)]," *Notes
          and Queries*, Ninth Series X, No. 238 (July 19, 1902),
          50-51.   [B]

[1801]   Dixon, Ronald.   "[Untitled, following item 1800]," *Notes
          and Queries*, Ninth Series X, No. 238 (July 19, 1902),
          51.   [B]

[1802]   Edgcumbe, Richard.   "Shelley's Ancestry.   (9th S. ix. 381,
          509; x. 50.)," *Notes and Queries*, Ninth Series X, No. 247
          (September 20, 1902), 229-231.   [B]

[1803]   Knipe, M.   "Shelley at Bracknell.," *Notes and Queries*, Ninth
          Series X, No. 247 (September 20, 1902), 229.   [B]

[1804]   Stimson, John Ward.   "The Democracy of Shelley and Keats,"
          The Arena, XXVIII, No. 4 (October, 1902), [354]-369.
          [C]

Books:

[1805]   Joline, Adrian H[offman].   *Meditations of an Autograph Collec-
          tor*.   [vi]+316pp.   New York: Harper & Brothers, 1902.
          [M: 177-178]

[1806] Laughlin, Clara E. *Stories of Authors' Loves*. 2 vols.
Philadelphia: J. B. Lippincott Company, 1902. [B:
"Shelley, the Skylark Poet," II, 166-200]

[1807] Salt, Henry S[tephens]. *Shelley as a Pioneer of Humanitarianism*
15pp. London: Humanitarian League, 1902. [C; rptd.
from item 1788]

[1808] Williams, Edward Ellerker. *Journal of Edward Ellerker Williams*
[/] *Companion of Shelley and Byron in 1821 and 1822*. Edited
with a Introduction by Richard Garnett. [68]pp.
London: Elkin Mathews, 1902. [B]

1903

Periodicals:

[1809] Woodberry, George Edward. "The Poe-Chivers Papers," *The
Century Magazine*, New Series XLIII [whole number LXV],
No. 3 (January, 1903), 435-447. [M; first of two
parts]

[1810] Woodberry, George Edward. "The Poe-Chivers Papers," *The
Century Magazine*, New Series XLIII [whole number LXV],
No. 4 (February, 1903), 545-558. [M; second of two
parts]

[1811] [Anonymous]. " *Journal of Edward Ellerker Williams, Companion of
Shelley and Byron in 1821 and 1822*. With an Introduction
by Richard Garnett, C.B., LL.D. (Elkin Mathews.)," *The
Athenaeum*, No. 3928 (February 7, 1903), 171-172. [R:
item 1808]

[1812] Garnett, R[ichard]. "The Williams Diary.," *The Athenaeum*,
No. 3929 (February 14, 1903), 210. [C, in reply to
item 1811]

[1813] [Anonymous]. "Shelley's 'Sophocles.,'" *The Book-Lover* [San
Francisco], IV, No. 1 (March-April, 1903), 14. [B:
a photograph of Lady Shelley's gift to the Bodleian
Library]

[1814] Le Galliene, Richard. "Old Love Stories Retold. V.
Shelley and Mary Godwin," *The Cosmopolitan*, XXXV, No. 3
(July, 1903), [291]-297. [B; rptd.: item 1852]

[1815] Lynn, W. T. "Shelley and Astronomy," *Notes and Queries*, Ninth
Series XII, No. 311 (December 12, 1903), 467. [C]

Books:

[1816] Gosse, Edmund. *From the Age of Johnson to the Age of Tennyson.*
[*English Literature* [/] *An Illustrated Record* [/] *In Four Volumes.*
Volume IV.] xii+462pp. London: William Heinemann,
1903. [C: 122-134]

[1817] Hazlitt, William. *The Collected Works of William Hazlitt.*
Edited by A. R. Waller and Arnold Glover. 13 vols.
London: J. M. Dent & Company, 1903. [C and M: V, 378,
rptd. from item 47; VI, 149; 285, rptd. from item 74;
VII, 208, 246; 378-379, rptd. from item 47; VIII, 474;
X, 256, rptd. from item 24; XII, 179, rptd. from item
90; 341, rptd. from item 122]

[1818] Locock, C[harles] D[ealtry]. *An Examination of the Shelley
Manuscripts in the Bodleian Library* [/] *Being a collation thereof
with printed texts, resulting in the publication of several long
fragments hitherto unknown, and the introduction of many improved
readings into Prometheus Unbound, and other poems.* iv+75pp.
Oxford: At the Clarendon Press, 1903. [T]

[1819] Morley, John. *The Life of William Ewart Gladstone.* 3 vols.
New York: The Macmillan Company, 1903. [?M]

[1820] Rossetti, William Michael , ed. *Rossetti Papers* [/] *1862 to
1870.* xxiii+559pp. New York: Charles Scribner's Sons,
1903. [C and M: over one hundred indexed references]

[1821] Ruskin, John. *The Works of John Ruskin.* ["Library Edition."]
Edited by E. T. Cook and Alexander Wedderburn. 39
vols. London: George Allen, 1903-1912. [C and M:
see "General Index," under "Shelley, Percy Bysshe,"
XXXIX, 560-561]

[1822] Shelley, [Percy Bysshe]. *Shelley. Adonais.* Edited with
Introduction and Notes by William Michael Rossetti.
A New Edition revised with the assistance of A. O.
Prickard. viii, 162pp. Oxford: At the Clarendon
Press, 1903. [T,C]

[1823] Slicer, Thomas R. *Percy Bysshe Shelley* [/] *An Appreciation.*
82pp. New York: privately printed [The Literary
Collector Press], 1903. [C,T]

[1824] Wooldridge, Henry. *Fine Engraving of a Newly Discovered Bust of
Percy Bysshe Shelley* [/] *with Collected Family and Contemporary
"Word Portraits."* 16pp. Stourbridge, Eng.: Henry Woold-
ridge, 1903. [B]

[1825] Yeats, W[illiam] B[utler]. *Ideas of Good and Evil.* vii+341pp.
London: A. H. Bullen, 1903. [C: "The Philosophy of
Shelley's Poetry," 90-141]

Periodicals:

[1826] Steichen, Lilian. "A Study of Shelley's 'Prometheus Un-
        bound.,'" *The Sewanee Review*, XII, No. 1 (January, 1904),
        [44]-51. [C]

[1827] Roberts, W. "Shelley's Mother.," *Notes and Queries*, Tenth
        Series I, No. 23 (January 23, 1904), 68. [B]

[1828] Hill, M. Kirby. "Shelley at Home," *Temple Bar*, CXXIX (Feb-
        ruary, 1904), 225-228. [B]

[1829] Norlin, George. "Greek Sources of Shelley's Adonais," *The
        University of Colorado Studies*, I, No. 4 (February, 1904),
        [305]-321. [C]

[1830] [Anonymous]. " *Shelley's Adonais*. Edited, with introduction
        and notes, by W. M. Rossetti and A. O. Prickard. Second
        edition. Oxford: Clarendon Press; New York: H. Frowde
        1903.," *The Nation*, LXXVIII, No. 2020 (March 17, 1904),
        218-219. [R: item 1822]

[1831] [Signed "A.B.S.]. "Samuel Shelley.," *Notes and Queries*, Tenth
        Series I, No. 12 (March 19, 1904), 227. [B]

[1832] Coleman, Everard Home. "Samuel Shelley (10th S. i. 227).,
        Notes and Queries, Tenth Series I, No. 14 (April 2, 1904)
        278. [B]

[1833] [Anonymous]. "Some Recent Shelley Literature.," *The Athen-
        aeum*, No. 3991 (April 23, 1904), 522-524. [R: items
        1818, 1822, 1849, and a reprint of the Pisa edition
        of *Adonais* (Methuen & Co., London, 1904)]

[1834] Streatfeild, R. A. "Hogg's 'Shelley at Oxford,'" *The Athen-
        aeum*, No. 3992 (April 30, 1904), 562-563. [C]

[1835] Browning, Robert. "Shelley," *The Book-Lover* [San Francisco]
        V, No. 5 (May, 1904), 528. [A sixteen line poem]

[1836] Symons, Arthur. "Shelley's 'Tower of Famine.,'" *The Athen-
        aeum*, No. 3993 (May 7, 1904), 593. [T]

[1837] [Anonymous]. "Notes.," *The Nation*, LXXVIII, No. 2028 (May
        12, 1904), 371-373. [R: item 1849]

[1838] Rossetti, W[illia]m M[ichael]. "Shelley's 'Tower of
        Famine.,'" *The Athenaeum*, No. 3994 (May 14, 1904), 626.
        [T]

[1839]   Winstanley, Lilian. "Shelley as Nature Poet," *Englische Studien*, XXXIV, No. 1 ([July], 1904), 17-51. [C]

[1840]   Hill, M. Kirby. "Shelley at Bracknell," *Temple Bar*, CXXX (August, 1904), 199-203. [B]

[1841]   McMahan, Anna Benneson. "The Last Home of Shelley," *The Dial*, XXXVII, No. 435 (August 1, 1904), 55. [B]

[1842]   [Signed "A. S—r."]. "Italian Lines in Shelley.," *Notes and Queries*, Tenth Series II, No. 40 (October 1, 1904), 268. [T]

[1843]   Steuart, A. Francis. "Jane Clairmont's Grave.," *Notes and Queries*, Tenth Series II, No. 41 (October 8, 1904), 284. [B]

[1844]   Vaughan, Percy. "Early Shelley Pamphlets. IV.—The Irish Pamphlets.," *The Literary Guide and Rationalist Review*, [New Series] No. 101 (November 1, 1904), 169-170. [C; rptd.: item 1878]

[1845]   [Signed "Vox Clamantis"]. "The Ethical and Political Teachings of Shelley," *The Westminster Review*, CLXIII, No. 6 (December, 1904), [675]-682. [C]

[1846]   [Anonymous]. "Our Library Table," *The Athenaeum*, No. 4024 (December 10, 1904), 804-805. [R of item 1850: 805]

Books:

[1847]   Dowden, Edward. *The Life of Robert Browning.* ["The Temple Biographies"]. xvi+404pp. London: J. M. Dent & Co., 1904. [C: 144-148]

[1848]   Emerson, Ralph Waldo. *Letters and Social Aims.* [Volume VIII of the Concord (or Centenary) Edition of the Works of Ralph Waldo Emerson, 12 vols.]. xiii+441pp. Boston: Houghton, Mifflin and Company, 1904. [M: "Poetry and Imagination," 1-75, Shelley: 25; "Immortality," (323)-352, Shelley: 325-326]

[1849]   Hogg, Thomas Jefferson. *Shelley at Oxford.* Edited with an introduction by R. A. Streatfeild. xii+229pp. London: Methuen & Co., 1904. [B; rptd. from items 175, 176, 180, 184, 202, 215, 233, and 664 (vol I, 48-135, 213-236]

[1850]   Jack, Adolphus Alfred. *Shelley* [/] *An Essay.* 127pp. London: Archibald Constable & Co., Ltd., 1904. [C]

[1851] Kuhns, Oscar. *Dante and the English Poets from Chaucer to Tenny-
        son.* vii+277pp. New York: Henry Holt and Company,
        1904. [C: "Shelley.," 173-197; rptd. from item 1724]

[1852] Le Galliene, Richard. *Old Love Stories Retold.* 183pp. New
        York: The Baker & Taylor Co., 1904. [B: "Shelley and
        Mary Godwin," rptd. from item 1814]

[1853] Shelley, Percy Bysshe. *The Complete Poetical Works of Shelley* [,
        *Including Materials Never Before Printed in Any Edition of the
        Poems* [/] *Edited with Textual Notes by Thomas Hutchinson.*
        [xxix]+1023pp. Oxford: The Clarendon Press, 1904.
        [T]

[1854] Stephen, Leslie. *Hours in a Library.* 4 vols. ["New Edition
        with Additions"]. New York: G. P. Putnam's Sons, 1904.
        [C: "Godwin and Shelley," III, 356-406; rptd. from item
        1041]

[1855] Swinburne, Algernon Charles. "Percy Bysshe Shelley," 107-
        118 in Volume III in *Chambers's Cyclopaedia of English
        Literature.* New Edition by David Patrick. 3 vols.
        Philadelphia: J. B. Lippincott Company, 1904. [B,C]

[1856] Ward, Wilfred [Philip], ed. *Aubrey de Vere* [/] *A Memoir* [/]
        Based on His Unpublished Diaries and Correspondence. x+428pp.
        London: Longmans, Green, and Co., 1904. [C: 333-338;
        M: 12, 265, 303]

                                1905

Periodicals:

[1857] [Woodberry, George Edward]. "Notes," *The Nation*, LXXX,
        No. 2066 (February 2, 1905), 92-94. [R of item 1818:
        92]

[1858] [Anonymous]. "Our Library Table," *The Athenaeum*, No. 4039
        (March 25, 1905), 369. [R: item 1853]

[1859] Forman, H[arry] B[uxton]. "Shelley's Stanza-Numbering in
        the 'Ode to Naples,'" *The Athenaeum*, No. 4043 (April 22,
        1905), 497-498. [T]

[1860] Koszul, A[ndre Henri]. "The Sources of Shelley's Ro-
        mances.," *The Athenaeum*, No. 4045 (May 6, 1905), 561-562.
        [C]

[1861] Cook, Albert S. "Notes on Shelley," *MLN*, XX, No. 6 (June,
        1905), 161-162. [C]

[1862] [Signed "A.S."]. "Sir James Lawrence's 'Empire of the
        Nairs,' 1811.," *Notes and Queries*, Tenth Series III,
        No. 77 (June 17, 1905), 463-464. [C]

[1863] Bradley, A[ndrew] C[ecil]. "Notes on Passages in Shelley,"
        The Modern Language Review, I, No. 1 (October, 1905), [25]-
        42. [T]

[1864] Croft, Margaret L. "A Strange Adventure of Shelley's and
        Its Belated Explanation," *Century Magazine*, New Series
        XLVIII [whole number LXX], No. 6 (October, 1905), 905-
        909. [B]

[1865] Dunn, N. P. "Unknown Pictures of Shelley," *Century Magazine*,
        New Series XLVIII [whole number LXX], No. 6 (October,
        1905), 909-917. [B]

[1866] Forman, H[arry] Buxton. "'Queen Man' and 'The Daemon of
        the World.,'" *The Athenaeum*, No. 4068 (October 14, 1905),
        507-508. [T]

[1867] [Anonymous]. "A Hitherto Unpublished Portrait of Shelley,"
        Current Literature, XXXIX, No. 5 (November, 1905), 505-
        506. [B]

Books:

[1868] Barker, George. *Essays by George Barker*. Edited by Julia
        Wickham. 52pp. Oxford: Parker and Son, 1905. [C:
        "A Comparison Between Shelley and Keats," (1)-31]

[1869] Brandes, George. *Naturalism in England* [Volume IV of *Main
        Currents in Nineteenth Century Literature*]. viii+356pp.
        New York: The Macmillan Company, 1905 [translated from
        the Danish (Copenhagen, 1875)]. [C: "Radical Natural-
        ism," 207-250]

[1870] Brown, J[ohn] Macmillan. *The "Prometheus Unbound" of Shelley* [/]
        A Study. 187pp. Christchurch, New Zealand: Whitcombe
        and Tombs, [1905]. [C]

[1871] Edgar, Pelham. "II. Shelley's Debt to Eighteenth Century
        Thought.," *Proceedings and Transactions of the Royal Society
        of Canada*, Second Series X (1904 [Toronto: The Copp-
        Clark Co., 1905]), Transactions, Section II, 187-199.
        [C]

[1872] Groser, Horace G. "Percy Bysshe Shelley," [515]-532 in
        Volume II [*Robert Southey to Percy Bysshe Shelley*] of *The
        Poets and Poetry of the Nineteenth Century*. Edited by Alfred
        H. Miles. 12 vols. London: George Routledge & Sons,
        Ltd., 1905-1907. [C]

[1873]   Higginson, Thomas Wentworth.   *Parts of a Man's Life.* vii+
         311pp.   Boston: Houghton, Mifflin and Company, 1905.
         [M: 220-221]

[1874]   Miles, Alfred H., ed.   *The Poets and the People* [/] *A Selection
         of Patriotic and Democratic Verse . . . Illustrating and Chroni-
         cling the Development of the Democratic Movement during the
         Nineteenth Century.*   [47]pp.   London: The Liberal Publi-
         cation Department, 1905.   [T: 9]

[1875]   Poe, Edgar Allan.   *The Works of Edgar Allan Poe.*   Edited by
         Edmund Clarence Stedman and George Edward Woodberry.
         10 vols.   Chicago: Stone & Kimball, 1905.   [C: "Miss
         Barrett's 'A Drama of Exile, and Other Poems,'" VI,
         288-320]

[1876]   Shelley, Percy Bysshe.   *The Complete Poetical Works of Percy
         Bysshe Shelley.*   Edited by Thomas Hutchinson.   ["Oxford
         Standard Authors" Series].   xxiii+918pp.   London:
         Oxford University Press, 1905.   [T; rptd. from item
         1853]

[1877]   Smith, Nowell C., ed.   *Wordsworth's Literary Criticism.*   xxi+
         260pp.   London: Oxford University Press [/] Humphrey
         Milford, 1905.   [M: 259]

[1878]   Vaughan, Percy.   *Early Shelley Pamphlets.*   [Reprinted from the
         "Literary Guide"].   32pp.   London: Watts & Co., 1905.
         [C, T; includes item 1844]

[1879]   Watson, William.   *The Poems of William Watson.*   2 vols.   New
         York: John Lane Company, 1905.   [Three poems:
         "Shelley's Centenary," I, 52-56, rptd. from item 1553;
         "Shelley," II, 26; "Shelley and Harriet," II, 105]

[1880]   Woodberry, George Edward.   *The Torch* [/] *Eight Lectures on Race
         Power in Literature Delivered Before the Lowell Institute of
         Boston MCMIII.*   217pp.   New York: McClure, Phillips & Co.
         1905.   [C: "The Titan Myth I," 57-81, Shelley: 66-80;
         "Shelley," 193-217]

                                1906

Periodicals:

[1881]   Forman, H[arry] Buxton.   "Shelley.," *The Bookman* [London],
         XXIX, No. 172 (January, 1906), [153]-160.   [C,T]

[1882]   Taylor, John Warner.   "Sources of Shelley's 'Queen Mab.,'"
         The Sewanee Review, XIV, No. 3 (July, 1906), [324]-351.
         [C]

[1883] Young, A. B. "Shelley and M. G. Lewis," *The Modern Language Review*, I, No. 4 (July, 1906), [322]-324. [C]

[1884] [Anonymous]. "The Keats-Shelley Memorial," *The Outlook*, LXXXIII (July 14, 1906), 585-586. [M]

[1885] [Anonymous]. "A Poet's Shrine," *The Dial*, XLI, No. 483 (August 1, 1906), [57]-58. [B]

[1886] Koszul, A[ndre Henri]. "Notes and Corrections to Shelley's 'History of a Six Weeks' Tour' (1817).," *The Modern Language Review*, II, No. 1 (October, 1906), 61-62. [T]

*[1887] Quinn, James Keenan. "[?]," *The Weekly Freeman's Journal* [Dublin], [?] (November [?], 1906), [?p]. [B]

Books:

[1888] Garnett, Richard. "Shelley's Voyages," *The Hampstead Annual* [/] *1905-1906* [London: C. Mayle, 1906], 57-71. [B]

*[1889] Gilman, Lawrence. *Edward Macdowell* [/] *A Study*. xii+190pp. New York: John Lane Company, 1906. [?M]

[1890] Hogg, Thomas Jefferson. *The Life of Percy Bysshe Shelley by Thomas Jefferson Hogg* [/] *With an Introduction by Professor Dowden and an Index*. xix+585pp. London: George Routledge & Sons Limited, 1906. [B; rptd. from item 664]

[1891] Hutton, Richard Holt. *Brief Literary Criticisms*. Selected from the *Spectator* and edited by his niece Elizabeth Roscoe. vii+417pp. New York: The Macmillan Company, 1906. [C: "Shelley as Prophet," 97-103, rptd. from item 1632; "What is a Lyric," 104-118, Shelley: 108-109]

*[1892] Nicoll, W. Robertson, and Thomas Seccombe. *A History of English Literature*. 2 vols. London: [?], 1906. [C: II, 431-437]

*[1893] Rossetti, William Michael. *Some Reminiscences of William Michael Rossetti*. 2 vols. London: Brown Langham & Co., 1906. [?C]

1907

Periodicals:

[1894] Lang, Andrew. "Shelley's Oxford Martyrdom," *The Fortnightly Review*, New Series LXXXI [whole number LXXXVII], No. cccclxxxii (February, 1907), [230]-240. [B]

[1895]   Lang, Andrew.   "Shelley as a Proofreader," *The Academy*,
         LXXII, No. 2013 (February 2, 1907), 118-119.   [T]

[1896]   Young, A. S.   "Shelley and Peacock," *The Modern Language
         Review*, II, No. 3 (April, 1907), [228]-232.   [B,C]

[1897]   Johnson, R. U.   "The Keats-Shelley Memorial," *The Nation*,
         LXXXIV, No. 2186 (May 23, 1907), 474.   [M]

[1898]   Forman, H[arry] Buxton.   "Shelley's 'Stanzas Written in
         Dejection near Naples.,'" *The Athenaeum*, No. 4163
         (August 10, 1907), 155-156.   [T]

[1899]   Forman, H[arry] Buxton.   "Shelley's 'Indian Serenade.,'"
         The Athenaeum, No. 4166 (August 31, 1907), 239-240.   [T]

[1900]   Dunn, N. P.   "An Artist of the Past [/] William Edward West
         and His Friends at Home and Abroad," *Putnam's Monthly*,
         II, No. 6 (September, 1907), 658-669.   [B]

[1901]   Dunn, N. P.   "To the New-Found Picture of Shelley [/]
         Painted by Wm. Edward West," *Putnam's Monthly*, II, No. 6
         (September, 1907), 669.   [A sonnet]

[1902]   Knapp, George L.   "Shelley," *Lippincott's Monthly Magazine*,
         LXXX, No. 477 (September, 1907), 376-382.   [B,C]

[1903]   Symons, Arthur.   "Shelley," *The Atlantic Monthly*, C, No. 3
         (September, 1907), 347-356.   [C; excerpted: item 1907;
         revised and rptd.: item 1980]

[1904]   [Signed "A.E.A."].   "Shelley's 'Sensitive Plant.,'" *Notes
         and Queries*, Tenth Series VIII, No. 195 (September 21,
         1907), 231.   [T]

[1905]   Revell, William F.   "Shelley's 'Prometheus Unbound': A
         Reading," *The Westminster Review*, CLXVIII, No. 4 (October,
         1907), [415]-427.   [C]

[1906]   Spurgeon, Caroline F. E.   "Art. VI. —Mysticism in English
         Poetry.," *The Quarterly Review*, CCVII, No. 413 (October,
         1907), 427-459.   [C; Shelley: 434-436]

[1907]   [Symons, Arthur].   "'The One Perfect Illustration of the
         Poetic Nature,'" *Current Literature*, XLIII, No. 4 (October
         1907), 408-409.   [C; excerpted from item 1903]

[1908]   Grierson, H[erbert] J. C.   "A Shelley MS at Aberdeen.," *The
         Athenaeum*, No. 4172 (October 12, 1907), 443-444.   [T]

[1909]   [Anonymous].   "Literary Gossip," *The Athenaeum*, No. 4174
         (October 26, 1907), 521.   [T]

[1910]   Rossetti, William Michael. "A Shelley MS. at Aberdeen,"
          The Athenaeum, No. 4174 (October 26, 1907), 519. [T]

[1911]   [Anonymous]. "Unpublished Letters From an Autograph Col-
          lector's Manuscripts," *Pearson's Magazine*, XVIII, No. 5
          (November, 1907), 568-570. [T]

[1912]   Forman, H[arry] Buxton. "Shelley, Matastasio, and Mozart:
          'The Indian Serenade.,'" *The Athenaeum*, No. 4175 (Novem-
          ber 7, 1907), 550-551. [T]

Books:

[1913]   Brooke, Stopford [Augustus]. *Studies in Poetry.* 253pp.
          New York: G. P. Putnam's Sons, 1907. [C: "Inaugural
          Address to the Shelley Society, London, 1886," 115-
          143, rptd. from item 1281; "Lyrics of Shelley," 144-
          175; "Epipsychidion," 176-201, rptd. from item 1378]

[1914]   Huchon, Rene. *George Crabbe and His Times 1754-1832* [/] *A Critical
          and Biographical Study.* Trans. Frederick Clarke. xvi+
          561pp. London: John Murray, 1907. [M: 478-481]

[1915]   Payne, William Morton. *The Greater English Poets of the Nine-
          teenth Century.* vi+388pp. New York: Henry Holt and
          Company, 1907. [C: "Percy Bysshe Shelley," 33-63]

[1916]   Rannie, David Watson. *Wordsworth and His Circle.* xii+360pp.
          New York: G. P. Putnam's Sons, 1907. [C: 261-272]

[1917]   Reed, Myrtle. *Love Affairs of Literary Men.* vi+204pp. New
          York: G. P. Putnam's Sons, 1907. [B: "Percy Bysshe
          Shelley," 151-177]

*[1918]   Van Dyke, Henry. *Four Sonnets Dedicated to the Class of 1907,
          Princeton University.* 3pp. [?]: privately printed, 1907.
          [A sonnet]

[1919]   Yolland, Arthur B[attishill]. *Shelley's Poetry.* 19pp.
          Budapest: Stephaneum Printing Co., 1907. [C]

                                1908

Perodicals:

[1920]   Crawford, F. Marion. "Beatrice Cenci [/] The True Story of
          a Misunderstood Tragedy: With New Documents," *The
          Century Magazine*, LXXV, No. 3 (January, 1908), 449-466.
          [M]

[1921]   Bradley, A[ndre] C[ecil]. "Shelley's View of Poetry," *The*
         Albany Review, II, No. 11 (February, 1908), 511-530. [C;
         rptd.: items 1944, 1972]

[1922]   Simboli, Raffaele. "Keats and Shelley in Rome," *Putnam's*
         Monthly, II, No. 5 (February, 1908), 537-542. [B]

[1923]   Cooper, Lane. "Dryden and Shelley on Milton," *MLN*, XXIII,
         No. 3 (March, 1908), 93. [C]

[1924]   [Anonymous]. "Shelley and Elizabeth Hitchener," *The Times*
         Literary Supplement [London], No. 321 (March 5, 1908),
         76-77. [R: item 1945]

[1925]   Cooper, Lane. "Notes on Byron and Shelley," *MLN*, XXIII,
         No. 4 (April, 1908), 118-119. [C]

[1926]   Gile, F. H. "Prometheus Bound and Unbound: A Study in
         Advancing Civilization," *The Arena*, XXXIX, No. 221
         (April, 1908), 430-436. [C]

[1927]   Catty, Corbet Stacey. "Shelley's 'I Arise from Dreams of
         Thee' and Miss Sophia Stacey.," *The Athenaeum*, No. 4199
         (April 18, 1908), 478. [B]

[1928]   Nicholson, Arthur P. "Shelley 'Contra Mundum,'" *The Nine-*
         teenth Century, LXIII, No. 375 (May, 1908), 794-810. [C]

[1929]   Thompson, Francis. "Shelley," *The Dublin Review*, CXLIII,
         No. 286 (July, 1908), 25-49. [C; rptd.: item 1982]

[1930]   [Anonymous]. "Was Shelley an Atheist?" *Current Literature*,
         XLV, No. 2 (August, 1908), 190-191. [R: item 1945]

[1931]   Menzies, W. G. "The First Editons of Shelley Part I.,"
         The Connoisseur, XXI, No. 84 (August, 1908), 258-260. [T]

[1932]   [Anonymous]. "Literary Gossip," *The Athenaeum*, No. 4216
         (August 15, 1908), 185. [M]

[1933]   Edgcumbe, Richard. "Harriet Shelley.," *The Athenaeum*,
         No. 4218 (August 29, 1908), 241-242. [B]

[1934]   Mead, William Edward. "XVIII. —Italy in English Poetry.,"
         PMLA, XXIII, No. 3 (September, 1908), 421-470. [C;
         Shelley: 442-444]

[1935]   Menzies, W. G. "The First Editions of Shelley Part II.,"
         The Connoisseur, XXII, No. 85 (September, 1908), 10-12.
         [T]

[1936]   [Anonymous]. "Our Library Table," *The Athenaeum*, No. 4220
         (September 12, 1908), 300-303. [R of item 1945: 302]

[1937]   Young, A. B.   "'Original Poetry by Victor and Cazire.,'"
          Notes and Queries, Tenth Series X, No. 247 (September 19,
          1908), 224-225.   [C]

[1938]   Willoughby, Leonard.   "The Treasures of Avington [/] The
          Seat of Sir John Shelley, Bart.," *The Connoisseur*, XXII,
          No. 86 (October, 1908), 73-82.   [B]

[1939]   Potter, A. G.   "Persian Translation by Shelley.," *Notes and
          Queries*, Tenth Series X, No. 253 (October 31, 1908),
          349.   [T]

[1940]   [Anonymous].   "Francis Thompson's Tribute to Shelley,"
          Current Literature, XLV, No. 5 (November, 1908), 515-517.
          [Excerpt and paraphrase of item 1929]

[1941]   Gardner, Edmund G.   "The Mysticism of Shelley," *The Catholic
          World*, LXXXVIII, No. 524 (November, 1908), [145]-155.
          [C]

[1942]   Potter, A. G.   "Persian Translation by Shelley (10 S. x.
          368).," *Notes and Queries*, Tenth Series X, No. 257
          (November 28, 1908), 438.   [T]

Books:

[1943]   Bates, Ernest Sutherland.   *A Study of Shelley's Drama the Cenci.*
          [Columbia University Studies in English, Series II,
          Volume III, Number 1].   xi+103pp.   New York: Columbia
          University Press, 1908.   [C]

[1944]   Bradley, A[ndrew] C[ecil].   *Shelley's View of Poetry [/] A
          Lecture.* The English Association, Leaflet No. 4.   20pp.
          [London: The English Association, 1908].   [C; rptd.
          from item 1921]

[1945]   Dobell, Bertram, ed.   *Letters from Percy Bysshe Shelley to Eliza-
          beth Hitchener. Now First Published. With an Introduction and
          Notes.*   li+351pp.   London: Bertram Dobell, 1908.   [C,
          B, T]

[1946]   Foster, Claude E[dward].   *Shelley, A Poem. With a Biographical
          Sketch of Shelley.*   xii+105pp.   London: Joun Ouseley, Ltd.,
          1908.   [A Poem, B, C]

[1947]   Hinchman, Walter S., and Francis B. Gummere.   *Lives of Great
          English Writers [/] from Chaucer to Browning.*   vi+569pp.
          Boston: Houhgton, Mifflin and Company, 1908.   [B:
          "Percy Bysshe Shelley," (383)-398]

*[1948]   Woodberry, George Edward.   *Studies of a Litterateur.*   [?]pp.
          New York: Harcourt, Brace & Company, 1908.   [C]

1909

[1949]   Petty, S. L.   "Persian Translation by Shelley (10 S. x.
         349, 438).," *Notes and Queries*, Tenth Series XI, No. 270
         (February 27, 1909), 178.   [T]

[1950]   Forman, H[arry] Buxton.   "How Leigh Hunt Treated Shelley's
         Letters.," *The Athenaeum*, No. 4250 (April 10, 1909), 439-
         440.   [T]

[1951]   [Anonymous].   " *Shelley*. By Francis Thompson. With an In-
         troduction by the Right Hon. George Wyndham.   (Burns &
         Oates).," *The Athenaeum*, No. 4252 (April 24, 1909),
         490-491.   [R: item 1982]

[1952]   [Anonymous].   "The Keats-Shelley Memorial," *The Outlook*,
         XCII (May 1, 1909), 12.   [M]

[1953]   Mabie, Hamilton Wright.   "To a Skylark [/] by Percy Bysshe
         Shelley [/] The Sixth of a Series of Great Poems [/]
         with Introductions by Hamilton Wright Mabie," *The Out-
         look*, XCII (May 22, 1909), [205]-[213].   [C, T]

[1954]   Forman, H[arry] Buxton.   "More Shelley Crumbs.," *The Athen-
         aeum*, No. 4258 (June 5, 1909), 674.   [T]

[1955]   McMahan, Anna Benneson.   "Shelley the 'Enchanted Child,'"
         The Dial, XLVI, No. 552 (June 16, 1909), 399-401.   [R:
         item 1982]

[1956]   Bryant, Fitch C.   "America Honors Keats and Shelley," *The
         World To-Day*, XVII, No. 2 (August, 1909), 836-838.   [B]

[1957]   [Anonymous].   "Shelley's Letters," *The Times Literary Supplemen*
         [London], No. 400 (September 9, 1909), 324.   [R: item
         1977]

[1958]   [Anonymous].   "Musings without Method," *Blackwood's Edinburgh
         Magazine*, CLXXXVI, No. mcxxviii (October, 1909), 570-
         580.   [R of item 1977: 576-580]

[1959]   Saintsbury, [George].   "Shelley's Letters.," *The Bookman*
         [London], XXXVII, No. 217 (October, 1909), 29-20.   [R:
         item 1977]

[1960]   Quantock, Elizabeth.   "Sent Down.," *T.P.'s Weekly* [?Oxford],
         (October 1, 1909), 433-434.   [B]

[1961]   [Signed "I.M.L."].   "Matthew Arnold, Shelley, Keats, and
         the Yew.," *Notes and Queries*, Tenth Series XII, No. 302

(October 9, 1909), 287. [C]

[1962] Boothroyd, Norman. "Matthew Arnold, Shelley, Keats and the Yew (10 S. xii. 287).," *Notes and Queries*, Tenth Series XII, No. 304 (October 23, 1909), 336. [C]

[1963] [Signed "C.C.B."]. "[Untitled, following item 1962]," *Notes and Queries*, Tenth Series XII, No. 304 (October 23, 1909), 336. [C]

[1964] Pinchbeck, W. H. "[Untitled, following item 1963]," *Notes and Queries*, Tenth Series XII, No. 304 (October 23, 1909), 336. [C]

[1965] [Bailey, John Cann]. "Shelley," *The Times Literary Supplement* [London], No. 408 (November 4, 1909), [405]-406. [R: item 1974; rptd.: items 1970, 2027]

[1966] [Anonymous]. "*The Letters of Percy Bysshe Shelley*. Collected and edited by Roger Ingpen. 2 vols. Illustrated. (Sir Isaac Pitman & Sons.)," *The Athenaeum*, No. 4280 (November 6, 1909), 550-551. [R: item 1977]

[1967] [Signed "M.C.L."]. "Matthew Arnold, Shelley, Keats, and the Yew (10 S. xii. 287, 336).," *Notes and Queries*, Tenth Series XII, No. 308 (November 20, 1909), 414-415. [C]

[1968] [Anonymous]. "Shelley's Letters.," *The Spectator*, CIII, No. 4,248 (November 27, 1909), 889-890. [R: item 1977]

[1969] [Anonymous]. " *Shelley, the Man and the Poet*. By A. Clutton-Brock. Illustrated. (Methuen & Co.)," *The Athenaeum*, No. 4286 (December 18, 1909), 753-754. [R: item 1974]

[1970] [Bailey, John Cann]. "Shelley," *The Living Age*, Seventh Series XLV [whole number CCLXIII], No. 3415 (December 18, 1909), 746-750. [R: item 1974; rptd. from item 1970].

Books:

[1971] Blake, R. [pseud. of Robert Hely Thompson]. *Kant and Shelley*. [4]pp. London: privately printed, 1909. [C]

[1972] Bradley, A[ndrew] C[ecil]. *Oxford Lectures on Poetry*. viii+ 395pp. London: Macmillan and Co., 1909. [C: "Shelley's View of Poetry," 151-174; rptd. from item 1921]

[1973] Brett-Smith, H. F. B., ed. *Peacock's Memoirs of Shelley with Shelley's Letters to Peacock*. London: Henry Frowde [Oxford University Press], 1909. [B,T,C; B rptd. from items

653, 684, 687, 688, 721]

[1974] Clutton-Brock, A[rthur]. *Shelley* [/] *The Man and the Poet.*
xxiii+294pp. London: Methuen & Co., 1909. [B,C; re-
vised edition, 1923]

[1975] Emerson, Ralph Waldo. *Journals of Ralph Waldo Emerson with
Annotations.* Edited by Edward Waldo Emerson and Waldo
Emerson Forbes. 10 vols. Boston: Houghton Mifflin
Company, 1909-1914. [M: IV, 198; V, 344; VI, 114-115;
VII, 284-285]

[1976] Garnett, Richard. "The Life of Percy Bysshe Shelley," 551-
569 in *Representative Biographies of English Men of Letters.*
Chosen and Edited by Charles Townsend Copeland and Frank
Wilson Cheney Hersey. x+642pp. New York: The Macmillan Company, 1909. [B; rptd. from item 1709]

[1977] Ingpen, Roger, ed. *The Letters of Percy Bysshe Shelley.* Collected and Edited by Roger Ingpen. 2 vols. London:
Sir Isaac Pitman & Sons, Ltd., 1909. [T; revised
editions, 1911, 1914]

[1978] McLean, Charles Mossman. "The Poet Shelley," 144-149 in
Representative College Orations. xi+403pp. New York:
Macmillan Company, 1909. [C]

[1979] Shawcross, John, ed. *Shelley's Literary and Philsophical Criticism.* xlv+244pp. London: Henry Frowde, 1909. [C,T]

[1980] Symons, Arthur. *The Romantic Movement in English Poetry.* xi+
344pp. New York: E. P. Dutton and Company, 1909.
[C: "Percy Bysshe Shelley (1792-1822)," 268-286;
revised and rptd. from item 1903]

[1981] Toynbee, Paget. *Dante in English Literature* [/] *From Chaucer to
Cary* [/] *(C. 1380-1844).* 2 vols. London: Methuen & Co.,
1909. [C: "Percy Bysshe Shelley," II, 214-230, 716-
717]

[1982] Thompson, Francis. *Shelley.* With an Introduction by the
Rt Honorable George Wyndham. Edited, with Notes by
W[ilf d] M[eynell]. 91pp. London: Burns & Oates,
1909. [C; rptd. from item 1929]

[1983] Wagstaff, Blanche Shoemaker. *Atys* [/] *A Grecian Idyl and Other
Poems.* 58pp. New York: Mitchell Kennerley, 1909.
[Twenty line poem: "Shelley's House at Pisa," 22]

[1984] Woodberry, George Edward, ed. *The Cenci* [/] *By Percy Bysshe
Shelley.* [The Belles Lettres Series; general editor
George Pierce Baker]. xxxv+159pp. Boston: D. C.
Heath & Co., 1909. [T, C]

[1985]   McMahan, Anna Benneson. "New Revealments of Shelley,"
         The Dial, XLVIII, No. 565 (January 1, 1910), 15-17.
         [R: item 1977]

[1986]   [Anonymous]. "Musings without Method," *Blackwood's Edinburgh
         Magazine*, CLXXXVII, No. mcxxxii (February, 1910), 294-
         308. [C: 296-298]

[1987]   [Anonymous]. "New Efforts to Explain the Dual Nature of
         Shelley," *Current Literature*, XLVIII, No. 2 (February,
         1910), 207-210. [R: items 1974, 1977]

[1988]   Digeon, Aurélien A. "Shelley and Peacock," *MLN*, XXV, No. 2
         (February, 1910), 41-45. [B]

[1989]   M[ore], P[aul] E[lmer]. "Shelley. I.," *The Nation*, XC,
         No. 2328 (February 10, 1910), 133-136. [C; revised
         and rptd.: item 2010]

[1990]   M[ore], P[aul] E[lmer]. "Shelley. II.," *The Nation*, XC, No.
         2329 (February 17, 1910), 157-159. [C; revised and
         rptd.: item 2010]

[1991]   [Anonymous]. "The Keats-Shelley Memorial," *The Dial*, XLVIII,
         No. 570 (March 16, 1910), 185-186. [B]

[1992]   Winstanley, L[ilian]. "*The Romantic Movement in English Poetry*.
         By Arthur Symons. London: Constable, 1909. 8vo.
         344pp.," *Modern Language Review*, V, No. 2 (April, 1910),
         234-241. [R: item 1980; Shelley: 239-240]

[1993]   Bayley, A. R. "B. R. Haydon and Shelley," *Notes and Queries*,
         Eleventh Series I, No. 24 (June 11, 1910), 461-463.
         [B]

[1994]   Abrahams, Aleck. "B. R. Haydon and Shelley (11 S. i.
         461)," *Notes and Queries*, Eleventh Series II, No. 29
         (July 16, 1910), 53. [B]

[1995]   Tew, E. L. H. "Mr. W. Graham and Jane Clermont," *Notes and
         Queries*, Eleventh Series II, No. 32 (August 6, 1910),
         108-109. [B]

[1996]   Hadow, G. E. "*Peacock's Memoir of Shelley, with Shelley's Letters
         to Peacock*. Edited by H. F. B. Brett-Smith. Oxford:
         Clarendon Press. 1909. 8vo. xxviii+219pp.," *Modern
         Language Review*, V, No. 4 (October, 1910), 529-530. [R:
         item 1973]

Books:

[1997]   Austin, Alfred. *The Bridling of Pegasus* [/] *Prose Papers on*
         Poetry. vii+252pp. London: Macmillan and Co., Limited,
         1910. [M: 54, 179-180]

[1998]   Browning, Oscar. *Memories of Sixty Years at Eton Cambridge and*
         Elsewhere. x+364pp. London: John Lane [/] The Bodley
         Head, 1910. [M: 119, 170, 203, 311, 312]

[1999]   Byron, May Clarissa. *A Day with the Poet Percy Bysshe Shelley.*
         47pp. London: Hodder & Stoughton, 1910. [B]

[2000]   Chapman, Edward Mortimer. *English Literature in Account with*
         Religion 1800-1900. xii+578pp. Boston: Houghton Mifflin
         Company, 1910. [C: "The Apostles of Revolt: Byron
         and Shelley," (91)-126]

[2001]   Clarke, Helen Archibald. *Ancient Myths in Modern Poets.* 360pp.
         New York: The Baker & Taylor Company, 1910. [C: "II (/)
         The Prometheus Myth from Hesiod to Shelley (/) Poetic
         Treatment of the Myth in Shelley and Other Modern
         Poets," 55-182]

[2002]   Courthope, W[illiam] J[ohn]. *A History of English Poetry* [/]
         Volume VI [/] *The Romantic Movement in English Poetry* [/] *Effects*
         of the French Revolution. London: Macmillan and Co.,
         Limited, 1910 [6 vols., 1985-1910]. [C: "Romanticism
         in English Poetry (/) The Poetry of Revolutionary
         Idealism: Percy Bysshe Shelley," VI, 278-319]

[2003]   Dobell, Bertram. *A Century of Sonnets.* viii+102pp. London:
         Bertram Dobell, 1910. [A sonnet: "Shelley," 79]

[2004]   Forman, H[arry] Buxton. "Poetry in the Making [/] The
         Three Shelley Notebooks," *Bibliophile Society Yearbook,*
         IX ([Boston: Bibliophile Society,] 1910), 83-108.
         [C,T]

[2005]   Harrison, Frederic. *Studies in Early Victorian Literature.*
         224pp. London: Edward Arnold, 1910. [C: 21; rptd.
         from item 1647]

[2006]   Hewlett, Maurice. *Open Country* [/] *A Comedy with a Sting.* x+
         321pp. New York: Charles Scribner's Sons, 1910.
         [Parallel and allusions to *Prometheus Unbound* throughout]

[2007]   Hobhouse, John Cam. *Recollections of a Long Life by Lord Brough-*
         ton (John Cam Hobhouse) with Additional Extracts from His Private
         Diaries. Edited by his daughter Lady Dorchester.
         6 vols. London: John Murray, 1909-1910 [Volume III:
         1910]. [M: III, 2, 69]

[2008] Koszul, A[ndre] H[enri]. *Shelley's Prose in the Bodleian Manuscripts*. 148pp. London: H. Frowde [Oxford University Press], 1910. [T]

[2009] Miller, Barnett. *Leigh Hunt's Relations with Byron, Shelley and Keats*. [Columbia University Studies in English, No. 26]. vii+169pp. New York: Columbia University Press, 1910. [B]

[2010] More, Paul Elmer. *Shelburne Essays [/] Seventh Series*. iii+269pp. New York: G. P. Putnam's Sons, 1910. [C: "Shelley," 1-26; revised and rptd. from items 1989, 1990]

[2011] Peacock, Thomas Love. *Letters to Edward Hookham and Percy B. Shelley with Fragments of Unpublished MSS. Thomas Love Peacock*. Edited by Richard Garnett. 250pp. Boston: Bibliophile Society, 1910. [B, C, T]

[2012] Rodd, Rennell, and H. Nelson Gay, eds. *Bulletin of the Keats-Shelley Memorial [/] Rome No. 1*. v+187pp. New York: Macmillan & Co., Ltd., 1910. [B,C, and catalogue of volumes in the Keats-Shelley Memorial House, Rome]

[2013] Saintsbury, George. *A History of English Prosody [/] From the Twelfth Century to the Present Day*. 3 vols. London: Macmillan and Co., Limited, 1910. [C: III, 102-116]

[2014] Stedman, Laura, and George M. Gould. *Life and Letters of Edmund Clarence Stedman*. 2 vols. New York: Moffat, Yard and Company, 1910. [M: II, 114; B: II, 418-430]

[2015] Trelawny, Edward John. *Letters of Edward John Trelawny*. Edited with a brief Introduction and Notes by H[arry] Buxton Forman. xxiv+306pp. London: Henry Frowde [/] Oxford University Press, 1910. [M: over fifty, fully indexed]

1911

Periodicals:

[2016] Edgcumbe, Richard. "Shelley and Leigh Hunt," *Notes and Queries*, Eleventh Series III, No. 14 (January 14, 1911), 21-22. [B]

[2017] [Anonymous]. "Percy Bysshe Shelley [/] from the miniature in the collection of Mr. J. Pierpont Morgan," *The Century Magazine*, New Series LX [whole number LXXXII], No. 2 (June, 1911), [215]. [Color reproduction of the portrait, no text]

[2018] Verrall, Margaret de G. "Allusions in 'Adonais' to the
        Poems of Keats," *Modern Language Review*, VI, No. 3
        (July, 1911), [354]-359. [C]

[2019] [Anonymous]. " *The Diary of Dr. John William Polidori, 1816, rela-
        ting to Byron, Shelley, &c.* Edited and Elucidated by Wil-
        liam Michael Rossetti. (Elkin Mathews.)," *The Athenaeum*,
        No. 4374 (August 26, 1911), 236-237. [R: item 2035]

[2020] [Anonymous]. "Shelley in Italy," *The Times Literary Supplement*
        [London], No. 503 (August 31, 1911), 318. [R: item
        2026]

[2021] [Anonymous]. "Poetry and Life Series.," *The Athenaeum*, No.
        4375 (September 2, 1911), 266. [R: item 2029]

[2022] Darbishire, Helen. " *A History of English Poetry*. By W. J.
        Courthope. Vols. V and VI. London: Macmillan. 1905-
        10. 8vo. xxviii+464, xxiv+471pp.," *Modern Language
        Review*, VI, No. 4 (October, 1911), [520]-524. [R:
        item 2002; Shelley: 523]

[2023] Woods, Margaret L. "Shelley at Tan-yr-allt," *The Nineteenth
        Century*, LXX, No. 417 (November, 1911), 890-903. [B]

[2024] Stanley, Carleton W. "Shelley's Debt to Plato," *The Univer-
        sity Magazine*, X, No. 4 (December, 1911), [655]-668. [C]

[2025] [Anonymous]. "Shelley.," *The Spectator*, CVII, No. 4,357
        (December 30, 1911), 1154-1155. [R: item 2034]

Books:

[2026] Angeli, Helen [Maria Madox] Rossetti. *Shelley and His Friends
        in Italy*. With sixteen illustrations by Maxwell Arm-
        field, eight of which are in colour. xiii+326pp.
        London: Methuen & Co., Ltd., 1911. [B]

[2027] Bailey, John [Cann]. *Poets and Poetry [/] Being Articles Reprint-
        ed from the Literary Supplement of 'The Times.'* Oxford:
        Clarendon Press, 1911. [C: "Shelley," (157)-169; rptd.
        from item 1965]

*[2028] Carter, John [pseud.]. *Hard Labor and Other Poems [/] of Prison
        Life*. viii+79pp. New York: The Baker & Taylor Company,
        1911. [A poem: "Shelley," (?p)]

[2029] Edmunds, E[dward] W[illiam]. *Shelley & His Poetry*. [Poetry
        & Life Series, No. 4]. 144pp. London: George G.
        Harrap & Company, 1911. [C,B,T]

[2030]   Forman, H[arry] Buxton, ed. *Notebooks of Percy Bysshe Shelley.*
          From the Originals in the Library of W. K. Bixby. Deciphered,
          Transcribed, and Edited, With a full Commentary by H.
          Buxton Forman. 3 vols. [Boston: Bibliophile Society],
          1911.   [C,T]

[2031]   Furnivall, Frederick James.   *A Volume of Personal Record.*
          3+lxxx+215pp. London: Henry Frowde [/] Oxford Univer-
          sity Press, 1911. [M: lxxiii-lxxvi, 17, 88]

[2032]   Godwin, William. *The Elopement of Percy Bysshe Shelley and Mary*
          Wollstonecraft Godwin [/] *As Narrated by William Godwin* [/] *With*
          Commentary by H. Buxton Forman, C.B. 24pp. [Boston: Biblio-
          phile Society, 1911]. [B]

[2033]   Gribble, Francis. *The Romantic Life of Shelley and the Sequel.*
          xi+387pp. London: Eveleigh Nash, 1911. [B]

[2034]   Locock, C[harles] D[ealtry], and A[rthur] Clutton-Brock, eds
          The Poems of Percy Bysshe Shelley. Edited with Notes by C.
          D. Locock [/] With an Introduction by A. Clutton-Brock
          [/] In Two Volumes. London: Methuen and Co., Ltd.,
          1911. [T; C: "Introduction,": I, v-xxvii]

[2035]   Polidori, John William. *The Diary of Dr. John William Polidori*
          [/] *1816* [/] *Relating to Byron, Shelley, etc.* Edited and
          Elucidated by William Michael Rossetti. 228pp.
          London: Elkin Mathews, 1911. [B]

[2036]   Porteous, Gilbert. *The Use of Mythological Subjects in Modern*
          Poetry. 59pp. London: University of London Press,
          1911. [C: 8-22]

[2037]   Stevenson, Robert Louis. *The Letters of Robert Louis Stevenson.*
          Edited by Sidney Colvin. 4 vols. New York: Charles
          Scribner's Sons, 1911. [M: II, 317, 357, 358; III,
          177]

[2038]   Thomas, Edward. *Feminine Influence on the Poets.* 352pp. New
          York: John Lane Company, 1911. [B: 38-45, 66-68, 77-
          78, 130-131, 188, 199-227]

[2039]   [Wallis, Henry]. *Thomas Love Peacock on the Portraits of Shelley.*
          2pp.+portrait. London: Bernard Quaritch, 1911. [B]

                              1912

Periodicals:

[2040]   Hughes, A[rthur] M[ontague] D['Urban]. "*Shelley's Zastrozzi*
          and St Irvyne.," *Modern Language Review*, VII, No. 1 (January,
          1912), [54]-63. [C]

[2041]   [Anonymous]. "Shelley.," *The Nation*, XCIV, No. 2427
          (January 4, 1912), 12-14. [R: items 2026, 2033]

*[2042]   [Many authors, including William Hale White]. *Keats-
          Shelley Memorial Souvenir*. [A special issue of *The Bookman*
          (London)]. [?p]. June 20, 1912. [C,B,T; contains
          reprints of several items, among them item 1042]

[2043]   Hughes, A[rthur] M[ontague] D['Urban]. "The Nascent
          Mind of Shelley," *Englische Studien*, XLV, No. 1 ([July],
          1912), 61-74. [C]

[2044]   Hughes, A[rthur] M[ontague] D['Urban]. "La Jeunesse de
          Shelley. Par A. Koszul. Paris: Bloud. 1910. 8vo.
          xxii+439pp.," *Modern Language Review*, VII, No. 3 (July,
          1912), 383-387. [R: as indicated; no English trans-
          lation was ever published]

*[2045]   Randall, A. E. "Shelley and Nihilism," *The New Age*, [?],
          ([?July], 1912), [?p]. [C; resumé in item 2049]

[2046]   Edgcumbe, Richard. "The Death of Shelley," *Notes and Quer-
          ies,* Eleventh Series VI, No. 132 (July 6, 1912), 9.
          [B]

[2047]   [Signed "G.B.M."]. "The Death of Shelley," *Notes and Quer-
          ies*, Eleventh Series VI, No. 135 (July 27, 1912), 76.
          [B]

[2048]   Potter, A. G. "[Untitled, following item 2047]," *Notes and
          Queries*, Eleventh Series VI, No. 135 (July 27, 1912),
          76. [B]

[2049]   [Randall, A. E.]. "Shelley As the Laureate of Nihilism,"
          Current Literature, LIII, No. 2 (August, 1912), 226-227.
          [C; a resumé of item 2045]

[2050]   Hughes, A[rthur] M[ontague] D['Urban]. "Some Recent
          English Shelley Literature," *Englische Studien*, XLV,
          No. 2 ([September], 1912), [293]-299. [C]

[2051]   [Anonymous]. "News Notes.," *The Bookman* [London], XLIII,
          No. 253 (October, 1912), 1-8. [B: 6, reproduction of
          the Wyon portrait of Shelley from item 301]

[2052]   Hughes, A[rthur] M[ontague] D['Urban]. "Shelley's 'Witch
          of Atlas.,'" *Modern Language Review*, VII, No. 4 (October,
          1912), [508]-516. [C]

[2053]   [Signed "C.H."]. "Shelley Portrait," *Notes and Queries*,
          Eleventh Series VI, No. 154 (December 7, 1912), 448.
          [B]

Books:

[2054]   Birkhead, Edith. "Imagery and Style in Shelley," 54-87 in
         Primitiae [/] *Essays in English Literature* [/] *By Students of the*
         University of Liverpool. Liverpool: The University Press,
         1912. [C]

[2055]   [Bradley, Andrew Cecil]. *Short Bibliographies of Wordsworth,*
         Coleridge [/] *Byron, Shelley, Keats.* [The English Associa-
         tion, Leaflet No. 23]. 13pp. [Oxford: The English
         Association, 1912]. [C: "Shelley," 10-12]

[2056]   Elton, Oliver. *A Survey of English Literature* [/] *1780-1830.*
         2 vols. London: Edward Arnold, 1912. [C: "Chapter
         XVIII. Percy Bysshe Shelley," II, 183-224; revised
         and rptd.: item 2355]

[2057]   MacDonald, Daniel J. *The Radicalism of Shelley and Its Sources.*
         [A dissertation submitted to the Faculty of Philosophy
         of the Catholic University of America in partial ful-
         fillment of the requirements for the degree of Doctor
         of Philosophy]. 143pp. Washington, D.C.: privately
         printed, 1912. [C; rptd.: items 2164, 2175, 2190,
         2192, 2195, 2206, 2207, 2212, 2215, 2217, 2221]

[2058]   Meredith, George. *Letters of George Meredith* [/] *Collected and*
         Edited by His Son [W. H. Meredith]. 2 vols. New York:
         Charles Scribner's Sons, 1912. [M: I, 34, 49, 68]

*[2059]   Reed, Edward Bliss. *English Lyrical Poetry.* [?]pp. New
         Haven, Conn.: [?], 1912. [?C]

[2060]   Stewart, J[ohn] A[lexander]. "Platonism in English Poet-
         ry," [25]-48 in *English Literature and the Classics.* Col-
         lected by G[eorge] S[tuart] Gordon. 252pp. Oxford:
         At the Clarendon Press, 1912. [C]

[2061]   Suddard, S[arah] J[ulie] Mary. *Keats Shelley and Shakespeare*
         [/] *Studies & Essays in English Literature.* 308pp. Cambridge,
         Eng.: At the University Press, 1912. [C: "The *Hymn to*
         Intellectual Beauty," (86)-91; "Shelley's Transcendental-
         ism," (100)-108; "Shelley's Idealism," (109)-112; "The
         Images in Shelley's *Hellas*," (113)-127]

*[2062]   Williams, Orlo. *Lamb's Friend the Census-Taker. Life and Letters*
         of John Rickman by Orlo Williams. xiii+330pp. London:
         Constable and Company, 1912. [?M]

1913

Periodicals:

[2063]   Darbishire, Helen.   "*Poets and Poetry*. By John Bailey.
         Oxford: Clarendon Press. 1911. 8vo. 217pp.," *Modern
         Language Review*, VIII, No. 1 (January, 1913), 113-115.
         [R: item 2027; Shelley: 114-115]

[2064]   Thompson, Elbert N. S.   "IV. The Theme of Paradise Lost,"
         PMLA, XXVIII, No. 1 (March, 1913), 106-120.   [M: 114]

[2065]   Moore, Charles Leonard.   "Shelley Once More," *The Dial*, LV,
         No. 654 (September 16, 1913), 193-195.   [C]

[2066]   Tew, E. L. H.   "'Last Links with Byron, Shelley, and
         Keats.,'" *Notes and Queries*, Eleventh Series VIII,
         No. 195 (September 20, 1913), 228.   [B]

[2067]   Lonsdale, H.   "Graham's 'Last Links with Byron, Shelley,
         and Keats.,'" *Notes and Queries*, Eleventh Series VIII,
         No. 196 (September 27, 1913), 249.   [B]

Books:

[2068]   [Bradlaugh, Charles].   "Biography of Percy Bysshe Shel-
         ley.," 184-195 in *Biographies of Ancient and Modern Celebrated
         Freethinkers* [/] *Reprinted from an English Work, Entitled "Half
         Hours with the Freethinkers." By "Iconoclast," Collins* [pseud.]
         (brackets in original), *and Watts*. [No. 8 in "Library of
         Famous Literature"]. 387pp. New York: P. Eckler,
         [1913]. [B,C; rptd. from item 627]

[2069]   Brailsford, Henry Noel.   *Shelley, Godwin, and Their Circle*.
         256pp. London: Williams and Norgate, [1913].   [C]

[2070]   Buck, Philo M., Jr.   *Social Forces in Modern Literature*. vii+
         254pp. Boston: Ginn and Company, 1913. [C: "The
         Empire of Beauty—Shelley," 205-244]

[2071]   Medwin, Thomas.   *The Life of Percy Bysshe Shelley* [/] *By Thomas
         Medwin* [/] *A New Edition printed from a copy copiously emended
         by the Author and left unpublished at his death* [/] *With an
         Introduction and Commentary by H. Buxton Forman, C.B.* xxxii+
         542pp. London: Humphrey Milford, Oxford University
         Press, 1913. [B; revised edition of item 477]

[2072]   Rhys, Ernest.   *Lyric Poetry*. viii+374pp. London: J. M.
         Dent & Sons Ltd., 1913. [C: "Percy Bysshe Shelley—
         Leigh Hunt—John Keats," 313-325; Shelley: 313-321]

[2073]   Rodd, Rennell, and H. Nelson Gay, eds. *Bulletin and Review of the Keats-Shelley Memorial* [/] *Rome*. [No. 2]. viii+190pp. London: Macmillan & Co., Ltd., 1913. [B, C, catalogue of volumes in the library of the Keats-Shelley House, Rome]

[2074]   Santayana, George. *Winds of Doctrine* [/] *Studies in Contemporary Opinion*. 215pp. London: J. M. Dent & Sons, 1913. [C: "Shelley: Or the Poetic Value of Revolutionary Principles," 155-185]

[2075]   Schelling, Felix E. *The English Lyric*. ix+335pp. Boston: Houghton Mifflin Company, 1913. [C: 173-178]

[2076]   Winstanley, L[ilian M.]. "Platonism in Shelley," *Essays and Studies by Members of the English Association* [Oxford: Clarendon Press], IV (1913), [72]-100. [C]

[2077]   Waterlow, Sydney. *Shelley*. [People's Books Series]. 94pp. London: T. C. & E. C. Jack, 1913. [B]

1914

Periodicals:

[2078]   Routh, James. "Notes on the Sources of Poe's Poetry: Coleridge, Keats, Shelley.," *MLN*, XXIX, No. 3 (March, 1914), 72-75. [C: "III. Shelley and Poe.," 73-75]

*[2079]   [Anonymous]. "Shelley and Byron.," *The Observer* [London], [?], (April 12, 1914), [?p]. [B]

[2080]   Bradley, A[ndrew] C[ecil]. "Notes on Shelley's 'Triumph of Life,'" *Modern Language Review*, IX, No. 4 (October, 1914), [441]-456. [C]

[2081]   Hepple, Norman. *"Primitiae: Essays in English Literature*. By Students of the University of Liverpool. Liverpool: The University Press (London: Constable). 1912. 8vo. 287pp.," *Modern Language Review*, IX, No. 4 (October, 1914), 536-539. [R: item 2054; Shelley: 538]

Books:

[2082]   Stawell, F. Melian. "Shelley's 'Triumph of Life.,'" *Essays and Studies by Members of the English Association* [Oxford: Clarendon Press], V (1914), [104]-131. [C]

Periodicals:

[2083]   Graham, Walter. "Wordsworth and Shelley," *Notes and Queries,*
         Eleventh Series XI, No. 266 (January 30, 1915), 83-84.
         [C]

[2084]   Snow, Francis Haffkina. "Shelley in Italian [/] Shelley,
         Tradotto da Antonio Calitri. [/] York Printing Company
         —Casa Editrice di F. J. Dassori, [/] New York, 1914.,"
         The University Magazine, XIV, No. 2 (April, 1915), [254]-
         261. [R as indicated]

[2085]   Richardson, G. F. "A Neglected Aspect of the English
         Romantic Revolt," *University of California Publication in
         Modern Philology,* III, No. 3 (May 20, 1915), 247-360.
         [C]

[2086]   Campbell, Gertrude H. "The Swinish Multitude," *MLN,* XXX,
         No. 6 (June, 1915), [161]-164. [C]

[2087]   [Signed "G.L.de St.M.W."]. "Shelley's 'Pecksie.,'" *Notes
         and Queries,* Eleventh Series XII, No. 307 (November 13,
         1915), 378. [B]

Books:

[2088]   Herford, Charles Harold. "Shelley," 63-68 in Volume XII,
         The Cambridge History of English Literature. Edited by Sir
         A. W. Ward and A. R. Waller. 15 vols. Cambridge, Eng.:
         Cambridge University Press, 1915. [C]

[2089]   Lounsbury, Thomas R. *The Life and Times of Tennyson* [*From 1809
         to 1850*] (brackets in the original). xvi+660pp. New
         Haven, Conn.: Yale University Press, 1915. [M: 56, 87,
         117, 122, 128, 138, 145, 150-161, 174, 223, 224, 304,
         305, 354, 371, 373, 484, 485, 552]

[2090]   Price, Lawrence Marsden. *The Attitude of Gustav Freytag and
         Julian Schmidt toward English Literature (1848-1862).* [*Hesperia
         (/) Schriften zur germanischen Philologie. No. 7*]. viii+119pp.
         Gottingen: Vandenhoeck & Ruprecht, 191-. [C: "Shelley
         and his school.," 33-36; M: numerous, indexed]

[2091]   Powys, John Cowper. *Visions and Revisions* [/] *A Book of Literary
         Devotions.*   298pp. New York: G. Arnold Shaw, 1915.
         [C: "Shelley," (167)-180]

[2092]   Rutherford, Mark [pseud. of William Hale White]. *Last Pages
         From a Journal* [/] *With Other Papers.* Edited by his Wife

[Dorothy V. White]. vii+321pp. London: Oxford
University Press [/] Humphrey Milford, 1915. [B:
"Notes on Shelley's Birthplace," (219)-233; rptd.
from item 1042]

1916

Periodicals:

[2093] Collison-Morley, Lacy. "Some English Poets in Modern
        Italian Literature.," *Modern Language Review*, XI, No. 1
        (January, 1916), [48]-60. [C]

[2094] Benham, Allen R. "Shelley and Spinoza," *The Nation*, CII,
        No. 2641 [Special Supplement, 18pp.] (February 10,
        1916), 16-17. [C]

[2095] [Anonymous]. "Shelley Was With Us.," *The Times Literary
        Supplement* [London], No. 736 (February 24, 1916), [85].
        [C]

[2096] Legge, J. E. "Shelley.," *The Times Literary Supplement* [Lon-
        don], No. 737 (March 2, 1916), 105. [C]

[2097] Smith, E. T. Murray. "Shelley," *The Times Literary Supplement*
        [London], No. 738 (March 9, 1916), 117. [C]

[2098] Battersby, J. C. " *Essays and Studies by Members of the English
        Association.* Vol. V. Collected by Oliver Elton. Ox-
        ford: Clarendon Press, 1914. 8vo. vi + 171pp.," *Modern
        Language Review*, XI, No. 2 (April, 1916), [222]-230. [R:
        item 2082]

[2099] Cooke, Margaret W. "Schiller's 'Robbers' in England,"
        Modern Language Review, XI, No. 2 (April. 1916), [156]-
        175. [C: 174-175]

[2100] Kooistra, J. "Shelley's *Prometheus Unbound*," *Neophilologus*, I,
        No. 3 ([April], 1916), 213-222. [C]

[2101] Martin, L. C. "A Crashaw and Shelley Parallel," *Modern
        Language Review*, XI, No. 2 (April, 1916), 217. [C]

[2102] Desai, Hiralal N. "Shelley and Kalâpi," *East & West*, XV,
        Part II, No. 177 (July, 1916), 632-646. [C]

[2103] E.W. [Edith Franklin Wyatt]. "Shelley in His Letters,"
        Poetry: A Magazine of Verse, VIII, No. 4 (July, 1916), 204-
        208. [R: item 1977 (revised ed., 1915)]

[195]

[2104] van Kranendonk, A. G. "Demogorgon in Shelley's *Prometheus Unbound*," *Neophilologus*, II, No. 1 ([October], 1916), 59-62. [C]

[2105] Pelo, Florence Boylston. "Some Unpublished Letters of Mary Shelley," *The North American Review*, CCIV, No. 732 (November, 1916), [727]-740. [T]

Books:

[2106] Thayer, Mary Rebecca. *The Influence of Horace on the Chief English Poets of the Nineteenth Century.* 117pp. New Haven, Conn.: Yale University Press, 1916. [C: "Percy Bysshe Shelley," (85)-92]

[2107] Wylie, Laura Johnson. *Social Studies in English Literature.* [Vassar Semi-Centennial Series]. 216pp. Boston: Houghton Mifflin Company, 1916. [C: "Shelley's Democracy," (167)-210]

1917

Periodicals:

[2108] Wyatt, Edith [Franklin]. "Shelley and Claire Clairmont," *The North American Review*, CCV, No. 734 (January, 1917), [118]-130. [B]

[2109] Griffith, John H. Sandham. "Shelley's Copy of Abbe Barruel's Work on Secret Societies," *Notes and Queries*, Twelfth Series III, No. 59 (February 10, 1917), 108. [C,T]

[2110] [Anonymous]. "Shelley and His Father.," *The Times Literary Supplement* [London], No. 790 (March 8, 1917), 115. [R: item 2124]

[2111] Dodds, M. H. "Shelley's Use of Abbe Barruel's Work on Secret Societies (12 S. iii. 108).," *Notes and Queries*, Twelfth Series III, No. 63 (March 10, 1917), 196. [C]

[2112] MacSweeney, Joseph J. "[Untitled, following item 2111]," *Notes and Queries*, Twelfth Series III, No. 63 (March 10, 1917), 196. [C]

[2113] Bayley, A. R. "[Untitled, following item 2112]," *Notes and Queries*, Twelfth Series III, No. 63 (March 10, 1917), 196-197. [C]

[2114]   Butterworth, G. "Shelley in England," *The Bookman* [London],
          LII, No. [?] (April, 1917), 15-16. [R: item 2124]

[2115]   Elton, Oliver. "*The Cambridge History of English Literature.*
          Edited by A. W. Ward and A. R. Waller. Vol. XII. The
          Nineteenth Century, I. Cambridge: University Press.
          1915. 8vo. xi+565pp.," *Modern Language Review,* XII,
          No. 2 (April, 1917), 236-242. [R: item 2088; Shelley:
          239]

[2116]   Frere, John [Hookham]. "A Talk with Coleridge. [/]
          Abstract of a discourse with Mr. Coleridge on the state
          of the country in December 1830, written at the time
          by John Frere. [Edited by E. M. Green]," *The Cornhill
          Magazine,* XLII, New Series No. 250 (April, 1917), 402-
          410. [C: 409]

[2117]   Buell, Llewellyn M. "Byron and Shelley," *MLN,* XXXII, No. 5
          (May, 1917), 312-313. [C]

[2118]   Burch, Rousseau A. "The Case of Shelley v. Westbrooke,"
          Case and Comment [/] *Lawyer's Magazine* [Rochester, N.Y.],
          XXIII (June, 1916-May, 1917), 181-187. [B]

[2119]   Kelly, Florence Finch. "Being Dead Yet Liveth," *The Bookman*
          [New York], XLV, No. 3 (May, 1917), [289]-292. [R:
          item 2124]

[2120]   Pollard, Alfred W. "Review. [/] *Letters about Shelley inter-
          changed by three friends—Edward Dowden, Richard Garnett and W.
          Michael Rossetti. Edited, with an introduction, by R. S. Garnett.
          Hodder & Stoughton, London, New York, Toronto. 1917. pp.
          271.,*" *The Library,* Third Series VIII, No. 31 (July,
          1917), 288. [R: item 2123]

[2121]   MacFarlane, Charles. "Shelley in Italy: A Personal
          Memory of Him," *The Book Monthly,* XIII, No. 4 (Spring &
          Summer, 1917), 259-262. [Rptd. from item 2125]

[2122]   C[hew], S[amuel] C. "[Untitled item under general title
          of "Brief Mention"]," *MLN,* XXXII, No. 7 (November,
          1917), 445-447. [R: item 2124]

Books:

[2123]   Dowden, Edward, Richard Garnett, and William Michael Ros-
          setti. *Letters about Shelley* [/] *Interchanged by Three Friends
          —Edward Dowden* [/] *Richard Garnett and Wm. Michael Rossetti.*
          Edited, with an introduction by R[obert] S. Garnett.
          271pp. London: Hodder and Stoughton, 1917. [C,B,T]

[2124]   Ingpen, Roger. *Shelley in England* [/] *New Facts and Letters from*
          the Shelley-Whitton Papers. 2 vols. Boston: Houghton
          Mifflin Company, 1917. [B,T; one volume edition,
          London: Kegan Paul, Trench, Trübner & Co., Ltd., 1917]

[2125]   MacFarlane, Charles. *Reminiscences of a Literary Life. By*
          Charles MacFarlane [/] *1799-1858* [/] *Author and Traveller* [/]
          with an introduction by John F. Tattersall. xviii+
          303pp. London: John Murray, 1917. [B: "Chapter I:
          Percy Bysshe Shelley," (1)-12; rptd.: item 2121]

[2126]   Stratton, Clarence. "The Cenci Story in Literature and
          Fact," 130-160 in *Studies in English Drama*. Edited by
          Allison Gaw. [Publications of the University of
          Pennsylvania (/) Series in Philology and Literature,
          XIV]. [Philadelphia]: University of Pennsylvania,
          1917. [C: 136-138]

                                1918

Periodicals:

[2127]   Brooke, Stopford A[ugustus]. "Shelley's Interpretation
          of Christ and His Teaching [1902]," *The Hibbert Journal*
          [Boston], XVI, No. 3 (April, 1918), 366-376. [C;
          rptd.: item 2183]

[2128]   Stockley, V. "Shelley: Schubart.," *Notes and Queries*, Twelfth
          Series IV, No. 79 (April, 1918), 102. [C]

[2129]   Chew, Samuel C. "Byroniana," *MLN*, XXXIII, No. 5 (May,
          1918), 306-309. [C]

[2130]   Colvin, Sidney. "Shelley and Keats: A Correction.," *The*
          Times Literary Supplement [London], No. 851 (May 9, 1918),
          220. [T]

[2131]   Hepburn, Blanche E. "Shelley and Keats.," *The Times Literary*
          Supplement [London], No. 852 (May 16, 1918), 233. [T]

[2132]   Henry Sotheran and Co. "The Shelley Letter in the Red
          Cross Sale.," *The Times Literary Supplement* [London],
          No. 853 (May 23, 1918), 245. [T]

[2133]   Hughes, A[rthur] M[ontague] D['Urban]. "Shelley and
          Nature," *The North American Review*, CCVIII, No. 753
          (August, 1918), [287]-295. [C]

[2134]   Gingerich, S[olomon] F[rancis]. "XVII. Shelley's Doc-
          trine of Necessity *Versus* Christianity," *PMLA*, XXXIII,
          No. 3 (September, 1918), 444-473. [C]

[2135]   Wilson, W. E.   "Shelley: Schubart (12 S. iv. 102).," *Notes
          and Queries*, Twelfth Series IV, No. 86 (November, 1918),
          315.   [C]

Books:

[2136]   Harvey, Alexander.   *Shelley's Elopement* [/] *A Study of the
          Most Romantic Episode in Literary History.* 288pp.   New York:
          A. A. Knopf, 1918.   [B]

[2137]   Shelley, Mary Wollstonecraft.   *Letters of Mary Wollstonecraft
          Shelley (Mostly Published).* With Introduction and Notes by
          Henry H. Harper.   191pp.   Boston: privately printed
          [Bibliophile Society], 1918.   [T]

[2138]   Swinburne, Algernon Charles.   *The Letters of Algernon Charles
          Swinburne.*   Edited by Edmund Gosse and Thomas James Wise.
          2 vols.   London: William Heinemann, 1918.   [M: I, 4,
          192, 225, 241; II, 165, 166, 170, 178]

                              1919

Periodicals:

[2139]   Harding, Anna Trail.   "Shelley's *Adonais* and Swinburne's
          Ave Atque Vale," *The Sewanee Review*, XXVII, No. 1 (January,
          1919), [32]-42.   [C]

[2140]   van Maanen, W.   "Shelley-Translations," *English Studies*, I,
          No. 1 (February, 1919), 9-16.   [C]

[2141]   Anderson, G. A.   "A Shelley Letter.," *The Times Literary
          Supplement* [London], No. 890 (February 6, 1919), 70.   [C]

[2142]   Butterworth, S.   "A Shelley Letter.," *The Times Literary
          Supplement* [London], No. 896 (March 20, 1919), 153.   [C]

[2143]   van Kranendonk, A. G.   "Some Notes on the Metre of
          Shelley's *Sensitive Plant.*," *Neophilologus*, IV, No. 3
          ([April], 1919), 267-274.   [C]

[2144]   Bourdillon, F. W.   "A Misprint in Shelley?" *The Times Liter-
          ary Supplement* [London], No. 906 (May 29, 1919), 296.
          [T]

[2145]   Colgan, W. H.   "A Misprint in Shelley?" *The Times Literary
          Supplement* [London], No. 907 (June 5, 1919), 313.   [T]

[2146]   Farrington, B.   "The Text of Shelley's Translation of the
          'Symposium' of Plato.," *Modern Language Review*, XIV, No. 3

(July, 1919), 325-326. [T]

[2147] Campbell, Olwen W[ard]. "A Critic of Shelley," *The Times
Literary Supplement* [London], No. 936 (December 25, 1919),
781. [C]

*[2148] Taylor, Eugene C. "Shelley as Myth-maker," *Journal of
Abnormal Psychology*, XIV (1919), 64-90. [C]

Books:

[2149] Babbitt, Irving. *Rousseau and Romanticism.* xxiii+476pp.
Boston: Houghton Mifflin Company, 1919. [C: numerous
references, fully indexed]

[2150] Browning, Elizabeth Barrett. *Edgar Allan Poe [/] A Criticism
[/] With Remarks on the Morals and Religion of Shelley and Leigh
Hunt.* Edited by T[homas] J[ames] Wise. 15pp. London:
privately printed [Richard Clay and Sons], 1919. [C]

*[2151] Madariaga, Salvador de. "Shelley and Calderon," [?p] in
*Transactions and Report of the Royal Society of Literature of the
United Kingdom.* Volume XXXVII. London: Humphrey Milford,
1919. [C; rptd.: item 2186]

[2152] Osborn, Andrew R[ule]. *Shelley.* 128pp. Melbourne: Whit-
combe & Tombs, 1919. [C,B]

1920

Periodicals:

[2153] Ingpen, Roger. "Shelley and His Publishers [/] (with Some
new Letters)," *The London Mercury*, I, No. 3 (January,
1920), 291-300. [B, T]

[2154] [Signed "L.M.M."]. "Leigh Hunt on Shelley," *Notes and
Queries*, Twelfth Series VI, No, 101 (February, 1920),
37. [M]

[2155] Pancoast, Henry S. "Shelley's Ode to the West Wind," *MLN*,
XXXV, No. 2 (February, 1920), 97-100. [C]

[2156] Peck, Walter Edwin. "More Shelley Letters with Correc-
tions of Previously Published Texts: The Whole from
MSS.," *The Athenaeum*, No. 4709 (July 30, 1920), 135-136.
[T]

[2157] Allen, B. Sprague. "XVII. —William Godwin and the
Stage," *PMLA*, XXXV, No. 3 (September, 1920), 358-374.

[M: 370-371]

[2158] [Anonymous]. "A Poet's Pamphlet.," *The Nation*, XXVII,
No. 26 (September 25, 1920), 780-781. [C; rptd.:
item 2166]

[2159] [Anonymous]. "Shelley on Politics," *The Times Literary
Supplement* [London], No. 977 (October 7, 1920), [641].
[C]

[2160] Waterlow, Sydney. "Shelley as Politician. [/] A Philosophical View of Reform. By Percy Bysshe Shelley.
With Introduction and Appendix by T. W. Rolleston.
(Milford.)," *The Athenaeum*, No. 4720 (October 15, 1920),
513-514. [R: item 2187]

[2161] Peck, Walter Edwin. "Shelley and Reform," *The Athenaeum*,
No. 4721 (October 22, 1920), 563. [T]

[2162] [Signed "G.G.L."]. "A Poem of Shelley," *Notes and Queries*,
Twelfth Series VII, No. 132 (October 23, 1920), 331.
[C]

[2163] Falconer, J. P. E. "The Cremation of Shelley.," *The Times
Literary Supplement* [London], No. 980 (October 28, 1920),
702. [B]

[2164] McDonald [*sic*], Daniel J. "The Radicalism of Shelley and
Its Sources," *The Catholic Educational Review*, XVIII, No. 9
(November, 1920), 545-551. [C; rptd. from item 2057]

[2165] Elliot, Hugh. "The Cremation of Shelley," *The Times Literary
Supplement* [London], No. 981 (November 4, 1920), 719.
[B]

[2166] [Anonymous]. "An Unpublished Pamphlet by Shelley," *The
Living Age*, CCCVII, No. 3983 (November 6, 1920), 363-
366. [C; rptd. from item 2158]

[2167] Hutchison, W. A. "A Poem of Shelley (12 S. vii. 331).,"
Notes and Queries, Twelfth Series VII, No. 134 (November
6, 1920), 375. [C]

[2168] [Signed "C.C.B."]. "[Untitled, following item 2167],"
Notes and Queries, Twelfth Series VII, No. 134 (November
6, 1920), 375. [C]

[2169] Benington, Wilson. "The Cremation of Shelley.," *The Times
Literary Supplement* [London], No. 982 (November 11, 1920),
739. [B]

[2170] Panton, J. E. "The Cremation of Shelley.," *The Times Literary Supplement* [London], No. 983 (November 18, 1920), 759.
[B]

[2171] [Signed "P.G.R."]. "[Untitled, following item 2170],"
The Times Literary Supplement [London], No. 983 (November
18, 1920), 759. [B]

[2172] Peck, W[alter] E[dwin]. "Scott and Shelley," *The Athenaeum*,
No. 4725 (November 19, 1920), 706. [T]

[2173] Panton, J. E. "The Cremation of Shelley.," *The Times Literary Supplement* [London], No. 984 (November 25, 1920),
779. [B]

[2174] Haines, C. R. "[Untitled, following item 2173]," *The Times
Literary Supplement* [London], No. 984 (November 25, 1920),
779. [B]

[2175] McDonald [*sic*], Daniel J. "The Radicalism of Shelley and
Its Sources," *The Catholic Educational Review*, XVIII, No. 9
(December, 1920), 575-582. [C; rptd. from item 2057]

[2176] Syers, Edgar. "Shelley and the Thames—with Some Digres-
sions," *The National Review*, LXXVI, No. 454 (December,
1920), [503]-513. [B]

[2177] Falconer, J. P. E. "The Cremation of Shelley.," *The Times
Literary Supplement* [London], No. 985 (December 2, 1920),
799. [B]

[2178] McFadden, A. G. "[Untitled, following item 2177]," *The
Times Literary Supplement* [London], No. 985 (December 2,
1920), 799. [B]

[2179] Peck, Walter Edwin. "The Cremation of Shelley.," *The Times
Literary Supplement* [London], No. 986 (December 9, 1920),
838-839. [B]

[2180] Panton, J. E. "[Untitled, following item 2179]," *The Times
Literary Supplement* [London], No. 986 (December 9, 1920),
839. [B]

[2181] Griffiths, John S. "[Untitled, following item 2180]," *The
Times Literary Supplement* [London], No. 986 (December 9,
1920), 839. [B]

[2182] [Signed "K.C.B."]. "The Cremation of Shelley.," *The Times
Literary Supplement* [London], No. 987 (December 16, 1920),
859. [B]

Books:

[2183] Brooke, Stopford [Augustus]. *Naturalism in English Poetry.*
viii+310pp. London: J. M. Dent & Sons, 1920. [C:
"Wordsworth, Shelley and Byron," 165-194; "Poetry of
Shelley," 195-224; "Shelley's Interpretation of

Christianity," 218-233, rptd. from item 2127]

[2184]   Browning, Robert. *An Opinion on the Writings of Alfred Lord Tennyson* [/] *with a Statement of His Changed Views Regarding Percy Bysshe Shelley.* Edited by T[homas] J[ames] Wise. 18pp. London: privately printed [Richard Clay and Sons], 1920. [C]

[2185]   Lynd, Robert. *The Art of Letters.* 240pp. London: T. Fisher Unwin, Ltd, 1920. [C: "Aspects of Shelley," 106-121]

[2186]   Madariaga, Salvador de. *Shelley & Calderon* [/] *and Other Essays on English and Spanish Poetry.* zii+198pp. London: Constable & Company Limited, 1920. [C: "Shelley and Calderon," (1)-48; rptd. from item 2151]

[2187]   Shelley, Percy Bysshe. *A Philosophical View of Reform by Percy Bysshe Shelley (Now printed for the first time) together with an Introduction and Appendix by T. W. Rolleston.* xi+94pp. London: Humphrey Milford [/] Oxford University Press, 1920. [T; C: "Introduction," (iii)-xi]

[2188]   Thomson, James Alexander Kerr. "The Religious Background of the *Prometheus Vinctus,*" *Harvard Studies in Classical Philology,* XXXI (1920), 1-37. [M]

[2189]   Woodberry, George Edward. *Literary Essays.* 338pp. New York: Harcourt, Brace and Howe, 1920. [C: "Shelley's work," 107-127; rptd. from item 1565]

1921

Periodicals:

[2190]   McDonald [*sic*], Daniel J. "The Radicalism of Shelley and Its Sources," *The Catholic Educational Review,* XIX, No. 1 (January, 1921), 23-38. [C; rptd. from item 2057]

[2191]   White, Newman I[vey]. "The Historical and Personal Background of Shelley's Hellas," *The South Atlantic Quarterly,* XX, No. 1 (January, 1921), [52]-60. [C,B]

[2192]   McDonald [*sic*], Daniel J. "The Radicalism of Shelley and Its Sources," *The Catholic Educational Review,* XIX, No. 2 (February, 1921), 89-98. [C; rptd. from item 2057]

[2193]   Gosse, Edmund. "New Fragments of Shelley," *The Times Literary Supplement* [London], No. 997 (February 24, 1921), 126. [T]

[2194]   Graham, Walter. "III. —The Politics of the Greater
         Romantic Poets," *PMLA*, XXXVI, No. 1 (March, 1921),
         60-78. [C; Shelley: 75-78]

[2195]   McDonald [*sic*], Daniel J. "The Radicalism of Shelley and
         Its Sources," *The Catholic Educational Review*, XIX, No. 3
         (March, 1921), 154-166. [C; rptd. from item 2057]

*[2196] White, O. E. "[?]," *The Bookman* [London], LXIX, No. [?]
         (March, 1921), 229-230. [R]

[2197]   Garnett, R[obert] S. "New Fragments of Shelley," *The Times
         Literary Supplement* [London], No. 998 (March 3, 1921),
         144. [T]

[2198]   Toynbee, Paget. "[Untitled, following item 2197]," *The
         Times Literary Supplement* [London], No. 998 (March 3, 1921).
         144. [T]

[2199]   Peck, Walter Edwin. "New Fragments of Shelley," *The Times
         Literary Supplement* [London], No. 999 (March 10, 1921),
         160. [T]

[2200]   Buttrick, E. G. "Shelley and Keats: Bibliographies
         Wanted," *Notes and Queries*, Twelfth Series VIII, No. 153
         (March 19, 1921), 230. [C]

[2201]   Peck, Walter Edwin. "New Shelley Papers.," *The Nation &
         The Athenaeum*, No. 4742 (March 19, 1921), 876-877. [T;
         rptd.: item 2205]

[2202]   Case, R. H. "Transactions and Report of the Royal Society
         of Literature of the United Kingdom. Vol. XXXVII.
         London: Humphrey Milford. 1919. 8vo. 8s.," *Modern
         Language Review*, XVI, No. 2 (April, 1921), 178-180. [R:
         item 2151]

[2203]   Hewitt, E. P. "Shelley and Westminster Abbey," *The National
         Review*, LXXVII, No. 458 (April, 1921), [225]-232. [B]

[2204]   Peck, Walter E[dwin]. "The Source Book of Shelley's
         'Adonais'?" *The Times Literary Supplement* [London],
         No. 1,003 (April 7, 1921), 228-229. [C]

[2205]   Peck, Walter Edwin. "New Shelley Manuscripts," *The Living
         Age*, CCCIX, No. 4008 (April 30, 1921), 303-308. [T;
         rptd. from item 2201]

[2206]   McDonald [*sic*], Daniel J. "The Radicalism of Shelley and
         Its Sources," *The Catholic Educational Review*, XIX, No. 5
         (May, 1921), 325-337. [C; rptd. from item 2057]

[2207]   McDonald [*sic*], Daniel J. "The Radicalism of Shelley and
         Its Sources," *The Catholic Educational Review*, XIX, No. 6

(June, 1921), 381-397. [C; rptd. from item 2057]

[2208] Peck, Walter Edwin. "A Note on Shelley and Peacock," *MLN*,
        XXXVI, No. 6 (June, 1921), 371-373. [C]

[2209] Peck, Walter E[dwin]. "Shelley's Autograph Corrections
        of 'The Daemon of the World,'" *The Times Literary Supplement*
        [London], No. 1,014 (June 23, 1921), 404. [T]

[2210] Wise, Thomas J[ames]. "Shelley's 'Queen Mab,'" *The Times
        Literary Supplement* [London], No. 1,015 (June 30, 1921),
        421. [T]

[2211] Deford, Miriam Allen. "A Poet's Science," *The Open Court*,
        XXXV, No. 9 [whole number 784] (September, 1921),
        [549]-551. [C]

[2212] McDonald [*sic*], Daniel J. "The Radicalism of Shelley and
        Its Sources," *The Catholic Educational Review*, XIX, No. 7
        (September, 1921), 464-473. [C; rptd. from item 2057]

[2213] Peck, Walter Edwin. "XVI. Shelley and the Abbé Barruel,"
        PMLA, XXXVI, No. 3 (September, 1921), 347-353. [C]

[2214] White, Newman I[vey]. "XV. Shelley's Swell-foot the
        Tyrant in Relation to Contemporary Political Satires,"
        PMLA, XXXVI, No. 3 (September, 1921), 332-346. [C]

[2215] McDonald [*sic*], Daniel J. "The Radicalism of Shelley and
        Its Sources," *The Catholic Educational Review*, XIX, No. 8
        (October, 1921), 517-532. [C; rptd. from item 2057]

[2216] [Anonymous]. "Poets on Poetry.," *The Times Literary Supplement*
        [London], No. 1,032 (October 27, 1921), [685]-686. [R:
        H. F. B. Brett-Smith's edition of *A Defence of Poetry*
        (London, 1921)]

[2217] McDonald [*sic*], Daniel J. "The Radicalism of Shelley and
        Its Sources," *The Catholic Educational Review*, XIX, No. 9
        (November, 1921), 580-591. [C; rptd. from item 2057]

[2218] Markland, Russell. "Dr. Johnson and Shelley," *Notes and
        Queries*, Twelfth Series IX, No. 186 (November 5, 1921),
        368. [C]

[2219] [Anonymous]. "Poets and Philosophy.," *The Times Literary
        Supplement* [London], No. 1,034 (November 10, 1921),
        731 (R: item 2222]

[2220] Gilbert, Allan H. "A Note on Shelley, Blake, and Milton,"
        MLN, XXXVI, No. 8 (December, 1921), 505-506. [C]

[2221] McDonald [*sic*], Daniel J. "The Radicalism of Shelley and
        Its Sources," *The Catholic Educational Review*, XIX, No. 10

(December, 1921), 646-659. [C; rptd. from item 2057]

Books:

[2222] Strong, Archibald T.   *Three Studies in Shelley* [/] *and an Essay
        on Nature in Wordsworth and Meredith.*   189pp. London: Oxford
        University Press [/] Humphrey Milford, 1921. [C: "The
        Faith of Shelley," (9)-66; "Shelley's Symbolism," (67)-
        106; "The Sinister in Shelley," (107)-147]

                                1922

Periodicals:

[2223] Forman, W. Courthope. "Shelley's First Wife: The Unpub-
        lished Letter," *The Cornhill Magazine*, New Series LII
        [whole number CXXV], No. 307 (January, 1922), 28-32.
        [T,B]

[2224] Stuwe, J. R. Van. "A Shelley Letter.," *The Times Literary
        Supplement* [London], No. 1,046 (February 2, 1922), 76.
        [T]

[2225] Mitchell, Stewart. "A Century of Shelley," *The Dial*, LXXII
        (March, 1922), [246]-258. [C]

[2226] Herford, C[harles] H[arold]. "The Centenary of Shelley's
        Death," *The Times Literary Supplement* [London], No. 1,056
        (April 13, 1922), 244. [B]

[2227] Evans, B. I. "The Persistent Image in Shelley," *The Nine-
        teenth Century*, XCI, No. 543 (May, 1922), 791-797. [C]

[2228] Pendlebury, P. J. "D'Annunzio and Shelley.," *The Times
        Literary Supplement* [London], No. 1,059 (May 4, 1922),
        292. [C]

[2229] Elliot, G[eorge] R[ay]. "How Poetic Is Shelley's Poetry?
        [/] (A Centenary View)," *PMLA*, XXXVII, No. 2 (June,
        1922), 311-323. [C]

[2230] Shanks, Edward. "Shelley," *The London Mercury*, VI, No. 32
        (June, 1922), 154-165. [B]

[2231] [Anonymous]. "The Gossip Shop," *The Bookman* [New York],
        LV, No. 5 (July, 1922), 552-560. [M: 552]

[2232] [Signed "Brother Leo"]. "Percy Bysshe Shelley.," *The
        Catholic World*, CXV, No. 688 (July, 1922), [468]-480.
        [C,B]

[2233]   [Signed "Prometheus"].   "Percy Bysshe Shelley," *The English Review*, XXXV (July, 1922), 16-21.   [C; rptd.: item 2259]

[2234]   Beach, Joseph Warren.   "Latter-Day Critics of Shelley," *The Yale Review*, New Series XI, No. 4 (July, 1922), [718]-731.   [C]

[2235]   Elton, Oliver.   "*Three Studies in Shelley, and an Essay on Nature in Wordsworth and Meredith.* By Archibald T. Strong.   Oxford: Oxford University Press.   1921.   8vo.   189pp.   10s. 6d.," *Modern Language Review*, XVII, No. 3 (July, 1922), 307-310.   [R: item 2222]

[2236]   Ingpen, Roger.   "Shelley in London.," *The Bookman* [London], LXII, No. 370 (July, 1922), 163-164 [with supplementary illustration on 165].   [B]

[2237]   Liveing, Edward.   "The Fate of a Great Lyric Poet—I," *Discovery [/] A Monthly Popular Journal of Knowledge*, III, No. 31 (July, 1922), 183-188.   [C]

[2238]   Meynell, Wilfrid.   "'Shelley Plain.,'" *The Review of Reviews*, LXVI, No. 391 (July, 1922), [43]-60.   [B,C]

[2239]   Millar, A. H.   "Mary Godwin in Dundee.," *The Bookman* [London], LXII, No. 370 (July, 1922), 161-162.   [B]

[2240]   M[onroe], H[arriet].   "Shelley," *Poetry: A Magazine of Verse*, XX, No. 4 (July, 1922), 206-214.   [C]

[2241]   Powys, Llewelyn.   "Percy Bysshe Shelley," *The Century Magazine*, New Series LXXXII [whole number CIV], No. 3 (July, 1922), 459-462.   [C]

[2242]   Slaughter, Gertrude.   "Percy Bysshe Shelley [/] 1822-1922," *The North American Review*, CCXVI, No. 800 (July, 1922), [67]-82.   [C]

[2243]   Thomas, Gilbert.   "Shelley the Prophet.," *The Bookman* [London], LXII, No. 370 (July, 1922), [159]-160.   [C]

[2244]   White, Newman I[vey].   "Shelley's *Charles the First*," *The Journal of English and Germanic Philology*, XXI, No. 3 (July, 1922), 431-441.   [C]

[2245]   Jordan, Charlotte Brewster.   "Shelley after a Hundred Years," *The New York Times Book Review* (July 2, 1922), 3.   [C]

[2246]   C[lutton]-B[rock], A[rthur].   "Percy Bysshe Shelley.," *The Times Literary Supplement* [London], No. 1,068 (July 6, 1922), [433]-434.   [C; rptd.: item 2448]

[2247] Peck, Walter Edwin. "Shelley's 'Philosophical View of
        Reform.,'" *The Times Literary Supplement* [London], No.
        1,068 (July 6, 1922), 444. [T]

[2248] [Anonymous]. "The Shelley Centenary," *The Saturday Review*,
        CXXXIV, No. 3480 (July 8, 1922), 53-54. [C]

[2249] Blunden, Edmund. "Shelley and His Friends.," *The Nation and
        the Athenaeum*, XXXI, No. 15 (July 8, 1922), 506-507. [B]

[2250] B[radley], A[rthur] G[ranville]. "Shelley in Wales," *The
        Saturday Review*, CXXXIV, No. 3480 (July 8, 1922), 58. [B]

[2251] Chisholm, Hugh. "A Note on the 'Ineffectual Angel,'" *The
        Saturday Review*, CXXXIV, No. 3481 (July 15, 1922), 96-97.
        [C]

[2252] de Gruyter, J. "Shelley and Dostoievsky," *English Studies*,
        IV, No. 4 ["Shelley Centenary Number"] (August, 1922),
        [129]-151. [C]

[2253] Grant, L. "The Mysticism of Shelley," *Occult Review*, XXXVI,
        No. 2 (August, 1922), 88-91. [C]

[2254] Kooistra, J. "The Pan-erotic Element in Shelley," *English
        Studies*, IV, No. 4 ["Shelley Centenary Number"] (August,
        1922), 171-176. [C,B]

[2255] Kooistra, J. "Shelley-Bibliography. 1908-1922.," *English
        Studies*, IV, No. 4 ["Shelley Centenary Number"] (August,
        1922), 177-181. [C]

[2256] Liveing, Edward. "The Fate of a Great Lyric Poet—II,"
        Discovery [/] *A Monthly Popular Journal of Knowledge*, III, No.
        32 (August, 1922), 215-218. [B]

*[2257] Teall, Gardner. "Keats and Shelley: A Frustrated Friend-
        ship," *The Bookman's Journal*, [?] (August, 1922), 145-147.
        [B]

[2258] Verwey, Albert. "Alastor or the Spirit of Solitude [/]
        Translated into Dutch," *English Studies*, IV, No. 4
        ["Shelley Centenary Number"] (August, 1922), 152-170.
        [T,C]

[2259] [Signed "Prometheus"]. "Percy Bysshe Shelley," *The Living
        Age*, Eighth Series XXVII [whole number CCXIV], No. 4075
        (August 12, 1922), 415-418. [C; rptd. from item 2233]

[2260] [Anonymous]. "News Notes.," *The Bookman* [London], LXII,
        No. 372 (September, 1922), [231]-236. [B: 234]

[2261] Bradley, A[rthur] G[ranville]. "Shelley in Wales," *The
        National Review*, LXXX, No. 475 (September, 1922), [127]-

132. [B]

[2262] Umis, N. "Shelley. [/] 1822-1922.," *The Irish Monthly*, LI, No. 591 (September, 1922), [353]-363. [C]

[2263] Marshall, William E. "In Memory of Shelley," *The Dalhousie Review*, II, No. 3 (October, 1922), 302-312. [B,C]

[2264] Veldkamp, J. "A Pilgrimage to the Remains of Shelley and Keats (1822(1)-1922 [*sic*].," *English Studies*, IV, No. 5 (October, 1922), 200-201. [B]

[2265] [Signed "J.D."]. "In Defence of Shelley.," *The Irish Monthly*, LI, No. 593 (November, 1922), 472-477. [C]

[2266] White, Newman I[vey]. "Shelley's Debt to Alma Murray," *MLN*, XXXVII, No. 7 (November, 1922), 411-415. [C]

[2267] Hutchison, W. A. "Shelley—Esdaile.," *Notes and Queries*, Twelfth Series XI, No. 238 (November 4, 1922), 368. [B]

[2268] Lehman, H. H. "XXIX. The Doctrine of Leadership in the Greater Romantic Poets," *PMLA*, XXXVII, No. 4 (December, 1922), 639-661. [C; Shelley: 639, 652-655, 660]

[2269] Shipp, Horace. "Shelley and Chevalier," *The English Review*, XXXV (December, 1922), 525. [C]

[2270] Turner, W. J. "Chronicles [/] Drama," *The London Mercury*, VII, No. 38 (December, 1922), 199-201. [R of performance of *The Cenci*: 201]

[2271] White, Newman I[vey]. "XXXI. An Italian 'Imitation' of Shelley's *The Cenci*," *PMLA*, XXXVII, No. 4 (December, 1922), 683-690. [C]

[2272] [Anonymous]. "Shelley in German," *The Times Literary Supplement* [London], No. 1,092 (December 21, 1922), 852. [R of *Dichtungen von Shelley*. In neuer Übertragung von Alfred Wolfenstein. (Berlin: Paul Cassirer, 1922)]

Books:

[2273] Gosse, Edmund. *Aspects and Impressions*. [300]pp. London: Cassell and Company, Ltd, 1922. [C: 177, 180]

[2274] Gutteling, Johanna Frederika. *Hellenic Influence on the English Poetry of the Nineteenth Century*. 144pp. Amsterdam: H. G. Van Dorssen, [1922]. [C: 18-19, 25-29, 86, 90-96, 112-114, 132-140]

[2275] Havens, Raymond Dexter. *The Influence of Milton on English*

Poetry. xii+720pp. Cambridge, Mass.: Harvard University Press, 1922. [C: 42, 201, 228-231, 536-537, 555,
567]

[2276] Herford, C[harles] H[arold]. "Romanticism in the Modern
World," [107]-134 in *Essays and Studies by Members of the
English Association*, VIII. 167pp. Oxford: At the Claren-
don Press, 1922. [C: 130-134]

[2277] Hewlett, Maurice. *Extemporary Essays*. 256pp. London:
Humphrey Milford [/] Oxford University Press, 1922.
[C: "Shelley's Swan-song," (22)-26]

*[2278] Peck, Walter Edwin. "Shelley in Edinburgh," *The Book of
Old Edinburgh Club*, II (1922), [?pp]. [B]

[2279] Miller, Joaquin. *Trelawny with Shelley and Byron*. [The Ramapo
Press Publications, No. 1]. 24pp. Pompton Lakes,
N.J.: The Biblio Company, 1922. [B]

[2280] Moore, Thomas Verner. *Percy Bysshe Shelley* [/] *An Introduction
to the Study of Character*. [Psychological Review Publica-
tions (/) Psychological Monographs (/) Volume XXXI,
No. 2 (/) Psychological Studies from the Catholic
University of America (/) No. 6]. 62pp. Princeton,
J.J.: Psychological Review Company, 1922. [B]

[2281] Prescott, Frederick Clarke. *The Poetic Mind*. xx+308pp.
New York: The Macmillan Company, 1922. [C: nearly
fifty references, fully indexed]

[2282] Quiller-Couch, Arthur. *Studies in Literature* [/] *Second Series*.
310pp. Cambridge, Eng.: At the University Press, 1922.
[C: "Shelley," (31)-87]

[2283] Saito, Takeshi, ed. *The Shelley Memorial Volume by Members of the
English Club, Imperial University of Tokyo*. [237]pp. [Tokyo:
(?privately printed), 1922]. [C]

*[2284] *Shisei Shelley*. [In Honor of Immortal Shelley]. Collections
of Contributions by Prominent Students of English
Literature in Japan. 110pp. Tokyo: [?], 1922. [C]

[2285] Ward, F. W. Orde. *Percy Bysshe Shelley (1792-1822)*. With a
memorial Forward by Russell Markland. 16pp. Lytham:
N. Ling & Co., 1922. [C]

1923

Periodicals:

[2286] Walters, J. Cuming. "Shelley: A Centenary Tribute.," *The

[210]

Manchester Quarterly, [XLII], No. clxv (January, 1923), [1]-20.   [C]

[2287]   Woollen, Wilfrid H.   "Dr. Hume, the Guardian of Shelley's Children," *Notes and Queries*, Twelfth Series XII, No. 252 (February 10, 1923), 109-110.   [B]

[2288]   [Signed "G.F.R.B."].   "Dr. Hume, the Guardian of Shelley's Children (12 S. xii. 109).," *Notes and Queries*, Twelfth Series XII, No. 254 (February 24, 1923), 156.   [B]

[2289]   Peck, Walter, Edwin.   "On the Origin of the Shelley Society," *MLN*, XXXVIII, No. 3 (March, 1923), 159-163.   [B]

[2290]   Peck, Walter Edwin.   "The Biographical Element in the Novels of Mary Wollstonecraft Shelley," *PMLA*, XXXVIII, No. 1 (March, 1923), 196-219.   [B]

[2291]   Woollen, Wilfrid H.   "The Grave of Shelley's Daughter, Ianthe.," *Notes and Queries*, Twelfth Series XII, No. 257 (March 17, 1923), 213.   [B]

[2292]   Massey, B[ernard] W[ilfrid] A[rbuthnot].   "The 'O.E.D.' and Some Adjectives of Shelley and Keats.," *Notes and Queries*, Twelfth Series XII, No. 259 (March 31, 1923), 243-244.   [C]

[2293]   Allen, L. H.   "Plagiarism, Sources, and Influences in Shelley's 'Alastor.,'" *Modern Language Review*, XVIII, No. 2 (April, 1923), [133]-151.   [C]

[2294]   Benham, Allen R.   "Shelley's Prometheus Unbound [/] An Interpretation," *The Personalist*, IV, No. 2 (April, 1923), 110-120.   [C]

[2295]   Kooistra, J.   "Supplement to the Shelley-Bibliography 1908-1922.," *English Studies*, V, No. 2 (April, 1923), 79-80.   [C]

[2296]   Severn, Nigel B.   "Keats and Shelley: About Certain Portraits.," *The Bookman* [London], LXIV, No. 379 (April, 1923), 16-17.   [B]

[2297]   Majid, Jamila.   "Shelley's Heart.," *Notes and Queries*, Twelfth Series XII, No. 264 (May 5, 1923), 352.   [B]

[2298]   [Anonymous].   "The Challenge to Poetry.," *The Times Literary Supplement* [London], No. 1,113 (May 17, 1923), [329]-330.   [C]

[2299]   Woollen, Wilfrid H.   "Letters of Shelley," *Notes and Queries*, Twelfth Series XII, No. 266 (May 19, 1923), 391.   [T]

[2300]   Woollen, Wilfrid H.   "Shelley's Heart (12 S. xii. 352).,"
          Notes and Queries, Twelfth Series XII, No. 266 (May 19,
          1923), 396.   [B]

[2301]   de Selincourt, E[rnest].   "Shelley's Knowledge of Music.,"
          The Times Literary Supplement[London], No. 1,114 (May 24,
          1923), 355.   [C]

[2302]   Woollen, Wilfrid H.   "Shelley's Knowledge of Music.," *The
          Times Literary Supplement* [London], No. 1,116 (June 7,
          1923), 388.   [C]

[2303]   Massey, B[ernard] W[ilfrid] A[rbuthnot].   "Compound Ad-
          jectives of Shelley and Keats," *Notes and Queries*, Twelfth
          Series XII, No. 270 (June 16, 1923), 464-468.   [C]

[2304]   Goldberry, A. J.   "Shelley's Knowledge of Music.," *The
          Times Literary Supplement* [London],   No. 1,118 (June 21,
          1923), 422.   [C]

[2305]   [Anonymous].   "Ariel.," *The Times Literary Supplement* [London],
          No. 1,119 (June 28, 1923), 437.   [R: Andre Maurois'
          Ariel; ou La Vie de Shelley (Paris: Bernard Grasset, 1923),
          trans. (1924): item 2361]

[2306]   [Anonymous].   "The Grolier Club Shelley Catalogue.," *The
          Times Literary Supplement* [London], No. 1,119 (June 28,
          1923), 444.   [R: item 2317]

[2307]   Wylie, Elinor.   "Shelley's Grandson and Some Others,"
          The Bookman [New York], LVII, No. 6 (August, 1923), 611-
          612.   [B]

[2308]   Woollen, Wilfrid H.   "'Last Links with Byron, Shelley and
          Keats.' (See 11 S. ii. 108; viii. 228, 249.)," *Notes and
          Queries*, Thirteenth Series I, No. 17 (October 27, 1923),
          323-326.   [B]

[2309]   Peck, Walter Edwin.   "Shelley Defends Keats," *MLN*,
          XXXVIII, No. 7 (November, 1923), 443-445.   [B]

*[2310]   Peck, Walter Edwin.   "Note on Shelley," *The Literary Review*
          [published by the *New York Evening Post*], [?] (November 3,
          1923), 221.   [C]

[2311]   Peck, Walter E[dwin].   "Publications of the Shelley
          Society.," *The Times Literary Supplement* [London], No.
          1,140 (November 22, 1923), 790.   [C; bibliography of
          the Shelley Society's publications]

[2312]   Benham, Allen R.   "Shelley and Browning," *MLN*, XXXVIII,
          No. 8 (December, 1923), 503.   [C]

[2313]   Hespelt, E. Herman.   "XL.   Shelley and Spain,"   *PMLA*,
          XXXVIII, No. 4 (December, 1923), 887-905.   [C]

[2314]   Cœuroy, Andre.   "The Musical Inspiration of Shelley,"
          [trans. Theodore Baker], *Musical Quarterly*, IX, No. 1
          (January, 1923), 82-95.   [C]

Books:

[2315]   Alden, Raymond Macdonald.   "The Romantic Defense of
          Poetry," 19-33 in *Schelling Anniversary Papers* [/] By His
          Former Students.   x+341pp.   New York: The Century Co.,
          1923.   [C: 25-33]

[2316]   Bailey, John [Cann].   *The Continuity of Letters*.   viii+273pp.
          Oxford: At the Clarendon Press, 1923.   [C: "Prometheus
          in Poetry," (101)-138]

[2317]   Granniss, Ruth S[hepard].   *A Descriptive Catalogue of the First
          Editions in Book Form of the Writings of Percy Bysshe Shelley* [/]
          *Based on a Memorial Exhibition Held at the Grolier Club from
          April 20 to May 20, 1922*.   xx+133pp.   New York: Grolier
          Club [Gillis Press], 1923.   [T]

[2318]   Kellett, Ernest Edward.   *Suggestions* [/] *Literary Essays*.
          212pp.   Cambridge, Eng.: At the University Press, 1923.
          [C: "Imaginative: 'The Witch of Atlas,'" (109)-136;
          "The Plastic Stress," (137)-154]

[2319]   Ker, William Paton.   *The Art of Poetry* [/] *Seven Lectures* [/]
          1920-1922.   Oxford: At the Clarendon Press, 1923.   [C:
          "Shelley," (29)-52]

[2320]   Massey, B[ernard] W[ilfrid] A[rbuthnot].   *The Compound
          Epithets of Shelley and Keats* [/] *Considered from the Structural,
          the Historical, and the Literary Standpoints, with Some Compari-
          sons from the Greek, the Old English and the German*.   [Poznan-
          skie Towarzystwo Przyjaciol Nauk.   Prace Komisji Filo-
          logicznej.   Volume II.   No. 4].   xv+256pp.   Poznan,
          Poland: Nakladem Poznanskiego Towarz, Przyjaciol Nauk,
          1923.   [C]

[2321]   Pottle, Frederick A.   *Shelley and Browning* [/] *A Myth and Some
          Facts*.   [With a Foreword by William Lyon Phelps].
          94pp.   Chicago: The Pembroke Press, 1923.   [C]

[2322]   Reul, Paul de.   "The Centenary of Shelley.," 69-88 in
          *Essays by Divers Hands, Being the Transations of the Royal Society
          of Literature of the United Kingdom*.   New Series.   Vol. iii.
          Edited by F[rederick] S[amuel] Boas.   xi+119pp.
          London: Oxford University Press, 1923.   [C]

1924

Periodicals:

[2323]   Keith, Arthur L.   "The Imagery of Shelley," *The South Atlan-
          tic Quarterly*, XXIII, No. 1 (January, 1924), [61]-72.
          [C; first of two parts]

[2324]   Nash, J. V.   "Shelley—After One Hundred Years," *The Open
          Court*, XXXVIII, No. 1 [whole number 812] (January,
          1924), [1]-7.   [C]

[2325]   White, Newman I[vey].   "The Shelley Society Again," *MLN*,
          XXXIX, No. 1 (January, 1924), 18022.   [B]

[2326]   Woollen, Wilfrid H.   "Article on Shelley in 'The Prospec-
          tive Review.,'" *Notes and Queries*, CXLVI [Thirteenth
          Series II], No. 29 (January 19, 1924), 46.   [C]

[2327]   [Anonymous].   "Shelley and Romance," *The Times Literary
          Supplement* [London], No. 1,149 (January 24, 1924), 51.
          [R: item 2353]

[2328]   [Anonymous].   "Recent Books in Brief Review," *The Bookman*
          [New York], LVIII, No. 6 (February, 1924), 668-676.
          [R: item 2361]

[2329]   Peck, Walter Edwin.   "Shelley's Reviews Written for the
          Examiner," *MLN*, XXXIX, No. 2 (February, 1924), 118-119.
          [T]

[2330]   Walker, A. Stanley.   "A Sidelight on Shelley," *MLN*, XXXIX,
          No. 2 (February, 1924), 121.   [B]

[2331]   Wise, Thomas J[ames].   "Two Shelley Forgeries.," *The Times
          Literary Supplement* [London], No. 1,152 (February 14,
          1924), 96.   [T]

[2332]   Dickinson, G. Lowes.   "Shelley and Science," *The Nation and
          Athenaeum*, XXXIV, No. 20 (February 16, 1924), 703.   [R:
          item 2353]

[2333]   Adler, E. N.   "Two Shelley Forgeries.," *The Times Literary
          Supplement* [London], No. 1,153 (February 21, 1924),
          112.   [T]

[2334]   Peck, walter Edwin.   "Trelawny's 'Recollections,'" *The
          Times Literary Supplement* [London], No. 1,153 (February 21,
          1924), 112.   [B]

[2335]   Faussett, Hugh I'A.   "Shelley and Romanticism.," *The Bookman*
          [London], LXV, No. 390 (March, 1924), 309-310. [R:

item 2353]

[2336] Grierson, H[erbert] J. C. "Shelley and the Unromantics," *The Times Literary Supplement* [London], No. 1,158 (March 27, 1924), 192. [R: item 2353]

[2337] Keith, Arthur L. "The Imagery of Shelley [/] (Concluded," *The South Atlantic Quarterly*, XXXIII, No. 2 (April, 1924), [166]-176. [C; second of two parts]

[2338] Kirtlan, Ernest J. B. "The Political and Religious Creed of Shelley," *The London Quarterly Review*, Fifth Series XXVII [whole number CXLI], [No. 2] (April, 1924), 225-234. [C]

[2339] O'Neill, Moira. "Shelley," *Blackwood's Edinburgh Magazine*, CCXV, No. mcccii (April, 1924), 510-532. [R: items 2353, 2361]

[2340] Peck, Walter E[dwin]. "Keats, Shelley and Mrs. Radcliffe," *MLN*, XXXIX, No. 4 (April, 1924), 251-252. [C]

[2341] Woollen, Wilfrid H. "Shelley and the Unromantics.," *The Times Literary Supplement* [London], No. 1,159 (April 3, 1924), 208. [R: item 2353]

[2342] [Anonymous]. "Shelley in French.," *The Times Literary Supplement* [London], No. 1,161 (April 17, 1924), 236. [R of *Odes, Poèmes, Fragments Lyriques Choisis*, edited and trans. by A. Fontaines (Paris, 1923)]

[2343] Campbell, Olwen W[ard]. "Shelley and the Unromantics.," *The Times Literary Supplement* [London], No. 1,162 (April 24, 1924), 253. [B]

[2344] Peck, Walter Edwin. "On the Origin of the Shelley Society (Postscript)," *MLN*, XXXIX, No. 5 (May, 1924), 312-314. [B]

[2345] Gutteling, J[ohanna] F[rederika] C[ornelia]. "Demogorgon in Shelley's *Prometheus Unbound*," *Neophilologus*, IX, No. 4 ([July], 1924), 283-285. [C]

[2346] Hoffman, Harold. "An Angel in the City of Dreadful Night," *The Sewanee Review*, XXXII, No. 3 (July, 1924), [317]-335. [C]

[2347] J[espersen], O[tto]. "[Untitled subsection of "Minor Notices," 385-391]," *Modern Language Review*, XIX, No. 3 (July, 1924), 386-387. [R: item 2320]

[2348] Donelson, John. "Burying Poets," *The Bookman* [New York], LIX, No. 6 (August, 1924), 740-741. [R: items 2353, 2361]

[2349]   Porterfield, Allen W. "Foreign Notes and Comment," *The Bookman* [New York], LX, No. 3 (November, 1924), 361-365. [R of item 2360: 364]

[2350]   [Signed "'Mimnermus.'"]. "Slandering Shelley.," *The Freethinker* (November 9, 1924), 707-708. [C]

[2351]   Peck, Walter Edwin. "An Essay by Shelley.," *The Times Literary Supplement* [London], No. 1,193 (November 27, 1924), 797-798. [T]

[2352]   Peck, Walter Edwin. "XLII. Unpublished Passages from the Pforzheimer MS. of Shelley's *Philosophical View of Reform*," *PMLA*, XXXIX, No. 4 (December, 1924), 910-918. [T]

Books:

[2353]   Campbell, Olwen Ward. *Shelley and the Unromantics.* xi+307pp. London: Methuen & Co., Ltd., 1924. [B,C]

[2354]   Chew, Samuel C. *Byron in England* [/] *His Fame and After-Fame.* vii+415pp. New York: Charles Scribner's Sons, 1924. [B,C; fully indexed]

[2355]   Elton, Oliver. *Shelley.* viii+96pp. London: Edward Arnold, 1924. [C; revised and rptd. from item 2056]

[2356]   Gingerich, Solomon Francis. *Essays in the Romantic Poets.* 276pp. New York: The Macmillan Company, 1924. [C: "Shelley," (193)-239]

[2357]   Gordon, George. "Warton Lecture on English Poetry [/] XIV [/] Shelley and the Oppressors of Mankind," [257]-269 in *Proceedings of the British Academy* [/] *1921-1923.* [Volume X]. xx+579pp. London: Humphrey Milford, Oxford University Press, [1924]. [C,B]

*[2358]   Hulme, T. E. *Speculations.* [?]pp. London: [?], 1924. [M]

[2359]   Klein, John W. *Shelley* [/] *A Drama in Five Acts.* [Plays for a People's Theatre, XXIV]. 288pp. London: The C. W. Daniel Company, 1924. [Fictionalized dramatization]

[2360]   Liptzin, Solomon. *Shelley in Germany.* [Columbia University Germanic Studies]. vii+97pp. New York: Columbia University Press, 1924. [C]

[2361]   Maurois, André [pseud. of Emile Salomon Wilhelm Herzog]. *Ariel* [/] *The Life of Shelley.* Translated by Ella D'Arcy. 336pp. New York: D. Appleton and Company, 1924. [B;

also issued as *Ariel* [/] *A Shelley Romance*]

*[2362] Noyes, Alfred. *Some Aspects of Modern Poetry*. [?]pp. New
         York: Frederick A. Stokes Company, 1924. [C: "The
         Poet of Light," (?p)]

[2363] Wise, Thomas James. *A Shelley Library* [/] *A Catalogue of Printed
        Books, Manuscripts and Autograph Letters* [/] *By Percy Bysshe
        Shelley* [/] *Harriet Shelley* [/] *and Mary Wollstonecraft Shelley*
        [/] *Collected by Thomas James Wise* [/] *Honorary Fellow of
        Worcester College, Oxford*. xvii+164pp. London: privately
        printed, 1924. [T,C]

                          1925

Periodicals:

[2364] Beers, H[enry Augustin]. "Shelley," *The Yale Review*, New
        Series XIV, No. 2 (January, 1925), 373-377. [R: items
        2353, 2361]

[2365] Clarke, George Herbert. "Refocussing Shelley," *The Sewanee
        Review*, XXXIII, No. 1 (January, 1925), [88]-94. [R:
        revised edition of item 1974, and items 2353, 2360,
        2361]

[2366] White, Newman I[vey]. "The Beautiful Angel and His Biog-
        raphers," *The South Atlantic Quarterly*, XXIV, No. 1 (Janu-
        ary, 1925), 73-85. [B]

[2367] White, Newman I[vey]. "Literature and the Law of Libel:
        Shelley and the Radicals of 1840-1842," *Studies in
        Philology*, XXII, No. 1 (January, 1925), 34-47. [C]

[2368] Peck, Walter Edwin. "Shelley's Lost Satire on the Prince
        Regent," *The New York Times Book Review*, XXX, No. 2 (Janu-
        ary 11, 1925), 2. [T]

[2369] Turnbull, John M. "An Essay by Shelley.," *The Times Literary
        Supplement* [London], No. 1,203 (February 5, 1925), 88.
        [T]

[2370] [Anonymous]. "The Psychology of Shelley," *The Times Literary
        Supplement* [London], No. 1,204 (February 12, 1925), 100.
        [R: item 2396]

[2371] Irving, R. C. "An Essay by Shelley.," *The Times Literary
        Supplement* [London], No. 1,204 (February 12, 1925), 104.
        [T]

[2372]　Babington, Percy L.　"The *Errata* Leaf in Shelley's
　　　　Posthumous Poems," *The Library*, Fourth Series V, No. 4
　　　　(March, 1925), 365.　[T]

[2373]　Graham, Walter.　"VIII. Shelley's Debt to Leigh Hunt and
　　　　the *Examiner*," *PMLA*, XL, No. 1 (March, 1925), 185-192.
　　　　[C]

[2374]　Peck, Walter Edwin.　"VI.　Shelley, Mary Shelley, and
　　　　Rinaldo Rinaldini," *PMLA*, XL, No. 1 (March, 1925), 165-
　　　　171.　[C]

[2375]　Walker, A. Stanley.　"V. Peterloo, Shelley and Reform,"
　　　　PMLA, XL, No. 1 (March, 1925), 128-164.　[C]

[2376]　White, Newman I[vey].　"VII. Shelley's *Prometheus Unbound* or
　　　　Every Man His Own　Allegorist," *PMLA*, XL, No. 1 (March,
　　　　1925), 172-184.　[C]

[2377]　Peck, Walter Edwin.　"Shelley's Indebtedness to Sir
　　　　Thomas Lawrence," *MLN*, XL, No. 4 (April, 1925), 246-
　　　　249.　[C]

[2378]　S[tokoe], F[rank] W.　"[Untitled subsection of "Minor
　　　　Notices," 231-239]," *Modern Language Review*, XX, No. 2
　　　　(April, 1925), 236-237.　[R: item 2360]

[2379]　[Anonymous].　"Memorabilia," *Notes and Queries*, CXLVIII
　　　　[Thirteenth Series IV], No. 14 (April 4, 1925), 235-
　　　　236.　[M: 235]

[2380]　[Anonymous].　"Documents and Records [/] A [/] The
　　　　'Reserved' Shelley Papers in the Bodleian Library," *The
　　　　Bodleian Quarterly Record*, IV, No. 45 (May 15, 1925),
　　　　[218]-222.　[T]

[2381]　Woollen, Wilfrid H.　"'Blackwood' and 'Adonais.,'" *The
　　　　Times Literary Supplement* [London], No. 1,217 (May 14,
　　　　1925), 335.　[C]

[2382]　Chew, Samuel C.　"XXVI.　A Note on Peterloo," *PMLA*, XL,
　　　　No. 2 (June, 1925), 490.　[C]

[2383]　[Anonymous].　"Documents and Records [/] A [/] The
　　　　'Reserved Shelley Papers in the Bodleian Library," *The
　　　　Bodleian Quarterly Record*, IV, No. 46 (July 31, 1925),
　　　　[246]-250.　[T]

[2384]　Hirst, G. M.　"The Text of Shelley.," *The Times Literary
　　　　Supplement* [London], No. 1,231 (August 20, 1925), 545.
　　　　[T]

[2385]　Fowler, H[enry] W.　"The Text of Shelley.," *The Times Liter-
　　　　ary Supplement* [London], No. 1,233 (September 3, 1925),
　　　　569.　[T]

[2386]   [Anonymous].   "Memories of Shelley.," *The Times Literary Supplement* [London], No. 1,235 (September 17, 1925), 597.   [R: item 2395]

[2387]   Woollen, Wilfrid Henry.   "Memories of Shelley.," *The Times Literary Supplement* [London], No. 1,236 (September 24, 1925), 619.   [B]

[2388]   Beston, Henry.   "The Pirate and the Poets [/] Glimpses of Edward John Trelawny," *The Bookman* [New York], LXII, No. 2 (October, 1925), 132-136.   [B]

[2389]   Graham, Walter.   "Some Infamous Tory Reviews," *Studies in Philology*, XXII, No. 4 (October, 1925), 500-517.   [C; Shelley: 503-506]

[2390]   Damon, S. Foster.   "Three Generations of One Line," *MLN*, XL, No. 7 (November, 1925), 441.   [C]

[2391]   [Anonymous].   "In Brief Review," *The Bookman* [London], LXII, No. 4 (December, 1925), 504-511.   [R of item 2396: 510-511]

[2392]   Graham, Walter.   "Shelley and the *Empire of the Nairs*," *PMLA*, XL, No. 4 (December, 1925), 881-891.   [C]

[2393]   Von Wiegand, Charmion.   "Emilia Viviani [/] A Romantic Drama in One Act," *Poet-Lore*, XXXVI, [No. 4] (Winter [December], 1925), 552-568.   [Fictionalized dramatization]

*[2394]   Peck, Walter Edwin.   "Unpublished Shelley Poems Are Discovered at Harvard," *The Boston Herald*, [?] (December 21, 1925), 12.   [T]

Books:

[2395]   Blunden, Edmund [Charles], ed.   *Shelley and Keats* [/] *As They Struck Their Contemporaries* [/] *Notes partly from Manuscript Sources.*   [x]+94pp.   London: C. W. Beaumont, 1925.   [B: 1-65; rptd. from, among others, item 739]

[2396]   Carpenter, Edward, and George Barnfield [pseud. of Edward Carpenter].   *The Psychology of the Poet Shelley.*   126pp.   London: George Allen & Unwin Ltd., 1925.   [B,C]

[2397]   Drinkwater, John.   *The Muse in Council* [/] *Being Essays on Poets and Poetry.*   x+303pp.   Boston: Houghton Mifflin Company, 1925.   [C: "Percy Bysshe Shelley," (143)-155]

[2398]   Newton, A[lfred] Edward.   *The Greatest Book in the World* [/] *and Other Papers.*   407pp.   Boston: Little, Brown, and Company, 1925.   [B: "XII. Skinner Street News," (343)-407]

[2399] Quiller-Couch, Arthur. *Adventures in Criticism*. Revised
        edition. viii+234pp. New York: G. P. Putnam's
        Sons, 1925. [C: "The Popular Conception of a Poet,"
        133-139; "Poets on Their Own Art," 140-145]

[2400] Rolleston, Maud. *Talks with Lady Shelley*. 137pp. London:
        G. G. Harrap & Co., 1925. [B]

*[2401] Trant, Clarissa. *The Journal of Clarissa Trant 1800-1832*.
        Edited by C. G. Luard. With Illustrations in Colour,
        etc. London: John Lane, [1925]. [B]

[2402] Whitehead, Alfred North. *Science and the Modern World* [/]
        Lowell Lectures, 1925. xii+304pp. New York: The
        Macmillan Company, 1925. [C: 120-134]

                        1926

Periodicals:

[2403] Spiller, Robert E. "The English Literary Horizon: 1815-
        1835 [/] (As Seen by the American Traveler)," *Studies in
        Philology*, XXIII, No. 1 (January, 1926), 1-15. [M: 8]

[2404] Burriss, Eli Edward. "The Classical Culture of Percy
        Bysshe Shelley," *The Classical Journal*, XXI, No. 5 (Febru-
        ary, 1926), 344-354. [C]

[2405] [Anonymous]. "[Untitled subsection of "Memorabilia"],"
        Notes and Queries, CL, No. 12 (March 20, 1926), 199-200.
        [C]

[2406] Peck, Walter Edwin. "An Unpublished Ballad by Percy
        Bysshe Shelley," *Philological Quarterly*, V, No. 2 (April,
        1926), 114-118. [T]

[2407] Atkins, Elizabeth. "XXII. Points of Contact Between
        Byron and Socrates," *PMLA*, XLI, No. 2 (June, 1926),
        402-423. [M: 404]

*[2408] Ingpen, Roger. "The Shelley Correspondence in the Bod-
        leian Library," *The Library Association Review*, New Series
        IV (June, 1926), 96-98. [R: item 2418]

[2409] Gray, W. Forbes. "An Unpublished Literary Correspond-
        ence," *The Cornhill Magazine*, LXI, New Series No. 361
        [whole number 789] (July, 1926), 77-93. [T]

[2410] [Anonymous]. "[Untitled subsection of "Memorabilia," 37-
        38]," *Notes and Queries*, CLI, No. 3 (July 17, 1926), 37.
        [B]

[2411]   [Anonymous].   "[Untitled subsection of "Memorabilia,"
          73-74]," *Notes and Queries*, CLI, No. 5 (July 31, 1926),
          73-74.   [T]

[2412]   Woollen, Wilfrid H.   "The 'Julian' Shelley," *The Times
          Literary Supplement* [London], No. 1,281 (August 19, 1926),
          549.   [B]

[2413]   Knickerbocker, William S.   "Shelley's Oxford," *The Sewanee
          Review*, XXXIV, No. 4 (October-December, 1926), [466]-
          475.   [B]

[2414]   Woollen, Wilfrid H.   "Shelley and Catholic Emancipation,"
          The Downside Review [Exeter], New Series XXV [whole
          number XLIV] ([no month given], 1926), [271]-284.
          [B,C]

Books:

[2415]   Brinton, [Clarence] Crane.   *The Political Ideas of the English
          Romanticists.*   242pp.   London: Oxford University Press,
          1926.   [C: 163-195]

[2416]   Dowden, Edward.   *The Life of Percy Bysshe Shelley.*   viii+602pp.
          London: Kegan Paul, Trench, Trübner & Co., Ltd., 1926.
          [B; rptd. from item 1692]

[2417]   Hardy, Thomas.   *Collected Poems of Thomas Hardy.*   xxviii+818pp.
          New York: The Macmillan Company, 1926.   [Two Poems:
          "Shelley's Skylark (1887)," 92; "Rome (/) At the
          Pyramid of Cestius near the Graves of Shelley and
          Keats (1887)," 95]

[2418]   Hill, R[eginald] H[arrison], ed.   *The Shelley Correspondence
          in the Bodleian Library [/] Letters of Percy Bysshe Shelley and
          others, mainly published, from the Collection presented to the
          Library by Lady Shelley in 1892.   Edited by R. H. Hill [...] with
          a chronological table of the collection and a list of other Shel-
          ley manuscripts & relics in the library.*   xv+48pp.   Oxford:
          Printed for the Bodleian Library [/] By John Johnson,
          Printer to the University, 1926.   [T]

[2419]   Ingpen, Roger, and Walter Edwin Peck, eds.   *The Complete Works
          of Percy Bysshe Shelley [/] Newly Edited by Roger Ingpen and
          Walter E. Peck [/] In Ten Volumes.*   ["The Julian Edition"].
          London: Ernest Benn Ltd., 1926-1928.   [T, B]

[2420]   Marshall, Elizabeth Glass.   *Poetical Theories and Criticisms of
          the Chief Romantic Poets [/] as expressed in their Personal
          Letters; with some account of the Poets' Opinions of the Periodi-
          cal Reviews of their Works.*   [A Dissertation presented to
          the Academic Faculty of the University of Virginia in

candidacy for the degree of Doctor of Philosophy (/)
April 15, 1925]. 170pp. Ann Arbor, Michigan: Edwards
Brothers, [1926]. [C]

[2421] Monroe, Harriet. *Poets and Their Art.* xiii+301pp. New
York: The Macmillan Company, 1926. [C:"Shelley," 155-162]

[2422] Newbolt, Henry. *Studies in Green and Gray.* viii+295pp.
London: Thomas Nelson and Sons, Ltd., 1926. [C: "Notes
on Certain Poets (/) II. Shelley," 248-257]

*[2423] Peck, Walter Edwin, ed. *Letters of Elizabeth Hitchener to
Percy Bysshe Shelley.* [?p]. New York: privately printed,
1926. [T]

[2424] Powell, A. E. [Mrs. E. R. Dodds]. *The Romantic Theory of
Poetry. An Examination in the Light of Croce's Æsthetic.* viii+
263pp. London: Edward Arnold & Company, 1926. [C:
"Shelley," 183-221]

[2425] Stokoe, F[rank] W. *German Influence in the English Romantic
Period [/] 1788-1818 [/] with Special Reference to Scott, Cole-
ridge, Shelley and Byron.* x+202pp. Cambridge, Eng.:
At the University Press, 1926. [C: "Percy Bysshe
Shelley (1792-1822)," (144)-158]

1927

Periodicals:

[2426] de S[elincourt], E[rnest]. *"The Shelley Correspondence in the
Bodleian Library.* Edited by R. H. Hill. Oxford: Printed
for the Bodleian Library. Pp. xv. + 48. 5s.," *The
Review of English Studies*, III, No. 9 (January, 1927), 110-
111. [R: item 2418]

[2427] S[mith], G. C. M[oore]. "[Untitled subsection of "Short
Notices," (116)-120]," *Modern Language Review*, XXII, No. 1
(January, 1927), 117-118. [R: item 2418]

[2428] [Anonymous]. "[Untitled subsection of "Memorabilia," 145-
146]," *Notes and Queries*, CLII, No. 9 (February 26, 1927),
146. [T]

[2429] Bald, Marjory A. "The Psychology of Shelley," *The Contemporary Review*, CXXXI (March, 1927), 359-366. [B,C]

[2430] Wylie, Elinor. "Mr. Shelley Speaking," *The Bookman* [New
York], LXV, No. 1 (March, 1927), 29-33. [C]

[2431]   Grabo, Carl H.   "Electricity, the Spirit of the Earth,
         in Shelley's *Prometheus Unbound*," *Philological Quarterly*,
         VI, No. 2 (April, 1927), 133-150.   [C]

[2432]   Herring, Robert.   "Percy's Little Circle," *The London
         Mercury*, XVI, No. 92 (June, 1927), 179-192.   [B]

[2433]   [Anonymous].   "Satire.," *The Times Literary Supplement* [London],
         No. 1.325 (June 23, 1927), [429]-430.   [M: 430]

[2434]   [Anonymous].   "The Correspondence of Shelley," *The Times
         Literary Supplement* [London], No. 1,327 (July 7, 1927),
         [461]-462.   [R: item 2419]

[2435]   Douglas, Alfred.   "'Satire.,'" *The Times Literary Supplement*
         [London], No. 1.327 (July 7, 1927), 472.   [C]

[2436]   Ingpen, Roger.   "The Correspondence of Shelley.," *The Times
         Literary Supplement* [London], No. 1,328 (July 14, 1927),
         488.   [T]

[2437]   Douglas, Alfred.   "Satire.," *The Times Literary Supplement*
         [London], No. 1,330 (July 28, 1927), 520.   [C]

[2438]   Peck, Walter Edwin.   "A Shelley Poem?" *The Times Literary
         Supplement* [London], No. 1,338 (September 22, 1927),
         647.   [T]

[2439]   King, R. W.   "A Shelley Poem?" *The Times Literary Supplement*
         [London], No. 1,339 (September 29, 1927), 667.   [T]

[2440]   Woollen, Wilfrid H.   "An Essay by Shelley.," *The Times
         Literary Supplement* [London], No. 1,229 (September 29,
         1927), 667.   [T]

*[2441] Dunn, Waldo H.   "Shelley Once More," *The London Quarterly
         Review*, CXLVII, No. [?] (October, 1927), 145-[?].   [R:
         item 2452]

[2442]   Grabo, Carl H.   "Astronomical Allusions in Shelley's *Prome-
         theus Unbound*," *Philological Quarterly*, VI, No. 4 (October,
         1927), 362-378.   [C]

*[2443] Gosse, Edmund.   "Shelley.," *The* [London] *Sunday Times*, [?],
         (November 27, 1927), [?p].   [R: item 2419, vol. vi]

[2444]   [Anonymous].   "The Biography of Shelley.," *The Times Literary
         Supplement* [London], No. 1.348 (December 1, 1927), [893]-
         894.   [R: item 2452]

*[2445] Sadler, Michael.   "Shelley, Copleston and Oxford.," *The*
         [London] *Sunday Times*, [?], (December 4, 1927), [?p].
         [B]

[2446]   [Signed "The Reviewer"]. "A Shelley Letter.," *The Times*
         Literary Supplement [London], No. 1,351 (December 22,
         1927), 977. [T]

*[2447]   [?Anonymous]. "A Shelley Discovery," *Book-Notes*, V, ([?],
         1927), 111. [B]

Books:

[2448]   Clutton-Brock, A[rthur]. *Essays on Literature & Life*. vii+
         [216]pp. New York: E. P. Dutton and Company, [1927].
         [C: "Percy Bysshe Shelley," 92-102; rptd. from item
         2446]

[2449]   de Ricci, Seymour. *A Bibliography of Shelley's Letters, Pub-
         lished and Unpublished*. 296pp. Bois-Colombes [Paris]:
         privately printed, 1927. [T]

[2450]   Hunt, Leigh. *Leigh Hunt's Letter on Hogg's Life of Shelley* [/]
         With Other Papers. [Edited by Luther A. Brewer]. 32pp.
         Cedar Rapids, Iowa: privately printed, 1927. [T,B]

[2451]   Murray, Gilbert. *The Classical Tradition in Poetry*. [The
         Charles Eliot Norton Lectures]. xi+274pp. Cambridge,
         Mass.: Harvard University Press, 1927. [C: 68, 98,
         151, 183, 247, 248, 260; M: 7, 45, 50, 117, 118, 132,
         134-138, 143, 145, 198, 247, 249, 254, 256, 259]

[2452]   Peck, Walter Edwin. *Shelley* [/] *His Life and Work*. 2 vols.
         Boston: Houghton Mifflin Company, 1927. [B,C,T]

[2453]   Prescott, Frederick Clarke. *Poetry & Myth*. 190pp. New
         York: The Macmillan Company, 1927. [C: 3, 43, 47, 52,
         78-88, 122-125]

*[2454]   Rhys, Ernest. *Prelude to Poetry*. [?]pp. London: [?],
         1927. [C]

[2455]   Solve, Melvin T. *Shelley* [/] *His Theory of Poetry*. xv+207pp.
         Chicago: University of Chicago Press, 1927. [C]

                              1928

Periodicals:

[2456]   Farrington, B. "Shelley's Translation from the Greek
         [/] With Observations on his Classical Scholarship,"
         The Dublin Magazine, New Series III, No. 1 (January-
         March, 1928), 3-18. [C]

[2457]   Purdie, Edna.   *"German Influence in the English Romantic Period,*
          1788-1818. With Special Reference to Scott, Coleridge, Shelley,
          and Byron. By F. W. Stokoe. Cambridge: University
          Press, 1926. x + 202pp. 12s6d.," *Modern Language Review,*
          XXIII, No. 1 (January, 1928), 80-82. [R: item 2425]

[2458]   Freeman, John. "Shelley Plain.," *The Bookman* [London],
          LXXIII, No. 437 (February, 1928), 257-259. [R: item
          2452]

[2459]   Maurois, André [pseud. of Emile Salomon Wilhelm Herzog],
          "Biographies in Counterpoint," *The Bookman* [New York],
          LXVII, No. 1 (March, 1928), 88-89. [R: items 2452,
          2455]

[2460]   Peck, Walter Edwin.   *"The Shelley Correspondence in the Bodleian*
          Library. Edited by R. H. Hill. Printed for the Bod-
          leian Library, Oxford, 1926. Pp. xv + 48.," *MLN,* XLIII,
          No. 3 (March, 1928), 208-209. [R: item 2418]

[2461]   [Anonymous]. "Shelley's Theory of Poetry," *The Times*
          Literary Supplement [London], No. 1,364 (March 22, 1928),
          206. [R: item 2455]

[2462]   Brown, C. A. "Notes for *Prometheus Unbound,*" *Philological Quar-*
          terly, VII, No. 2 (April, 1928), 195-198. [C]

[2463]   Campbell, Oscar James. *"German Influence in the English Romantic*
          Period 1788-1818, with special reference to Scott, Coleridge,
          Shelley and Byron. By F. W. Stokoe. Pp. x + 174 + 5
          appendices and bibliographies. Cambridge University
          Press, 1926.," *MLN,* XLIII, No. 4 (April, 1928), 262-
          263. [R: item 2425]

[2464]   Clarke, George Herbert. "The Search for Shelley," *The*
          Virginia Quarterly Review, IV, No. 2 (April, 1928), 285-
          292. [R: item 2452]

[2465]   King, R. W. "Crabb Robinson's Opinion of Shelley," *The*
          Review of English Studies, IV, No. 14 (April, 1928), 167-
          172. [C]

[2466]   Weatherhead, Leslie D. "Shelley's Hell Complex," *The London*
          Quarterly Review, Fifth Series XXXV [whole number CXLIX]
          (April, 1928), 201-210. [B,C]

[2467]   [Anonymous]. "Bibliography of Shelley Letters.," *The Times*
          Literary Supplement [London], No. 1,372 (May 17, 1928),
          384. [R: item 2449]

[2468]   Koszul, A[ndre Henri]. " *Shelley, His life and Work.* By Walter
          Edwin Peck. Houghton Mifflin Co., Boston, 1927.
          2 vols. xiii, 532, vii, 490 pp.," *MLN,* XLIII, No. 6

(June, 1928), 394-399. [R: item 2452]

[2469] [Anonymous]. "Leigh Hunt's 'Examiner.,'" *The Times Literary Supplement* [London], No. 1,382 (July 26, 1928), 549. [R: items 2479, 2483]

[2470] Eiloart, Arnold. "Shelley's 'The Question.,'" *Notes and Queries*, CLV, No. 10 (September 8, 1928), 165-169. [C]

[2471] Steuart, A. Francis. "Mount Coffee House.," *Notes and Queries*, CLV, No. 10 (September 8, 1928), 171. [B]

[2472] Smith, G. C. Moore. "The Mount Coffee House (clv. 171)," *Notes and Queries*, CLV, No. 12 (September 22, 1928), 208-209. [B]

[2473] Forman, W. Courthope. "[Untitled, following item 2472]," *Notes and Queries*, CLV, No. 12 (September 22, 1928), 209. [B]

[2474] Forman, W. Courthope. "The Mount Coffee House (clv. 171, 208).," *Notes and Queries*, No. 14 (October 6, 1928), 247. [B]

[2475] McPharlin, Paul. "Shelley's 'The Question': Black Flowers (clv. 165)," *Notes and Queries*, CLV, No. 16 (October 20, 1928), 284. [C]

[2476] Moore, T. Sturge. "Mr. T. S. Eliot and Shelley's Skylark.," *The Times Literary Supplement* [London], No. 1,402 (December 13, 1928), 991. [C]

[2477] [Signed "A.E.H."]. "Shelley's Skylark.," *The Times Literary Supplement* [London], No. 1,403 (December 20, 1928), 1011. [C]

Books:

[2478] Bald, Marjory A. "Shelley's Mental Progress," *Essays and Studies by Members of the English Association*, XIII, ([Oxford: At the Clarendon Press], 1928), [112]-137. [B, C]

[2479] Blunden, Edmund. *Leigh Hunt's "Examiner" Examined [/] Comprising Some Account of that Celebrated Newspaper's Contents, &c. 1808-25 [/] And [/] Selections, by or concerning Leigh Hunt, Lamb, Keats, Shelley, and Byron, Illustrating the Literary History of that Time, for the most part previously unreprinted.* xi+263pp. London: Cobden-Sanderson, 1928. [C,B]

[2480] Church, Richard. *Mary Shelley.* [92]pp. London: Gerald Howe Ltd., 1928. [B]

[2481]   Fairchild, Hoxie Neale.   *The Noble Savage¯[/] A Study in
         Romantic Naturalism.* xi+535pp. New York: Columbia Univer-
         sity Press, 1928. [C: 137, 223, 236-237, 238, 239,
         304, 305-312, 345, 346, 348-355, 361, 366, 371, 379,
         389-390, 394, 395, 416, 506]

[2482]   Huxley, Aldous. *Point Counterpoint.* 432pp. New York:
         Doubleday, Doran & Co., 1928 [C: the character of Rampion
         is a satire of Shelley]

[2483]   Johnson, R[eginald] Brimley.   *Shelley-Leigh Hunt [/] How
         Friendship Made History and Extended the Bounds of Human Freedom
         and Thought [/] Being Reviews from* The Examiner, *etc. [/]
         with intimate Letters between the Shelleys and Leigh Hunt, partly
         from unpublished manuscripts.* xviii+346pp. London: Ingpen
         and Grant, 1928. [B,C,T; revised edition: item 2507]

[2484]   Smith, Robert Metcalf, ed.   *Types of Philosophical Drama.*
         vi+524pp. New York: Prentice-Hall, Inc., 1928. [C,
         T: "Prometheus Unbound," (341)-439]

[2485]   Young, George.   *An English Prosody on Inductive Lines.* xiv+
         296pp. Cambridge, Eng.: At the University Press, 1928.
         [C: 249-253, 265-267]

                                1929

Periodicals:

[2486]   Dawson, R. V. "Beethoven and Shelley," *Music and Letters,*
         X, No. 1 (January, 1929), [35]-45. [C]

[2487]   Koszul, A[ndre Henri]. "Another Plagiarism in Shelley's
         'Original Poetry by Victor and Cazire,'" *MLN,* XLIV,
         No. 1 (January, 1929), 42-43. [T]

[2488]   Moore, T. Sturge. "Shelley's Skylark.," *The Times Literary
         Supplement* [London], No. 1,405 (January 3, 1929), 12. [C]

[2489]   Luce, Morton. "Shelley's Skylark.," *The Times Literary Sup-
         plement* [London], No. 1,407 (January 17, 1929), 44. [C]

[2490]   Banerjee, Jaygopal. "The Philosophy of Shelley," *The
         Calcutta Review,* Third Series XXX, No. 2 (February,
         1929), 220-248. [C]

[2491]   [Anonymous]. "*A Bibliography of Shelley's Letters,* published
         and unpublished. Compiled by Seymour de Ricci. Pri-
         vately printed, 1927.," *The Library,* Fourth Series IX,
         No. 4 (March, 1929), 425-426. [R: item 2449]

[2492] Banerjee, Jaygopal. "The Philosophy of Shelley," *The Calcutta Review*, Third Series XXX, No. 3 (March, 1929), 367-381. [C]

[2493] Banerjee, Jaygopal. "The Philosophy of Shelley," *The Calcutta Review*, Third Series XXXI, No. 2 (May, 1929), 215-231. [C]

[2494] [Anonymous]. "Poetry Revisited," *The Times Literary Supplement* [London], No. 1,422 (May 2, 1929), 353. [R: item 2504]

[2495] Banerjee, Jaygopal. "The Philosophy of Shelley," *The Calcutta Review*, Third Series XXXII, No. 2 (August, 1929), 265-276. [C]

[2496] Marsh, George L. "The Early Reviews of Shelley," *Modern Philology*, XXVII, No. 1 (August, 1929), 73-95. [C]

[2497] Banerjee, Jaygopal. "The Philosophy of Shelley," *The Calcutta Review*, Third Series XXXII, No. 3 (September, 1929), 408-421. [C]

[2498] Banerjee, Jaygopal. "The Philosophy of Shelley," *The Calcutta Review*, Third Series XXXIII, No. 1 (October, 1929), 96-105. [C]

[2499] Dodds, A. E. [Powell]. "*Papers on Shelley, Wordsworth, and Others.* By J. A. Chapman. Oxford University Press. 1929. Pp. v + 171. Price 6s. net.," *The Review of English Studies*, V, No. 20 (October, 1929), 491-492. [R: item 2504]

[2500] Banerjee, Jaygopal. "The Philosophy of Shelley," *The Calcutta Review*, Third Series XXXIII, No. 2 & 3 (November-December, 1929), 324-337. [C]

[2501] Leslie, Shane. "The Lost Bust of Shelley [/] Lost, Stolen or Strayed?" *Landmark* [/] *The Monthly Magazine of the English Speaking Union*, XI, No. 11 (November, 1929), [671]-674. [B]

Books:

[2502] Bates, Ernest Sutherland. "Mad Shelley: a Study in the Origins of English Romanticism," 117-140 in *The Fred Newton Scott Anniversary Papers*. Contributed by former students and colleagues of Professor Scott and presented to him in celebration of his thirty-eighth year of distinguished service in the University of Michigan, 1888-1926. [With a portrait and a bibliography]. ix+319pp. Chicago: University of Chicago Press, 1929. [C]

[2503] Bradley, A[ndrew] C[ecil]. *A Miscellany.* 267pp. London:
        Macmillan and Co., 1929. [C: "Shelley and Arnold's
        Critique," 139-162; "Odours and Flowers in the Poetry
        of Shelley," 163-170; "Coleridge-Echoes in Shelley's
        Poems," 171-176]

[2504] Chapman, J. A. *Papers on Shelley* [/] *Wordsworth* [/] *& Others.*
        171pp. London: Oxford University Press [/] Humphrey
        Milford, 1929. [C: "Shelley and Francis Thompson,"
        (1)-18; "Publishing Lyrical Poetry," (155)-163; "In
        Conclusion," 164-171]

[2505] Elliott, G[eorge] R[ay]. *The Cycle of Modern Poetry* [/] *A
        Series of Essays Toward Clearing Our Present Poetic Dilemma.*
        xv+194pp. Princeton, N.J.: Princeton University Press,
        1929. [C: "The Solitude of Shelley," (1)-24]

[2506] Huxley, Aldous. *Do What You Will* [/] *Essays.* 310pp. London:
        Chatto & Windus, 1929. [C: "Fashions in Love," 130-
        142; Shelley: 138]

[2507] Johnson, R[eginald] Brimley. *Shelley-Leigh Hunt* [/] *How
        Friendship Made History* [/] *Extending the bounds of Human Freedom
        and Thought* [/] *A Record of revolt against relgious and political
        tyranny in* The Examiner, The Indicator, *and Shelley's Prose
        Pamphlets, with intimate Letters between the Shelleys and Leigh
        Hunt, partly from unpublished manuscripts.* [Second edition,
        revised, with additions]. xviii+352pp. London: Ingpen
        and Grant, 1929. [B,C,T; revised and rptd. from item
        2483]

[2508] Royce, Josiah. *Fugitive Essays.* [?]pp. Cambridge, Mass.:
        Harvard University Press, 1929. [?M]

[2509] Solve, Melvin T. "Shelley and the Novels of Brown," 141-
        156 in *The Fred Newton Scott Anniversary Papers.* Contributed
        by former students and colleagues of Professor Scott
        and presented to him in celebration of his thirty-
        eighth year of distinguished service in the University
        of Michigan, 1888-1926. [With a portrait and a bibli-
        ography]. xi+319pp. Chicago: University of Chicago
        Press, 1929. [C]

[2510] Van Dyke, Henry. *The Man Behind the Book: Essays in Understand-
        ing.* xi+357pp. New York: Charles Scribner's Sons,
        1929. [B: "A Knight Errant of Dreams," (201)-226]

[2511] Woodberry, George Edward. *The Shelley Notebook in the Harvard
        College Library* [/] *Reproduced with Notes and a Postscript.* 22+
        [107]pp. Cambridge, Mass.: John Barnard Associates,
        1929. [T; revised and rptd. from item 1459]

1930

Periodicals:

[2512] Hotson, Leslie. "Shelley's Lost Letters to Harriet," *The Atlantic Monthly*, CXLV (January, 1930), 122-133. [T; rptd.: item 2542]

[2513] [Anonymous]. "Shelley's Critics," *The Times Literary Supplement* [London], No. 1.457 (January 2, 1930), 9. [R of privately circulated reprint of item 2496]

[2514] Banerjee, Jaygopal. "The Philosophy of Shelley," *The Calcutta Review*, Third Series XXXIV, No. 2 (February, 1930), 255-279. [C]

[2515] Hotson, Leslie. "Shelley's Lost Letters to Harriet. II. *The Atlantic Monthly*, CXLV (February, 1930), 166-177. [T; rptd.: item 2542]

[2516] Banerjee, Jaygopal. "The Philosophy of Shelley [/] Part II," *The Calcutta Review*, Third Series XXXIV, No. 3 (March, 1930), 430-445. [C]

[2517] Hotson, Leslie. "A Footnote to Shelley," *The Atlantic Monthly*, CXLV (March, 1930), 350-358. [B; rptd.: item 2542]

[2518] Stovall, Floyd. "Shelley's Doctrine of Love," *PMLA*, XLV, No. 1 (March, 1930), 283-303. [C,B]

[2519] [Anonymous]. "The Lover, and the Poet," *The Times Literary Supplement* [London], No. 1,468 (March 20, 1930), 239. [R: items 2511, 2542]

[2520] Banerjee, Jaygopal. "The Philosophy of Shelley," *The Calcutta Review*, Third Series XXXV, No. 1 (April, 1930), 133-149. [C]

[2521] Havens, Raymond D[exter]. "Shelley's 'Birthday,'" *MLN*, XLV, No. 4 (April, 1930), 225. [B]

[2522] Roberts, R. Ellis. "Shelley and Harriet.," *The Bookman* [London], LXXVIII, No. 463 (April, 1930), 21-22. [R: item 2542]

[2523] Banerjee, Jaygopal. "The Philosophy of Shelley," *The Calcutta Review*, Third Series XXXV, No. 2 (May, 1930), 253-263. [C]

[2524] [Anonymous]. "[Untitled subsection of "Literary"]," *The Times Literary Supplement* [London], No. 1,474 (May 1, 1930), 373-374. [R: item 2538]

[2525]   [Anonymous]. "The Figure of Shelley," *The Times Literary Supplement* [London], No. 1,476 (May 15, 1930), 411. [R: item 2545]

[2526]   Stout, G. D. "*Papers on Shelley, Wordsworth, and Others.* By J. A. Chapman. New York, Oxford University Press, 1929. Pp. 171. $2.25. *The Profession of Poetry, and Other Lectures.* By H. W. Garrod. New York, Oxford University Press, 1929. Pp. x + 270. $4.50.," *MLN*, XLV, No. 6 (June, 1930), 415-417. [R: item 2504]

[2527]   White, Newman I[vey]. "Shelley and the Active Radicals of the Early Nineteenth Century," *The South Atlantic Quarterly*, XXXIX, No. 3 (July, 1930), [248]-261. [C,B]

[2528]   [Anonymous]. "Trelawny Interpreted," *The Times Literary Supplement* [London], No. 1,484 (July 10, 1930), 571. [R: item 2544]

[2529]   Sketchley, R. E. D. "The Friend of Shelley," *The Times Literary Supplement* [London], No. 1,486 (July 24, 1930), 611. [B]

[2530]   Massingham, H[arold] J[ohn]. "The Friend of Shelley," *The Times Literary Supplement* [London], No. 1,487 (July 31, 1930), 628. [B]

[2531]   Ellis, S. M. "Edward John Trelawny.," *The Bookman* [London], LXXVIII, No. 467 (August, 1930), 284-285. [R: item 2544]

[2532]   Rader, Melvin M. "Shelley's Theory of Evil Misunderstood," [*Western Reserve Studies (/) A Miscellany*] *Western Reserve University Bulletin*, XXXIII, No. 16 (September 15, 1930), 25-32. [C]

[2533]   Havens, Raymond D[exter]. "*Julian and Maddalo*," *Studies in Philology*, XXVII, No. 4 (October, 1930), 648-653. [C]

[2534]   Havens, Raymond D[exter]. "Shelley's *Alastor*," *PMLA*, XLV, No. 4 (December, 1930), 1698-1115. [C]

[2535]   Sickels, Eleanor. "Shelley and Charles Brockden Brown," *PMLA*, XLV, No. 4 (December, 1930), 1116-1128. [C]

[2536]   [Anonymous]. "Memorabilia," *Notes and Queries*, CLIX, No. 25 (December 20, 1930), 433-434. [M: 433]

[2537]   Sen, Amiyakumar. "Godwin and Shelley," *Journal of the Department of Letters* [University of Calcutta], XX (1930), [1]-123. [C; rptd.: item 2715]

Books:

[2538] Clarke, John Henry. *The God of Shelley and Blake.* 36pp. London: John M. Watkins, 1930. [C]

[2539] Clary, William Webb. *Some Remarks about Andrew Lang [/] with Excerpts from his writings concerning the Poet Shelley.* 15pp. Los Angeles: privately printed [Ampersand Press], 1930. [C]

[2540] Empson, William. *Seven Types of Ambiguity.* 325pp. London: Chatto and Windus, 1930. [C: 197-204]

[2541] Grabo, Carl. *A Newton Among Poets [/] Shelley's Use of Science in Prometheus Unbound.* xii+208pp. Chapel Hill, N.C.: The University of North Carolina Press, 1930. [C]

[2542] Hotson, Leslie, ed. *Shelley's Lost Letters to Harriet.* [90]pp. London: Faber & Faber Limited, 1930. [T, B; rptd. from items 2512, 2515, 2517]

*[2543] Kerlin, Robert Thomas. *Theocritus in English Literature.* xii+203pp. Lynchburg, Va.: J. P. Bell Co., 1930. [C]

[2544] Massingham, H[arold] J[ohn]. *The Friend of Shelley [/] A Memoir of Edward John Trelawny.* xiii+350pp. London: Cobden-Sanderson, 1930. [B]

[2545] Ullman, James Ramsey. *Mad Shelley.* [121]pp. Princeton, N.J.: Princeton University Press, 1930. [C]

1931

Periodicals:

[2546] Havens, Raymond D[exter]. "*Rosalind and Helen,*" *The Journal of English and Germanic Philology,* XXX, No. 2 (April, 1931), 218-222. [C]

[2547] Jones, F[rederick] L. "*Adonais:* The Source of XXVII-XXVIII," *MLN,* XLVI, No. 4 (April, 1931), 236-239. [C]

[2548] [Anonymous]. "Shelley's Scientific Allusions," *The Times Literary Supplement* [London], No. 1,525 (April 23, 1931), 326. [R: item 2541]

[2549] Eiloart, A[rnold]. "Shelley's 'Skylark': The 'Silver Sphere.,'" *Notes and Queries,* CLXI, No. 1 (July 4, 1931), 4-8. [C]

[2550] [Signed "S"]. "Queries on Shelley," *Notes and Queries*, CLXI, No. 2 (July 11, 1931), 29. [T]

[2551] Wier, Marion Clyde. "8. Shelley's 'Alastor' Again," *PMLA*, XLVI, No. 3 (September, 1931), 947-950. [C]

[2552] Havens, Raymond D[exter]. "[Untitled, follwing item 2551]," *PMLA*, XLVI, No. 3 (September, 1931), 950-951. [C]

[2553] Loane, George G. "Shelley and Livy," *The Times Literary Supplement* [London], No. 1,545 (September 10, 1931), 683. [C]

[2554] Pettegrove, J. P. "The Text of Shelley," *The Times Literary Supplement* [London], No. 1,561 (December 31, 1931), 1053. [T,C]

Books:

[2555] Brett, George S. "Shelley's Relation to Berkeley and Drummond," 170-202 in *Studies in English by Members of University College, Toronto*. Collected by Principal Malcolm W[illiam] Wallace. 254pp. Toronto: University of Toronto Press, 1931. [C]

*[2556] Ebeling, Elizabeth. *Shelley's Imaginative Use of His Sources in Prometheus Unbound with Special Reference to Calderon*. [An unpublished Master of Arts essay , University of Minnesota]. Minneapolis, 1931. [C]

[2557] Fairchild, Hoxie Neale. *The Romantic Quest*. viii+444pp. New York: Columbia University Press, 1931. [C: "Shelley and Transcendentalism," (373)-401; M: numerous and fully indexed]

[2558] Keats, John. *The Letters of John Keats*. Edited by Maurice Buxton Forman. 2 vols. London: Humphrey Milford [/] Oxford University Press, 1931. [M: I, xxxvi, 27, 56, 77-78, 81, 94, 107, 110, 114, 115; II, 308, 354, 551, 552-553, 560, 570]

[2559] Levin, Harry. *The Broken Column* [/] *A Study in Romantic Hellenism*. [76]pp. Cambridge, Mass.: Harvard University Press, 1931. [C: "The Poet Unbound," 51-64]

[2560] Rutland, William R. *Swinburne* [/] *A Nineteenth Century Hellene* [/] *With some reflections on the Hellenism of modern Poets*. viii+410pp. Oxford: Basil Blackwell, 1931. [C: 58-91]

[2561] Rylands, George. "English Poets and the Abstract," *Essays*

and *Studies by Members of the English Association*, XVI (1931),
[53]-84. [C: 67-73]

[2562] Stovall, Floyd. *Desire and Restraint in Shelley*. ix+308pp.
Durham, N.C.: Duke University Press, 1931. [B,C]

1932

Periodicals:

[2563] Strout, Alan Lang. "*Maga*, Champion of Shelley," *Studies
in Philology*, XXIX, No. 1 (January, 1932), 95-119. [C]

[2564] Smith, Nowell. "The Text of Shelley," *The Times Literary
Supplement* [London], No. 1.562 (January 7, 1932), 12.
[C,T]

[2565] Houlden, W. H. "A Vindication of Shelley: I," *The Poetry
Review*, XXIII, No. 2 (March-April, 1932), 129-138. [C]

[2566] [Anonymous]. "Memorabilia," *Notes and Queries*, CLXII, No.
10 (March 5, 1932), 163. [M]

[2567] Andrade, E. N. da C. "*A Newton Among Poets*. By Carl Grabo.
The University of North Carolina Press; London: H.
Milford. 1930. Pp. xiv + 208. 13s 6d. net.," *The
Review of English Studies*, VIII, No. 30 (April, 1932),
233-235. [R: item 2541]

[2568] Houlden, W. H. "A Vindication of Shelley: II," *The Poetry
Review*, XXIII, No. 3 (May-June, 1932), 213-222. [C]

[2569] [Anonymous]. "The Conflicts of Shelley," *The Times Literary
Supplement* [London], No. 1,580 (May 12, 1932), 346. [R:
item 2562]

[2570] Weaver, Bennett. "XXXIX. Shelley Works Out the Rhythm
of 'A Lament,'" *PMLA*, XLVII, N0. 2 (June, 1932), 570-
576. [C]

[2571] Darbishire, Helen. "*The Shelley Note-Book in the Harvard College
Library*. Reproduced with Notes and a Postscript by
George Edward Woodberry. Cambridge, Mass.: John
Barnard Associates; London: Humphrey Milford. 1929.
Pp. ii + 134. 35s. net.," *The Review of English Studies*,
VIII, No. 31 (July, 1932), 352-354. [R: item 2511]

[2572] Houlden, W. H. "A Justification of Shelley: III," *The
Poetry Review*, XXIII, No. 4 (July-August, 1932), 332-338.
[C]

[2573]   Jorgenson, Chester Eugene.   "Emerson's Paradise under the
         Shadow of Swords," *Philological Quarterly*, XI, No. 3 (July,
         1932), 274-292.   [C: 287-289]

[2574]   Houlden, H. W.   "A Justification of Shelley: IV," *The Poetry
         Review*, XXIII, No. 5 (September-October, 1932), 390-
         398.   [C]

[2575]   Tillyard, E. M. W.   "Shelley's *Prometheus Unbound* and Plato's
         Statesman," *The Times Literary Supplement* [London], No.
         1,600 (September 29, 1932), 691.   [C]

[2576]   Lees, George Frederic.   "Recollections of an Anglo-
         Parisian Bibliophile [/] III—The Great Shelley For-
         gery," *The Bookman* [London], LXXXIII, No. 493 (October,
         1932), 31-33.   [T]

[2577]   Sampson, George.   "Shelley's 'Prometheus Unbound,'" *The
         Times Literary Supplement* [London], No. 1,603 (October 20,
         1932), 762.   [C]

Books:

[2578]   Buck, Philo M., Jr.   "Goethe and Shelley," *The Goethe Centen-
         ary at the University of Wisconsin: University of Wisconsin
         Studies in Language and Literature*, Number 34 (1932), 84-
         100.   [C]

[2579]   Gingerich, Solomon F.   "The Conception of Beauty in the
         Works of Shelley, Keats, and Poe," 169-194 in *University
         of Michigan Publications* [/] *Language and Literature* [/] *Volume
         VIII* [/] *Essays and Studies in English and Comparative Literature*
         [/] By Members of the English Department of the Univer-
         sity of Michigan. 231+xpp. Ann Arbor, Mich.: Univer-
         sity of Michigan Press, 1932.   [C]

*[2580]   Grove, Harriet [later Mrs. Helyar].   *The Journal of Harriet
         Grove for 1809-1810*.   Edited by Roger Ingpen.   London:
         privately printed, 1932.   [T]

*[2581]   Neumann, Robert.   *Passion; Six Literary Marriages*. Translated
         from the German [1897] by Brian W. Downs.   213pp.
         New York: Harcourt, Brace and Company, 1932.   [B]

[2582]   Sen, Amiya Kumar [*sic*].   "Shelley and the French Revolu-
         tion," *Journal of the Department of Letters* [University of
         Calcutta], XXII (1932), [1]-64.   [C; rptd.: item 2715]

[2583]   Shaw, [George] Bernard.   *Pen Portraits and Reviews*. vi+
         [305]pp.   London: Constable and Company Limited, 1932.
         [C: "Shaming the Devil about Shelley," 236-246; rptd.
         from item 1579]

[2584]   Sickels, Eleanor M. *The Gloomy Egotist* [/] *Moods and Themes*
          of Melancholy from Gray to Keats. Columbia University
          Studies in English and Comparative Literature [Number
          110]. x+456pp. New York: Columbia University Press,
          1932. [C: 324-330; M: forty, fully indexed]

[2585]   Weaver, Bennett. *Toward the Understanding of Shelley.* Univer-
          sity of Michigan Publications [/] Language and Litera-
          ture [/] Volume IX. xii+258pp. Ann Arbor, Mich.:
          The University of Michigan Press, 1932. [C]

[2586]   Weaver, Bennett. "The Williams Transcription of *Hellas,*"
          151-168 in *University of Michigan Publications* [/] *Language*
          and Literature [/] *Volume VIII* [/] *Essays and Studies in English*
          and Comparative Literature [/] *By Members of the English Depart-*
          ment of the University of Michigan. 231+xpp. Ann Arbor,
          Mich.: University of Michigan Press, 1932. [T]

                              1933

Periodicals:

[2587]   Koszul, A[ndre Henri]. " *A Newton Among Poets—Shelley's Use*
          of Science in Prometheus Unbound. By Carl Grabo. Univer-
          sity of North Carolina Press, 1930. pp. xii + 208
          $3.00," *Modern Language Notes,* XLVIII, No. 1 (January,
          1933), 50-53. [R: item 2541]

[2588]   Cousins, James H. "The Message of Shelley's 'Prometheus
          Unbound,'" *The Calcutta Review,* Third Series XLVI, No. 2
          (February, 1933), [155]-170. [C; revised and rptd.:
          item 2612]

[2589]   Propst, Louise. *An Analaytical Study of Shelley's Versification.*
          University of Iowa Studies [/] *Humanistic Studies,* V, No. 3
          (February 15, 1933), [75]pp. Iowa City, Iowa: [Uni-
          versity of Iowa Press], 1933. [C]

[2590]   Yeats, W[illiam] B[utler]. "'Prometheus Unbound,'" *The*
          Spectator, CL, No. 5,464 (March 17, 1933), 366-367. [C]

[2591]   [Anonymous]. "Shelley's Biographers," *The Times Literary*
          Supplement [London], No. 1626 (March 30, 1933), 221.
          [R: item 2620]

[2592]   Chilton, Eleanor Carroll. "'A Power Girt Round with
          Weakness,'" *The English Review,* LVI (April, 1933), 453-
          455. [R: item 2620]

[2593]   Wright, Herbert G. " *Toward the Understanding of Shelley.* By

                              [236]

Bennett Weaver. Ann Arbor: University of Michigan
Press, 1932. xii + 258pp. $2.50," *Modern Language Review*,
XXVIII, No. 2 (April, 1933), 264. [R: item 2586]

[2594] Clark, David Lee. "Shelley and Bacon," *PMLA*, XLVIII, No. 2
(June, 1933), 529-546. [C]

[2595] Solve, Melvin T. *"Toward the Understanding of Shelley*. By
Bennett Weaver. Ann Arbor: University of Michigan
Press, 1932. pp. xii + 258 + viii. $2.50 [/] *The
Best of Shelley*. Edited with an Introduction and Notes
by Newman I. White. New York: Thomas Nelson and Sons,
1932. Pp. xlvi + 532. [/] *An Analytical Study of Shelley's
Versification*. By Louise Propst. Iowa City: University
of Iowa Press, 1933. Pp. 74. $0.75 (University of
Iowa Studies.) [/] *Desire and Restraint in Shelley*. By
Floyd H. Stovall. Durham, N.C.: Duke University Press,
1931. Pp. xi + 308. $3.50.," *MLN*, XLVIII, No. 6 (June,
1933), 408-413. [R: items 2585, 3261 , 2589, 2562]

[2596] Jones, Fred[erick] L. "The Revision of *Laon and Cythna*,"
The Journal of English and Germanic Philology, XXXII, No. 3
(July, 1933), 366-372. [T]

[2597] Harrison, T. P., Jr. "Spenser and Shelley's 'Adonais,'"
Studies in English, Number 13 [*The University of Texas Bulletin*
No. 3226] (July 8, 1933), [54]-63. [C]

[2598] [Anonymous]. "Alastor," *The Times Literary Supplement* [London],
No. 1644 (August 3, 1933), 523. [R: item 2616]

[2599] Kessel, Marcel. "The Revising of Shelley's 'Laon and
Cythna,'" *The Times Literary Supplement* [London], No. 1649
(September 7, 1933), 592. [B,T]

[2600] Brett-Smith, H. F. B. "Shelley's 'Laon and Cythna,'" *The
Times Literary Supplement* [London], No. 1651 (September 21,
1933), 631. [B,T]

[2601] Hoffman, Harold Leroy. "Shelley's 'Alastor,'" *The Times
Literary Supplement* [London], No. 1651 (September 21,
1933), 631. [C]

[2602] Brown, Leonard. "The Genesis, Growth, and Meaning of
Endymion," *Studies in Philology*, XXX, No. 4 (October, 1933),
618-653. [C]

[2603] K[ing], R. W. "Short Notices," *Modern Language Review*,
XXVIII, No. 4 (October, 1933), [544]-548. [R: item
2589]

[2604] Wright, Herbert G. "La Poesia di Shelley. Da Michele
Renzulli. Foligno: Franco Campitelli. 1932. 448pp.
L. 20.," *Modern Language Review*, XXVIII, No. 4 (October,
1933), 529-530. [R, as indicated]

[2605]   Gregory, Horace. "A Defense of Poetry," *The New Republic*,
          LXXVI, No. 984 (October 11, 1933), 235-238. [R:
          item 2620]

[2606]   Young, Stark. "Poetry of Defense," *The New Republic*, LXXVI,
          No. 987 (November 1, 1933), 334-336. [C]

[2607]   Kessel, Marcel. "Shelley's 'Laon and Cythna,'" *The Times
          Literary Supplement* [London], No. 1658 (November 9, 1933),
          774. [B,T]

[2608]   White, Newman I[vey]. "Shelley at Oxford," *The Times Liter-
          ary Supplement* [London], No. 1659 (November 16, 1933),
          795. [B]

[2609]   Gregory, Horace, and Stark Young. "Shelley Unbound," *The
          New Republic*, LXXXVII, No. 991 (November 29, 1933), 75-
          76. [C]

Books:

[2610]   Batho, Edith C. *The Later Wordsworth*. x+417pp. Cambridge,
          Eng.: At the University Press, 1933. [M: 38, 78, 100-
          101, 101n, 374, 384

[2611]   Blunden, Edmund. *Charles Lamb and His Contemporaries* [/] *Being
          the Clark Lectures Delivered at Trinity College* [/] *Cambridge
          1932*. ix+215pp. Cambridge, Eng.: At the University
          Press, 1933. [M: 215]

*[2612]   Cousins, James H. *The Work Promethean: Interpretations and
          Applications of Shelley's Poetry*. [?]pp. Madras: Ganesh
          & Company, 1933. [C; Chapter II, "The Message of
          Prometheus Unbound," (?p), rptd. from item 2588]

[2613]   Croce, Benedetto. *The Defence of Poetry* [/] *Variations on the
          Theme of Shelley*. Translated by E. F. Carritt. 31pp.
          Oxford: At the Clarendon Press, 1933. [C]

[2614]   Dodd, Catherine I[sabel]. *Eagle-Feather*. 313pp. New York:
          D. Appleton and Company, 1933. [Fictionalized B]

[2615]   Eliot, T[homas] S[tearns]. *The Use of Poetry and the Use of
          Criticism* [/] *Studies in the Relation of Criticism to Poetry in
          England* [/] The Charles Eliot Norton Lectures for 1932-
          1933. viii+149pp. Cambridge, Mass.: Harvard Univer-
          sity Press, 1933. [C: "Shelley and Keats," (78)-94]

[2616]   Hoffman, Harold Leroy. *An Odyssey of the Soul* [/] *Shelley's
          Alastor*. [Columbia University Studies in English
          and Comparative Literature]. viii+173pp. New York:
          Columbia University Press, 1933. [C]

*[2617]   Knight, G. Wilson. *The Christian Renaissance.*   374pp.
          Toronto: Macmillan Company, 1933. [C]

[2618]   Kurtz, Benjamin P. *The Pursuit of Death* [/] *A Study of
          Shelley's Poetry.* xxii+339pp. New York: Oxford Univer-
          sity Press, 1933. [C]

[2619]   Praz, Mario. *The Romantic Agony.* Translated by Angus
          Davidson.   xvii+454pp. London: Oxford University
          Press [/] Humphrey Milford, 1933. [Original Italian
          (1930); C: 4, 11, 25-26, 28, 31, 46n, 57, 76, 87n,
          88n, 90n, 114-116, 249, 285n]

[2620]   Wolfe, Humbert, ed.   *The Life of Percy Bysshe Shelley, as
          Comprised in The Life of Shelley by Thomas Jefferson Hogg, The
          Recollections of Shelley & Byron by Edward John Trelawny, Memoirs
          of Shelley by Thomas Love Peacock.* 2 vols. London: J. M.
          Dent & Co., 1933. [B; rptd. from items 664, 669, 935]

                                1934

Periodicals:

[2621]   Renzulli, Michele. "On the Criticism of Shelley's
          Poetry," *The Poetry Review*, XXV, No. 1 (January-February,
          1934), 35-43. [Rptd. from the "Preface" of Renzulli's
          La Poesia di Shelley (Foligno: Franco Campitelli, 1932),
          translated by Frederick T. Wood; C]

[2622]   Mueschke, Paul, and Earl L. Griggs. "Wordsworth as the
          Prototype of the Poet in Shelley's *Alastor*," *PMLA*, XLIX,
          No. 1 (March, 1934), 229-245. [C]

[2623]   Waller, Ross D. *"An Odyssey of the Soul. Shelley's Alastor.* By
          Harold Leroy Hoffman. New York: Columbia University
          Press; London: H. Milford. 1933. x + 174pp. 16s 6d.,"
          Modern Language Review, XXIX, No. 2 (April, 1934), 208-210.
          [R: item 2616]

[2624]   [Anonymous]. "Shelley and Byron," *The Times Literary Supple-
          ment* [London], No. 1688 (June 7, 1934), 404. [R: item
          2637]

[2625]   [Anonymous]. "The Newdigate," *The Times Literary Supplement*
          [London], No. 1689 (June 14, 1934), [413]-414. [M:
          (413)]

[2626]   [Anonymous]. "After Shelley," *The Times Literary Supplement*
          [London], No. 1691 (June 28, 1934), 456. [R: item
          2639]

[2627]   Bush, Douglas. "Notes on Shelley," *Philological Quarterly*,
         XIII, No. 3 (July, 1934), 299-302. [C]

[2628]   Lotspeich, Henry G. "Shelley's 'Eternity' and Demogor-
         gon," *Philological Quarterly*, XIII, No. 3 (July, 1934),
         309-311. [C]

[2629]   Praz, Mario. *"Toward the Understanding of Shelley*. By Bennett
         Weaver. Ann Arbor: University of Michigan Press.
         (University of Michigan Publications, Language and
         Literature, Vol. IX.) 1932. Pp. xii + 258. $2.50.
         [/] *La Poesia di Shelley*. By Michele Renzulli (dell'
         Universita di Temple, Philadelphia, Pa.). Foligno:
         Campitelli. 1932. Pp. iv + 448. Lire 20.," *The
         Review of English Studies*, X, No. 39 (July, 1934), 365-
         366. [R: item 2585]

[2630]   White, Newman I[vey]. "Shelley's Biography: The Primary
         Sources," *Studies in Philology*, XXXI, No. 3 (July, 1934),
         472-486. [B]

[2631]   [Anonymous]. "Shelley: Verse and Prose," *The Times Literary
         Supplement* [London], No. 1,693 (July 12, 1934), 489.
         [R: items 2636, 2643]

[2632]   Jones,Frederick L. *"Alastor* Foreshadowed in *St. Irvyne*,"
         PMLA, XLIX, No. 3 (September, 1934), 969-971. [C]

*[2633]   Leavis, F[rank] R[aymond]. "Shelley's Imagery," *The Bookman*
         [London], LXXXVI, No. [?] (September, 1934), 278. [C]

[2634]   Tempest, N. R. *"An Analytical Study of Shelley's Versification*.
         By Louise Propst, Ph.D. (University of Iowa Humanities
         Studies, Vol. V, No. 3). U.S.A. 1933. Pp. 74.
         $ .75.," *The Review of English Studies*, X, No. 40 (October,
         1934), 493-494. [R: item 2589]

[2635]   Weaver, Bennett. "Shelley: Values and Imagination,"
         The American Scholar, III, No. 4 (Autumn, 1934), 404-412.
         [C]

Books:

[2636]   Bailey, Ruth. *Shelley*. ["Great Lives," No. 39]. 143pp.
         London: Duckworth, 1934. [B]

[2637]   Clarke, Isabel C[onstance]. *Shelley and Byron, A Tragic
         Friendship*. 324pp. London: Hutchinson and Co., 1934.
         [B, C]

[2638]   Goodchild, William. *Shelley / A Play in Three Acts With a
         Prologue and an Epilogue*. 152pp. Oxford: Basil Blackwell,
         1934. [Fictionalized B]

[2639]   Hogg, Thomas Jefferson.   *After Shelley* [/] *The Letters of*
         Thomas Jefferson Hogg to Jane Williams.   Edited with a Bio-
         graphical Introduction by Sylva Norman.   xlvi+94pp.
         London: Oxford University Press [/] Humphrey Milford,
         1934.   [B,T]

[2640]   Murry, John Middleton.   "Percy Bysshe Shelley [/] 1792-
         1822," [585]-502 in *Great Democrats*.   Edited by A[lfred]
         Barratt Brown.   704pp.   London: Ivor Nicholson and
         Watson, 1934.   [C; rptd.: item 2793]

[2641]   Rossetti, William Michael.   *Letters of William Michael Rossetti*
         [/] *Concerning Whitman, Blake, and Shelley to Anne Gilchrist and*
         Her Son Herbert Gilchrist [/] *With Appendices Containing a Letter*
         to President Cleveland and an Uncollected Whitman Circular.   xi+
         201pp.   Durham, N.C.: Duke University Press, 1934. [C:
         25, 44, 50-51, 52, 62, 66, 69, 70n, 71-72, 82, 83n, 91-
         92, 94, 104, 108, 113, 116, 150]

[2642]   Sen, Amiyakumar.   "Locke, Hume and Shelley," *Journal of the*
         Department of Letters [University of Calcutta], XXIV (1934)
         [1]-117.   [C; rptd.: item 2715]

[2643]   Shelley-Rolls, John C. E., and Roger Ingpen, eds.   *Verse*
         and Prose from the Manuscripts of Percy Bysshe Shelley.   xiii+
         159pp.   London: privately printed [Curwin Press], 1934.

[2644]   Tillyard, E. M. W.   *Poetry* [/] *Direct and Oblique*.   viii+286pp
         London: Chatto & Windus, 1934.   [C: 5, 38, 39-40, 50,
         97, 124-128, 157-166, 172-173, 177, 180, 196-197, 227-
         228, 240, 257]

                              1935

Periodicals:

[2645]   Jones, Claude E.   "Christ a Fury?" *MLN*, L, No. 1 (January,
         1935), 41.   [C]

[2646]   Jones, Frederick L.   "Two Notes on *Epipsychidion*," *MLN*, L,
         No. 1 (January, 1935), 40.   [C]

[2647]   Shepard, Odell.   "*La Poesia di Shelley*. By Michele Renzulli.
         Rome: Campitelli, 1932.   Pp. iv + 450.   L. 20.," *MLN*,
         L, No. (January, 1935), 66-67.   [R as indicated]

[2648]   Kessel, Marcel.   "Shelley's 'To Constantia Singing,'" *The*
         Times Literary Supplement [London], No. 1,720 (January 17,
         1935), 33.   [T]

[2649]   Lemmi, Charles W.   "The Serpent and the Eagle in Spenser
         and Shelley," *MLN*, No. 3 (March, 1935), 165-168.   [C]

[2650]   Kitchin, G. "*The Pursuit of Death: a Study of Shelley's Poetry.*
         By Benjamin P. Kurtz. New York: Oxford University
         Press. 1933. xxii + 339pp. 13s. 6d.," *Modern Language
         Review*, XXX, No. 2 (April, 1935), 235-237. [R: item
         2618]

[2651]   Jones, Frederick L. "Mrs. Shelley's 'Lodore,'" *The Times
         Literary Supplement* [London], No. 1,731 (April 4, 1935),
         228. [B]

[2652]   Glenn, Keith. "Shelley's 'To Constantia Singing,'" *The
         Times Literary Supplement* [London], No. 1,732 (April 11,
         1935), 244. [T]

[2653]   Grylls, R[osalie]. "Mrs. Shelley's Novels," *The Times
         Literary Supplement* [London], No. 1,732 (April 11, 1935),
         244. [M]

[2654]   Jones, Frederick L. "Shelley's *Leonora*," *Modern Philology*,
         XXXII, No. 4 (May, 1935), 391-395. [T]

[2655]   Robb, N. A. "Shelley's Dante," *The Times Literary Supplement*
         [London], No. 1,739 (May 30, 1935), 348. [T]

[2656]   Leavis, F[rank] R[aymond]. "Revaluations (VIII):
         Shelley," *Scrutiny*, IV, No. 1 (June, 1935), 158-180.
         [C; rptd.: item 2713]

[2657]   Richards, Irving T. "A Note on Source Influences in
         Shelley's *Cloud* and *Skylark*," *PMLA*, L, No. 2 (June,
         1935), 562-567. [C]

[2658]   Robb, N. A. "Shelley's Copy of Dante," *Notes and Queries*,
         CLXVIII, No. 22 (June 1, 1935), 385. [T]

[2659]   Heron-Allen, Edward. "Shelley Family.," *Notes and Queries*,
         CLXVIII, No. 23 (June 8, 1935), 403. [B]

[2660]   [Anonymous]. "Shelley in France," *The Times Literary Supple-
         ment* [London], No. 1,743 (June 27, 1935), 412. [R of
         Henri Peyre's *Shelley et la France* (Paris and Cairo,
         1935)]

[2661]   Ebeling, Elizabeth. "A Probable Paracelsian Element in
         Shelley," *Studies in Philology*, XXXII, No. 3 (July,
         1935), 508-525. [C]

*[2662] Wright, C. E. "Manuscripts of T. J. Hogg and E. E.
         Williams," *The British Museum Quarterly*, IX, No. 3 (July,
         1935), 78-81. [T]

[2663]   Davies, David W. "Herschel and the Poets," *Notes and Queries*,
         CLXIX, No. 2 (July 13, 1935), 28. [C]

[2664] Mabbott, T[homas] O. "Shelley's Copy of Dante (clxviii. 385)," *Notes and Queries*, CLXIX, No. 2 (July 13, 1935), 34. [C]

[2665] [Signed "F.S."]. "Shelley Family (clxviii. 403).," *Notes and Queries*, CLXIX, No. 5 (August 3, 1935), 88. [B]

[2666] Bush, Douglas. "Notes on Keats's Reading," *PMLA*, L, No. 3 (September, 1935), 785-806. [C: 792]

[2667] Spencer, Theodore. "Shelley on 'Hamlet.,'" *Notes and Queries*, CLXIX, No. 11 (September 14, 1935), 190. [T]

[2668] [Anonymous]. "Shelley's Electrical Universe," *The Times Literary Supplement* [London], No. 1,756 (September 26, 1935), 593. [R: item 2675]

[2669] Lind, L. Robert "Shelley Reappraised," *The Sewanee Review*, XLIII, No. 4 (October-December, 1935), [413]-435. [C]

[2670] [Anonymous]. "Memorabilia," *Notes and Queries*, CLXIX, No. 14 (October 5, 1935), 235-236. [C of item 2657]

[2671] Mabbctt, T[homas] O. "An Early American Printing of Shelley," *Notes and Queries*, CLXIX, No. 14 (October 5, 1935), 242. [T]

[2672] Ballman, Adele B. "The Dating of Shelley's Prose Fragments—'On Life,' 'On Love,' 'On the Punishment of Death,'" *ELH*, II, No. 4 (December, 1935), 332-335. [T]

[2673] Leavis, Q. D. "The Critical Writings of George Santayana: An Introductory Note," *Scrutiny*, IV, No. 3 (December, 1935), 278-295. [C: 285]

*[2674] Jones, Frederick L. "Shelley and Christianity," *The Crozer Quarterly*, XII (1935), [?p]. [C]

Books:

[2675] Grabo, Carl. *The Meaning of the Witch of Atlas*. ix+158pp. Chapel Hill, N.C.: The University of North Carolina Press, 1935. [C]

[2676] Grabo, Carl. *Prometheus Unbound* [/] *An Interpretation*. ix+ 205pp. Chapel Hill, N.C.: The University of North Carolina Press, 1935. [C]

[2677] [Griffith, R. H.]. *An Account of An Exhibition of Books and Manuscripts of Percy Bysshe Shelley* [/] *With Something of Their Literary History* [/] *Their Present Condition and Their Provenance*. 40pp. Austin, Texas: The University of Texas [The Library of the University of Texas], 1935. [T]

[2678]   Origo, Iris [Scott]. *Allegra*. 119pp. London: Hogarth
         Press, 1935. [B]

[2679]   Pratt, Willis Winslow. *Shelley Criticism in England* [/] *1810-*
         1890. [A Thesis Presented to the Faculty of the Gradu-
         ate School of Cornell University for the degree of
         Doctor of Philosophy]. 290pp. Ithaca, N.Y.: [unpub-
         lished, Cornell University Library], 1935. [C]

[2680]   Thompson, L. C. *More Magic Dethroned*. 16pp. + 6 charts.
         London: privately printed [Warner Press], 1935. [C]

[2681]   Weaver, Bennett. "Shelley's Biblical Extracts: A Lost
         Book," *Papers of the Michigan Academy of Science, Arts & Letters*,
         XX (1935), 523-528.

[2682]   Winwar, Frances [Mrs. Frances Vinciguerra Grebanier]. *The*
         Romantic Rebels. viii+507pp. Boston: Little, Brown, and
         Company, 1935. [B]

                                1936

Periodicals:

[2683]   Jones, Frederick L. "Shelley's Boat," *The Times Literary*
         Supplement [London], No. 1772 (January 18, 1936), 55.
         [B]

[2684]   [Signed "Wigwam"]. "A Disciple of Shelley," *Blackwood's*
         Edinburgh Magazine, CCXXXIX, No. mccccxliv (February,
         1936), 199-206. [M; fiction]

[2685]   [Signed "G.H.D."]. "Shelley on 'Hamlet' (clxix. 190).,"
         Notes and Queries, CLXX, No. 6 (February 8, 1936), 104.
         [T]

[2686]   [Anonymous]. "In Defence of Shelley [/] New Essays by
         Mr. Hebert Read," *The Times Literary Supplement* [London],
         No. 1777 (February 22, 1936), 157. [R: item 2713]

[2687]   Kessel, Marcel. "The Poet in Shelley's *Alastor*: A
         Criticism and a Reply," *PMLA*, LI, No. 1 (March, 1936),
         302-310. [C]

[2688]   Mueschke, Paul, and Earl Leslie Griggs. "Reply," *PMLA*,
         LI, No. 1 (March, 1936), 310-312. [C]

[2689]   Smith, John Harrington. "Shelley and Milton's 'Chariot
         of Paternal Deity,'" *MLN*, LI, No. 4 (April, 1936),
         215-217. [C]

[2690] Cook, Davidson. "Sadak the Wanderer [/] An Unknown Shel-
        ley Poem," *The Times Literary Supplement* [London], No. 1789
        (May 16, 1936), 424. [T]

[2691] Ingpen, Roger. "*The Pursuit of Death.* A Study of Shelley's
        Poetry. By Benjamin P. Kurtz. New York: Oxford Uni-
        versity Press, 1933. Pp. xxii + 339.," *MLN*, LI, No. 6
        (June, 1936), 393-395. [R: item 2618]

[2692] Mason, H. A. "Ontogenic Criticism," *Scrutiny*, V, No. 1
        (June, 1936), 90-92. [R: item 2714]

[2693] Notopoulos, James A. "XXXV. Shelley and Thomas Taylor,"
        PMLA, LI, No. 2 (June, 1936), 502-517. [C]

[2694] Pottle, Frederick A. "Shelley and Wordsworth," *The Times
        Literary Supplement* [London], No. 1794 (June 20, 1936),
        523. [C]

[2695] [Signed "G.G.L."]. "Shelley and Scott," *Notes and Queries*,
        CLXXI, No. 4 (July 25, 1936), 60. [C]

[2696] Kessel, Marcel. "Shelley-Leigh Hunt," *The Times Literary
        Supplement* [London], No. 1804 (August 29, 1936), 697.
        [T]

[2697] Van Doren, Carl. "Elinor Wylie [/] A Portrait from Mem-
        ory," *Harper's Monthly Magazine*, CLXXIII (September,
        1936), [358]-367. [B]

[2698] Kessel, Marcel. "The Harvard Shelley Notebook," *The Times
        Literary Supplement* [London], No. 1805 (September 5,
        1936), 713. [T]

[2699] Darbishire, Helen. "The Harvard Shelley Notebook," *The
        Times Literary Supplement* [London], No. 1806 (September
        12, 1936), 729. [T]

[2700] DuBois, Arthur E. "Alastor: The Spirit of Solitude," *The
        Journal of English and Germanic Philology*, XXXV, No. 4
        (October, 1936), 530-545. [C]

[2701] Mousel, M. Eunice. "Falsetto in Shelley," *Studies in
        Philology*, XXIII, No. 4 (October, 1936), 587-609. [C]

[2702] [Signed "T.C.C."]. "'Shelleyty [*sic* for Shelleyfy].,'"
        Notes and Queries, CLXXI, No. 21 (November 21, 1936), 368.
        [M]

[2703] Kapstein, I[srael] J[ames]. "LXX. The Symbolism of the
        Wind and the Leaves in Shelley's 'Ode to the West
        Wind,'" *PMLA*, LI, No. 4 (December, 1936), 1069-1079.
        [C]

*[2704] Clark, Eleanor Grace. "Radical Poets: Old Style—New
         Style," *Catholic World*, CXLIII, No. 854 ([?], 1936),
         178-181. [C]

*[2705] Gnudi, Martha T. "Shelley and Carducci," *Italica*, XIII
         ([?], 1936), 79-84. [C]

*[2706] Grabo, Carl. "Shelley Reconsidered," *The New Humanist*,
         IX ([?], 1936), 1-5. [C]

Books:

 [2707] Beach, Joseph Warren. *The Concept of Nature in Nineteenth-
         Century English Poetry*. xii+618pp. New York: The
         Macmillan Company, 1936. [C: "Shelley's Naturalism,"
         209-241; "Shelley's 'Platonism,'" 242-275]

*[2708] Buck, Philo Melvin. "When We Dead Awake: Shelley," 69-
         91 in *The World's Great Age: The Story of a Century's Search
         for a Philosophy of Life*. xv+382pp. New York: The Macmil-
         lan Company, 1936. [C]

 [2709] Cowling, George. *Shelley and Other Essays*. [176]pp. Mel-
         bourne: Melbourne University Press, 1936. [B: "Shel-
         ley," 13-108]

 [2710] Dangerfield, Elma. *"Mad Shelley"* [/] *A Dramatic Life in Five
         Acts*. [262]pp. London: Michael Joseph Ltd., 1936.
         [Dramatized biography]

 [2711] Ervine, StJohn [*sic*]. "Shelley as a Dramatist.," [77]-
         106 in *Essays by Divers Hands* [/] *Being Transactions of the
         Royal Society of Literature of the United Kingdom*. [Edited by
         Hugh Walpole]. New Series XV. viii+202pp. London:
         Humphrey Milford [/] Oxford University Press, 1936.
         [C]

 [2712] Grabo, Carl. *The Magic Plant* [/] *The Growth of Shelley's Thought*.
         ix+450pp. Chapel Hill, N.C.: The University of North
         Carolina Press, 1936. [C]

 [2713] Leavis, F[rank] R[aymond]. *Revaluation: Tradition and Develop-
         ment in English Poetry*. viii+275pp. London: Chatto &
         Windus, 1936. [C: "VI. Shelley," 203-240; rptd. from
         item 2656]

 [2714] Read, Herbert. *In Defence of Shelley & Other Essays*. 282pp.
         London: William Heinemann, 1936. [C: "In Defence of
         Shelley," (1)-86]

 [2715] Sen, Amiyakumar. *Studies in Shelley*. xvi+343pp. Calcutta:
         University of Calcutta, 1936. [C: "Locke, Hume and

Shelley," (1)-104, rptd. from item 2642; "Baron D'Hol-
bach and Shelley," (105)-114; "Godwin and Shelley,"
(115)-242, rptd. from item 2537; "Shelley and Indian
Thought," (243)-270; "Shelley and the French Revolution," (271)-335, rptd. from item 2582]

[2716] Somervell, D[avid] C[hurchill]. *English Thought in the
Nineteenth Century.* [xii]+242pp. New York: Longmans,
1936. [C: 60-62, 71-72]

1937

Periodicals:

[2717] Gates, Eunice Joiner. "Shelley and Calderon," *Philological
Quarterly*, XVI, No. 1 (January, 1937), 49-58. [C]

[2718] Thompson, D. W. "Ozymandias," *Philological Quarterly*, XVI,
No. 1 (January, 1937), 59-64. [C]

[2719] [Anonymous]. "The True Tale of Shelley's 'Emily' [/] The
Dream and the Reality," *The Times Literary Supplement* [Lon-
don], No. 1825 (January 23, 1937), 55. [R of della
Robbia's *Vita di una Donna* (Florence, 1936), a biography
of Emilia Viviani]

*[2720] App, A. J. "How Six Famous Poets Were Treated," *Catholic
World*, CXLIV, No. [?] (February, 1937), 582-589.

[2721] Ballman, Adele B. *"The Meaning of 'The Witch of Atlas.'* By
Carl Grabo. Chapel Hill: University of North Carolina
Press, 1935. Pp. x + 158. $2.50," *MLN*, LII, No. 2
(February, 1937), 144-146. [R: item 2675]

[2722] Kurtz, Benjamin P. *"Shelley et la France.* Lyrisme anglais
et lyrisme francais au XIXe siecle. Par Henry Peyre.
Le Caire: Barbey, 1935. Pp. 509.," *MLN*, LII, No. 3
(February, 1937), 146-147. [R, as indicated]

[2723] Kapstein, Israel James. "Shelley and Canabis," *PMLA*, LII,
No. 1 (March, 1937), 238-243. [C]

[2724] Koller, Kathrine [*sic*]. "A Source for Portions of *The
Witch of Atlas*," *MLN*, LII, No. 3 (March, 1937), 157-161.
[C]

[2725] Wellek, Rene. "Literary Criticism and Philosophy,"
Scrutiny, V, No. 4 (March, 1937), 375-383. [C of item
2713; Shelley: 380-383]

[2726] Norman, Sylva. "A Forged Shelley Letter," *The Times Literary Supplement* [London], No. 1833 (March 20, 1937), 222. [T]

[2727] De Ricci, Seymour. "A Forged Shelley Letter," *The Times Literary Supplement* [London], No. 1834 (March 27, 1937), 240. [T]

[2728] [Signed "H.F."]. "'Shelley's a Trademark Used on Sheets,'" *Notes and Queries*, CLXXII, No. 13 (March 27, 1937), 228. [C]

[2729] [Jones, Frederick L.]. "The Letters of Mary W. Shelley in the Bodleian Library," *The Bodleian Quarterly Record*, VIII, No. 93 (Spring, 1937), [297]-310.

[2730] Carver, P. L. *"An Odyssey of the Soul: Shelley's Alastor*. By Harold Leroy Hoffman. New York: Columbia University Press; London: H. Milford. 1933. Pp. viii + 173. 16s. 6d. net.," *The Review of English Studies*, XIII, No. 50 (April, 1937), 243-245. [R: item 2616]

[2731] Norman, Sylva. "A Forged Shelley Letter," *The Times Literary Supplement* [London], No. 1836 (April 3, 1937), 256. [T]

[2732] De Ricci, Seymour. "A Forged Shelley Letter," *The Times Literary Supplement* [London], No. 1835 (April 10, 1937), 275. [T]

[2733] Pollard, Graham. "A Forged Shelley Letter," *The Times Literary Supplement* [London], No. 1837 (April 17, 1937), 292. [T]

[2734] De Ricci, Seymour. "A Forged Shelley Letter," *The Times Literary Supplement* [London], No. 1838 (April 24, 1937), 308. [T]

[2735] Besterman, Theodore. "[Untitled, following item 2734]," *The Times Literary Supplement* [London], No. 1838 (April 24, 1937), 308. [T]

[2736] Sen, Devendrakumar. "On Prometheus Unbound," *The Calcutta Review*, LXIII, No. 2 (May, 1937), [159]-162. [C]

[2737] Pollard, Graham. "A Forged Shelley Letter," *The Times Literary Supplement* [London], No. 1840 (May 8, 1937), 364. [T]

[2738] Kessel, Marcel. "A Forged Shelley Letter," *The Times Literary Supplement* [London], No. 1843 (May 29, 1937), 412. [T]

[2739] Cox, R. G. "The Great Reviews (I)," *Scrutiny*, VI, No. 1 (June, 1937), 2-20. [C: 11-16]

[2740]   Jones, Frederick L.   "Hogg and *The Necessity of Atheism*,"
          PMLA, LII, No. 2 (June, 1937), 423-426.   [C,T]

[2741]   Norman, Sylva.   "A Forged Shelley Letter," *The Times Literary
          Supplement* [London], No. 1844 (June 5, 1937), 428.   [T]

[2742]   [Jones, Frederick L.].   "The Letters of Mary W. Shelley in
          the Bodleian Library   (continued)," *The Bodleian Quarterly
          Record*, VIII, No. 94 (Summer, 1937), [360]-371.   [T]

[2743]   Jones, Frederick L.   "A Letter from Claire Clairmont," *The
          Times Literary Supplement* [London], No. 1849 (July 10,
          1937), 512.   [T]

[2744]   Jones, Frederick L.   "A Shelley Letter," *The Times Literary
          Supplement* [London], No. 1850 (July 17, 1937), 528.   [T]

*[2745] [Signed "H. McC."].   "A First Edition of Shelley," *More
          Books, The Bulletin of the Boston Public Library*, XII (Septem-
          ber, 1937), 312.   [T]

[2746]   Marjarum, E. Wayne.   "9. The Symbolism of Shelley's 'To a
          Skylark,'" *PMLA*, LII, No. 3 (September, 1937), 911-913.
          [C]

[2747]   [Jones, Frederick L.].   "The Letters of Mary W. Shelley in
          the Bodleian Library," *The Bodleian Quarterly Record*, VIII,
          No. 95 (Autumn, 1937), [412]-420.   [T]

[2748]   Kernahan, Coulson.   "'The Cross Leads Generations On' [/]
          The changed attitude, towards Christianity, of two
          great poets, Swinburne and Shelley; and the influence
          for good, upon Swinburne," *London Quarterly and Holborn
          Review*, Sixth Series VI [whole number CLXII], [No. 4]
          (October, 1937), 456-476.   [C]

[2749]   Waller, Ross D.   *"The Magic Plant. The Growth of Shelley's
          Thought.* By Carl Grabo. Chapel Hill: University of
          North Carolina Press; London: H. Milford. 1936. xii
          + 450 pp. 18s. [/] *Shelley's Religion.* By Ellsworth
          Barnard. Minneapolis: University of Minnesota Press;
          London: H. Milford. 1937. xii + 320pp. 16s. [/]
          Power and Elusiveness in Shelley. By Oscar W. Firkins.
          Minneapolis: University of Minnesota Press; London:
          H. Milford. 1937. iv + 188pp. 11s. 6d.," *The Modern
          Language Review*, XXXII, No. 4 (October, 1937), 622-625.
          [R: items 2712, 2752, 2758]

*[2750] Garnier, Charles-Marie.   "A Metrical Study of the Lyrical
          Parts in Shelley's 'Prometheus Unbound,'" *Revue de l'En-
          seignement des Langues Vivantes*, LIV, No. [?] ([?March],
          1937), 97-102.   [C]

*[2751]   Garnier, Charles-Marie. "A Metrical Study of the Lyrical
           Parts in Shelley's 'Prometheus Unbound,'" *Revue de l'En-
           seignement des Langues Vivantes*, LIV, No. [?] ([?April],
           1937), 145-157. [C]

Books:

 [2752]   Barnard, Ellsworth. *Shelley's Religion*. xii+320pp. Min-
           neapolis, Minn.: The University of Minnesota Press,
           1937. [C]

 [2753]   Benet, Laura. *The Boy Shelley*. viii+307pp. New York:
           Dodd, Mead and Company, 1937. [B]

 [2754]   Bush, Douglas. *Mythology and the Romantic Tradition in English
           Poetry*. [Harvard Studies in English, XVIII]. xvi+647pp.
           Cambridge, Mass.: Harvard University Press, 1937. [C:
           "Shelley," (129)-168]

 [2755]   Charnwood, [Dorothea Mary Roby Thorpe], Baroness. *Call
           Back Yesterday*. vii+320pp. London: Eyre and Spottis-
           woode, 1937. [T: 201-206]

*[2756]   Caudwell, Christopher. *Illusion and Reality: A Study of the
           Sources of Poetry*. [?]pp. New York and London: Macmil-
           lan and Co., 1937. [C: Chapter IV]

*[2757]   Colum, May Maguire. *From These Roots: The Ideas that Have Made
           Modern Literature*. [?]pp. New York: Charles Scribner's
           Sons, 1937. [C: 146-148, 340]

 [2758]   Firkins, Oscar W. *Power and Elusiveness in Shelley*. 187pp.
           Minneapolis, Minn.: The University of Minnesota Press,
           1937. [C]

 [2759]   Freeman, Martin Joseph. *A Text of Shelley's Prometheus Un-
           bound*. A Part of a Dissertation Submitted to the Fac-
           ulty of the Division of the Humanities in Candidacy
           for the Degree of Doctor of Philosophy [/] Department
           of English Language and Literature [/] 1934. 50pp.
           Chicago: privately printed [The University of Chicago
           Libraries], 1937. [T]

*[2760]   Hamilton, G[eorge] Rostrevor. *Poetry and Its Contemplation* [/]
           A New Preface to Poetics. Cambridge, Eng.: At the Uni-
           versity Press, 1937. [C: 104-105]

 [2761]   James, D[avid] G[wilym]. *Skepticism and Poetry* [/] *An Essay
           on the Poetic Imagination*. 274pp. London: George Allen &
           Unwin Ltd., 1937. [C: 115-120, 133, 244, 270]

*[2762] Johnson, Edgar. *One Mighty Torrent: The Drama of Biography*.
        [?]pp. New York: Stackpole Sons, 1937. [C: 237-244,
        252-259, 268-270]

[2763] Lucas, F. L. *The Decline and Fall of the Romantic Ideal.* [ix]+
        236pp. Cambridge, Eng.: At the University Press,
        [second printing:] 1937.   [C: 13, 39, 46, 51, 60, 98,
        113-114, 117, 148, 207-208, 231]

[2764] Mason, Francis Claiborne. *A Study of Shelley Criticism* [/]
        *An Examination of the Principal Interpretations of Shelley's
        Art and Philosophy in England from 1818 to 1860.*   [A Disserta-
        tion Presented to the Academic Faculty of the   Univer-
        sity of Virginia in Candidacy for the Degree of Doctor
        of Philosophy. 1929]. 176pp. Mercersburg, Penn.:
        privately printed, 1937. [C]

[2765] Pollock, J[ohn] H[ackett]. *The Moth and the Star* [/] *A
        Surmise.* 337pp. Dublin: The Talbot Press Limited,
        1937. [Fictionalized B]

[2766] Spender, Stephen. "Keats and Shelley," 574-587 in *From
        Anne to Victoria* [/] *Essays by Various Hands.*   Edited by
        Bonamy Dobree. x+630pp. London: Cassell and Co.,
        Ltd., 1937. [C]

                              1938

Periodicals:

[2767] White, Newman I[vey]. *"Studies in Shelley.* By Amiyakumar
        Sen. Calcutta: Calcutta University Press, 1936. Pp.
        xvi + 343.," *MLN*, LIII, No. 1 (January, 1938), 71-72.
        [R: item 2715]

[2768] De Ricci, Seymour. "Shelley Letter," *The Times Literary
        Supplement* [London], No. 1875 (January 8, 1938), 28.   [T]

[2769] Carlson, C. Lennert. "Shelley et la France. By Henri
        Peyre. Le Caire: Imprimerie Paul Barbey, 1935. Pp.
        509.," *Modern Philology*, XXXV, No. 3 (February, 1938),
        342-344. [R, as indicated]

[2770] Fleisher, David. "Shelley Letter," *The Times Literary
        Supplement* [London], No. 1882 (February 26, 1938), 140.
        [T]

*[2771] Church, Richard. "More Than the Wife of Shelley," *The
        Christian Science Monitor*, Magazine Section (March 9,
        1938), 10.   [?B]

[2772] Hort, G. M. "'Never to Remove,'" *English*, II, No. 7
        ([Spring], 1938), 29-40. [Fictionalized B, on Fanny
        Godwin]

[2773] Pettit, Henry Jewett. "Shelley and Denon's 'Voyage dans
        la Haute et la Basse Egypte,'" *Revue de la Littérature
        Comparée*, XVIII, No. 2 (April-June, 1938), 326-334.

[2774] Verkoren, L[ucas]. "A Note on the Shelley Bibliography
        1908-1922," *English Studies*, XX, No. 2 (April, 1938),
        61. [C]

[2775] [Booth, Bradford A.]. "Shelley and Mary," *The Times Liter-
        ary Supplement* [London], No. 1891 (April 30, 1938), 304.
        [T]

[2776] Nitchie, Elizabeth. "Mary Shelley," *The Times Literary Sup-
        plement* [London], No. 1891 (April 30, 1938), 296. [B,
        T]

*[2777] Lea, F[rank] A[lfred]. "Shelley and Pacifism," *New Adelphi*,
         XIV (May, 1938), 231-235. [C]

[2778] [Anonymous]. "The Expulsion of Shelley," *The Times Literary
        Supplement* [London], No. 1896 (June 4, 1938), 388. [R:
        item 2788]

[2779] Carver, P. L. *"The Magic Plant: The Growth of Shelley's Thought.*
        By Carl Grabo. Chapel Hill: University of North Caro-
        lina Press; London: Oxford University Press. 1936.
        Pp. viii + 450. $4.00; 18s.," *The Review of English
        Studies*, XIV, No. 55 (July, 1938), 365-370. [R: item
        2712]

[2780] Parker, W. M. "A Shelley Letter," *The Times Literary Supple-
        ment* [London], No. 1903 (July 23, 1938), 494. [T]

[2781] [Signed "Hibernicus."]. "Actaeon: Myth and Moralizing,"
        Notes and Queries, CLXXV, No. 4 (July 30, 1938), 74-76.
        [C]

[2782] [Anonymous]. "Shelley and His Contemporaries [/] A Col-
        lection of Criticisms," *The Times Literary Supplement* [Lon-
        don], No. 1907 (August 20, 1938), 544. [R: item 2797]

[2783] White, Newman I[vey]. "Unpublished Letters," *The Times
        Literary Supplement* [London], No. 1910 (September 10,
        1938), 584. [M]

[2784] Carver, P. L. *"Shelley's Religion.* By Ellsworth Barnard.
        Minneapolis: University of Minnesota Press; London:
        H. Milford. 1937. Pp. xiii + 320. $3.50; 16s. net.,"
        The Review of English Studies, XIV, No. 56 (October, 1938),
        480-487. [R: item 2752]

[2785]   Verkoren, L[ucas].   "The Unextinguished Hearth.   Shelley
         and His Contemporary Critics.   By Newman I. White.
         XVI and 397 pp.   8 vo.   Duke University Press, Durham,
         North Carolina.   1938 $3.00," *English Studies*, XX, No. 5
         (October, 1938), 228-230.   [R: item 2797]

[2786]   Verkoren, L[ucas].   "Erratum [for item 2774]," *English
         Studies*, XX, No. 5 (October, 1938), 230.   [C]

[2787]   Clark, David Lee.   "Shelley and *Pieces of Irish History*," *MLN*,
         LIII, No. 7 (November, 1938), 522-525.   [T]

Books:

[2788]   Blunden, Edmund, Gavin de Beer, and Sylva Norman.   *On
         Shelley*.   vi+99pp.   London: Humphrey Milford [/] Oxford
         University Press, 1938.   [B,C: Edmund Blunden, "Shelley
         Is Expelled," (1)-33; Gavin de Beer, "The Atheist: An
         Incident at Chamonix," (35)-54; Sylva Norman, "Mary
         Shelley: Novelist and Dramatist," (55)-99]

*[2789]   Brewer, Luther Albertus.   *My Leigh Hunt Library* [/] *The Holo-
         graph Letters*.   vi+421pp.   Iowa City, Iowa: University
         of Iowa Press, 1938.   [B]

[2790]   Cappon, Alexander Patterson.   *The Scope of Shelley's Philosoph-
         ical Thinking* [/] A part of a dissertation submitted to
         the faculty of the humanities in candidacy for the
         degree of Doctor of Philosophy [/] Department of
         English Language and Literature [/] 1935.   [7pp.   num-
         bered 135-141].   Chicago: "Private Edition, Distrib-
         uted by The University of Chicago Libraries," 1938.
         [C]

[2791]   Grylls, R[osalie] Glynn.   *Mary Shelley* [/] *A Biography*.
         xvi+345pp.   London: Oxford University Press, 1938.   [B]

[2792]   MacNeice, Louis.   *Modern Poetry* [/] *A Personal Essay*.   xix+
         205pp.   Oxford: At the Clarendon Press, 1938.   [C:
         3-4, 50, 87, 202]

[2793]   Murry, John Middleton.   *Heroes of Thought*.   xiii+368pp.
         New York: Julian Messner, 1938.   [C: "Shelley (/) Means
         and Ends," 294-312; published in England as *Heaven—and
         Earth*.   383pp.   London: J. Cape, (1938), "Percy Bysshe
         Shelley 1792-1822 (/) Chapt. XXIII (/) Means and Ends,"
         305-323; revised and rptd. from item 2640]

*[2794]   Ransom, John Crowe.   *The World's Body*.   [?]pp.   New York:
         Charles Scribner's Sons, 1938.   [C: 244-245]

[2795]   Roy, P. N.   *Shelley's Epipsychidion* [/] *A Study*.   53pp.
         Calcutta: The Modern Publishing Syndicate, 1938.   [C]

[2796]   Starkie, Walter.   *The Waveless Plain* [/] *An Italian Autobiog-*
         raphy.   xviii+509pp.   New York: E. P. Dutton & Co.,
         1938.   [M: xiii-xv, xvii, 107]

[2797]   White, Newman Ivey.   *The Unextinguished Hearth* [/] *Shelley and*
         His Contemporary Critics.   xvi+397pp.   Durham, N.C.: Duke
         University Press, 1938.   [C]

*[2798]   Workman, A. Maud.   *Percy Bysshe Shelley.*   [?]pp.   Bristol:
         [?], 1938.   [?B]

                                1939

Periodicals:

*[2799]   [Anonymous].   "Shelley is Permitted to Return," *The Canadian*
         Bookman, XXI, No. [?] ([?], 1939), 9.   [M]

[2800]   Carver, P. L.   *"Power and Elusiveness in Shelley.*   By O. W.
         Firkins.   Minneapolis: University of Minnesota Press;
         London: H. Milford.   1937.   Pp. iv + 187. $2.50;
         11s. 6d. net.," *The Review of English Studies*, XV, No. 57
         (January, 1939), 108-110.   [R: item 2758]

[2801]   Clark, David Lee.   "The Date and Source of Shelley's *A*
         Vindication of Natural Diet," *Studies in Philology*, XXXVI,
         No. 1 (January, 1939), 70-76.   [T,C]

[2802]   Clark, David Lee.   *"The Unextinguished Hearth, Shelley and his*
         Contemporary Critics.   By Newman I. White.   Durham, N.C.:
         Duke University Press, 1938.   Pp. xvi + 397. $3.00.,"
         MLN,   LIV, No. 1 (January, 1939), 71-72.   [R: item 2797]

[2803]   Davenport, William H.   "Shelley and the British Govern-
         ment," *Notes and Queries*, CLXXVI, No. 2 (January 14,
         1939), 26.   [B]

[2804]   Millhauser, Milton.   "Shelley: A Reference to Ricardo in
         'Swellfoot the Tyrant.,'" *Notes and Queries*, CLXXVI,
         No. 2 (January 14, 1939), 25-26.   [C]

[2805]   Partington, Wilfred.   "Some Marginalia," *The Times Literary*
         Supplement [London], No. 1930 (January 28, 1939), 64.
         [B]

[2806]   White, William.   "Fifteen Years of Shelley Scholarship:
         A Bibliography, 1923-1938," *English Studies*, XXI, No. 1
         (February, 1939), 8-11.   [C]

[2807]   Burke, Charles Bell.   "Coleridge and Shelley," *Notes and*
         Queries, CLXXVI, No. 6 (February 11, 1939), 98-99.   [C]

[2808] Clark, David Lee. "XIII. Shelley and Shakespeare," *PMLA*,
        LIV, No. 1 (March, 1939), 261-287. [C]

[2809] Goodspeed, George T. "The 'First American' Queen Mab,"
        Colophon, New Graphic Series I (March, 1939), 25-32.
        [T]

[2810] Prescott, F. C. "What Shelley Said," *The Saturday Review
        of Literature*, XIX, No. 19 (March 4, 1939), 9. [C]

[2811] [Signed "T.C.C."]. "Coleridge and Shelley (clxxvi. 98).,"
        Notes and Queries, CLXXVI, No. 9 (March 4, 1939), 159.
        [C]

[2812] Notopoulos, James A. "The Datings of Shelley's Notes and
        Translations from Plato," *Modern Language Review*, XXXIV,
        No. 2 (April, 1939), 245-248. [T]

[2813] Davenport, William H. "Footnote for a Political Letter of
        Shelley.," *Notes and Queries*, CLXXVI, No. 14 (April 8,
        1939), 236-237. [T]

[2814] Jones, Frederick L. "Shelley and the Don Juan," *The Times
        Literary Supplement* [London], No. 1942 (April 22, 1939),
        233. [B]

[2815] Moorman, Lewis J. "Percy Bysshe Shelley: Tuberculosis
        and Genius," *Annals of Medical History* [New York], Third
        Series I, No. 3 (May, 1939), 260-282. [B; rptd.: item
        2854]

[2816] [Anonymous]. "Memorabilia," *Notes and Queries*, CLXXVI, No.
        8 (May 6, 1939), 307. [C of item 2808]

[2817] [Anonymous]. "The Poet's Defence. By J. Bronowski.
        (Cambridge University Press. 7s 6d. net.)," *Notes and
        Queries*, CLXXVI, No. 20 (May 20, 1939), 359-360. [R:
        item 2833]

[2818] Verkoren, L[ucas], and William White. "Addenda to the
        Shelley Bibliography, 1923-1938," *English Studies*, XXI,
        No. 3 (June, 1939), 120. [C]

[2819] Verkoren, L[ucas]. "*On Shelley*. By Edmund Blunden, Gavin
        de Beer, and Sylva Norman. VI and 99pp. With a fron-
        tispiece. Oxford University Press, 1938. 5s. net.,"
        English Studies, XXI, No. 3 (June, 1939), 140. [R:
        item 2788]

[2820] [Anonymous]. "Shelley Returns to Eton," *The Times Literary
        Supplement* [London], No. 1949 (June 10, 1939), 341. [B]

[2821] Grylls, R[osalie] Glynn. "A Shelley Portrait," *The Times
        Literary Supplement* [London], No. 1950 (June 17, 1939),

358. [B]

[2822] Notopoulos, James A. "Note on the Text of Shelley's Translation of the 'Symposium,'" *Modern Language Review*, XXXIV, No. 3 (July, 1939), 421-422. [T]

[2823] White, Newman I[vey]. "Probable Dates of Composition of Shelley's 'Letter to Maria Gisborne' and 'Ode to a Skylark,'" *Studies in Philology*, XXXVI, No. 3 (July, 1939), 524-528. [T]

[2824] Quercus, P. E. G. "Trade Winds," *The Saturday Review of Literature*, XX, No. 37 (July 8, 1939), 24. [B]

[2825] Nitchie, Elizabeth. "Shelley in 'Fraser's' and the Annuals," *The Times Literary Supplement* [London], No. 1960 (August 26, 1939), 503. [T]

[2826] Smith, John Harrington. "Shelley and Claire Clairmont," *PMLA*, LIV, No. 3 (September, 1939), 785-814. [B,C]

[2827] Davenport, William H. "Notes on Shelley's Political Prose: Sources, Bibliography, Errors in Print.," *Notes and Queries*, CLXXVII, No. 13 (September 23, 1939), 223-225. [T]

[2828] Doughty, Oswald. "*Mary Shelley*. A Biography. By R. Glynn Grylls. London: Oxford University Press. 1938. xvi + 345pp. 18s. [/] *The Unextinguished Hearth. Shelley and his Contemporary Critics*. By Newman Ivey White. Durham, N.C.: Duke University Press. 1938. xvi + 397pp. $3.00. [/] *On Shelley*. London: Oxford University Press. 1938. vii + 99pp. 5s.," *The Modern Language Review*, XXXIV, No. 4 (October, 1939), 600-603. [R: items 2791, 2797, 2788]

[2829] Skeat, W. W. "To a Hedge-Cricket," *Notes and Queries*, CLXXVII, No. 24 (December 9, 1939), 417. [C]

[2830] Jones, Frederick L. "The Illustrious Obscure," *The Times Literary Supplement* [London], No. 1975 (December 16, 1939), 731. [B]

*[2831] Sayers, George. "The Critic's Shelley," *Blackfriars*, XX, No. [?] ([?], 1939), 24-33. [?R]

Books:

*[2832] Brooks, Cleanth. *Modern Poetry and the Tradition*. [?]pp. Chapel Hill, N.C.: University of North Carolina Press, 1939. [C]

[2833] Bronowski, J[acob]. *The Poet's Defence*. 258pp. Cambridge: At the University Press, 1939. [C: "Sidney & Shelley," (17)-86 ("Percy Bysshe Shelley," [57]-86)]

[2834] Grylls, R[osalie] Glynn. *Claire Clairmont [/] Mother of Byron's Allegra*. xii+304pp. London: John Murray, 1939. [B]

[2835] Hughes, A[rthur] M[ontague] D['Urban]. "Warton Lecture on English Poetry [/] The Theology of Shelley [/] By A. M. D. Hughes [/] Read 26 October 1938," [191]-203 in *Proceedings of the British Academy [/] 1938*. [Volume XXIV]. xvi+422pp. London: Humphrey Milford [/] Oxford University Press, [1939]. [C]

[2836] Lewis, C[live] S[taples]. *Rehabilitations [/] And Other Essays*. viii+197pp. London: Oxford University Press, 1939. [C: "Shelley, Dryden, and Mr. Eliot," (3)-34]

[2837] Oras, Ants. "On Some Aspects of Shelley's Poetic Imagery," *Acta et Commentationes Universitatis Tartuensis* [Tartu, Estonia: University of Tartu], B, XLIII, No. 4 (1939), 1-71. [C]

1940

Periodicals:

[2838] Fairchild, Hoxie N[eale]. "The Romantic Movement in England," *PMLA*, LV, No. 1 (March, 1940), 20-26. [C]

[2839] Knickerbocker, William S. "Arnold, Shelley, and Joubert," *MLN*, LV, No. 3 (March, 1940), 201. [C]

[2840] Lowes, John Livingston. "IX. *The Witch of Atlas* and *Endymion*," *PMLA*, LV, No. 1 (March, 1940), 203-206. [C]

[2841] Notopoulos, James A. "The Dating of Shelley's Fragment, 'The Moral Teachings of Jesus Christ,'" *Modern Language Review*, XXXV, No. 2 (April, 1940), 215-216. [T]

[2842] Braunlich, Alice F. "Parallels to Some Passages in *Prometheus Unbound*," *MLN*, LV, No. 6 (June, 1940), 428-429. [C]

[2843] Watson, Sara Ruth. "6. Shelley and Shakespeare: An Addendum. —A Comparison of *Othello* and *The Cenci*," *PMLA*, LV, No. 2 (June, 1940), 611-614. [C]

[2844] Welker, John J. "The Position of the Quarterlies on Some Classical Dogmas," *Studies in Philology*, XXXVII, No. 3 (July, 1940), 542-562. [M: 542-543]

[2845]   Armstrong, Margaret. "Trelawny," *The Atlantic Monthly*, CLXVI,
         No. 2 (August, 1940), 177-188. [B]

[2846]   Baker, Carlos [Heard]. "The Permanent Shelley," *The Sewanee
         Review*, XLVIII, No. 4 (October-December, 1940), [512]-
         516. [C]

[2847]   Evans, III, Frank B. "Shelley, Godwin, Hume, and the
         Doctrine of Necessity," *Studies in Philology*, XXXVII,
         No. 4 (October, 1940), 632-640. [C]

[2848]   Baker, Carlos [Heard]. "A Note on Shelley and Milton,"
         MLN, LV, No. 8 (December, 1940), 585-589. [C]

[2849]   Aldington, Richard. "Percy B. Shelley," *The Saturday Review
         of Literature*, XXIII, No. 7 (December 7, 1940), 7. [R:
         item 2863]

[2850]   [Anonymous]. "Poet of Revolution," *Time*, XXXVI, No. 25
         (December 16, 1940), 98 and 101. [R: item 2863]

Books:

[2851]   Armstrong, Margaret. *Trelawney* [sic] [/] *A Man's Life*. 380pp.
         New York: The Macmillan Company, 1940. [B]

[2852]   Evans, B. Ifor. *Tradition and Romanticism* [/] *Studies in English
         Poetry from Chaucer to W. B. Yeats*. London: Methuen & Co.
         Ltd., 1940. [C: "Shelley," (139)-155]

*[2853] Irvine, Magnus. *The Unceasing Quest*. [?]pp. London:
         Thynne, 1940. [C]

[2854]   Moorman, Lewis J. *Tuberculosis and Genius*. xxxv+[272]pp.
         Chicago: The University of Chicago Press, 1940. [B:
         "Percy Bysshe Shelley," 192-234; rptd. from item 2815]

[2855]   Nitchie, Elizabeth. *The Reverend Colonel Finch*. 109pp. New
         York: Columbia University Press, 1940. [B]

[2856]   Noyes, Alfred. *Pageant of Letters*. 356pp. New York: Sheed
         & Ward, 1940. [C: "Shelley," 107-150]

[2857]   Power, Julia. *Shelley in America in the Nineteenth Century: His
         Relation to American Critical Thought and His Influence*. [*Univer-
         sity of Nebraska Studies*, XL, No. 2 (April, 1940)]. vii+
         225pp. Lincoln, Neb.: University of Nebraska Press,
         1940. [C]

[2858]   Robinson, Edwin Arlington. *Selected Letters of Edwin Arlington
         Robinson*. Edited by Ridgely Torrance. x+191pp. New
         York: The Macmillan Company, 1940. [M: 86]

[2859]   Saurat, Denis. *Literature and the Occult Tradition* [/] *Studies in Philosophical Poetry*. Translated by Dorothy Bolton. viii+[246]pp. London: G. Bell and Sons Ltd., 1940. [Numerous M: 6-70, fully indexed]

[2860]   Shuster, George N. *The English Ode from Milton to Keats*. [Columbia University Studies in English and Comparative Literature, Number 150]. vi+314pp. New York: Columbia University Press, 1940. [C: 243n-244n, 257-262, 272-273]

*[2861]   Starrett, Vincent. "Murder and Sudden Death," 95-97 in *Books Alive: A Profane Chronicle of Literary Endeavor and Literary Misdemeanor*. With an Informal Index by Christopher Morley. New York: Random House, 1940. [B]

*[2862]   Wells, Henry W. *New Poets from Old: A Study in Literary Genetics*. [?]pp. New York: Columbia University Press, 1940. [C]

[2863]   White, Newman Ivey. *Shelley*. 2 vols. New York: Alfred A. Knopf, 1940. [B; revised edition, London: Secker & Warburg, 1947]

                              1941

Periodicals:

[2864]   Notopoulos, James A. "Shelley's Translation of the 'Ion' of Plato," *The Modern Language Review*, XXXVI, No. 1 (January, 1941), 98-105. [T]

[2865]   Notopoulos, James A. "Additional Note [/] Shelley's Translation of the 'Ion' of Plato (pp. 98-105 above)," *The Modern Language Review*, XXXVI, No. 1 (January, 1941), 155. [T]

[2866]   Baker, Carlos [Heard]. "Spenser, the Eighteenth Century, and Shelley's *Queen Mab*," *Modern Language Quarterly*, II, No. 1 (March, 1941), 81-98. [C]

[2867]   Cameron, Kenneth N[eill]. "XI. A Major Source of *The Revolt of Islam*," *PMLA*, LVI, No. 1 (March, 1941), 175-206. [C]

[2868]   C[lark], D[avid] L[ee]. "White, Newman Ivey. Shelley. New York. Alfred Knopf. 2 vols. Pp. 748; 642 + index.," *ELH*, VIII, No. 1 (March, 1941), 19-21. [R: item 2863]

[2869]   Glasheen, Francis J. "Shelley's Use of Gray's Poetry," *MLN*, LVI, No. 3 (March, 1941), 192-196. [C]

[2870]   Harper, Robert D.   "The Shelley Biography," *Poetry: A Magazine of Verse*, LVII, No. 6 (March, 1941), 386-389.   [R: item 2863]

[2871]   Wright, Walter Francis.   "Shelley's Failure in *Charles I*," *ELH*, VIII, No. 1 (March, 1941), 41-46.   [C]

[2872]   Griggs, Earl Leslie.   "Seeing Shelley Plain," *The Virginia Quarterly Review*, XVII, No. 2 (Spring, 1941), 310-313.   [R: item 2863]

[2873]   [Anonymous].   "Reprints," *The Times Literary Supplement* [London], No. 2045 (April 12, 1941), 183.   [M]

*[2874]   Trilling, Lionel.   "Shelley Plain," *The New Republic*, CIV, No. [?] (May 5, 1941), 637-638.   [R: item 2863]

[2875]   Baker, Carlos [Heard].   "XXVIII. Literary Sources of Shelley's *The Witch of Atlas* [/] I. Spenser and *The Witch of Atlas*," *PMLA*, LVI, No. 2 (June, 1941), 472-479.   [C]

[2876]   Clark, David Lee.   "[XXVIII. Literary Sources of Shelley's *The Witch of Atlas*] II. What Was Shelley's Indebtedness to Keats?" *PMLA*, LVI, No. 2 (June, 1941), 479-494.   [C]

[2877]   [Anonymous].   "Memorabilia," *Notes and Queries*, CLXXX, No. 23 (June 7, 1941), 397.   [M]

[2878]   [Anonymous].   "More About Shelley   [/] From Star Gold to Earth Dust," *The Times Literary Supplement* [London], No. 2055 (June 21, 1941), 302.   [R: item 2863]

[2879]   Cline, C[larence] L[ee].   "Unpublished Notes on the Romantic Poets by Isaac D'Israeli," *Studies in English* [*The University of Texas Publication; No. 4126*] (July 8, 1941), [138]-146.   [C]

[2880]   Cluck, Julia.   "XLV. Elinor Wylie's Shelley Obsession," *PMLA*, LVI, No. 3 (September, 1941), 841-860.   [C]

[2881]   Tinker, Chauncey Brewster.   "Shelley Once More," *The Yale Review*, New Series XXXI, No. 1 (September, 1941), [87]-94.   [C; rptd.: item 3177]

[2882]   Jones, Frederick L.   "Shelley in Rome," *The Times Literary Supplement* [London], No. 2069 (September 27, 1941), 483.   [B]

[2883]   Cameron, Kenneth N[eill].   "A New Source of Shelley's *A Defence of Poetry*," *Studies in Philology*, XXXVIII, No. 4 (October, 1941), 629-644.   [C]

[2884] Carver, P. L. *"Shelley in America in the Nineteenth Century.* By
Julia Power. (University Studies. Published by the
University of Nebraska, Vol. xl, No. 2.) Lincoln, Neb:
The University of Nebraska, 1940. Pp. viii + 225.
$1.50.," *The Review of English Studies*, XVII, No. 68 (Octo-
ber, 1941), 485-487. [R: item 2857]

[2885] Harper, George McLean. "Professor White's 'Shelley,'"
The Times Literary Supplement [London], No. 2070 (October 4,
1941), 495. [R: item 2863]

[2886] Glasheen, Francis [J]. "Shelley and Peacock," *The Times
Literary Supplement* [London], No. 2072 (October 18, 1941),
524. [C]

[2887] [Signed "N."]. "Shelley's 'Adonais.,'" *Notes and Queries*,
CLXXXI, No. 16 (October 18, 1941), 218. [T]

[2888] Notopoulos, James A. "Notes on the Text of Shelley's
Translations from Plato," *MLN*, LVI, No. 7 (November,
1941), 536-541. [T]

[2889] Beall, Chandler B. "A Tasso Quotation in Shelley,"
Modern Language Quarterly, II, No. 4 (December, 1941),
609-610. [C]

[2890] Siegel, Paul. "'A Paradise with Thee" in Milton, Byron,
and Shelley," *MLN*, LVI, No. 8 (December, 1941), 615-
617. [C]

[2891] White, Newman I[vey]. *"Shelley in America in the Nineteenth
Century: His Relation to American Critical Thought and His
Influence.* By Julia Power. Lincoln: University of
Nebraska, 1940. Pp. viii + 224. $1.50.," *MLN*, LVI,
No. 8 (December, 1941), 638. [R: item 2857]

[2892] Caldwell, James R[alston]. "The Solemn Romantics," *The
University of California Publications in English*, VIII, No. 2
([?], 1941) [Berkeley, Calif.: University of California
Press, 1941], 251-271. [C]

Books:

[2893] Daniels, Earl. *The Art of Reading Poetry.* vii+579pp. New
York: Rinehart & Company, Inc., 1941. [C: 354-359,
392-395]

[2894] Hicks, Arthur C. "An American Performance of *The Cenci*,"
287-311 in *Standford Studies in Language and Literature*.
Edited by Hardin Craig. vi+387pp. [Palo Alto], Calif:
[School of Letters] Stanford University Press, 1941.
[C; a special miscellany issued to commemorate the
fiftieth anniversary of Stanford University, and not

to be confused with a journal of the same title]

[2895] Hungerford, Edward B. *Shores of Darkness.* 314pp. New
        York: Columbia University Press, 1941. [C: "Shelley's
        Prometheus," (163)-215; "Shelley's Adonais," (216)-
        239]

*[2896] Jenney, Shirley Carson. *Great War Cloud.* [?]pp. North
        Devon, Eng.: Arthur H. Stockwell, 1941. [A clairaudi-
        tor's transcription of material purportedly by Percy
        Bysshe Shelley]

[2897] Knight, G. Wilson. *The Starlit Dome* [/] *Studies in the Poetry
        of Vision.* 314pp. London: Oxford University Press,
        1941. [C: "The Naked Seraph: An Essay on Shelley,"
        (179)-257]

*[2898] Ransom, John Crowe. *The New Criticism.* [?]pp. Norfolk,
        Conn.: New Directions, 1941. [C: 208, 249-250, 302]

*[2899] Schnittkind, Henry Thomas, and Dana Arnold Schnittkind.
        Living Biographies of Great Poets. [?]pp. Garden City,
        N.Y.: The Garden City Publishing Company, 1941. [B:
        "Percy Bysshe Shelley," 139-151]

[2900] Tate, Allen. *Reason in Madness* [/] *Critical Essays.* [?]pp.
        New York: G. P. Putnam's Sons, 1941. [C: 65, 97]

[2901] Woods, George B., Homer A. Watt, and George K. Anderson,
        eds. *The Literature of England* [/] *An Anthology and a History.*
        2 vols. Chicago: Scott, Foresman and Company, [second
        edition] 1941. [C, T: "Percy Bysshe Shelley," II,
        254-279]

                                1942

Periodicals:

*[2902] Spender, Stephen. "Shelley's Adonais," *The Listener*, [?]
        (January 22, 1942), [?p]. [?C]

[2903] [Anonymous]. "*The Starlit Dome.* By G. Wilson Knight. (Ox-
        ford University Press. 16s. net.)," *Notes and Queries*,
        CLXXXII, No. 5 (January 31, 1942), 56. [R: item 2897]

[2904] Nitchie, Elizabeth. "*Shelley.* By Newman Ivery White.
        2 vols. New York: A. A. Knopf, 1940. Pp. xvi + 748,
        x + 642 + cxlvii. 12.50.," *MLN*, LVII, No. 3 (March,
        1942), 221-223. [R: item 2863]

[2905] Gutteling, J[ohanna] F[rederika] C[ornelia]. "Shelley's
        Idealism—and Its Reverse," *Neophilologus*, XXVII, No. 3

(April, 1942), 213-220. [C]

[2906] Cameron, Kenneth Neill. "Shelley and *Ahrimanes*," *Modern Language Quarterly*, III, No. 2 (June, 1942), 287-295. [C]

[2907] Baker, Carlos [Heard]. *"Shores of Darkness*. By Edward B. Hungerford. New York: Columbia University Press, 1941. Pp. 314. $3,00.," *Modern Language Quarterly*, III, No. 2 (June, 1942), 338-340. [R: item 2895]

[2908] Cameron, Kenneth Neill. "XXX. Shelley *vs.* Southey: New Light on an Old Quarrel," *PMLA*, LVII, No. 2 (June, 1942), 489-512. [C]

[2909] Cherubini, William. "Shelley's 'Own Symposium': *The Triumph of Life*," *Studies in Philology*, XXXIX, No. 3 (July, 1942), 559-570. [C]

[2910] [Signed "P.F."]. "The Education of Keats and Shelley: A Note with Some Queries," *Notes and Queries*, CLXXXIII, No. 2 (July 18, 1942), 45. [B]

[2911] Grabo, Carl. "Spinoza and Shelley," *The Chicago Jewish Forum*, I, No. 1 (Fall, 1942), 43-50. [C]

[2912] Jones, Frederick L. "Shelley and Spenser," *Studies in Philology*, XXXIX, No. 4 (October, 1942), 662-669. [C]

[2913] The Editors [John P. Kirby]. "5. Shelley's *Lines Written Among the Euganean Hills*," *The Explicator*, I, No. 1 (October, 1942), [unnumbered page]. [C]

[2914] Pfeiffer, Karl G. "Landor's Critique of *The Cenci*," *Studies in Philology*, XXXIX, No. 4 (October, 1942), 670-679. [C]

[2915] Cameron, Kenneth Neill. "The Social Philosophy of Shelley," *The Sewanee Review*, L, No. 4 (October, 1942), [457]-466. [C]

[2916] The Editors [George Arms]. "22. Shelley's *Adonais*," *The Explicator*, I, No. 3 (December, 1942), [unnumbered page]. [C]

[2917] Cameron, Kenneth Neill. "Shelley and the *Conciones ad Populum*," *MLN*, LVII, No. 8 (December, 1942), 673-674. [C]

[2918] Jordan, John E. "Wordsworth and *The Witch of Atlas*," *ELH*, IX, No. 4 (December, 1942), 320-325. [C]

Books:

*[2919] Blunden, Edmund. "Romantic Poetry and the Fine Arts,"

(Warton Lecture on English Poetry), 103-118 in *Proceedings of the British Academy*, XXVIII. [?]pp. London: Humphrey Milford [/] Oxford University Press, (1942). [C]

*[2920] Grabo, Carl H., and Martin J. Freeman, eds. *The Reader's Shelley: Selections with Introduction, Bibliography and Notes.* [?]pp. New York: The American Book Company, 1942. [T,C]

[2921] Miles, Josephine. *Pathetic Fallacy in the Nineteenth Century [/] A Study of a Changing Relation Between Object and Emotion.* [University of California Publications in English, XII, No. 2]. vi+[183-]304pp. Berkeley, Calif.: University of California Press, 1942. [C: 206-212, 256-258; M]

*[2922] Roy, P. N. *Shelley and Italian Literature [/] A Study in Poetical Derivation.* [?]pp. London: Arthur Probsthain, 1942. [C]

*[2923] Van Doren, Mark. *The Private Reader: Selected Articles and Reviews.* [?]pp. New York: Henry Holt & Co., 1942. [B; "Shelley's First Child," 174-177]

[2924] Woolf, Virginia. *The Death of the Moth and other Essays.* 157pp. London: The Hogarth Press, 1942. [C: "'Not One of Us,'" 78-83, a review of item 2452]

1943

Periodicals:

[2925] Cameron, Kenneth Neill. "*Rasselas* and *Alastor:* A Study in Transmutation," *Studies in Philology*, XL, No. 1 (January, 1943), 58-78. [C]

[2926] Glasheen, Adeline E., and Francis J. Glasheen. "The Publication of the 'Wandering Jew,'" *Modern Language Review*, XXXVIII, No. 1 (January, 1943), [11]-17. [T]

[2927] Super, R. H. "Landor's Critique of *The Cenci*—A Correction," *Studies in Philology*, XL, No. 1 (January, 1943), 101. [C]

[2928] Cameron, Kenneth Neill. "A Reference to Shelley in *The Examiner*," *Notes and Queries*, CLXXXIV, No. 2 (January 16, 1943), 42. [C]

[2929] Dudley, Fred A. "31. Shelley's *Stanzas Written in Dejection Near Naples*," *The Explicator*, I, No. 4 (February, 1943), [unnumbered page]. [C]

[2930]   Mukherjee, K.   "Shelley and India," *The New Review* [Cal-
         cutta], XVII, No. 98 (February, 1943), [101]-114.   [C]

[2931]   Dudley, Fred A.   "Q 23.   Shelley's *Lines: 'When the Lamp Is
         Shattered,'" The Explicator*, I, No. 5 (March, 1943), [unnum-
         bered page].   [C]

[2932]   [Dick, Hugh G.]   "[Untitled, following item 2931]," *The
         Explicator*, I, No. 5 (March, 1943), [unnumbered page].
         [C]

[2933]   Nitchie, Elizabeth.   "39.   Shelley's Adonais," *The Explica-
         tor*, I, No. 5 (March, 1943), [unnumbered page].   [C]

[2934]   Mabbot, T[homas] O.   "[Untitled, following item 2933],"
         The Explicator, I, No. 5 (March, 1943), [unnumbered page].
         [C]

[2935]   Elwin, Malcolm.   "Robert Southey," *The Times Literary Supple-
         ment* [London], No. 2,147 (March 27, 1943), 151.   [B]

[2936]   Boas, Louise Schutz.   "48.   Shelley's *Lines: 'When the Lamp
         Is Shattered,'" The Explicator*, I, No. 6 (April, 1943),
         [unnumbered page].   [C]

[2937]   Cameron, Kenneth Neill.   "Shelley Cobbett, and the Na-
         tional Debt," *The Journal of English and Germanic Philology*,
         XLII, No. 2 (April, 1943), 197-209.   [C]

[2938]   Roberts, John Hawley.   "49.   Shelley's *Epipsychidion*," *The
         Explicator*, I, No. 6 (April, 1943), [unnumbered page].
         [C]

[2939]   Murison, J. W.   "Author and Context Wanted," *Notes and
         Queries*, CLXXXIV, No. 16 (April 24, 1943), 262.   [T]

[2940]   Gibson, Daniel.   "51.   Shelley's *Lines: 'When the Lamp Is
         Shattered,'" The Explicator*, I, No. 7 (May, 1943), [unnum-
         bered page].   [C]

[2941]   Philbrick, F. A.   "[Untitled, following item 2940]," *The
         Explicator*, I, No. 7 (May, 1943), [unnumbered page].   [C]

[2942]   Macbeth, Gilbert.   "[Untitled, following item 2941]," *The
         Explicator*, I, No. 7 (May, 1943), [unnumbered page].   [C]

[2943]   Looker, Samuel J.   "Author and Context Wanted (clxxiv.
         262.)," *Notes and Queries*, CLXXXIV, No. 20 (May 22, 1943),
         325.   [T]

[2944]   Baker, Carlos [Heard].   "The Traditional Background of
         Shelley's Ivy-Symbol," *Modern Language Quarterly*, IV, No. 2
         (June, 1943), 205-208.   [C]

[2945] Notopoulos, James A. "XXVI. The Dating of Shelley's Prose," *PMLA*, LVIII, No. 2 (June, 1943), 477-498. [T]

[2946] Notopoulos, James A. "8. The Platonic Sources of Shelley's 'Hymn to Intellectual Beauty,'" *PMLA*, LVIII, No. 2 (June, 1943), 582-584. [C]

[2947] [Signed "A.W.V."]. "Voice and Verse," *Notes and Queries*, CLXXXIV, No. 22 (June 5, 1943), 344. [C]

[2948] Nitchie, Elizabeth. "Mary Shelley's *Mathilda*: An Unpublished Story and Its Biographical Significance," *Studies in Philology*, XL, No. 3 (July, 1943), 447-462. [B]

[2949] Rajan, B. "The Motivation of Shelley's Prometheus Unbound," *The Review of English Studies*, XIX, No. 75 (July, 1943), 297-301. [C]

[2950] [Signed "Psychologist"]. "Voice and Verse (clxxiv. 344).," *Notes and Queries*, CLXXXV, No. 1 (July 3, 1943), 28. [C]

[2951] Cameron, Kenneth Neill. "XL. The Political Symbolism of *Prometheus Unbound*," *PMLA*, LVIII, No. 3 (September, 1943), 728-753. [C]

[2952] Gay, Robert M. "6. Shelley's *Lines: 'When the Lamp Is Shattered,'*" *The Explicator*, II, No. 1 (October, 1943), [unnumbered page]. [C]

[2953] Jones, Frederick L. "Mary Shelley and Claire Clairmont," *The South Atlantic Quarterly*, XLII, No. 4 (October, 1943), [406]-412. [B]

[2954] Ridley, M. R. "*Shores of Darkness*. By Edward B. Hungerford. New York: Columbia University Press, 1942. Pp. x + 314. 20s. net.," *The Review of English Studies*, XIX, No. 76 (October, 1943), 439. [R: item 2895]

[2955] [Signed "W.W.F."]. "Q 8. Shelley's *Prometheus Unbound*," *The Explicator*, II, No. 2 (November, 1943), [unnumbered page]. [C]

[2956] [Signed "W.J.M."]. "Q 12. Shelley's *Ode to Liberty*," *The Explicator*, II, No. 2 (November, 1943), [unnumbered page]. [C]

[2957] Kessel, Marcel. "An Early Review of the Shelleys' 'Six Weeks' Tour,'" *MLN*, LVIII, No. 8 (December, 1943), 623. [C]

[2958] Mabbott, T[homas] O. "24. Shelley's *Prometheus Unbound*, III, iv," *The Explicator*, II, No. 3 (December, 1943), [unnumbered page]. [C]

[2959] Friedland, Louis S. "[Untitled, following item 2958],"
        The Explicator, II, No. 3 (December, 1943), [unnumbered
        page]. [C]

*[2960] Marsh, George L. "The 'Peter Bell' Parodies of 1819,"
        Modern Philology, XL, No. [?] ([?], 1943), 267-274. [M]

Books:

*[2961] Barzun, Jaques. *Romanticism and the Modern Ego.* [?]pp.
        Boston: Little, Brown and Co., 1943. [M]

*[2962] Bowra, C[ecil] M[aurice]. *The Heritage of Symbolism.* [?]pp.
        London: Macmillan and Co. Ltd., 1943. [C: 29, 30, 35,
        180, 223, 228]

[2963] Larrabee, Stephen A. *English Bards and Grecian Marbles* [/] *The
        Relationship Between Sculpture and Poetry Especially in the
        Romantic Period.* ix+312pp. New York: Columbia University
        Press, 1943. [C: "Shelley (/) Greece: 'The Crystalline
        Sea of Thought,'" (175)-203]

[2964] Maurois, André [pseud. of Emile Salomon Wilhelm Herzog].
        "The Ethics of Biography," 6-28 in *English Institute
        Annual* [/] *1942.* xi+207pp. New York: Columbia Univer-
        sity Press, 1943. [B]

[2965] Scott, Walter Sidney, ed. *The Athenians* [/] *Being Correspondence
        between Thomas Jefferson Hogg and His Friends Thomas Love Peacock,
        Leigh Hunt, Percy Bysshe Shelley, and Others.* 86+1pp. London:
        The Golden Cockerel Press, 1943. [T,B; revised and
        rptd.: item 3175]

[2966] White, Newman I[vey]. "The Development, Use and Abuse of
        Interpretation in Biography," 29-58 in *English Institute
        Annual* [/] *1942.* xi+207pp. New York: Columbia Univer-
        sity Press, 1943. [B]

1944

Periodicals:

[2967] Smith, John Harrington. "Shelley and Claire Again," *Studies
        in Philology*, XLI, No. 1 (January, 1944), 94-105. [B]

[2968] Stevenson, Lionel. "Tennyson, Browning, and a Romantic
        Fallacy," *University of Toronto Quarterly*, XIII, No. 2
        (January, 1944), 175-195. [C]

[2969] B[lunden], E[dmund]. "Sir Timothy Shelley," *Notes and
        Queries*, CLXXXVI, No. 1 (January 1, 1944), 23. [B]

[2970]   [Signed "R.H."].   "'Love's Philosophy.,'" *Notes and Queries*,
         CLXXXVI, No. 2 (January 15, 1944), 49.   [C]

[2971]   Glasheen, Adeline E.   "Shelley's First Published Review of
         Mandeville," *MLN*, LIX, No. 3 (March, 1944), 172-173.
         [T]

[2972]   Guerard, Jr., Albert.   "Prometheus and the Aeolian Lyre,"
         The Yale Review, New Series XXXIII, No. 3 (March, 1944),
         [482]-497.   [C]

[2973]   Nitchie, Elizabeth.   "Variant Readings in Three of Shel-
         ley's Poems," *MLN*, LIX, No. 4 (April, 1944), 274-277.
         [T]

[2974]   Sackville-West, Edward.   "Books in General," *New Statesman
         and Nation*, XXVII, No. 684 (April 1, 1944), 227.   [C]

[2975]   [Anonymous].   "Friends of Shelley [/] T. Jefferson Hogg's
         Claim to Fame   [/]   Light from a Long-Hidden Letter,"
         The Times Literary Supplement [London], No. 2,203 (April 22,
         1944), 198.   [R: item 2965]

[2976]   Glasheen, Francis J.   "An Early Quotation from Shelley,"
         MLN, LIX, No. 5 (May, 1944), 335.   [T]

[2977]   Boas, Louise Schutz.   "59.   Shelley's *Ode to Liberty*, Stanzas
         XVI and XVII," *The Explicator*, II, No. 8 (June, 1944),
         [unnumbered page].   [C]

[2978]   Jones, Frederick L.   "4.   Shelley and Shakespeare: A
         Supplement," *PMLA*, LIX, No. 2 (June, 1944), 591-596.
         [C]

[2979]   McElderry, Jr., B[ruce] R.   "Common Elements in Words-
         worth's 'Preface' and Shelley's *Defence of Poetry*," *Modern
         Language Quarterly*, V, No. 2 (June, 1944), 175-181.   [C]

[2980]   Mercedes, Sister Anna.   "Two Paths from Plato [/] Shelley
         and St. Augustine," *The Catholic World*, CLIX, No. 952
         (July, 1944), 326-328.   [C]

[2981]   Einstein, Lewis.   "Shelley and Stendahl," *The Times Literary
         Supplement* [London], No. 2,216 (July 22, 1944), 355.   [B,
         C]

[2982]   Earp. T. W.   "Shelley and Stendahl," *The Times Literary Sup-
         plement* [London], No. 2,217 (July 29, 1944), 367.   [B]

*[2983] Norman, Sylva.   "Confessions of Shelley,"   *Fortnightly
         Review*, New Series CXLVI [whole number CLXII], No.
         dccccxxxii (August, 1944), 116-120.   [R: item 2965]

*[2984] Nicolson, Harold. "Marginal Comment," *The Spectator*, CLXXIII, No. [?] (August 4, 1944), 102. [B]

[2985] Archer, Jerome W. "*Kubla Khan: Queen Mab*, II, 4-79; VIII, 70-103, and *Alastor*, 81-94; 163-172," *Studies in Philology*, XLI, No. 4 (October, 1944), 576-581. [C]

[2986] Frye, Northrop. "The Nature of Satire," *University of Toronto Quarterly*, XIV, No. 1 (October, 1944), 75-89. [C]

[2987] [Anonymous]. "Shelley Secrets [/] Harriet, Mary and T. J. Hogg," *The Times Literary Supplement* [London], No. 2,230 (October 28, 1944), 527. [R: item 3000]

[2988] Boas, Louise Schutz. "14. Shelley's *Lines Written Among the Euganean Hills*," *The Explicator*, III, No. 2 (November, 1944), [unnumbered page]. [C]

[2989] Kessel, Marcel. "13. Shelley's *Lines: 'When the Lamp Is Shattered,'*" *The Explicator*, III, No. 2 (November, 1944), [unnumbered page]. [C]

[2990] Spender, Stephen. "Books in General," *New Statesman and Nation*, XXVIII, No. 718 (November 25, 1944), 355. [B]

[2991] Jones, Frederick L. "Shelley's Revised Will," *MLN*, LIX, No. 8 (December, 1944), 542-544. [B]

[2992] Kaderly, Nat Lewis. "The Stoppage of Shelley's Income in 1821," *MLN*, LIX, No. 8 (December, 1944), 545-547. [B]

[2993] Notopoulos, James A. "A Shelleyan Symbol," *The Classical Journal*, XL, No. 3 (December, 1944), 170-172. [C]

[2994] Smith, Robert Metcalf. "A Chapter in The Shelley Legend [/] The Letter to Mary Shelley of December 16, 1816," *The Papers of the Bibliographical Society of America*, XXXVIII, No. 3 (December, 1944), 312-334 + 8 plates. [T]

[2995] Ward, William S. "Shelley and the Reviewers Once More," *MLN*, LIX, No. 8 (December, 1944), 539-544. [C]

[2996] Evans, Bergen. "Shelley and Sir William," *Time*, XLIV, No. 25 (December 18, 1944), 4. [C]

Books:

[2997] Beach, Joseph Warren. *A Romantic View of Poetry* [/] Being Lectures Given at Johns Hopkins University on the Percy Turnbull Memorial Foundation in November 1941. 133pp. Minneapolis, Minn.: The University of Minnesota Press, 1944. [C: "Poetry as Dialectic," 110-133; 40, 76-81]

[2998]   Grierson, Herbert J. C., and J. C. Smith. *A Critical History*
         of English Poetry. viii+539pp. New York: Oxford Univer-
         sity Press, [1944]. [C: "Shelley," 350-369]

[2999]   Peyre, Henri. *Writers and Their Critics: A Study of Misunder-*
         standing. xii+340pp. Ithaca, N.Y.: Cornell University
         Press, 1944. [C: 30-34; M: forty-two mentions, fully
         indexed]

[3000]   Scott, Walter Sidney, ed. *Harriet and Mary [/] Being the Rela-*
         tions Between Percy Bysshe Shelley, Harriet Shelley, Mary Shelley,
         and Thomas Jefferson Hogg [/] As Shown in Letters between Them
         Now Published for the First Time. 84pp. London: The Golden
         Cockerel Press, 1944. [T,B; revised and rptd.: item
         3175]

[3001]   Scott, Walter Sidney, ed. *Shelley at Oxford [/] The Early Cor-*
         respondence of P. B. Shelley with his Friend T. J. Hogg together
         with Letters of Mary Shelley and T. L. Peacock and a hitherto
         unpublished Prose Fragment by Shelley. 79pp. London: The
         Golden Cockerel Press, 1944. [T,B; revised and rptd.:
         item 3175]

[3002]   Shelley, Mary W[ollstonecraft]. *The Letters of Mary W.*
         Shelley. Edited by Frederick L. Jones. 2 vols.
         Norman, Okla.: University of Oklahoma Press, 1944.   [T]

[3003]   Thomas, Gilbert. *Builders and Makers [/] Occasional Studies.*
         219pp. London: The Epworth Press, 1944. [C: "Percy
         Bysshe Shelley," (150)-163]

                              1945

Periodicals:

[3004]   [Anonymous]. "The Idol of Completeness," *The Times Literary*
         Supplement [London], No. 2,240 (January 6, 1945), 7.   [M]

[3005]   [Anonymous]. "Mary Shelley: The Years After the Trag-
         edy," *The Times Literary Supplement* [London], No. 2,240
         (January 6, 1945), 8. [R: item 3002]

[3006]   Roberts, Harry. "Shelley and Harriet Wetsbrook," *The New*
         Statesman and Nation, XXIX, No. 731 (February 24, 1945),
         126.   [B]

[3007]   Cameron, Kenneth Neill. "Shelley and the Reformers," *ELH,*
         XII, No. 1 (March, 1945), 62-85.   [C]

[3008]   Hott [*sic* for Hort], G. M. "Shelley and Harriet West-
         brook," *The New Statesman and Nation,* XXIX, No. 732

(March 3, 1945), 142. [B]

[3009] Gamlen, J. C. B. "[Untitled, following item 3008]," *The New Statesman and Nation*, XXIX, No. 732 (March 3, 1945), 142. [B]

[3010] Hudleston, C. Roy. "Shelley and Harriet," *The New Statesman and Nation*, XXIX, No. 733 (March 10, 1945), 158. [B]

[3011] Roberts, Harry. "[Untitled, following item 3010]," *The New Statesman and Nation*, XXIX, No. 733 (March 10, 1945), 158. [B]

[3012] Meyerstein, E. H. W. "'Epipsychidion' and 'The Hound of Heaven,'" *The Times Literary Supplement* [London], No. 2,250 (March 17, 1945), 127. [C]

[3013] [Signed "Sayar"]. "Burying the Heart Separately," *Notes and Queries*, CLXXXVIII, No. 6 (March 24, 1945), 128. [M]

[3014] Leavis, F[rank] R[aymond]. "'Thought' and Emotional Quality [/] Notes in the Analysis of Poetry," *Scrutiny*, XIII, No. 1 (Spring, 1945), 53-71. [C: 59-61, 66-70]

[3015] Clark, David Lee. "An Unpublished Shelley Letter," *MLN*, LX, No. 5 (May, 1945), 330-333. [T]

[3016] [Anonymous]. "The Liberties of T. J. Hogg," *The Times Literary Supplement* [London], No. 2,257 (May 5, 1945), 212. [R: item 3001]

[3017] Hamilton, G[eorge] Rostrevor. "Shelley's Own," *English*, V, No. 29 (Summer, 1945), 149-153. [C]

[3018] Cameron, Kenneth Neill. "Shelley's Use of Source Material in *Charles I*," *Modern Language Quarterly*, VI, No. 2 (June, 1945), 197-210. [C]

[3019] Hort, G. M. "Firstborn of Ariel," *The Contemporary Review*, CLXIX, No. 966 (June, 1946), 362-366. [B]

[3020] Norman, Sylva. "Shelley and the Greeks," *The Nineteenth Century*, CXXXVII, No. 820 (June, 1945), 245-253. [R: item 2965]

[3021] Ward, William S. "XXXIX. Some Aspects of the Conservative Attitude Toward Poetry in English Criticism, 1798-1820.," *PMLA*, LX, No. 2 (June, 1945), 386-398. [C]

[3022] Jones, Frederick L. "Shelley and Hogg," *The Times Literary Supplement* [London], No. 2,264 (June 23, 1945), 295. [B, T]

[3023]   Norman, Sylva. *"Shelley at Oxford,"* *The Fortnightly*, New Series
         CLVIII [whole number CLXIV], No. 943 (July, 1945), 67-
         68. [R: item 3001]

[3024]   [Anonymous]. "Thoughts on Shelley," *The Times Literary
         Supplement* [London], No. 2,268 (July 21, 1945), 344.
         [R: item 3041]

[3025]   Fogle, Richard H[arter]. "Romantic Bards and Metaphysical
         Reviewers," *ELH*, XII, No. 3 (September, 1945), 221-250.
         [C]

[3026]   [Anonymous]. "Memorabilia," *Notes and Queries*, CLXXXIX,
         No. 6 (September 22, 1945), 111-112. [C]

[3027]   Meyerstein, E. H. W. "[Untitled subsection of "Correspon-
         dence"]," *English*, V, No. 30 (Autumn, 1945), 219-220.
         [C]

[3028]   Fogle, Richard H[arter]. "The Abstractness of Shelley,"
         Philological Quarterly, XXIV, No. 4 (October, 1945), 362-
         379. [C]

[3029]   [Signed "W.E.J."]. "Q 2. Shelley's 'Final Chorus' from
         'Hellas,'" *The Explicator*, IV, No. 2 (October, 1945), [un-
         numbered page]. [C]

[3030]   Thomson, James S. "The Unbinding of Prometheus," *Univer-
         sity of Toronto Quarterly*, XV, No. 1 (October, 1945), 1-
         16. [C]

[3031]   [Anonymous]. "'The Cenci' on the Stage," *The Times Literary
         Supplement* [London], No. 2,282 (October 27, 1945), 509.
         [R: item 3039]

[3032]   Forman, Elsa. "'The Cenci,'" *The Times Literary Supplement*
         [London], No. 2,284 (November 10, 1945), 535. [C]

[3033]   [Anonymous]. "Seeing Shelley Plainer," *Time*, XLVI, No. 21
         (November 19, 1945), 103 and 105. [R: item 3046]

[3034]   Dubu, Jean. "'The Cenci' on the Stage," *The Times Literary
         Supplement* [London], No. 2,286 (November 24, 1945), 559.
         [C]

[3035]   Ratchford, Fanny E[lizabeth], and William Manly. "Shelley
         Meets the Texas Legislature," *Southwest Review*, XXX, No. 2
         (Winter, 1945), 161-166. [T,C]

[3036]   Cameron, Kenneth N[eill], and Horst Frenz. "LXV. The
         Stage History of Shelley's *The Cenci*," *PMLA*, LX, No. 4
         (December, 1945), 1080-1105. [C]

[3037] Wilson, Jean C. S. "P. B. Shelley: Homo Not Too Sap-
iens," *The Saturday Review of Literature*, XXVIII, No. 51
(December 22, 1945), 8-9. [R: item 3046]

[3038] [Anonymous]. "The Larger Entente," *The Times Literary Supplement* [London], No. 2,291 (December 29, 1945), 619. [C]

Books:

[3039] Hicks, Arthur C., and R. Milton Clarke. *A Stage Version of
Shelley's Cenci.* 156pp. Caldwell, Idaho: The Caxton
Printers Ltd., 1945. [T,C]

[3040] Jenney, Shirley Carson. *The Fortune of Eternity [/] by Percy
Bysshe Shelley.* 124pp. New York: The William-Frederick
Press, 1945. [A clairauditor's transcription of material purportedly by Percy Bysshe Shelley; verse and
prose]

[3041] Lea, F[rank] A[lfred]. *Shelley [/] And the Romantic Revolution.*
ix+289pp. London: Routledge, 1945. [C]

[3042] Muir, Kenneth. "Shelley's Heirs," *The Penguin New Writing*,
[volume] 26 (1945), 117-132. [C]

*[3043] Nelson, Lawrence Emerson. *Our Roving Bible.* Nashville,
Tenn.: Abingdon Cokesbury Press, 1945. [C: "Our
Damaged Archangels," 143-144]

[3044] Read, Herbert. *A Coat of Many Colours.* viii+352pp. London:
G. Routledge & Sons, 1945. [C: "Shelley," 119-128]

*[3045] Rideout, John Granville. *Rhetoric, Symbolism, and Imagery in
the Poetry of Percy Bysshe Shelley.* [Unpublished doctoral
dissertation]. [?]pp. Providence, R.I.: [Brown University, 1945. [C]

[3046] Smith, Robert Metcalf, Martha Mary Schlegel, Theodore
George Ehrsam and Louis Addison Waters. *The Shelley
Legend.* vii+343pp. New York: Charles Scribner's Sons,
1945. [B,C,T]

[3047] Smith, Robert Metcalf. "Shelley's 'Proposal for Reform,'"
*Elizabethan Studies and Other Essays [/] In Honor of George F.
Reynolds [University of Colorado Studies*, Series B, *Studies
in the Humanities*, volume 2, No. 4 ([Boulder, Colo.]
October, 1945), 286-293. [C]

[3048] White, Newman Ivey. *Portrait of Shelley.* 482+xxiiipp.
New York: Alfred A. Knopf, 1945. [B; revised, con-
densed, unannotated version of item 2863]

Periodicals:

[3049] McAdam, E. L. "Smith, Robert Metcalf and others. *The Shelley Legend.*," *The Papers of the Bibliographical Society of America*, XL, No. 1 (January, 1946), 81-83. [R: item 3046]

*[3050] Pinto, V[ivian] de S[ola]. "The English Romantics and France," *The Spectator*, CLXXVI, No. [?] (January 4, 1946), 14. [C]

[3051] [Anonymous]. "Mary Shelley and G. H. Lewes," *The Times Literary Supplement* [London], No. 2,293 (January 12, 1946), 24. [B]

[3052] Hubach, Robert R. "Was Keats 'The Sensitive Plant'?" *Notes and Queries*, CXC, No. 3 (February 9, 1946), 49-51. [C]

[3053] Cameron, Kenneth Neill. "Shelley and Aristotle," *Notes and Queries*, CXC, No. 4 (February 23, 1946), 80. [C]

[3054] [Signed "S.B.P."]. "'The Witch of Atlas.,'" *Notes and Queries*, CXC, No. 4 (February 23, 1946), 76-79. [C]

[3055] [Signed "S.B.P."]. "Thamondacana.," *Notes and Queries*, CXC, No. 4 (February 23, 1946), 82. [C]

[3056] Fogle, Richard H[arter]. "X. Empathic Imagery in Keats and Shelley," *PMLA*, LXI, No. 1 (March, 1946), 163-191. [C]

[3057] B[lunden], E[dmund]. "Harriet Shelley.," *Notes and Queries*, CXC, No. 5 (March 9, 1946), 102. [B]

[3058] B[lunden], E[dmund]. "'The Witch of Atlas' (cxc. 76).," *Notes and Queries*, CXC, No. 6 (March 23, 1946), 126. [C]

[3059] [Signed "S.B.P."]. "[Untitled, following item 3058]," *Notes and Queries*, CXC, No. 6 (March 23, 1946), 126-127. [C]

[3060] [Signed "R.W."]. "Shelley, Emerson, and Sir William Osler.," *Notes and Queries*, CXC, No. 6 (March 23, 1946), 120-121. [C]

[3061] Esdaile, Arundel. "[Untitled, subsection of "Correspondence"]," *English*, VI, No. 31 (Spring, 1946), 40. [C]

[3062] Ellis-Fermor, Una. "A Stage Version of Shelley's 'Cenci'.

By Arthur C. Hicks and R. Milton Clarke. Caldwell, Idaho: The Caxton Printers. 1945. 156pp. $3.50.," *The Modern Language Review*, XLI, No. 2 (April, 1946), 212-213. [R: item 3039]

[3063] Gohn, Ernest Salisbury. *"A Stage Version of Shelley's Cenci.* By Arthur C. Hicks and R. Milton Clarke. Caldwell, Idaho: The Caxton Printers, Ltd., 1945. Pp 156. $3.50.," *MLN*, LXI, No. 4 (April, 1946), 287. [R: item 3039]

[3064] Sencourt, Robert. "Art 6. —Byron and Shelley at the Lake of Geneva.," *The Quarterly Review*, CCLXXXIV, No. 568 (April, 1946), 209-221. [B]

[3065] [Signed "D.Q."]. "Authors and Sources Wanted (clxxxiii. 138).," *Notes and Queries*, CXC, No. 8 (April 20, 1946), 175. [M]

[3066] Norman, Sylva. "Some Truths about Shelley," *The Fortnightly*, New Series CLXI [whole number CLXVII], [No. 953] (May, 1946), [353]-354. [R: item 3046]

[3067] [Anonymous]. "The Man Shelley," *The Times Literary Supplement* [London], No. 2,309 (May 4, 1946), 210. [R: item 3095]

[3068] [Anonymous]. "Memorabilia," *Notes and Queries*, CXC, No. 10 (May 18, 1946), 199. [M]

[3069] McNully, J. H. "The Man Shelley," *The Times Literary Supplement* [London], No. 2,312 (May 25, 1946), 247. [C]

[3070] Baker, Carlos [Heard]. "Shelley's Translation from Aristotle," *MLN*, LXI, No. 6 (June, 1946), 405-406. [T]

[3071] Thompson, L. C. "Shelley and Keats," *The Times Literary Supplement* [London], No. 2,317 (June 29, 1946), 307. [C]

[3072] Millhauser, Milton. "The Noble Savage in Mary Shelley's *Frankenstein*.," *Notes and Queries*, CXC, No. 12 (June 15, 1946), 248-250. [C]

[3073] [Signed "R.W.H."]. "Gift of Shelley Manuscripts," *The Bodleian Library Record*, II, No. 24 (July, 1946), 144-145. [T]

[3074] Havens, Raymond D[exter]. *"Hellas and Charles The First,"* *Studies in Philology*, XLIII, No. 3 (July, 1946), 545-550. [C]

[3075] White, Newman I[vey]. *"The Shelley Legend* Examined," *Studies in Philology*, XLIII, No. 3 (July, 1946), 522-524. [R: item 3046; rptd. in *An Examination of the Shelley Legend* (Philadelphia, 1951)]

[3076]   [Anonymous].   "Memorabilia," *Notes and Queries*, CXCI, No. 1
         (July 13, 1946), 1.   [T]

[3077]   Blunden, E[dmund].   "Harriet Shelley," *The Times Literary
         Supplement* [London], No. 2,319 (July 13, 1946), 331   [B]

[3078]   [Anonymous].   "Memorabilia," *Notes and Queries*, CXCI, No. 2
         (July 27, 1946), 23.   [R: item 3095]

[3079]   Ehrsam, Theodore G.   "Mary Shelley in Her Letters," *Modern
         Language Quarterly*, VII, No. 3 (September, 1946), 297-
         302.   [T]

[3080]   Jones, Frederick L.   "'The Shelley Legend,'" *PMLA*, LXI,
         No. 3 (September, 1946), 848-890.   [R: item 3046;
         rptd. in *An Examination of the Shelley Legend* (Philadelphia,
         1951)]

[3081]   Cameron, Kenneth Neill.   "A New Shelley Legend," *The Journal
         of English and Germanic Philology*, XLV, No. 4 (October,
         1946), 369-379.   [R: item 3046; rptd. in *An Examination
         of the Shelley Legend* (Philadelphia, 1951)]

[3082]   Verkoren, L[ucas].   "A Note on Shelley's Sonnet 'Lift not
         the painted veil,'" *English Studies*, XXVII, No. 5 (Octo-
         ber, 1946), 156.   [C]

[3083]   [Anonymous].   "An Oxford Poet," *The Times Literary Supplement*
         [London], No. 2.332 (October 12, 1946), 493.   [T]

[3084]   Gates, Payson G.   "In Defense of Leigh Hunt," *The Times
         Literary Supplement* [London], No. 2,332 (October 12,
         1946), 500.   [B]

[3085]   [Anonymous].   "Memorabilia," *Notes and Queries*, CXCI, No. 8
         (October 19, 1946), 155.   [M]

[3086]   [Anonymous].   "Shelley: How Legends Are Made," *The Times
         Literary Supplement* [London], No. 2,334 (October 26,
         1946), 522.   [R: item 3046]

[3087]   Brown, J. J.   "The Shelley Legend," *The Canadian Forum*, XXVI,
         No. 310 (November, 1946), 181.   [R: item 3046]

[3088]   Munby, A. N. L.   "Universal Suffrage, 1811," *The Times
         Literary Supplement* [London], 2,339 (November 30, 1946),
         596.   [T]

[3089]   [Signed "G.W."].   "Shelley: A Life Story. By Edmund
         Blunden. London and Toronto: Collins. 1946. Pp. 320.
         $4.00.," *Queen's Quarterly*, LIII, No. 4 (Winter, 1946-47),
         517-518.   [R: item 3095]

[3090]   Albrecht, William Price.   "23. Shelley's *Queen Mab*, VIII,
          109-111; *Ode to Liberty*, XVII, 246-247," *The Explicator*,
          V, No. 3 (December, 1946), [unnumbered page].   [C]

[3091]   Jones, Frederick L.   "The Inconsistency of Shelley's
          Alastor," *ELH*, XIII, No. 4 (December, 1946), 291-298.
          [C]

[3092]   Pratt, Willis W[inslow].   *"The Shelley Legend*, by Robert
          Metcalf Smith, in collaboration with Martha Mary
          Schlegel, Theodore George Ersham [*sic*], and Louis
          Addison Waters. New York: Charles Scribner's Sons,
          1945. Pp. xiv + 343. $5.00.," *MLN*, LXI, No. 8 (Decem-
          ber, 1946), 571-573.   [R: item 3046]

[3093]   Sterling, E. L.   "Shelley's Grave," *The Times Literary Supple-
          ment* [London], No. 2,341 (December 7, 1946), 603.   [B]

[3094]   Tyler, Henry.   "'Thrillers' at Eton," *The Times Literary
          Supplement* [London], No. 2,343 (December 28, 1946), 643.
          [B]

Books:

[3095]   Blunden, Edmund.   *Shelley. A Life Story*.   320pp. London:
          William Collins, Sons & Co., Ltd., 1946.   [B; New
          York: Viking Press, 1947]

*[3096]   Gordon, George.   *The Discipline of Letters*.   [?]pp. Oxford:
          At the Clarendon Press, 1946.   [C: "Shelley and the
          Oppressors of Mankind," 69-82; rptd. from item 2357]

[3097]   Grierson, Herbert J. C., and Sandys Wason.   *The Personal
          Note [/] Or [/] First and Last Words from Prefaces, Introductions
          [/] Dedications, Epilogues*.   viii+190pp. London: Chatto &
          Windus, 1946.   [T: "Percy Bysshe Shelley (/) Prometheus
          Unbound (/) A Lyrical Drama (/) 1820 (/) Audisne haec
          Amphiarae, sub terram abdite? (/) Preface," 123-127]

[3098]   Häusermann, H. W.   "W. B. Yeats's Idea of Shelley," 179-
          194 in *The Mint [/] A Miscellany of Literature, Art and
          Criticism*.   Edited by Geoffrey Grigson. xii+220pp.
          London: Routledge and Sons Ltd., 1946.   [C]

[3099]   Jenney, Shirley Carson.   *Moments with Shelley [/] Taken Thro'
          the Clairaudience of Shirley Carson Jenney Psychic*. 55pp.
          Culver City, Calif.: The Highland Press, [?1946].
          [A clairauditor's transcription of material purportedly
          by Percy Bysshe Shelley]

[3100]   Laird, John.   *Philosophical Incursions into English Literature*.
          223pp. Cambridge, Eng.: At the University Press, 1946.
          [C: "Shelley's Metaphysics," 116-135]

[3101]   Martin-Baynat, Robert.   *Shelley* [/] *A Prelude*.   ix+76pp.
         [Bournemouth]: privately printed, 1946.   [C]

*[3102]   Rollins, Hyder.   *Keats' Reputation in America to 1848*.   [?]pp
         Cambridge, Mass.: Harvard University Press, 1946.   [M]

                              1947

Periodicals:

[3103]   Jones, Frederick L.   "The Vision Theme in Shelley's
         Alastor and Related Works," *Studies in Philology*, XLIV,
         No. 1 (January, 1947), 108-125.   [C]

[3104]   Sencourt, Robert.   "Art 7. —Byron and Shelley in
         Venice.," *The Quarterly Review*, CCLXXXV, No. 571 (January,
         1947), 84-97.   [B]

[3105]   Fairchild, Hoxie N[eale].   "Tennyson and Shelley," *The
         Times Literary Supplement* [London], No. 2,345 (January 11,
         1947), 23.   [C]

[3106]   [Anonymous].   "Supreme Capacity," *Time*, XLIX, No. 2 (Janu-
         ary 13, 1947), 108, 110, and 112. [R: item 3095]

[3107]   Perkins, John Ward.   "Keats and Shelley," *The Times Literary
         Supplement* [London], No. 2,352 (February 15, 1947), 91.
         [B]

[3108]   Rashbrook, R. F.   "Keats and Others.," *Notes and Queries*,
         CXCII, No. 8 (April 19, 1947), 161-164.   [M]

[3109]   [Anonymous].   "The Youth of Shelley," *The Times Literary
         Supplement* [London], No. 2,360 (April 26, 1947), 195.
         [R: item 3136]

[3110]   Mead, Douglass S.   "Q 20. Shelley's *Ode to the West Wind*,"
         The Explicator, V, No. 7 (May, 1947), [unnumbered page].
         [C]

[3111]   Fremantle, Anne.   "Shelley: A Life Story. Edmund Blunden.
         Viking. $3.75.," *The Commonweal*, XLVI, No. 4 (May 9,
         1947), 96-97. [R: item 3095]

*[3112]   Baker, Carlos.   "Spender's Blue Plate," *The New York Times
         Book Review*, LII, No. [?] (May 18, 1947), 4 and 38.   [R:
         3141]

[3113]   Parker, W. M.   "Charles Ollier to William Blackwood," *The
         Times Literary Supplement* [London], No. 2,366 (June 7,
         1947), 288.   [B]

[3114]   Cohane, J. J.   "Shelley," *The Commonweal*, XLVI, No. 10
         (June 20, 1947), 238-239.   [C; reply to item 3111]

[3115]   [Anonymous].   "Two Poets," *The Times Literary Supplement* [Lon-
         don], No. 2,375 (August 9, 1947), 403.   [C]

[3116]   Griffiths, J. Gwyn.   "Shelley and Diodorus," *The Times
         Literary Supplement* [London], No. 2,376 (August 16,
         1947), 415.   [C]

[3117]   Jones, Frederick L.   "XLIII. Shelley's *On Life*," *PMLA*,
         LXII, No. 3 (September, 1947), 774-783.   [C]

[3118]   Häusermann, H. W.   "The Villa Diodati," *The Times Literary
         Supplement* [London], No. 2,381 (September 20, 1947),
         479.   [B]

[3119]   Wormhoudt, Arthur.   "1. Shelley's *Ode to the West Wind*,"
         The Explicator, VI, No. 1 (October, 1947), [unnumbered
         page].   [C]

[3120]   Fogle, Richard Harter.   "[Untitled, following item 3119],"
         The Explicator, VI, No. 1 (October, 1947), [unnumbered
         page].   [C]

[3121]   [Anonymous].   "Shelley in the South," *The Times Literary
         Supplement* [London], No. 2,384 (October 11, 1947), 523.
         [R: item 3137]

[3122]   [Anonymous].   "More of Mary Shelley," *The Times Literary
         Supplement* [London], No. 2,387 (November 1, 1947), 560.
         [R: item 3140]

[3123]   Benet, William Rose.   "Shelley's Mary," *The Saturday Review of
         Literature*, XXX, No. 45 (November 8, 1947), 13 and 45.
         [R: item 3140]

[3124]   Tyler, Henry.   "Hunt and Shelley," *The Times Literary Supple-
         ment* [London], No. 2,388 (November 8, 1947), 577.   [B]

[3125]   Gibson, Evan K.   "LXII. *Alastor*: A Reinterpretation," *PMLA*,
         LXII, No. 4, Part I (December, 1947), 1022-1046.   [C]

[3126]   Kapstein, I[srael] J[ames].   "The Meaning of Shelley's
         'Mont Blanc,'" *PMLA*, LXII, No. 4, Part I (December,
         1947), 1046-1060.   [C]

*[3127] Glicksberg, Charles I.   "Herbert Read: Reason and Roman-
         ticism," *The University of Toronto Quarterly*, XVI, No. [?]
         ([?], 1947), 60-67.   [M: 62]

*[3128] Henkin, Leo J.   "Pugilism and the Poets," *The Modern Language
         Quarterly*, VIII, No. [?] ([?], 1947), 69-79.   [B]

*[3129]   Lamont, Corliss. "Naturalism and the Appreciation of
           Nature," *The Journal of Philosophy*, XLIV, No. [?] ([?],
           1947), 597-608. [C]

*[3130]   Rideout, John G[ranville]. "An Oxford Poet and Modern
           Times," *The American Oxonian*, XXXIV, No. [?] ([?], 1947),
           15-20. [B]

Books:

*[3131]   Aveling, E[dward Bibbins], and E[leanor] M[arx] Aveling.
           Shelley's Socialism [/] Two Lectures. [?]pp. Manchester:
           Leslie Preger, 1948 [1947]. [C; rptd. from item 1413]

[3132]   Baker, Carlos Heard. "Shelley's Ferrarese Maniac," *English
           Institute Essays, 1946*, [New York: Columbia University
           Press, 1947], [41]-73. [C]

[3133]   Barrell, Joseph. *Shelley and the Thought of his Time. A
           Study in the History of Ideas*. [Yale Studies in English,
           Volume 106]. viii+210pp. New Haven: Yale University
           Press, 1947. [C]

[3134]   Evans, Bertrand. *Gothic Drama from Walpole to Shelley*. [Uni-
           versity of California Studies in English, XVIII].
           viii+257pp. Berkeley and Los Angeles: University of
           California Press, 1947. [C: "Shelley's Cenci," 228-
           232]

[3135]   Howe, P[ercival] P[resland]. *The Life of William Hazlitt*.
           xxvi+433pp. London: Hamish Hamilton, 1947. [M: 151,
           208, 287-288, 292, 319, 320, 334, 337, 338, 342, 401;
           first published, London: Martin Secker, 1922]

[3136]   Hughes, A[rthur] M[ontague] D['Urban]. *The Nascent Mind of
           Shelley*. vii+272pp. Oxford: At the Clarendon Press,
           1947. [C,B; New York: Oxford University Press, 1948]

[3137]   Lehmann, John, ed. *Shelley in Italy [/] An Anthology*.   294pp.
           London: John Lehmann, 1947. [T,B]

[3138]   Lunn, Arnold. *Switzerland in English Prose and Poetry*. xxiii+
           262pp. London: Eyre & Spottiswoode, 1947. [C: "Percy
           Bysshe Shelley," 35-44]

[3139]   Pratt, W[illis] W[inslow]. *Lord Byron and His Circle [/] A
           Calendar of Manuscripts in the University of Texas Library*.
           56pp. Austin, Texas: [University of Texas], 1947.
           [T,B]

[3140]   Shelley, Mary [Wollstonecraft]. *Mary Shelley's Journal*.
           Edited by Frederick L. Jones. xxi+257pp. Norman,
           Okla.: University of Oklahoma Press, 1947. [B]

*[3141]   Spender, Stephen, ed.   *A Choice of English Romantic Poetry*.
           [?]pp. New York: The Dial Press, 1947. [M: 7-30;
           T: 204-298]

                              1948

Periodicals:

*[3142]   [Anonymous]. "Keats-Shelley Memorial in Rome," *The Bulletin
           of the John Rylands Library, Manchester*, XXXI, No. 1 (Janu-
           ary, 1948), 13-14. [M]

[3143]   Gates, Payson G. "Leigh Hunt's Review of Shelley's *Post-
          humous Poems*," *The Papers of the Bibliographical Society*, XLII,
          No. 1 (January, 1948), 1-40. [C]

[3144]   Griffiths, J. Gwyn. "Shelley's 'Ozymandias' and Diodorus
          Siculus," *Modern Language Review*, XLIII, No. 1 (January,
          1948), 80-84. [C]

[3145]   Himelick, Raymond. "Cabell, Shelley, and the 'Incorri-
          gible Flesh,'" *The South Atlantic Quarterly*, XLVII, No. 1
          (January, 1948), [88]-95. [C]

[3146]   Laser, Melvin. "The Growth and Structure of Poe's Concept
          of Beauty," *ELH*, XV, No. 1 (March, 1948), 69-84. [C]

[3147]   Meldrum, Elizabeth. "The Classical Background of
          Shelley," *Contemporary Review*, CLXXIII (March, 1948),
          160-165. [C]

[3148]   Weeks, Donald. "Image and Idea in Yeats' *The Second Coming*,"
          PMLA, LXIII, No. 1 (March, 1948), 281-292. [C]

[3149]   Mizener, Arthur. "The Scrutiny Group," *The Kenyon Review*, X,
          No. 2 (Spring, 1948), [355]-360. [M: 358]

[3150]   Vail, Curtis C. D. "Shelley's Translations from Goethe,"
          The Germanic Review, XXIII, No. 2 (April, 1948), 91-103.
          [C]

[3151]   [Anonymous]. "Shelley's Philosophy," *The Times Literary
          Supplement* [London], No. 2,414 (May 8, 1948), 263. R:
          item 3133]

[3152]   Nitchie, Elizabeth. "9. Shelley's 'Hymn to Intellectual
          Beauty,'" *PMLA*, LXIII, No. 2 (June, 1948), 752-753. [C]

*[3153]   Origo, Iris, Marchesa. "Byron's Last Attachment," *The
          Listener*, [?] (June 24, 1948), 1014-1015. [B]

[3154]   Grabo, Carl H.   *"Shelley and the Thought of His Time: A Study
         in the History of Ideas.* By Joseph Barrell. New Haven:
         Yale University Press. 1947. Pp. 210. $3.00.," *The
         Journal of English and Germanic Philology*, XLVII, No. 3 (July,
         1948), 313-318. [R: item 3133]

[3155]   Priestley, F. E. L.   "Newton and the Romantic Concept of
         Nature," *University of Toronto Quarterly*, XVII, No. 4 (July,
         1948), 323-336. [M: 326]

[3156]   Wain, John. *"The Nascent Mind of Shelley.* By A. M. D. Hughes.
         Pp. vii + 272. Oxford: Clarendon Press, 1947. 15s.
         net.," *The Review of English Studies*, XXIV, No. 95 (July,
         1948), 258-260. [R: item 3136]

[3157]   Weaver, Bennett. "Pre-Promethean Thought in the Prose of
         Shelley," *Philological Quarterly*, XXVII, No. 3 (July,
         1948), [193]-208. [C]

[3158]   Cameron, Kenneth Neill. "The Planet-Tempest Passage in
         Epipsychidion," *PMLA*, LXIII, No. 3 (September, 1948),
         950-972. [C]

[3159]   Fogle, Richard Harter. "The Imaginal Design of Shelley's
         'Ode to the West Wind,'" *ELH*, XV, No. 3 (September,
         1948), 219-226. [C]

[3160]   Hughes, A[rthur] M[ontague] D['Urban]. "'Alastor, or
         the Spirit of Solitude,'" *Modern Language Review*, XLIII,
         No. 4 (October, 1948), [465]-470. [C]

[3161]   Hughes, A[rthur] M[ontague] D['Urban]. *"Shelley and the
         Thought of His Time, a Study of the History of Ideas.* By Joseph
         Barrell. New Haven: Yale University Press; London:
         Geoffrey Cumberlege. 1947. ix + 207pp. 16s.,"
         Modern Language Review, XLIII, No. 4 (October, 1948),
         533. [R: item 3133]

[3162]   Koszul, A[ndré]. *"Shelley.* By Newman Ivery White. Vol. i,
         pp. xvi + 748; vol. ii, pp. x + 642 + cxlvii. London:
         Secker & Warburg, 1947. 3½ gns. net.," *The Review of
         English Studies*, XXIV, No. 96 (October, 1948), 338-341.
         [R: item 2863, revised edition]

*[3163]   Christensen, Francis. "From Heaven or Near It," *College
         English*, X, No. [?] (November, 1948), 107. [C]

[3164]   Jones, Frederick [L.]. "The Nascent Mind of Shelley.
         By A. M. D. Hughes. Oxford: At the Clarendon Press,
         1947. Pp. vii + 277pp. $5.00," *MLN*, LXIII, No. 8
         (December, 1948), 569-571. [R: item 3136]

[3165]   [Anonymous]. "The Shelley Circle," *The Times Literary Supple-
         ment* [London], No. 2,444 (December 4, 1948), 682. [R:

item 3175]

[3166] Baker, Carlos [Heard]. *"Shelley and the Thought of His Time: A Study in the History of Ideas.* By Joseph Barrell. New Haven: Yale University Press, 1947. Pp. viii + 210. $3.00. (Yale Studies in English, 106.)," *MLN*, LXIII, No. 8 (December, 1948), 571-572. [R: item 3133]

[3167] Blunden, Edmund. "A Word for Kirke White II," *Notes and Queries*, CXCII, No. 26 (December 24, 1948), 564-566. [C]

[3168] B[lunden], E[dmund]. "Thomas Medwin.," *Notes and Queries*, CXCII, No. 26 (December 24, 1948), 568. [B]

[3169] Wingo, Alice Logan. "Hark, Hark, the Lark," *College English*, IX, No. [?] ([?], 1948), 217. [C]

Books:

[3170] Baker, Carlos [Heard]. *Shelley's Major Poetry: the Fabric of a Vision.* 307pp. Princeton, N.J.: Princeton University Press, 1948. [C]

*[3171] Connolly, Francis X., ed. *Literature [/] The Channel of Culture.* [?]pp. New York: [?], 1948. [A textbook; Shelley:(?)pp]

[3172] Durand, Anthony. *Shelley on the Nature of Poetry.* 251pp. Quebec: Editions de l'Université Laval, 1948. [C]

[3173] James, D[avid] G. *The Romantic Comedy.* xi+276pp. London: Oxford University Press [/] Geoffrey Cumberlege, 1948. [C: 65-154]

[3174] Safroni-Middleton, A[rnold]. *Two Shelleys [/] An Interpretation and an Apologia.* 38pp. London: World Wide Press, 1948. [C,B]

[3175] Scott, W[alter] S[idney], ed. *New Shelley Letters.* [170]pp. London: The Bodley Head, 1948. [T; rptd. from items 2965, 3000, 3001]

[3176] Thomson, J[ames] A[lexander] K[err]. *The Classical Background of English Literature.* 272pp. London: George Allen & Unwin Ltd., [1948]. [C: 26, 75, 229, 230-233, 251]

*[3177] Tinker, Chauncey Brewster. *Essays in Retrospect [/] Collected Articles and Addresses.* [?]pp. New Haven: Yale University Press, 1948. [C: "Shelley Once More," 43-51; rptd. from item 2881]

Periodicals:

[3178] Tillotson, Geoffrey. *"The Nascent Mind of Shelley.* A. M. D.
        Hughes. Oxford: Clarendon Press. 1947. viii + 272pp
        15s.," *Modern Language Review*, XLIV, No. 1 (January,
        1949), 115-116. [R: item 3136]

[3179] Witcutt, W. P. "Shelley and Introverted Intuition," *The
        Wind and the Rain*, V, No. 3 (Winter, 1948-49 [January,
        1949]), 178-183. [B]

[3180] Notopoulos, James A. "Shelley and the *Symposium*," *The
        Classical Weekly*, XLII, No. 7 (January 10, 1949), [98]-
        102. [C]

[3181] Häusermann, W. H. "An Unpublished Letter from Shelley to
        Medwin," *Notes and Queries*, CXCIV, No. 2 (January 22,
        1949), 23-28. [T]

[3182] Langston, Beach. "Shelley's Use of Shakespeare," *The
        Huntington Library Quarterly*, XII, No. 2 (February, 1949),
        163-190. [C]

[3183] Häusermann, W. H. "An Unpublished Letter from Shelley to
        Medwin," *Notes and Queries*, CXCIV, No. 3 (February 5,
        1949), 49-57. [B]

[3184] [Anonymous]. "Evergreen," *The Times Literary Supplement*
        [London], No. 2,456 (February 19, 1949), 121. [B]

[3185] Weaver, Bennett. *"Prometheus Bound* and *Prometheus Unbound*,"
        PMLA, LXIV, No. 1 (March, 1949), 115-133. [C]

[3186] White, William. "An Armenian Performance of Shelley's *The
        Cenci*," *MLN*, LXIV, No. 3 (March, 1949), 178-179. [C]

[3187] Scott, Noel. "Shelley: Enigma Variations," *Notes and
        Queries*, CXCIV, No. 5 (March 5, 1949), 96-99. [B]

[3188] Leopardi, E. R. "Keats-Shelley Memorial," *The Times Literary
        Supplement* [London], No. 2,458 (March 12, 1949), 169.
        [M]

[3189] [Anonymous]. "Chameleon Changes," *The Times Literary Supple-
        ment* [London], No. 2,460 (March 26, 1949), 202. [R:
        item 3170]

[3190] Jones, Frederick L. *"Shelley's Major Poetry: The Fabric of a
        Vision.* By Carlos Baker. Princeton, N.J.: Princeton
        University Press, 1948. 307pp. $5.00.," *MLN*, LXIV,
        No. 4 (April, 1949), 278-279. [R: item 3170]

[3191] van Maanen, W. "A Note on Shelley's *Ozymandias*," *Neophilologus*, XXXIII, No. 2 (April, 1949), 123-125. [C]

[3192] [Signed "L.M.W."]. "Shelley: Enigma Variations (cxciv. 96).," *Notes and Queries*, CXCIV, No. 9 (April 30, 1949), 195. [B]

[3193] Jones, Frederick L. *"Shelley and the Thought of His Time: A Study in the History of Ideas.* By Joseph Barrell. New Haven: Yale University Studies in English, Volume 106; London: Geoffrey Cumberlege, Oxford University Press, 1947. Pp ix + 210. $3.00.," *Modern Language Quarterly*, X, No. 2 (June, 1949), 241-242. [R: item 3133]

[3194] Treece, Henry. *"New Shelley Letters,"* *World Review*, New Series No. 4 (June, 1949), 73. [R: item 3175]

[3195] Scott, Noel. "Enigma Variations: Three Postcripts [*sic*] (see cxciv. 96, 195)," *Notes and Queries*, CXCIV, No. 12 (June 11, 1949), 257-259. [B]

[3196] Phillips, Mary. "Shelley: Enigma Variations (cxciv.).," *Notes and Queries*, CXCIV, No. 13 (June 25, 1949), 283-284. [B]

[3197] Hughes, A[rthur] M[ontague] D['Urban]. *"Shelley's Major Poetry: the Fabric of a Vision.* By Carlos Baker. London: Geoffrey Cumberlege, Oxford University Press. 1948. 307pp. 25s.," *The Modern Language Review*, XLIV, No. 3 (July, 1949), 404. [R: item 3170]

[3198] Mayor, Andreas. "A Suspected Shelley Letter," *The Library*, Fifth Series IV, No. 2 (September, 1949), 141-145. [T]

[3199] Scott, Noel. "Shelley [/] (cxciv. 96, 258)," *Notes and Queries*, CXCIV, No. 18 (September 3, 1949), 389-390. [B]

[3200] Ehrsam, Theodore G. "Shelley's Letter to Mary Godwin," *The Times Literary Supplement* [London], No. 2,487 (September, 1949), 633. [T]

[3201] Wilcox, Stewart C. "The Source, Symbolism, and Unity of Shelley's *Skylark*," *Studies in Philology*, XLVI, No. 4 (October, 1949), 560-576. [C]

[3202] Norman, Sylva. "Shelley's Letter to Mary Godwin," *The Times Literary Supplement* [London], No. 2,488 (October 7, 1949), 649. [T]

[3203] Scott, Noel. "Dr. Lind (see cxciv. 97, 283)," *Notes and Queries*, CXCIV, No. 22 (October 29, 1949), 478. [B]

[3204]   Scott, Noel.   "G. F. Cooke and the Theatre Royal, Windsor
         (see cxciv. 98, 259)," *Notes and Queries*, CXCIV, No. 22
         (October 29, 1949), 478.   [B]

[3205]   Wilcox, Stewart C.   "13. Shelley's *Adonais*, XX-XXI," *The
         Explicator*, VIII, No. 2 (November, 1949), [unnumbered
         page].   [C]

[3206]   Ehrsam, Theodore [G.].   "Shelley's Letter to Mary Godwin,"
         The Times Literary Supplement [London], No. 2,492 (November
         4, 1949), 715.   [T]

[3207]   Norman, Sylva.   "Shelley's Letter to Mary Godwin," *The
         Times Literary Supplement* [London], No. 2,493 (November 11,
         1949), 733.   [C of item 3206]

[3208]   Soleta, Chester A.   "Peacock and Shelley," *Notes and Queries*,
         CXCIV, No. 23 (November 12, 1949), 496-497.   [C]

*[3209]   Vail, Curtis C. D.   "Shelley's Translations from Goethe's
         'Faust,'" *Symposium*, III, No. [?] ([?], 1949), 187-213.
         [C]

Books:

[3210]   Bowra, C[ecil] M[aurice].   *The Romantic Imagination*.   The
         Charles Eliot Norton Lectures 1948-1949.   306pp.
         Cambridge, Mass.: Harvard University Press, 1949.   [C:
         "Prometheus Unbound," (103)-125]

[3211]   Clark, David Lee.   "The Dates and Sources of Shelley's
         Metaphysical, Moral, and Religious Essays," *The Univer-
         sity of Texas Studies in English*, XXVIII (1949), [160]-
         194.   [T]

[3212]   Fairchild, Hoxie Neale.   *Religious Trends in English Poetry*.
         [Volume III (/) 1780-1830 (/) Romantic Faith].   ix+
         549pp.   New York: Columbia University Press, 1949.
         [C: "Shelley," (328)-387]

[3213]   Fogle, Richard Harter.   *The Imagery of Keats and Shelley* [/]
         A Comparative Study.   x+296pp.   Chapel Hill, N.C.: The
         University of North Carolina Press, 1949.   [C]

[3214]   Highet, Gilbert.   *The Classical Tradition* [/] *Greek and Roman
         Influences on Western Literature*.   xxxviii+763pp.   New York:
         Oxford University Press, 1949.   [C: 418-423; M: fully
         indexed]

[3215]   MacGillivray, J. R.   *Keats: A Bibliography and Reference Guide
         with an Essay on Keats' Reputation*.   ix+210pp.   Toronto:
         University of Toronto Press, 1949.   [M: fully indexed]

[3216] Murry, John Middleton. *Katherine Mansfield and Other Literary Portraits*. v+242pp. London: Peter Nevill Limited, 1949. [C: "Keats and Shelley," 230-242]

[3217] Notopoulos, James A. *The Platonism of Shelley* [/] *A Study of Platonism and the Poetic Mind*. xiii+671pp. Durham, N.C.: Duke University Press, 1949. [C]

[3218] Rogers, Neville, ed. *Keats Shelley & Rome* [/] *An Illustrated Miscellany*. 76pp. London: Christopher Johnson, for the Keats-Shelley Memorial Association, 1949. [B]

[3219] Sackville-West, Edward. *Inclinations*. 246pp. New York: Charles Scribner's Sons, 1949. [C: "The Innocent Heart," 136-149]

[3220] Wormhoudt, Arthur. *The Demon Lover* [/] *A Psychoanalytical Approach to Literature*. [With an Introduction by Edmund Bergler]. 150pp. New York: The Exposition Press, 1949. [C: "Shelley (/) *Prometheus Unbound*," (88)-112]

1950

Periodicals:

[3221] Jones, Frederick L. "A Shelley and Mary Letter to Claire," *MLN*, LXV, No. 2 (February, 1950), 121-123. [T]

[3222] Wilcox, S. C. "The Prosodic Pattern of 'Ode to the West Wind,'" *Notes and Queries*, CXCV, No. 4 (February 18, 1950), 77-78. [C]

[3223] Blakeney, E. H. "The Dreaded Name of Demogorgon.," *Notes and Queries*, CXCV, No. 5 (March 4, 1950), 105. [C]

[3224] Jeffares, A. Norman. "A Source for 'A Woman Homer Sung,'" *Notes and Queries*, CXCV, No. 5 (March 4, 1950), 104. [C]

[3225] Maser, Frederick E. "Darkness and Light [/] An Examination into the Attitude of Percy Bysshe Shelley toward Christianity," *The London Quarterly and Holborn Review*, Sixth Series XIX, [whole number CLXXV], No. 2 (April, 1950), 139-147. [C]

[3226] Jones, Frederick L. "Hogg's Peep at Elizabeth Shelley," *Philological Quarterly*, XXIX, No. 4 (October, 1950), 422-426. [B]

*[3227]   Verkoren, L[ucas]. "Shelley Prometheus Unbound," *Levende
          Talen*, [?] (October, 1950), [?p]. [?C]

[3228]   Weaver, Bennett. "Pre-Promethean Thought in Three Longer
          Poems of Shelley," *Philological Quarterly*, XXIX, No. 4
          (October, 1950), 353-366. [C]

[3229]   Rulf, Donald J. "The Romantic Writers and Edmund Kean,"
          Modern Language Quarterly, XI, No. 4 (December, 1950),
          425-437. [C: 435-436]

Books:

[3230]   Bush, Douglas. *Science and English Poetry* [/] *A Historical
          Sketch, 1590-1950.* vii+166pp. New York: Oxford Univer-
          sity Press, 1950. [C: 103-104]

[3231]   Hamilton, G[eorge] Rostrevor. *The Tell-Tale Article* [/]
          A Critical Approach to Modern Poetry. xii+114pp. New York:
          Oxford University Press, 1950. [C: "Tradition and
          the Sense of Man's Greatness: The Work of T. S.
          Eliot," 63-94; Shelley: 68]

*[3232]   Saintsbury, George. *A Last Vintage* [/] *Essays and Papers.*
          Edited by John W. Oliver, Arthur Melville Clark, and
          August Muir. [?]pp. London: Methuen & Co. Ltd.,
          1950. [C: "Notes on Six Poets," 239-241; Shelley: 240]

[3233]   Vivante, Leone. *English Poetry* [/] *and its contribution to the
          knowledge of a creative principle.* xv+340pp. New York:
          The Macmillan Company, 1950. [C: "Percy Bysshe
          Shelley," 127-181]

[3234]   Woods, George Benjamin. *English Poetry and Prose of the
          Romantic Movement.* Revised edition. xxx+1538pp. Chi-
          cago: Scott, Foresman and Company, 1950. [Textbook;
          T: 653-777; C: 1335-1353; bibliography: 1445-1448]

1951

*The four following items, while outside the chronological scope of the
present bibliography, have been included here because they were overlooked
by the early bibliographers of the* Keats-Shelley Journal *in compiling entries
for 1951.*

[3235]   Joyce, Michael. "A Poet's Honeymoon," *Blackwood's Edinburgh
          Magazine*, CCLXIX, No. 1624 (February, 1951), 104-111.
          [B]

[3236]   Sharrock, Roger. "Short Notices," *The Modern Language Review,*

XLVI, No. 2 (April, 1951), 258-309. [R of Carl
Grabo's *Shelley's Eccentricities* (Albuquerque, N.M.:
University of New Mexico Press, 1950): 301-302]

[3237] Maxwell, J. C. "Shelley and Manzoni," *The Modern Language
Review*, XLVI, Nos. 3 & 4 (July and October, 1950),
442. [C,B]

[3238] Sharrock, Roger. *"The Platonism of Shelley: A Study of
Platonism and the Poetic Mind.* By James A. Notopoulos.
Durham, N.C.: Duke University Press, 1950. xiv+671pp.
56s. 6d.,*" The Modern Language Review*, XLVI, Nos. 3 & 4
(July and October, 1951), 495-497. [R: item 3217]

.

[3239]   [Boone, J. S.]. "The Liberal.—No. II., " *The Council of
          Ten*, III, No. ix (February, 1823), 88-93. [R of the
          second number of *The Liberal*; M, T: 92]

[3240]   [Signed "P.T.O."]. "The Rhyming Review for the Month.,"
          The John Bull Magazine, I, No. 1 (July, 1824), 32-37. [R
          of item 49: 36]

[3241]   [Anonymous]. "Prospectus and Specimen of a New Joe
          Miller.," *The John Bull Magazine*, I, No. 4 (October, 1824),
          [121]-124. [M: "5. Shelley's Poetry.," 123]

[3242]   [Anonymous]. "Further Specimens of the New Joe Miller.,"
          The John Bull Magazine, I, No. 5 (November, 1824), [159]-
          162. [M: "10. Prometheus Unbound.," 160]

*[3243]   [Hunt, Leigh]. "[Reply to item 24]," *McPhun's Glasgow Maga-
          zine*, [?] (November, 1824), [?p]. [C]

*[3244]   [Shelley, Mary Wollstonecraft]. *The Last Man.* By the Author
          of Frankenstein. 3 vols. London: Henry Colburn, 1826.
          [B: the character of Adrian, Earl of Windsor, is a fic-
          tionalized portrait of Shelley]

*[3245]   Shelley, Percy Bysshe. "[?]," in *The Pledge of Friendship.*
          [?]pp. London: [?], 1827. [T: 282]

*[3246]   Shelley, Percy Bysshe. "[?]," in *The Keepsake.* Edited by
          Frederick Mansel Reynolds. [?]pp. London: Longman,
          Orme, Brown, Green, and Longmans, 1829. [T: 47, 160,
          161, 162]

*[3247]   [Shelley, Mary Wollstonecraft]. *Frankenstein; or, The Modern
          Prometheus.* Standard Novels, No. IX. By the Author of
          The Last Man, Perkin Warbeck, &c. &c. Rev., cor., and
          Illustrated with a New Introduction, bu the Author.
          xii+202pp. London: H. Colburn and R. Bentley, 1831.
          [B: "Introduction," v-xii]

*[3248]   [Anonymous]. "[?]," *The Literary Journal and Weekly Register of
          Science and the Arts* [Providence, R.I.], I, No. [?]
          (September 14, 1833), 114. [M]

*[3249]   Brydges, Egerton. "Conversations in Purgatory.—No. II.,"
          The Court Magazine, and Belle·Assemblée, V, [No. 5] (Novem-
          ber, 1834), 180-184. [An imaginary conversation among
          Pope, Burns, Bloomfield, and Shelley]

*[3250]   [Neale, Erskine]. *Closing Scenes: or, Christianity and Infidelity
          Contrasted in the Last Hours of Remarkable Persons.* 2 vols.
          London: [?], 1848. [B,C]

*[3251] Scrymgeour, Daniel. *The Poetry and Poets of Britain, from Chaucer to Tennyson, with Biographical Sketches and a Rapid View of the Characteristic Attributes of Each. By Daniel Scrymgeour. Preceded by an Introductory Essay on the Origin and Progress of English Poetical Literature.* xxx+544pp. Edinburgh: Adam and Charles Black, 1850. [C]

*[3252] Redding, Cyrus. *Fifty Years' Recollections, Literary and Personal, with Observations on Men and Things.* 3 vols. London: Charles J. Skeet, 1858. [T: II, 363-366]

*[3253] [Anonymous]. "[?]," *The Law Magazine*, LIII, No. [?] ([?], 1861), [?p]. [?B]

*[3254] [Carr, J. Comyns]. "The Artistic Spirit in Modern English Poetry.," *The New Quarterly Magazine*, V, No. [?] (October, 1875), 146-165. [C; Shelley: 152-157; rptd.: item 1049]

*[3255] Sinclair, Thomas. *The Mount: Speech from Its English Heights.* vii+302pp. London: Trubner and Co., 1878. [M]

*[3256] Gilfillan, George. *Sketches Literary and Theological, Being Selections from an Unpublished MS. of the late Rev. George Gilfillan.* Edited by Frank Henderson. x+300pp. Edinburgh: David Douglass, 1881. [M]

[3257] Forman, H[arry] Buxton. *The Shelley Library [/] An Essay in Bibliography [/] By H. Buxton Forman [/] Shelley's own Books, Pamphlets & Broadsides [/] Posthumous Separate Issues and Posthumous Books wholly [/] Or mainly by Him.* 127pp. London: Published for the Shelley Society by Reeves and Turner, 1886. [T; Shelley Society Publications, Fourth Series, Miscellaneous, No. 1]

[3258] [Wise, Thomas James, and Harry Buxton Forman, eds.]. *Letters from Percy Bysshe Shelley to Robert Southey and Other Correspondents.* 32pp. London: privately printed, 1888.

[3259] [Anonymous]. *Keats-Shelley Memorial Exhibition & Concert. [/] Stafford House, St. James's, S.W. [/] Wednesday, 20th March, 1907. [/] By Kind Permission of the Duke and Duchess of Sutherland. [/] Catalogue. [/] of Relics, Portraits, Manuscripts and other [/] interesting articles connected with John Keats and Percy Bysshe Shelley [/] with the names of the owners who have kindly placed them for this occasion at the disposal of the Committee of the Keats-Shelley Memorial at Rome.* 8pp. [London: privately printed by Hunt, Barnard & Co., 1907]. [B,T]

[3260] Smith, Harry B. "Books and Autograph Letters of Shelley," *Scribner's Magazine*, LXXII, No. [?] ([?], 1922), 74. [T]

[3261] White, Newman Ivey, ed. *The Best of Shelley*. Edited with
        an Introduction and Notes by Newman I. White. xlvi+
        532pp. New York: Thomas Nelson and Sons, 1932. [T,C]

*[3262] Thompson, Denys. *Reading and Discrimination*. [?]pp. London:
        Chatto & Windus, 1934. [C]

*[3263] Gilbert, Katherine Everett, and Helmet Kuhn. *A History of
        Aesthetics*. xi+582pp. New York: The Macmillan Company,
        1939. [C: "Chapter XIII. Romantic Ideas and Social
        Programs in England and America"]

[3264] Bartholomew, A. T., revised by Roger Ingpen. "Percy
        Bysshe Shelley (1792-1822)," III, 212-218 in *The
        Cambirdge Bibliography of English Literature*. Edited by F. W.
        Bateson. 4 vols. Cambirdge, Eng.: At the University
        Press, 1940. [C: bibliography]

[3265] Leon, Howard. "Shelley in America in the Nineteenth
        Century," *Modern Language Quarterly*, II, No. 3 (September,
        1941), 516-517. [R: item 2857]

*[3266] Schorer, Mark. *William Blake* [/] *The Politics of Vision*. [?]pp.
        New York: Henry Holt & Company, 1946. [M]

[3267] Erdman, David V. "Byron and Revolt in England," *Science
        and Society*, XI, No. [?] ([?], 1947), 234-248. [M]

[3268] Stallman, Robert Wooster. "Keats the Apollinian: The
        Time-and-Space Logic of His Poems As Paintings,"
        The University of Toronto Quarterly, XVI, No. [?] ([?],
        1947), 143-156. [M]

[3269] Bernbaum, Ernest. *Guide Through the Romantic Movement*. Second
        Edition, Revised and Enlarged. xi+351pp. New York:
        The Ronald Press, 1949 [original edition, 1930]. [C
        "Percy Bysshe Shelley," 241-265]

*[3270] Gorton, John. *A General Biographical Dictionary*. 4 vols.
        London: Henry Bohn, 1851 [original edition, one volume,
        1828]. [B: IV, 430-431]

*[3271] Lower, Mark Antony. *Worthies of Sussex*. 346pp. [London:
        privately printed (G. P. Bacon), 1865]. [B]

INDEX

All items have been entered in the index by author, and
periodical items have been entered additionally under the
name of the periodical. All anonymous items have been
entered by title; all pseudonymous items have been entered
by pseudonym and, where identifiable, have been entered
under the author's real name. All items signed with the
author's initials have been entered under those initials
and, where identifiable, have been entered under the
author's full name. The names of editors and translators
have also been included, as have variant titles of periodicals where the variation might cause oversight.

A., 182
A., A., 487
A., A. E., 1904
A., I. S., 1317
Abraham, Hayward, 1153
Abrahams, Aleck, 1994
Academy, The, 875, 910, 998, 1013, 1016,
  1025, 1127, 1132, 1213, 1214, 1217,
  1219, 1257, 1269, 1274, 1279, 1316,
  1328, 1335, 1729, 1731, 1734, 1895
*Account of An Exhibition of Books and
  Manuscripts of Percy Bysshe Shelley,
  An*, 2677
Adams, Francis, 1554, 1588, 1747
Adler, E. N., 2333
Admirier of Shelley, An, 398
Age Reviewed: A Satire, The, 94
Ainger, Alfred, 1765
Alastor, 569, 570
Albany Review, The, 1921
Albemarle, The, 1579
Albrecht, William Price, 3090
Alden, Raymond Macdonald, 2315
Aldington, Richard, 2849
Aldrich, T. B., 1597, 1630
Alexander, James Waddell, 303
Alger, G. W., 1555
Alger, William Rounseville, 781
Allardyce, Alexander, 1429
Allen, B. Sprague, 2157
Allen, L. H., 2293
Allibone, S. Austin, 835
Allingham, William, 699, 1642
American, The, 1341
American Bibilical Repository, The
  (later *The Biblical Repository and
  Classical Review*), 304, 329, 437
American Bibliopolist, The, 806, 908,
  919, 922, 944
American Daily Advertiser, The, 144
American Literary Magazine, The, 498
American Monthly Magazine (see *Graham's
  American Monthly Magazine*)
American Oxonian, The, 3130
American Quarterly Review, The, 179,
  182, 264, 274
American Review: A Whig Journal, The,
  (variously titled *The American Review*,
  and *The American Whig Review*), 424,
  445, 458, 459, 500, 516, 531, 532,
  534, 537, 543
American Scholar, The, 2635

American Whig Review, The (see *The
  American Review: A Whig Journal*)
Amos, Andrew, 487
Anderson, G. A., 2141
Anderson, George K., 2901
Anderson, John P., 1377
Anderson, Melville B., 1439, 1444, 16.
Anderson, William, 341
Andover Review, The, 1595
Andrade, E. N. da C., 2567
Andrews, Samuel, 1199
*Anecdotes of Lord Byron, from Authent
  Sources, with Remarks Illustrative
  His Connection with the Principal
  Literary Characters of the Present
  Day*, 63
Angeli, Helen Maria Madox Rossetti,
  2026
Anglo-Saxon Review, The, 1760
Annals of Medical History, 2815
Anster, John Henry, 470, 480, 482
Antaeus, 1471
Antiquary, The, 1086, 1088, 1242
Antiquus, 236
App, A. J., 2720
Appleton, Thomas Gold, 1236
Appleton's Journal, 1043, 1064
Archer, Jerome W., 2985
Archivist, The, 1411
Arcturus, 376, 386
Arena, 1515, 1804, 1926
Armfield, Maxwell, 2026
Armitt, Annie, 1589
Arms, George, 2916
Armstrong, Edmund John, 1004
Armstrong, George Francis, 1004
Armstrong, Margaret, 2845, 2851
Arnold, Frederick, 891
Arnold, Matthew, 753, 1083, 1090, 110
  1386, 1392, 1393, 1412
Athenaeum, The, 98, 101, 103, 112, 13
  150, 171, 185, 186, 190, 192, 193,
  194, 195, 197, 198, 199, 203, 204,
  206, 209, 211, 212, 232, 237, 262,
  320, 335, 338, 390, 446, 447, 464,
  465, 485, 487, 490, 528, 545, 552,
  556, 558, 562, 564, 631, 633, 634,
  635, 641, 642, 670, 727, 729, 811,
  873, 895, 932, 958, 999, 1001, 1021
  1024, 1069, 1073, 1074, 1075, 1094,
  1095, 1098, 1101, 1102, 1115, 1116,
  1117, 1118, 1120, 1121, 1122, 1123,

Cloudesly: A Tale, 161
Clough, Arthur Hugh, 807
Cluck, Julia, 2880
Clutton-Brock, Arthur, 1974, 2034, 2246, 2448
Cobbler, A, 786
Cocke, W. Archer, 871
Coeuroy, André, 2314
Cohane, J. J., 3114
Colby, C. W., 1688
Cole, Henry, 935
Coleman, Everard Home, 1338, 1832
Coleridge, Derwent, 81
Coleridge, Rev. Derwent, 966
Colgan, W. H., 2145
College English, 3163, 3169
Collier, William Francis, 730
Collins, A., 627
Collins, John Churton, 1780
Collison-Morley, Lacy, 2093
Colophon, 2809
Colum, May Maguire, 2757
Colvin, Sidney, 2037, 2130
Commonweal, The, 3111, 3114
Congregational Review, The, 1318
Connoisseur, The, 1931, 1935, 1938
Connolly, Francis X., 2171
Conservator, The, 1652
Consideratis Considerandis, 1125
Contemporary Review, The, 984, 985, 990, 1000, 1191, 1757, 2429, 3019, 3147
Converse, Florence, 1671
Cooke, Albert S., 1525, 1623, 1861
Cook, Davidson, 2690
Cooke, E. T., 1821
Cooke, Margaret W., 2099
Cooper, Lane, 1923, 1925
Cooper's Journal, 514, 515
Copeland, Charles Townsend, 1976
Cope's Tobacco Plant, 1017, 1055
Cordery, A., 867
Cornhill Magazine, The, 795, 901, 916, 917, 1041, 1494, 2116, 2223, 2409
Corsair, The, 314, 319, 352, 356, 357
Corson, Hiram, 1600
Cosmopolitan, The, 1814
Cosmopolitan Art Journal, The, 650
Cotterill, Henry Bernard, 1135
Council of Ten, The, 1135
Court Journal, The, 275, 309
Court Magazine, and Belle Assemblée, The, 3246

Courthope, William John, 1208, 1238,
Cousins, James H., 2588, 2612
Cowling, George, 2709
Cox, R. G., 2739
Craik, George L., 431, 717
Crawford, F. Marion, 1920
Crawshay, Rose Mary, 1599
Creasy, Edward Shepherd, 521
Crewe, Earl of, 1721
Critic, A Weekly Review of Literature, Fine Arts, and the Drama, The, 121, 124
Critic, The, 1221, 1222, 1223, 1224, 1226, 1227, 1246, 1275, 2178, 1321, 1342, 1395, 1468, 1512, 1518, 1523, 1538, 1571, 1572, 1573, 1575, 1587, 1598, 1601, 1628, 1635, 1661, 1674, 1690, 1864
Croce, Benedetto, 2613
Croft, Margaret L., 1864
Crosse, Mrs. Andrew, 1601
Crosse, Cornelia A. H., 1601
Crozer Quarterly, The, 2674
Cunningham, Allan, 237, 247, 255
Cunningham, George Godfrey, 800
Current Literature, 1867, 1907, 1940, 1987, 2049
Curry, Otway, 317
Curtis, George H., 488
Cuthrie, William Norman, 1707

(Delta), 341
D., 273
D., C., 81
D., C., 957
D., E., 395
D., G. H., 2685
D., J., 2265
D., L., 389
D., L., 461
D., O. T., 775, 776, 785, 859
D., R. K., 941
D., W., 537
de S., E., 2426
Dahlia, 363
Daily News, The, 1770, 1771, 1772, 1773, 1776, 1790, 1791
Dalby, John Watson, 870, 996
Dalhousie Review, The, 2263
Dallas, Eneas Sweetland, 574
Damon, S. Foster, 2390
Dangerfield, Elma, 2710

Harting, J. E., 1548
Harvey, Alexander, 2136
Haselfoot, Edward, 29
Hasell, Elizabeth J., 924
Häusermann, H. W., 3098, 3118, 3181, 3183
Havens, Raymond Dexter, 2275, 2521, 2533, 2534, 2546, 2551, 3074
Hawtrey, Edward Craven, 506
Haydon, Benjamin Robert, 583, 965
Hayne, Paul Hamilton, 589, 700
Hayward, Abraham, 240
Hazlitt, William, 24, 47, 74, 82, 90, 122, 594, 1817
Headley, Joel Tyler, 475, 489
Hebb, John, 1723
Helyar, Harriet, 2580
Hemans, Felicia Dorothea, 277
Henderson, Frank, 3256
Henkin, Leo J., 3128
Hepburn, Blanche E., 2131
Hepple, Norman, 2081
Heraud, John Abraham, 152, 168, 223, 464, 465, 474
Herford, Charles Harold, 1480, 1492, 1710, 2088, 2276
Heron, Robert Matthew, 1190
Heron-Allen, Edward, 2659
Herring, Robert, 2432
Hersey, Frank Wilson Cheney, 1976
Herzog, Emile Salomon Wilhelm, 2361, 2459, 2964
Hespelt, E. Herman, 2313
Hesperian, The, 317
Hewitt, E. P., 2203
Hewlett, Maurice, 2006, 2277
Hibbert, James, 1176
Hibbert Journal, The, 2127
Hibernicus, 2781
Hicks, Arthur C., 2894, 3039
Higginson, Thomas Wentworth, 1711, 1873
Highet, Gilbert, 3214
Hill, M. Kirby, 1828, 1840
Hill, Reginald Harrison, 2418
Hillard, George Stillman, 584
Hime, Henry William Lovett, 1420
Himelick, Raymond, 3145
Hinchman, Walter S., 1947
Hirst, G. M., 2384
Hobhouse, John Cam, 2007
Hodgkin, John Eliot, 825
Hodgkins, Louise Manning, 1369

Hoffman, Frederick A., 1201
Hoffman, Harold Leroy, 2346, 2601, 2616
Hogg, James, 599
Hogg, Thomas Jefferson, 92, 175, 176, 177, 180, 181, 184, 188, 202, 215, 216, 233, 246, 664, 1849, 1890, 2639
Hogg's Instructor, 519, 523
Holland, R. A., 943
Holmes, Oliver Wendell, 718, 1606
Hood's Magazine, 444, 462, 466
Hook, Theodore, 165
Hope, Henry Gerald, 1469
Horatio, 1002
Horne, Richard Hengist, 555, 831
Hort, G. M., 2772, 3008, 3019
Hotson, Leslie, 2512, 2515, 2517, 2542
Hott, G. M., 3008
Houghton, Richard Monckton Milnes, Lord, 564, 935
Houlden, W. H., 2565, 2568, 2572, 2574
Houstoun, Matilda C., 1166
Howard, Leon, 3262
Howard, Philip H., 662
Howe, Percival Presland, 3135
Howitt, William, 476
Hubach, Robert R., 3052
Huchon, René, 1914
Hudleston, C. Roy, 3010
Hughes, Arthur Montague D'Urban, 2040, 2043, 2044, 2050, 2052, 2133, 2835, 3136, 3160, 3161, 3197
Hughes, T. Cann, 1163
Hughson, Shirley Carter, 1607
Hulme, T. E., 2358
Humane Review, The, 1788
Humanitarian Review, The, 1774
Hungerford, Edward B., 2895
Hunt, Leigh, 10, 38, 116, 191, 220, 299, 300, 302, 418, 522, 673, 674, 2450, 3243
Hunt, Thornton, 739
Hunter, James L., 411
Huntington Library Qyarterly, The, 3182
Hurst, John L., 1674
Hutchinson, Thomas, 1853, 1876
Hutchison, W. A., 2167, 2267
Hutton, Richard Holt, 738, 860, 1048, 1632, 1891
Huxley, Aldous, 2482

MacGillivray, J. R., 3215
Mackenzie, R. Shelton, 599
Mackie, John M., 380, 455
McLean, Charles Mossman, 1978
McMahan, Anna Benneson, 1584, 1841,
  1955, 1985
Macmillan's Magazine, 689, 694, 725,
  1042, 1056, 1059, 1061, 1090, 1346,
  1691
Macneice, Louis, 2792
Macnish, Robert, 148
McNully, J. H., 3069
McPharlin, Paul, 2475
McPhun's Glasgow Magazine, 3240
MacQuarey, Howard, 1515
MacSweeney, Joseph J., 2112
Madariaga, Salvador de, 2151, 2186
Madden, Richard Robertm 241
Magazine of Art, The, 1775
Maginn, William, 9, 11, 30, 37, 152,
  599, 1240
Majid, Jamila, 2297
Malleson, W. T., 1458
Mallock, William Hurrell, 849, 1759
Malone, John, 1561
Manchester Quarterly, The, 1111, 2286
Manly, William, 3035
Marius, 113
Marjarum, E. Wayne, 2746
Markland, Russell, 2218, 2285
Markley, John T., 1140
Marsh, Goerge L., 2496, 2960
Marshall, Edward H., 1178, 1234, 1443,
  1452, 1651
Marshall, Elizabeth Glass, 2420
Marshall, George W., 1088
Marshall, Julian, 1398
Marshall, Mrs. Julian, 1472
Marshall, William E., 2263
Martin, L. C., 2101
Martin-Baynat, Robert, 3101
Maser, Frederick E., 3225
Mason, Edward T., 1241
Mason, Francis Claiborne, 2764
Mason, H. A., 2692
Massachusetts Quarterly Review, The,
  502
Massey, Bernard Wilfrid Arbuthnot, 2292,
  2303, 2320
Massey, Gerald, 602
Massingham, Harold John, 2530, 2545
Masson, David, 694, 913

Maureen, 880
Maurois, André, 2361, 2459, 2964
Maxwell, J. C., 3237
Mayer, S. R. Townshend, 944, 946, 1006
Mayo, Amory D., 502
Mayor, Andreas, 2198
Mayor, Joseph Bickersteth, 1422, 1529
Mead, Douglass S., 3110
Mead, William Edward, 1934
Medical Adviser, The, 17
Medicina Simplex, 219
Medwin, Thomas, 48, 155, 156, 185, 186,
  190, 192, 193, 194, 242, 289, 319,
  375, 477, 2071
Melbrook, Geoffrey, 1009
Meldrum, Elizabeth, 3147
Meliora, 658, 677
Menzies, W. G., 1931, 1935
Mercedes, Sister Anna, 2980
Meredith, George, 540, 2058
Meredith, W. H., 2058
Merle, Gibbons, 381
Merle, William Henry, 485
Merriman, Josiah J., 517
Methodist Review, The, 1633, 1657
Metropolitan Journal, The, 276
Metropolitan Quarterly Magazine, The,
  81
Meyerstein, E. H. W., 3027
Meynell, Wilfrid, 1982, 2238
Middleton, Charles S., 634, 443, 1609
Miles, Alfred H., 1872, 1874
Miles, Josephine, 2921
Mill, John Stuart, 236, 681
Millar, A. H., 2239
Miller, Barnett, 2009
Miller, Joaquin, 2279
Millhauser, Milton, 2804, 3072
Milner, George, 1009, 1010
Milnes, Richard Monckton, 564, 935
Mimnermus, 2350
Minerva, 1072
Minto, William, 1132
Mirror, The, 35, 68, 229, 313, 360
Mitchell, Donald Grant, 1713
Mitchell, Stewart, 2225
Mitford, Mary Russell, 577
Mizener, Arthur, 3149
MLN, 1439, 1623, 1724, 1861, 1923, 1988
  2078, 2086, 2117, 2122, 2129, 2155,
  2208, 2220, 2266, 2289, 2309, 2312,
  2325, 2329, 2330, 2340, 2344, 2390,

(cont'd) 2112, 2113, 2128, 2135, 2154, 2162, 2168, 2200, 2218, 2267, 2287, 2288, 2291, 2292, 2299, 2300, 2303, 2308, 2326, 2379, 2405, 2410, 2411, 2428, 2470, 2471, 2472, 2473, 2475, 2536, 2549, 2550, 2566, 2658, 2659, 2663, 2664, 2665, 2667, 2670, 2671, 2685, 2695, 2702, 2728, 2781, 2803, 2804, 2807, 2811, 2813, 2816, 2817, 2829, 2877, 2887, 2903, 2910, 2928, 2939, 2943, 2947, 2950, 2969, 2970, 3013, 3026, 3052, 3053, 3054, 3055, 3057, 3057, 3059, 3060, 3065, 3068, 3072, 3076, 3078, 3085, 3108, 3167, 3168, 3181, 3183, 3187, 3192, 3195, 3196, 3199, 3203, 3205, 3208, 3222, 3223, 3224

Notopoulos, James A., 2693, 2812, 2822, 2841, 2864, 2865, 2888, 2945, 2946, 2993, 3180, 3217

Noyes, Alfred, 2362, 2856

O., J., 979
O., P. T., 3240
O., R. T., 888
O., S., 331
Oakley, J. H. I., 887
Observer, The, 2079
Occult Review, 2253
O'Conor, William Anderson, 1111, 1141, 1473
Odoherty, M., 11
O'Grady, Standish, 899, 933
Oldmixon, Jonathan, 3, 8
Oliphant, Margaret, 847, 864, 865, 868, 1142, 1310
Oliver, John W., 3232
O'Neill, Moira, 2339
Open Court, The, 1404, 1436, 2211, 2324
Oras, Ants, 2837
Origo, Iris, 2678, 3153
Orton, James, 569, 570
Osborn, Andrew Rule, 2152
Ossoli, Margaret Fuller, 453, 682
Ouida, 1482, 1679
Outlook, The, 1884, 1952, 1953
Oxenford, John, 633
Oxford and Cambridge Magazine, The, 613
Oxford University Magazine, The, 244

(Pi), 1340
P., 516

P., A., 93
P., H. S., 387
P., H. W., 500
P., N., 167
P., P., 107
P., P., 829
P., P., 952
P., P., 1235
P., S. B., 3054, 3055, 3059
P., T. R., 66
Page, John, 1009, 1010
Palgrave, Francis Turner, 726, 894, 1714
Pall Mall Budget, The, 1267, 1270
Pall Mall Gazette, The, 1067, 1211, 1249, 1250, 1252, 1389, 1390, 1569
Pancoast, Henry S., 2155
Panton, J. E., 2170, 2173, 2180
Papers of the Bibliographical Society of America, 2994, 3049, 3143
Papers of the Michigan Academy of Science, Art & Letters, 2681
Parker, W. M., 2870, 3113
Parkes, Bessie Rayner, 618, 744
Parkes, Kineton, 1097, 1423, 1434, 1529, 1543, 1562
Partington, Wilfred, 2805
Patmore, Coventry, 1268, 1506
Patmore, Peter George, 7, 19, 596
Paton, Joseph Noel, 419, 720
Patrick, David, 1855
Paul, Charles Kegan, 967, 974
Pauline; A Fragment of a Confession, 238
Payne, William Morton, 1311, 1681, 1915
Peabody, William Bourne Oliver, 118, 224
Peacock, Edward, 713, 1337
Peacock, Thomas Love, 653, 684, 687, 688, 721, 935, 1973, 2011, 2620
Pearson, Howard S., 1372
Pearson's Magazine, 1911
Peck, Walter Edwin, 2156, 2161, 2172, 2179, 2199, 2201, 2204, 2208, 2209, 2213, 2247, 2278, 2288, 2289, 2309, 2310, 2311, 2329, 2334, 2340, 2344, 2351, 2352, 2367, 2374, 2377, 2394, 2406, 2419, 2423, 2438, 2452, 2460
Peet, William H., 1177
Pelagius, 869
Pelo, Florence Boylston, 2105